FOOD FIGHTS OVER FREE TRADE

FOOD FIGHTS OVER FREE TRADE

HOW INTERNATIONAL INSTITUTIONS PROMOTE AGRICULTURAL TRADE LIBERALIZATION

Christina L. Davis

PRINCETON UNIVERSITY PRESS   PRINCETON AND OXFORD

Second printing, and first paperback printing, 2005
Paperback ISBN 0-691-12254-7

The Library of Congress has cataloged the cloth edition of this book as follows

Davis, Christina L., 1971–
Food fights over free trade : how international institutions promote agricultural trade
liberalization / Christina L. Davis.
p.   cm.
Includes bibliographical references and index.
ISBN 0-691-11505-2 (alk. paper)
1. Agriculture and state—United States.   2. Agriculture and state—France.
3. Agriculture and state—Japan.   4. Tariff on farm produce.   5. Produce trade—
Government policy.   I. Title.

HD1761.D32 2003
382'.41—dc21   2002042465

British Library Cataloging-in-Publication Data is available

This book has been composed in Sabon

Printed on acid-free paper. ∞

pup.princeton.edu

Printed in the United States of America

10 9 8 7 6 5 4 3 2

To Kosuke

Contents

Figures

Tables

Acknowledgments ⸻

THIS BOOK began as a dissertation, and along the way to completion many more people have helped than I can acknowledge here. Some deserve special mention. First, I want to thank Susan Pharr for her continual guidance and encouragement as my advisor during both undergraduate and graduate studies at Harvard. I am grateful to Lisa Martin, who sparked my interest in the study of how international institutions help nations cooperate. Her probing questions led me to think more critically about my ideas from the first stage of research design to the final analysis of results. I would also like to thank James Alt, Marc Busch, Robert Paarlberg, and Steven Vogel for reading multiple versions of my research and providing valuable suggestions for improvements. Ezra Vogel and Henry Rosovsky shaped my early interest in Japan, and their guidance has continued to foster the development of my academic career.

I benefited greatly from feedback on parts of the manuscript at different stages from Gabriel Aguilera, Lawrence Broz, William Grimes, Tom Havens, Shigeo Hirano, Ellis Krauss, John Odell, Aurelia George Mulgan, Saadia Pekkanen, Leonard Schoppa, Anne Sartori, Ethan Scheiner, and Michael Witt. At Harvard, the Political Economy Workshop provided intellectual exchange, deadlines to present my work, and tough questions on my research from fellow students and faculty.

The case studies of this research were possible because of the willingness of busy officials and politicians in Japan, Europe, and Washington, D.C., to share their time with me for interviews. In all, I conducted over one hundred interviews from 1996 to 2000. Many of those I interviewed not only answered my questions, but also supplied me with written materials and introductions to other officials; some met with me on several occasions to give me additional information as my research developed. Although they deserve to be acknowledged by name, many requested to remain anonymous, and I have respected their wishes by not giving their names in the text. It is a tribute to their dedication and generous spirit that so many individuals were willing to share their time and knowledge while receiving nothing in return.

There are a few of these individuals to whom I would like to give special thanks. Kōsuke Hori was generous with his time in sharing his experiences as a senior LDP politician engaged in agricultural policy issues. I am grateful to him for introducing me to other politicians and officials and providing me with important materials for my research. Three other Japanese politicians, Katsutoshi Kaneda, Keizō Takemi, and Masami Tanabu, were especially helpful in increasing my understanding of the practice of trade negotiations as seen from a politician's perspective.

For my research it was an invaluable opportunity to be able to speak with officials who held direct experience in some of the toughest agricultural trade negotiations. Nancy Adams, Hisao Azuma, Kevin Brosch, John Child, Yasuo Endō, Glen Fukushima, Carla Hills, Tomomitsu Iwakura, Joao Aguiar Machado, Toshiaki Masuta, Rolf Moehler, Joe O'Mara, Amelia Porges, Hiroya Sano, Takashi Shinohara, Jirō Shiwaku, Hiroshi Ueno, Alan Wolff, Frank Wolter, Seizo Yamazaki, Jun Yokota, and Yutaka Yoshioka were kind to share their views with me in interviews that extended well beyond the allocated time, and several of them met with me on repeated occasions. Each has such extensive personal knowledge about the topic of agricultural trade policy that they should write the analysis themselves. While my study cannot begin to convey the full history of their experiences or their insights about the political process, I hope that in a small way I can contribute to recording their knowledge.

During the year and a half that I spent doing field research in Japan, many individuals contributed to my ability to conduct research. I would like to thank my advisors at the University of Tokyo, Nobuhirō Hiwatari and Junko Katō. Yutaka Arai of the Japanese Ministry of Agriculture and Masaru Yamada of the *Nihon nōgyō shimbun* (Japan agriculture newspaper) took far too much time from their extremely busy schedules to help my research. With their help, I could share a window on the policy-making process. Masami Hasegawa of Keidanren was very kind to spend many hours helping me to learn more about his organization and its position toward agricultural policy. I would also like to thank Mitsuo Ebihara, Hidemi Higashi, Akira Inoue, Fumito Mizuma, Yūki Shirato, Yūko Satō, Aichy Tamori, and Kazuko Yamamoto for their friendship and help with my research. Mr. Yamazaki and Ms. Yamamoto of the *Nihon nōgyō shimbun* archive in Tokyo kindly gave me unlimited access to their newspaper clipping files. I am especially grateful to Sakichi Tarumi, a livestock veterinarian in the northern Hokkaido town of Shari, who took me with him on his rounds of the local farms. Over many repeat visits, he and his wife showed me the best of life in rural Japan. Fumiko and Takashi Imai, Seichirō and Mitsuko Sugizaki, and Ayuchi Takita helped me to feel at home while studying in a foreign country.

My two research trips to Europe were of shorter duration, but officials of the European Commission and national delegations were remarkably accommodating so that I could set up many interviews on a tight schedule. Heiner Thofern kindly assisted my research in Bonn, and Ann Maher of the European Union (EU) Directorate General for Agriculture library in Brussels helped me to find all of the documents that I needed. In particular, I am grateful to the chairman of the European Parliament Committee on Agriculture and Rural Development, Friedrich-Wilhelm Graefe zu Baringdorf, for inviting me to attend the public meetings of the committee for two days during my visit in July 2000. I had the good fortune to hear EU Trade Commissioner Pascal Lamy and French Agriculture Minister Jean Glavany take questions from the committee on issues related to the EU discussion of World Trade Organization (WTO) dispute cases and the upcoming trade round. Observing these exchanges gave me a firsthand view of the passionate opinions about agriculture and the complicated balance of European politics and institutions.

I am grateful to Charles Myers for his interest in my manuscript and guidance throughout the publishing process. I thank Anita O'Brien for her careful copy editing, Pam Bromley for checking the final proofs, Sylvia Coates for creating the index, and Mark Bellis for helping oversee production.

Funding for the research came from the following institutions: the Harvard University Edwin O. Reischauer Institute of Japan Studies, Weatherhead Center for International Affairs, Harvard University Center for European Studies, Fulbright Institute for International Education, U.S. Department of Education (Foreign Language and Area Studies Fellowship), and MacArthur Transnational Security Project, funded by the John D. and Catherine T. MacArthur Foundation. A postdoctoral fellowship from the Harvard University Program on U.S.-Japan Relations allowed me to finish the book in a timely manner.

Finally, my personal debts are the greatest. I thank my parents for encouraging me to challenge myself while always making me realize that I could never fail in their eyes. The support of my husband Kosuke from the beginning to the end of this project represents the greatest act of devotion. Although he was busy with his own graduate studies, Kosuke spent countless hours helping me with theoretical arguments, statistical analysis, Japanese language, and LaTeX. Most importantly, I could always depend on him to make life fun through the ups and downs of research. His encouragement and example have made me a better person and made this a better book.

Abbreviations

APEC	Asia–Pacific Economic Cooperation
BEUC	European Consumers' Organization
CAP	Common Agricultural Policy (EU)
CDU	Christliche Demokratische Union (Germany)
COGECA	General Committee for Agricultural Cooperation in the European Union
COPA	Committee of Agricultural Organisations in the European Union
Coreper	Committee of Permanent Representatives (EU Council of Ministers)
CSU	Christliche Soziale Union (Germany)
DBV	Deutscher Bauernverband (German farmers' association)
DG	Directorate General (European Commission)
DGI	Directorate General for External Relations (European Commission)
DGVI	Directorate General for Agriculture (European Commission)
DSP	Dispute Settlement Proceedings (GATT/WTO)
EC	European Community
EPA	Economic Planning Agency (Japan)
EU	European Union
EVSL	Early Voluntary Sectoral Liberalization (APEC)
FNSEA	Federation Nationale des Syndicats d'Exploitants Agricoles (France)
GATT	General Agreement on Tariffs and Trade
IWC	International Wheat Council
Keidanren	Japan Federation of Economic Organizations
LDP	Liberal Democratic Party (Japan)
MAFF	Ministry of Agriculture, Forestry, and Fisheries (Japan)
MITI	Ministry of International Trade and Industry (Japan)
MOFA	Ministry of Foreign Affairs (Japan)
Nōkyō	Agricultural Cooperative Union (Japan)
OECD	Organization for Economic Cooperation and Development

RMA   Rice Millers' Association (United States)
SPS   Sanitary and Phytosanitary Measures (WTO)
UNICE   Union of Industries of the European Community
USDA   United States Department of Agriculture
USTR   United States Trade Representative
WTO   World Trade Organization

FOOD FIGHTS OVER FREE TRADE

1

Introduction

WAVING BANNERS that proclaimed "Our life is important, our lifestyle is important — so we oppose agricultural liberalization!" Japanese farmers drove thirty-seven tractors through the streets of the Ginza shopping district of downtown Tokyo in November 1989 to protest U.S. demands for rice liberalization. By 1990 their representatives sent politicians petitions signed by nearly ten million supporters who urged the government to reject any increase of agricultural imports. In one instance, seventeen men carried over three hundred cardboard boxes full of petitions to deposit in the Diet members' office building. One year later, fifty thousand Japanese farmers filled the Tokyo Dome baseball stadium in an emergency meeting to rally support for the ban against rice imports. The focus of all this anger by farmers was the Uruguay Round trade negotiation in which negotiators from 115 countries were trying to strengthen the system of trade rules and negotiate lower trade barriers for industrial and agricultural goods as well as for services and investment.[1]

At the same time, European farmers were also protesting against U.S. demands in the Uruguay Round for European Union (EU) agricultural liberalization. French, German, Italian, and other European farmers battled with police dressed in riot gear as they demonstrated in the streets of Brussels where EU decision-makers would determine the future of agricultural policy for all EU member nations. Actions were even more radical in France. As U.S. and EU negotiators struggled to reach an agricultural trade agreement in November 1992, French farmers burned an American flag and ransacked a McDonald's restaurant in Paris. Over the year, twenty-nine bomb attacks were made against public buildings throughout France. European farm groups labeled the compromise agreement that emerged as a "death warrant" for farmers.[2]

Yet by the end of 1993 both Japan and the EU had accepted the

[1] These incidents are recorded in a publication by a Japanese agricultural interest group, Zennōrin (1997), "*Zennōrin 50 nenshi*," pp. 43–62.

[2] This description of events draws on the *Financial Times*, 4 December 1990, and a book by two European Commission officials, Hugo Paemen and Alexander Bensch (1995, 210).

Uruguay Round Agreement requiring that Japan partially open its rice market and that Europe reduce its subsidies to farmers. While the agreement represented less liberalization than the United States and developing countries had wanted, it also represented more agricultural liberalization than in any previous negotiation and a major political concession by Japanese and European leaders for the cause of free trade. Agricultural liberalization angers one of the most powerful domestic constituencies while offering little political reward. Nevertheless, amidst many setbacks over the long history of negotiations on agricultural trade, some negotiations such as the Uruguay Round have brought progress toward liberalization. Why have Japan and Europe ignored farmer protests in some negotiations when they accepted U.S. demands for greater access to their agricultural markets, and why have they risked trade wars in other negotiations by their refusal to change agricultural policies?

This question is of ongoing importance, especially because agriculture is once again taking center stage in the new World Trade Organization (WTO) trade round scheduled to end in 2005. The negotiation, which the World Bank estimates could add 2.8 trillion dollars to global economic activity, may hinge upon whether agreement can be reached on agricultural liberalization.[3] Agriculture negotiations not only are of vital concern to farmers and trade officials around the world, but they also offer insights into the study of comparative politics and international relations. Negotiations over agricultural policy typify the difficulty of balancing local interests with the pressures arising from participation in the global economy.

This book is about the politics of negotiations to open sensitive markets. In such negotiations, international pressure for liberalization meets resistance from strong interest groups, ministries with a stake in the status quo, and high levels of politicization. As governments struggle to find an agreement that both sides can accept, their interaction is constrained by the institutional context of the negotiation. Governments establish rules for international trade in order to facilitate economic cooperation, but how does an international institution like the WTO promote liberalization when it encounters opposition from strong political groups? Can features in the structure of the negotiation present the key to persuading reluctant governments to liberalize markets? Will all governments respond in the same way to similar negotiation strategies? Answers to these questions may be found by looking at the efforts by the United States to open agricultural markets in Japan and the EU.

[3] *International Herald Tribune*, 15 November 2001.

More broadly, the book is aimed to appeal to those interested in trade negotiations, the role of international institutions, and Japanese and EU politics.

Through a comparative study of the past thirty years of agricultural trade negotiations, the following chapters explain how the context of the trade negotiation can offset the passionate and well-organized demands of farmers to make it politically possible for politicians to accept liberalization. Although some agricultural liberalization has taken place through internal reforms without international involvement, much of the substantial policy change in this sector has been the subject of international negotiations. The focus here is on such *negotiated policy liberalization*. It will be shown that two kinds of negotiation structures make governments more likely to liberalize agricultural policies: when a negotiation links together agricultural and industrial issues into a package deal that makes liberalization in one area conditional upon liberalization of the other; or, when a negotiation frames the agricultural protection policy as a violation of international trade law. Issue linkage and legal framing represent distinct strategies to pursue liberalization by either broadening or narrowing the scope of a negotiation. While they apply contradictory pressures, both promote liberalization by adding to the stakes of the negotiation and changing the aggregation of domestic interests. At the same time, the effectiveness of linkage or leverage from international law interacts with domestic interests and policy processes.

When addressing disagreements over trade policies, states can utilize several different existing institutional arenas, and each setting varies in terms of the agenda, rules, and procedures that guide the conduct of the negotiation. The General Agreement on Tariffs and Trade (GATT) and its successor the World Trade Organization form the core international institution for trade issues.[4] Within the GATT framework, negotiations consist of comprehensive trade rounds or legalistic dispute settlement procedures (DSP). The former are major trade events that bring together over a hundred members to negotiate many issues. Launched with an opening declaration by members that provides an agenda for discussion of liberalization across sectors, a trade round proceeds as a mix of informal bargaining and consensus decisions that culminate in a multilateral agreement with binding commitments. Issue linkages are

---

[4] The creation of the WTO in 1995 marked the integration of a new organization with a rule framework that represents an amended version of the 1947 General Agreement on Tariffs and Trade. For simplicity I will use the term GATT as the reference to the general framework of trade rules inclusive of both systems. I will distinguish between GATT 1947 and the WTO when referring to aspects specific to either the old or new institutions.

integral to the process of bringing agreement among the diverse economic interests of members. In contrast, the DSP negotiations resemble adjudication. They begin with the filing of a legal complaint against a specific policy and end with an early settlement or a ruling passed by a panel of judges. The narrow focus on the legal status of a trade barrier tends to exclude linkage among issues. Outside of the GATT framework, other types of trade negotiations include loosely structured bilateral talks on either a single policy or a broad set of issues. In addition, meetings of regional trade associations share the comprehensive character of trade rounds but follow different procedures. For example, the Asia–Pacific Economic Cooperation (APEC) forum emphasizes the voluntary nature of participation in nonbinding agreements. Comparison of these different kinds of negotiations will demonstrate whether the features that shape the structure of a negotiation have an impact on liberalization outcomes.

Theories of international relations and trade policy emphasize the importance of distributional interests and coercive power.[5] However, such explanations cannot account for the variation in outcomes between the same pairs of countries over topics from one sector. If U.S. market power or alliance relations allow it to coerce liberalization by means of threats or persuasion, then one would expect most negotiations with Japan and the EU to bring favorable outcomes for the United States. On the other hand, if the strength of domestic resistance in Japan and Europe determines negotiation outcomes, then one would expect that Japan and the EU would refuse to liberalize agricultural markets. Instead, there is considerable variation in the degree of liberalization across U.S. agricultural trade negotiations with Japan and Europe. Even when controlling for interests and power, issue linkage and legal framing emerge as important factors to predict when countries will liberalize agricultural policies. This finding challenges the emphasis on economic interests and threats found in the literature while pointing to the need to give more attention to the agenda and rules that shape the negotiation process.

Agricultural Protection

Historically, agriculture stands out as a sector where countries stubbornly defend domestic programs. Even though tariffs on industrial goods have fallen during the postwar period to average from 5 to 10

---

[5] For studies with emphasis on the role of preferences derived from economic interests, see, for example, Rogowski (1989), Moravcsik (1997), and Milner (1988; 1997). For studies with emphasis on the structure of power and different forms of coercion in economic relations, see e.g., Gilpin (1981), Gowa (1994), and Drezner (2001).

percent, agricultural protection has remained high with tariffs averaging above 40 percent in 1998 (OECD 1999, 33). Nontariff barriers remained common in the agricultural sector long after they were eliminated for most industrial goods. Indeed, there is a paradoxical relationship in which nearly all industrialized countries raise the levels of protection for agriculture as the sector's size in the economy shrinks (Hayami and Anderson 1986).

High levels of agricultural protection have arisen because farm lobbies are an influential pressure group. Collective action incentives guarantee that farmers wield political strength beyond their numbers (Olson 1965). The economist Peter Lindert (1991, 63) says "the farm sector gets the most protection when it employs 3 to 4 percent of the employed labor force." He explains that as their numbers decline, farmers become better organized and have greater incentives to seek protection, and governments can more easily subsidize the small group of remaining farmers. Few voices are raised against agricultural protection given the lack of organization by consumers and their belief — true or not — that nationally produced food is safer and better. Moreover, electoral districting often biases political representation to favor rural constituencies. Once protection programs were put in place, farmers have used the backing of politicians from rural districts and the agriculture ministry to defend their vested interests in the status quo.

The costs of the resulting agricultural protection include expenditures for higher prices and taxes. Much money is wasted on inefficient programs that often do not help the farmers in most need because they reward higher levels of production rather than compensate for low income levels (Johnson 1991). In 1998 OECD nations spent a total of 362 billion dollars on their farm support policies and per capita expenditure on farm policies reached an astonishing 363 dollars in the United States, 381 dollars in Europe, and 449 dollars in Japan.[6] The most common forms of policy intervention are subsidies, price support measures, and trade barriers.

Protection also closes off valuable markets for agriculture exporters, which include the United States and many developing countries. Research by the U.S. Department of Agriculture (USDA) indicates that elimination of agricultural protection and support could increase the value of U.S. agricultural exports by 19 percent.[7] The USDA study also

[6] These figures are based on the "total support estimate" of the OECD that measures the value of all transfers from taxpayers and consumers arising from policy measures that support agriculture (OECD 1999, 88, 190–91).

[7] U.S. Department of Agriculture (2001), "Food and Agricultural Policy: Taking Stock for the New Century" (Washington, DC: USDA).

predicts that removal of global market distortions would increase global economic welfare by 56 billion dollars annually. Agricultural liberalization by wealthy countries would especially benefit many developing countries, which have been denied fair opportunities to export their goods while at the same time being forced to compete in their local markets with subsidized agricultural products from developed countries. Although many developing countries have a comparative advantage in agriculture and agricultural exports could play a major role in poverty reduction, the subsidies and trade barriers of rich countries have prevented these gains from trade.[8] At the Doha ministerial meeting in November 2001 that launched the new WTO trade round, one delegate said agricultural issues that "may lose elections in France are life and death in Tanzania."[9]

Trade friction represents another cost of agricultural protection, as these policies have given rise to a large number of controversial trade negotiations. Japan and Europe both have stood on the brink of trade wars with the United States over "food fights" that threaten the stability of the global trade system. In the context of the GATT, agricultural issues nearly blocked conclusion of successive trade rounds and generated the largest number of formal trade disputes. In December 1999 at the Seattle meeting of the WTO, when member states failed to agree on beginning a new trade round, agriculture formed one of the major lines of division. Two years later the meeting at Doha nearly ended in a similar failure as France declared that an agenda statement on phasing out agricultural subsidies was a "deal breaker."[10] Only a last-minute compromise allowed the meeting to go forward to establish the agenda for the upcoming round. This compromise included the controversial phrase on agriculture along with the qualification that the agenda would not prejudice the outcome of the negotiation.

The United States made little effort to stop the rise of agricultural protection until the 1960s. It is one of the ironies of postwar institutional development that the United States created the GATT exceptions for agricultural protection that later hindered its own efforts to promote agricultural liberalization. When Western leaders in the aftermath of

[8] A report by Oxfam International (2002, 96) condemns the double standards of developed nation agricultural protection, which have a harmful impact on the agriculture sector "where two-thirds of the poor in developing countries live and work." It cites the 2001 World Bank study, "World Development Report 2000/2001: Attacking Poverty," which provides evidence that annual welfare losses to developing countries from developed nation agricultural protection amount to $20 billion—equivalent to 40 percent the value of aid given these countries.

[9] *The Economist*, 17 November 2001, p. 65.

[10] *International Herald Tribune*, 15 November 2001.

World War II gathered to form the new economic order, their goal was to prevent the kind of competitive protectionist policies that were blamed for the economic turmoil of the 1930s. However, ambitious goals to promote liberalization in a multilateral trading system were modified by the political need to provide flexibility for domestic social policies (Ruggie 1982; Downs and Rocke 1995). In particular, Judith Goldstein (1993) explains that exceptions were closely fit to accommodate the needs of the U.S. agricultural sector. When officials negotiated the original 1947 GATT rules, U.S. agricultural policy used price supports and supply controls such that many products could not compete with imports and could only be exported with the aid of subsidies. Rather than change U.S. domestic policies, GATT rules were shaped around them. The GATT rules fully apply to the agricultural sector, but two clauses (article 11:2c and article 16:3) grant exemptions for primary products from the prohibition against quantitative restrictions and export subsidies under special circumstances.[11] This established the pattern for special treatment of the sector. Goldstein concludes that U.S. preferences shaped the GATT institution, but the institution locked in policies that were difficult to change later.

Although the United States had led the way to high agricultural trade barriers, U.S. interests shifted to favor liberalization in the late 1960s. Over the two decades following the creation of GATT, productivity gains and reformed national policies transformed U.S. agriculture into an internationally competitive, export-oriented sector.[12] By 1971 the Williams Commission, an expert group advising the president on economic problems, highlighted promotion of agricultural exports as a major part of the overall strategy to resolve the U.S. balance of payments deficit and urged the administration to pursue negotiations in GATT to address the barriers against U.S. agricultural exports.[13] Thereafter, while continuing to protect U.S. agricultural markets against imports, the gov-

[11] The conditions for granting the exemption are very specific for quantitative restrictions (quotas are justified when necessary for the function of a domestic supply reduction program), while the conditions are less specific for export subsidies. Hence panel rulings on the former have offered consistent strict interpretations of the rules, while there have been several cases where panels were unable to make a ruling on export subsidies. See Hudec (1993).

[12] See Ingersent and Rayner (1999) for an overview of changes in the pattern of agricultural policy in the United States and Europe. The major U.S. policy shift occurred through several legislative acts in the 1960s that moved farm policy away from supporting above-market price levels. Instead prices were allowed to fall to international market levels while loans and deficiency payments compensated farmers.

[13] "United States International Economic Policy in an Interdependent World," Report to the President submitted by the Commission on International Trade and Investment Policy, July 1971, cited in U.S. Senate Committee on Finance (1979b, 5).

ernment began to use export promotion as a means to support U.S. farmers.[14] The share of agricultural goods in the total value of U.S. exports rose to a high of 25 percent in 1973 (USDA 1999). Although agricultural goods in 1999 were a much smaller 8 percent of total U.S. exports, they remain a substantial export item and one of the largest contributors to the U.S. balance of trade. Among U.S. agricultural export markets, Japan ranked first and Europe ranked second as the recipients of, respectively, 18 percent and 16 percent of the 53.6 billion dollar value of U.S. agricultural exports in 1998.[15]

Japan and Europe faced a more severe agricultural adjustment problem than the United States, and this set the stage for the clash of interests in trade negotiations over agricultural policies. Table 1.1 highlights that both regions have a smaller land endowment and a larger share of the population remaining in the agricultural sector than the United States. As part of the process of postwar industrial growth and economic restructuring, Japanese and European societies experienced rapid decline in the number of farmers from levels of 20 to 30 percent of the population in 1961 to 4 to 5 percent of the population in 1999.[16] Through a combination of price support policies and import barriers, governments in both Japan and Europe intervened in agricultural markets with policies aimed to close the income gap between farmers and workers in other industries (Honma 1994; Grant 1997). Much of the agricultural sector in Europe and nearly all farms in Japan would be unable to compete in world markets without such government intervention. Consequently, U.S. demands for free trade in agriculture have been viewed as threats to the livelihood of farmers and the welfare of rural communities.

In Japan, the Agricultural Basic Law of 1961 sets forth the goals of government intervention in agriculture: to ensure food supply, preserve farm incomes at levels of parity with urban incomes, and preserve the vitality of the rural areas and agriculture (Moore 1990). Price support

---

[14] This does not deny that the United States also continues to protect some agricultural products. Dairy, sugar, and peanuts are a few of the most protected U.S. agricultural products.

[15] In 1998 Canada and Mexico were the next largest markets as recipients of, respectively, 13 percent and 11 percent of all U.S. agricultural exports. USDA Economic Research Service, *Outlook for U.S. Agricultural Trade* (USDA, 1999).

[16] In 1961 across the fifteen countries that are current EU members, farmers were 20 percent of the total population (West Germany and France had, respectively, 14 and 21 percent of the population active in farming). At this time in Japan, farmers were 30 percent of the population. The United States had already undergone much of the transition by 1961 when farmers were just 7 percent of the population. FAO (2001).

TABLE 1.1
Cross-national Comparison of Land and Farm Population in 1999

	Agricultural Land (million hectares)	Per Capita Farmland (hectares)	Farm Population
U.S.	418.25	1.49	2.3%
Japan	5.27	0.04	4.1
EU-15	143.02	0.38	4.5
France	29.90	0.51	3.5
Germany	17.01	0.21	2.6

Source: FAO (2001).

Note: The Farm Population is defined as all persons depending for their livelihood on agriculture, hunting, fishing or forestry (both workers and non-working dependents), and it is reported as percent of total population.

programs and import barriers maintain high farmer incomes despite inefficient production on small land plots (Honma 1994). The Japanese government supported development of a dual-structure agricultural economy with high dependence on imports of feed grains and protection against most other agricultural imports. The lack of any substantial agricultural exports simplifies the picture. Until reforms in the 1990s, the Food Control Agency and several quasi-state trading organizations managed the price-setting and wholesale purchase of several key commodities. Rice was among the most protected commodities and the government maintained self-sufficiency until 1995 with generous support policies, a government monopoly for sale and distribution, and a ban on imports (Hayami and Godo 1995).[17]

Agriculture has achieved a privileged position in Japanese politics. The powerful organizing role of the agriculture cooperatives provides farmers with a unified political voice. Their influence is also enhanced by an electoral system that gave rural votes as much as three times the weight of urban votes until reforms in 1993 partially redressed the imbalance (Mulgan 1997a, 882–883). Farmers are a key electoral base for the dominant Liberal Democratic Party (LDP), and few in Japan speak out against agricultural protection.[18] While consumers would benefit

---

[17] The policy not to purchase imported rice was set aside in 1993 when unusual weather produced a domestic crop shortfall and emergency imports became a temporary necessity.

[18] A majority of all LDP Diet members belong to the Agricultural Policy Committee. Within the ruling LDP's policy-making apparatus, the Comprehensive Agricultural Policy Investigation Committee has a membership including 55 percent of LDP Diet politicians, making it one of the largest among the policy committees that authorize all LDP-sponsored legislation (George 1988, 25).

from cheaper imports, opinion polls reveal little support for liberalization, and consumer organizations have actively opposed liberalization due to food safety and self-sufficiency concerns.[19] Industrial groups, especially the food-processing industry, also would benefit from lower food costs and reduced trade tensions over agricultural issues. However, for decades these antiprotection interests remained largely passive while agricultural protection programs expanded.

Agricultural protection is equally entrenched in Europe, where member nations negotiated a Common Agricultural Policy (CAP) during the process of European integration. The strength of farm groups within the member country governments is augmented by "disproportionate enfranchisement of EC agriculture" in decision-making of the Commission and Council of Ministers (Keeler 1996, 135–137). Since its establishment in 1962, CAP has taken on symbolic importance as the central pillar of European integration. CAP encompasses 90 percent of all European agricultural commodities and for most of the 1980s formed over 50 percent of the Community budget (Grant 1993, 257). The high price support policies of CAP led to chronic oversupply problems and the need to use export subsidies to dispose of the excess production. CAP transformed the Community from a net agricultural importer into a major exporter in less than a decade. In a major difference from Japan, the European agriculture economy encompasses large competitive farms as well as inefficient small farms, and agricultural policies have embraced both protection of the internal market and promotion of exports.

Although the EU is not entirely comparable to other national governments as an actor in world politics, agricultural trade is the policy area where the EU comes closest to resembling a national polity—albeit a federal-style and often divided polity.[20] Under CAP, everything from prices to production quotas is determined by the central EU policy process. Trade negotiations are also coordinated by European institutions as the European Commission acts as the "single voice" for the member states in consultation with the Council of Ministers.[21] This high level of

[19] Official of Shufuren (Housewive's Association). Interview by author. Tokyo, 9 August 1996. See also Vogel (1999).

[20] I refer generally to the European Union (EU), which became the common term upon the signing of the Treaty on European Union at Maastricht in December 1991 that changed the European Community (EC) into the European Union. When making specific references to earlier periods, I will use the term EC as appropriate.

[21] Two EU officials, Hugo Paemen and Alexander Bensch (1995, 94), write that "trade and agricultural policies are among the most integrated of all of the European Community's areas of responsibility. The Member States have transferred all their rights of action to the Community."

centralization at the EU level for agricultural trade facilitates the comparison of the EU in a cross-national study. This book treats the EU as a single entity for aggregate analysis and considers divided interests within the EU according to which national government holds the presidency of the Council of Ministers. Later, in case studies, more attention is given to the influence on EU policy by the different interests of member governments.

The strong opposition to liberalization in Japan and Europe makes it surprising to observe any agricultural liberalization. Indeed, agriculture remains highly protected compared to other sectors. However, *within* the agricultural sector, some liberalization is evident. In Japan, total imports of all agricultural products rose more than forty times in value from 1970 to 2000. Imports by fifteen European member nations doubled in just the fourteen years from 1986 to 2000 (see fig. 1.1).[22] The increasing share of imports in total food consumption provides further evidence of liberalization. Over the period 1970 to 1999, the average import dependency across the main food categories (meat, milk, fruits, vegetables, and cereals) increased from 21 percent to 42 percent for Japan, and from 18 percent to 33 percent for Europe.[23] However, there is also considerable variation by product category. For example, in contrast to growing import dependency for other products, EU import dependency in cereal grains declined as a result of CAP subsidies and trade barriers. Trade negotiations at best were able to reverse the decline slightly. Further variation is found in the aggregated categories. For example, Japan's import dependency for cereal grains exceeded 70 percent for most of the period, but its ban on rice imports guaranteed near complete self-sufficiency in rice production until 1993.[24] The reduc-

[22] The reported data are from FAO (2001). U.S. dollar values have been adjusted to 1995 prices. Since 1986, the FAO has compiled a single aggregate figure for the external trade of the following fifteen European nations, excluding their trade with each other: Austria, Belgium, Denmark, Finland, France, Germany, Greece, Ireland, Italy, Luxembourg, Netherlands, Portugal, Spain, Sweden, and the UK. Although Austria, Finland, and Sweden did not join the EU until 1995, their trade has been included in this figure since 1986.

[23] Author's calculations based on data from food balance sheets reported by FAO (2001). The import dependency for a given commodity group and year is based on the ratio of imports to total supply in terms of quantity for that commodity. The FAO calculates conversion back to the primary level for processed commodities. The aggregate figure given here is a simple average of the five commodity group ratios for the specified year and region. The FAO compiles a single import figure for the fifteen nations that form the current EU membership.

[24] Some imports were allowed into Okinawa for the production of a local variety of rice wine, but import dependency was 0.2 percent in 1992 according to the FAO data.

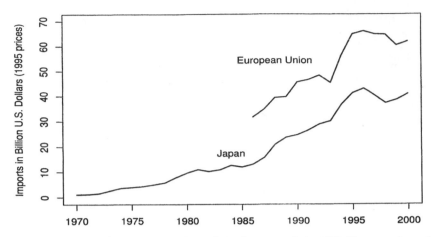

Figure 1.1: Agriculture Import Growth in Japan and the EU. Shows value of total agricultural imports in billion U.S. dollars adjusted to 1995 prices. EU figures are for trade by the fifteen EU members excluding intra-EU trade (data available beginning in 1986).

tion of trade barriers as well as changes in the structure of demand and supply account for the increase of food imports, which is evident in other industrial countries as well.

Although governments continue to favor farmers with subsidies and special programs, the trend is toward reducing such support. OECD statistics monitoring agricultural policies indicate that total support to agriculture as a share of GDP has fallen substantially (see table 1.2). In particular, market-distorting policies, such as price supports and export subsidies, are gradually being replaced by direct income payments. These changes have closed some of the gap between world market prices and the prices paid to farmers in Japan and Europe. For example, the ratio between internal and border prices for milk in Japan and the EU declined from respective levels of 7.7 and 3.3 in 1986 to 4.7 and 1.7 in the year 2000. Even where nominal protection remains large, market price support has declined. Over this period, Japan reduced market price support for rice by 39 percent and for beef by 56 percent, and the EU reduced market price support for wheat by 86 percent.[25] The variation by commodity and policy measure complicates evaluation of agricul-

---

[25] Figures are author's calculation based on the producer nominal protection coefficient and market price support data of the OECD Producer and Consumer Support Estimates Database.

TABLE 1.2
Reduction of Support to Agriculture

Region	1986–88	1999
Japan	2.6%	1.6%
EU	2.6	1.5
U.S.	1.4	1.0
OECD 24	2.2	1.3

Source: OECD (2000a).
Note: OECD Total Support estimates as share of GDP (percent) for Japan, the European Union, the United States, and the average of the twenty-four OECD members. The estimate includes financial transfers from taxpayers and consumers. The higher the percentage, the larger the share of national wealth used to support agriculture.

tural policy changes, but the OECD figures reported in table 1.2 show the overall reduction of support levels.

The significance of this increase of agricultural imports depends largely on the standard of evaluation. For governments trying to open Japanese and European agricultural markets, changes seem inadequate. Against an expectation that agricultural trade barriers should be reduced to the levels of industrial trade barriers, existing levels of protection of agriculture are far too high. In contrast, for farmers in Japan and Europe, their governments have conceded too much to foreign demands. Against an expectation that politically influential groups receive protection, a surprising amount of liberalization has taken place. In short, looking at the same policy outcome — for example, Japan's 1993 decision to import up to 8 percent of domestic rice consumption — one could consider this a small market share or a major political step.

Whether beginning from an expectation of zero or full liberalization, it is the variation in outcomes across different negotiations that is important. The two most recent GATT trade rounds illustrate the wide disparity in negotiation outcomes: the Tokyo Round ended with only small tariff concessions and modest expansion of import quotas in agriculture; in contrast, the Uruguay Round cut agricultural tariffs by 36 percent and domestic subsidies by 20 percent, and also converted nontariff barriers into tariff policies. In a series of negotiations, the Japanese government reduced the number of quotas on primary goods from fifty-eight in 1970 to five remaining quotas (MAFF 1997). Among these negotiations, in 1984 the Japanese government refused to end the quotas on beef and orange imports, but in 1988 agreed to end the quotas. The decision to end the rice import ban in the Uruguay Round was shortly followed by an APEC negotiation in which Japan refused to change its policies for fishery and forestry products. U.S. negotiations with the EU produced similarly contrasting outcomes. In 1986 European officials agreed to reduce duties against U.S. citrus products and to reduce export subsidies for European pasta products. However, despite retaliatory sanctions and a negative WTO ruling, the EU still refuses to modify the health regulation that prohibits the import of most U.S. beef.

In short, farmers are powerful, but not all-powerful. Some negotiations ended in deadlock with no policy change, others brought only partial changes in the level of protection, while others led to the overhaul of existing policy. This mix of liberalization outcomes within the agricultural sector challenges explanations based on domestic interest groups or foreign pressure alone. One must consider instead what factors in the context of each negotiation strengthen or weaken the relative influence of U.S. demands and political resistance in Japan and Europe.

Perspectives on Trade Negotiations

Negotiations are the most basic form of international cooperation. A negotiation can be anything from a simple conversation between diplomats over a disagreement to a formal meeting involving hundreds of countries and a broad agenda on a range of issues. Because the outcome may determine whether countries pursue war or peace and whether they open markets or close them, understanding why some negotiations are more successful than others is central to international relations. Do the more powerful states always win? Do strong domestic interests and values shape agreements? Such questions raised by the realist and liberal traditions of international relations theories address the larger forces that influence negotiations. Yet in the negotiation process, both power and interests are constrained by rules of the game that are recognized by all parties — it matters whether the negotiation takes place in an informal bartering session or in an international court. Therefore the study of negotiations should give attention not only to power and interests but also to the arena in which these forces face off against each other. Since power and interests tend to shift only slowly over time, attention to the details of the negotiation process offers more clues to explain individual negotiation outcomes and better advice for policy-makers about future strategies.

Trade policy offers a promising area for the study of negotiations. On the one hand, states can autonomously set their own commercial policies — the right to raise tariffs stands alongside the right to collect taxes as a basic function of governments. However, in order to gain access to foreign markets, states usually must grant access to their own markets. This gives rise to the need for negotiations to promote and/or restrain the forces of economic interdependence. Governments choose among different institutional fora and negotiating strategies: unilateral versus multilateral demands, threats versus legal complaints, single-sector versus multisector negotiations. The economic impact of changes in trade policies also means that political constraints at home bear directly on the negotiation. The large number of trade negotiations provides a broad sample of evidence to evaluate how these factors influence outcomes.

When explaining negotiations, different theoretical approaches emphasize the importance of the preferences of negotiating parties, the strategic interaction between governments in the negotiation, the two-level interaction between domestic groups and governments, and the institutional context of the negotiation. The next section will discuss these perspectives on the study of trade negotiations and justify the need to give more attention to the institutional context of the negotiation. The central claim is that international institutions that structure a negotiation change the balance of interests at the domestic level in a direction favoring liberalization. Counter to the expectations of both liberal and realist theories of international relations, rules persuade more than power — whether the power of politically influential interest groups or U.S. pressure.

Trade Policy Preferences

Economic interests and political institutions determine the goals put forth in each government's negotiation mandate at the outset of the negotiation. Understanding the source of preferences over trade policies is fundamental to international political economy and is the logical starting point for an examination of trade negotiations.

Economic approaches to trade policy instruct us that countries gain from trade by exporting those goods that hold a comparative advantage within the economy. The Ricardo-Viner model assumes it is difficult for factors to move (e.g., farmers are unable easily to change occupations and reallocate their assets), and therefore import-competing sectors lose from trade while export sectors gain from trade. The Hecksher-Ohlin model assumes land, labor, and capital are completely mobile so that relatively abundant factors will benefit from trade while relatively scarce factors will suffer. For land-scarce Japan, this implies that trade hurts landowners and benefits owners of capital. Political economy studies have drawn on these models to explain the pattern of social cleavages and preferences for trade policies (Rogowski 1989; Hiscox 2002). This division of the winners and losers from trade explains broad differences, such as why farmers in Japan and Europe oppose liberalization while their industrial manufacturers favor liberalization. However, what does this mean for policy outcomes? The declining share of agriculture in the economy and the losses suffered from trade weaken the sector and also strengthen its need for government intervention.

In the policy-making process, politicians consider not only the aggregate economic interests of their constituency but also the contributions and votes promised by those groups that lobby for narrow interests.[26] Many of the economic inefficiencies observed in policy outcomes are attributed to *collective action problems* that arise because groups representing a smaller segment of the population, such as farmers, have greater incentive and capacity to organize than broader groups in the population, such as consumers. Thus narrow interests are more likely to accept the costs of paying campaign contributions and organizing voter turnout in order to lobby for their policy goals. This dynamic explains why there is a political marketplace for protection even when it is not economically rational to protect that sector. From this perspective, the political organization of farmers accounts for their ability to earn more protection, and liberalization is unexpected.

Liberalization outcomes may reflect the decision to delegate to an executive representing broader interests. In U.S. politics, Congress is said to have delegated to the president in order to avoid its own protectionist tendencies and gain the benefits of liberalization (Lohmann and O'Halloran 1994). In the Japanese and European political context, some have described a policy process in which elite technocrats form a blueprint to guide economic policy according to a chosen trajectory for economic development (Johnson 1982; Haas 1958). However, for the most part, models of politicians abdicating control to bureaucrats in Japan and Europe have been dismissed. Not only do bureaucrats have interests that may diverge from objective national economic interests, but also they share influence with political actors that make decisions

---

[26] In the landmark study of the political forces for protection, Schattschneider (1935) says the advantage for concentrated interests over diffuse interests explained the support for the protectionist Smoot-Hawley Act. Olson (1965) offers the classic study of biased influence for organized groups in political action. For formal models of pressure group influence, see Becker (1983) and Grossman and Helpman (1994). Rodrik (1995) provides a review article of a range of studies. In an empirical evaluation of U.S. trade policy, Goldberg and Maggi (1999) show that the level of political organization and import penetration explain the structure of protection across sectors within the United States.

about when and how much authority to delegate (Cowhey and McCubbins 1995; Moravcsik 1998).

Politicians are usually unwilling to grant autonomy when there are divided interests and high political stakes, which means that the degree of delegation varies across policy areas and issues.[27] In trade negotiations, the interests at stake and nature of the policy process varies with the context of each negotiation. This creates different incentives for delegation. In Europe, the Council of Ministers has sometimes passed a strict mandate limiting the negotiation authority of the Commission, and at other times granted considerable flexibility (Meunier 2000). The Japanese Diet passed three resolutions against rice liberalization, which restrained the freedom of the government during the Uruguay Round. In other negotiations the Diet has largely been on the sidelines waiting for the outcome negotiators bring back. Rather than an a priori level of delegation, the balance between different government actors changes for each negotiation.

Institutions or ideas can strengthen the influence of one interest over another (Alt and Gilligan 1994; Goldstein and Keohane 1993). The electoral system shapes distributive politics for who receives the allocation of benefits from trade and the supply of protection policies. For example, in Japan electoral districting has led to overrepresentation of rural areas in the Diet, and multimember districts have magnified the influence of concentrated voting groups such as farmers (Mulgan 2001). It is also possible for institutions to reshape policy choices in ways that lead to mobilization of narrow interests favoring liberalization to counterbalance those for protection (Gilligan 1997). Prevailing ideology will shape what goals are pursued and which solutions are seen as likely to prove effective. An ideological notion about food security that calls for self-sufficiency in food supply and maintenance of family farms helps to explain the form of protection policies in Japan and Europe. The sum of domestic pressure on a given policy issue will reflect economic interests, collective action, bias in the political system, and ideas about how best to achieve social welfare. However, these factors better explain the persistence of agricultural protection policies in Japan and Europe, and leave as a puzzle the variation in negotiation outcomes and the emergence of greater liberalization.

A common assumption across many political economy models of trade policy is that countries set their trade policies autonomously. Even cross-national studies attribute variation in trade patterns to industry-

---

[27] See Epstein and O'Halloran (1999) for a thorough review of the literature on delegation and analysis of when the U.S. Congress has been more or less willing to delegate.

or country-specific characteristics (Ray and Marvel 1984; Lee and Swagel 1997). The focus on U.S. trade policy may account for this emphasis on the single-country determination of trade policy. Sheer market size allows considerable autonomy for the United States, such that it may indeed be possible for the United States to impose its preference for open markets or to adopt an optimal tariff (Kindleberger 1986; Conybeare 1987). However, for most countries, and even the United States, it is difficult and often undesirable to pursue unilateral trade policy.

International politics constrain trade policy choices because the options for export markets and the costs of protecting imports are directly related to the policies of other countries. Given the competing trade preferences within a country, not only domestic politics and institutions but also international politics and institutions interact to favor one policy over another. Thus while understanding trade preferences is a start to the analysis of trade policy, one must look further at the international bargaining that influences which preferences will be realized.

Interstate Bargaining

Whether a country can achieve its policy goal depends on the strategic interaction between national governments in the negotiation. In their analysis of international bargaining, many studies assume that preferences over trade policy are fixed and states are unitary actors. From this perspective, material power or strategic tactics provide bargaining leverage that determines negotiation outcomes.

Realist perspectives on bargaining emphasize that national interest and material power determine the distribution of gains in negotiations (Krasner 1991; Mearsheimer 1994–95; Steinberg 2002). In this view, threats or bribes coerce countries into making compromises they would not otherwise choose. When applied to economic negotiations, the size of the U.S. economy and its role as a superpower help the United States force other states to open their markets. Many studies of U.S.-Japan negotiations portray Japan as a "reactive state" that will submit to pressure when the United States threatens to deny access to U.S. markets and alliance cooperation (Calder 1988; Lincoln 1999). This approach seems persuasive for static comparison; Japan's higher level of dependence on U.S. markets may account for its greater responsiveness to U.S. pressure relative to the EU. However, it does not fit the general trend that liberalization has increased since 1970 even though the relative dependence of Japan and Europe on the U.S. market has declined.

Strategic dependence is also an unsatisfying explanation. Some of the most controversial and least successful trade negotiations have occurred when global security tension should have enhanced the importance of the alliance. For example, in 1963 at the height of Cold War politics, the United States and the EC engaged in a trade dispute over U.S. poultry exports to Germany, the so-called Chicken War, and both sides refused to back down. Decades later as the United States prepared to lead troops to fight in the Gulf War, Japan, Europe, and the United States caused an embarrassing negotiation failure when they steadfastly refused to compromise their positions on agriculture in a December 1990 GATT negotiation in Brussels. None of the alliance partners seemed to restrain their demands or make more generous concessions in order to maintain a common front. Indeed, it is quite difficult to say whether one would expect more or less liberalization because of a strategic relationship.

Although the United States has the capacity to coerce other countries, its interests may be mixed and its resources inappropriate for the task. In economic negotiations with allies and trade partners, military power is not relevant, and the denial of access to U.S. markets harms the United States and damages important relationships. Therefore, the United States may be willing to back down, depending on its own costs and its evaluation of whether the trade partner is bluffing or genuinely cannot politically afford to offer concessions (Odell 1993; Gawande and Hansen 1999). As a result, it may be difficult to determine negotiation outcomes even when U.S. goals and power vis-à-vis an ally are clearly understood.

While preferences and power constrain states in a negotiation, states' choice of strategies depends on beliefs about what the other actor will do. The strategic bargaining literature views negotiating strategies that rely on information and commitment as the source of bargaining leverage.[28] From this perspective, uncertainty is the biggest obstacle to international cooperation. Bargaining leverage derives from which side can make a credible threat, and cooperation is possible when states can make credible commitments. This focus on credibility arises because actors have incentives to misrepresent their preferences when it can help them achieve an outcome closer to their ideal point.

The realist approach, and most bargaining models of strategic interaction, assume the state is a unitary actor. Focusing only on the national level outcomes, this assumption ignores the variation in preferences among different domestic actors and the uncertainty over which group's

---

[28] For example, see Schelling (1960), Morrow (1994), Fearon (1998), and Lake and Powell (1999).

interests will be reflected in policy outcomes. Treating the domestic level as a black box seems especially inappropriate for the study of trade negotiations because distributional effects create opposing interests within a country, and the potential losses to some do not threaten national survival in a way that would force national unity. Domestic factors will influence the strategies of both sides as each negotiates while looking at their own domestic audience and their opponents' domestic costs.

Domestic Politics and International Negotiations

Negotiation agreement is possible only when it satisfies both domestic and international requirements. Robert Putnam (1988) introduced the analogy of "two-level games" to characterize the observation that a leader negotiates simultaneously over domestic constraints and the international bargain. Fundamentally, distributional consequences and interest group behavior in the domestic institutional context set the parameters for negotiation outcomes (Milner 1997; Moravcsik 1998). From a tactical perspective, a restrictive mandate from a critical home audience may help to push a foreign negotiating partner to offer more concessions (Schelling 1960, 28).[29] Domestic processes are also important because they convey information about state intentions. For example, legislative involvement in negotiations may increase the likelihood of cooperation because it allows governments to commit credibly to implement an agreement (Martin 2000).[30]

The importance of examining both international and domestic levels of the negotiation has been emphasized in analyses of Japanese and European foreign policy. Several studies demonstrate that *gaiatsu* (foreign pressure) is necessary to bring change in Japan but will work only when domestic groups support the foreign demand.[31] The policy process in Europe is even more complicated. Some have pointed to the need to understand EU trade politics as a "three-level game" in which there is the national process of preference determination, and then an EU pro-

---

[29] See Evans, Jacobson, and Putnam (1993) for several case study applications of two-level games analysis. See Iida (1993) and Tarar (2001) for bargaining models extending Schelling's argument.

[30] Iida (1993) and Tarar (2001) argue that domestic constraints can improve distributive outcomes for the constrained side. Milner (1997) uses an alternative bargaining model to show that domestic divisions could make cooperation more rather than less difficult.

[31] Mulgan (1997b) applies this argument to the study of agricultural trade negotiations. Mikanagi (1996) and Schoppa (1993, 1999) examine the effectiveness of foreign pressure in U.S.-Japan bilateral negotiations.

cess for aggregating these national policies into a single EU position, and finally an international negotiation for coordinating international policies (Moyer 1993; Patterson 1997). However, since the EU Council of Ministers brings together national representatives to form a single negotiating mandate, it is possible to consider a two-level analysis of the EU politics in the Council of Ministers and the international bargaining level that parallels the domestic-international balancing act of other governments participating in trade negotiations.[32]

When studies relax the unitary actor assumption in order to address the complexity of domestic politics and its effect on international cooperation, they often generalize about the international level. For example, in a study of domestic politics and international relations, Helen Milner (1997) argues that the distributional consequences of cooperation for domestic interest groups and the domestic institutions that filter the influence of these interests will determine when international cooperation occurs. However, she treats the international negotiation as an undifferentiated bargaining arena.[33] This disregards the possibility that factors related to the international level could change the costs of cooperation for domestic actors.

In another important study, John Odell (2000) finds that negotiations are likely to achieve better outcomes when negotiators pursue integrative strategies that present gains for both sides. He examines how market conditions, beliefs, and domestic politics influence these strategies. However, the options available to negotiators are also influenced by constraints in the negotiation context, and any individual state has limited freedom to restructure those constraints.

This leads to the question, *what if the negotiation context affects the domestic distributional consequences of the negotiation outcome?* When governments choose among mixed domestic preferences, they consider the influence of international level constraints. Not only do governments evaluate the bargaining constraints, but also different domestic actors respond to the stakes created by the international negotiation. Both mobilization by interest groups and the policy track for decision making change according to how the negotiation frames the issues.

For example, the institutions of the Uruguay Round trade negotiation established a comprehensive package for the negotiation of a single

---

[32] See Meunier (2000) for an example.

[33] Milner (1997, 70) writes, "The international game adopted does not have a well-defined institutional structure; politics on that level are assumed to be anarchic, and international negotiations are generally conducted without a constitutionally mandated sequence of moves."

agreement for agricultural, industrial, and service market liberalization. Linking different issues had important implications for the distributional consequences of the negotiation, as liberalization desired by some industrial groups was made conditional on liberalization opposed by agricultural groups. At the same time, the broad agenda of the negotiation expanded the policy jurisdiction to give trade ministers more access to influence agricultural policy decisions. If there had not been any constraints created by the negotiation structure, Japan and Europe could have bargained over industrial trade liberalization separate from agricultural trade liberalization. Under such a scenario, export-oriented industry groups would lobby for the industrial goods negotiation and ignore the agricultural goods negotiation, while autonomous agriculture ministries and strong farm group lobbying would dominate the decision making for the agricultural negotiation. Clearly the credible linkage between the two different trade issues that arose in the negotiation had important implications for the distributional consequences of the negotiation on interest groups and for the constraints of domestic institutions on state policies. This example points to the need to examine more closely the negotiation context.

The Institutional Context of the Negotiation

Negotiations do not occur in a vacuum. International institutions act as the rules of the game that provide the context for bargaining among states and among domestic actors. This book emphasizes the influence of the institutions specific to the negotiation—the agenda, rules, and procedures that regulate the interaction between states in the policy dispute. The analysis builds on a wider literature about the role of international institutions while deepening understanding of how institutions influence negotiation outcomes.

Douglass North (1994, 60) defines institutions as "the humanly devised constraints that structure human interaction. They are made up of formal constraints (e.g., rules, laws, constitutions), informal constraints (e.g., norms of behavior, conventions, self-imposed codes-of-conduct), and their enforcement characteristics. Together, they define the incentive structure of societies and specifically economies." The WTO forms the principal institution for trade, although it operates alongside many other economic institutions, including bilateral trade agreements, regional trade associations, and other organizations such as the OECD. The WTO is a multilateral organization with a secretariat based in Geneva and a membership that had grown to 144 countries and customs unions by the end of 2001. As an international institution, it consists of rules for trade policies that form the core of international trade law, procedures for dispute settlement, and a forum for negotiations on new rules and commitments.

The present international trade system finds its roots in the planning of the United States, United Kingdom, and other allies during World War II. Leaders sought to create an economic system that would prevent the kind of economic turmoil that had contributed to developments leading to war. The historic 1944 Bretton Woods conference focused on monetary and banking issues and also endorsed the need to regulate trade. Governments proved unable to reach consensus on an International Trade Organization, but in 1947 twenty-three governments signed as contracting parties to the GATT, which was a "provisional" arrangement that became the de facto trade rules for nearly half a century. This multilateral agreement contained schedules of individual tariff commitments that were generalized to all members by the obligation of most-favored-nation treatment. The GATT rules guided the conduct of trade by prohibiting discriminatory treatment and regulating the use of different kinds of trade policies.[34] The GATT also provided a forum with formal procedures and mediation for the resolution of disputes over trade issues related to these rules. Periodic trade rounds among all members brought new tariff reduction commitments and amendments to GATT rules. In 1994 the Uruguay Round established the WTO as a formal organization that would thereafter encompass both the obligations of the GATT 1947 system and the new agreements of the Uruguay Round.[35]

In his functional theory of institutions, Robert Keohane (1984) describes an array of functions performed by institutions such as the GATT that help nations cooperate. Building on the transaction cost economics literature, Keohane argues that international institutions lower transaction costs by providing information, linking issues, and making commitments more credible.[36] Transaction costs arise because of the risk from uncertainty and the time investment for deal making. For example, two countries may be unable to make a trade agreement because each has incentives to refuse to comply with the liberalization of its

[34] The general rules of GATT articles 2 through 17 apply to all products and address the following policy areas: antidumping and countervailing duties, valuation of goods for customs purposes, procedures for customs administration, marks of origin, quantitative restrictions, subsidies, and state trading monopolies (Jackson 1997, 51–52).

[35] This brief overview draws on Jackson (1997). For more on the WTO, see also Krueger (1998).

[36] Keohane highlights that international institutions perform functions that create the conditions necessary for voluntary agreements as specified in the theorem by Ronald Coase (1960): legal framework, perfect information, and zero transaction costs.

sensitive products. A commitment to abide by an agreement is more credible when there is a system for monitoring compliance and punishing violations. International institutions engage states in an ongoing process of repeated negotiations and provide information about reputations. Transactions will be less risky—and hence more likely to take place—if there is an external source of information, such as a neutral third party who can maintain records on past behavior (Milgrom, North, and Weingast 1990). International institutions also increase cooperation by linking issues to create mutually beneficial agreements— more quids make it easier to reach agreement in quid pro quo deal making (Keohane 1984, 91).

Norms and legitimacy are another mechanism by which institutions can favor some policies over others. Alongside the material context of the negotiation is the social context.[37] Some policies will appear more legitimate than others, and a foreign demand to change a policy will encounter more resistance if the domestic policy is held to be legitimate and the foreign demand unjustified (Bhagwati and Patrick 1990; Chayes and Chayes 1995). On the other hand, a judgment that a policy violates international law undermines the legitimacy of the policy if leaders and the public attribute value to having policies congruent with accepted international norms.[38] As states continue to participate in the international institution, socialization makes it more likely that leaders and the public will prefer cooperation. At the same time, the interest a state has in the continued integrity of the system of rules also motivates decisions to follow rules.

Institutional theories often aggregate together these multiple functions to explain the general pattern of cooperation. However, to understand the causal process it is necessary to examine variation in specific features of institutions. Recent studies point to the need to consider how international institutions such as the WTO create fora for bargain-

[37] See Schoppa (1999) for a discussion of social context influencing U.S.-Japan negotiations. For a broad theoretical review and analysis, see Johnston (2001).

[38] Theoretical models have shown that the presence of a sense of international obligation motivates countries to follow GATT rulings (Kovenock and Thursby 1992). This use of legitimacy does not require abandoning a rationalist framework. Keohane (1984, 89) refers to possible retaliation, reputation damage, and linkage with future agreements as some of the costs associated with taking illegitimate actions. From the standpoint of utility maximization, it is possible to view "duty" as part of preference ordering. For example, Downs (1957) included in his model of voting turnout a term, D, to represent citizen duty. Subsequent analysis of the calculus of voting has also used a sense of duty to explain why people take the trouble to vote even when their single vote has almost no chance of changing the outcome and providing gains in the traditional sense of utility optimization. See Aldrich (1993) for a discussion of different approaches in the voting literature.

ing and shape outcomes (Morrow 1994; Fearon 1998). This involves looking more closely at institutions to show which rules and norms influence behavior, and how they create incentives that favor particular policy outcomes over others.[39]

Despite the central role of negotiations in shaping the international political economy, little is known about institutions specific to negotiation structure. The tendency has been for scholars to analyze one particular kind of negotiation in isolation, such as negotiations initiated by unilateral U.S. trade policies (section 301 cases), GATT dispute settlement cases, GATT trade rounds, or the structured bilateral talks between Japan and the United States.[40] However, few studies examine the differences between negotiations conducted in a GATT trade round versus a GATT dispute settlement proceeding versus bilateral talks or a regional trade forum.

In addition to comparison across negotiations, a closer examination of the negotiation process is important. Many claim that institutions matter because incentives created by institutions influence state preferences (Krasner 1983a). Yet little is known about how this feedback process operates. Studies focus on either state-to-state interaction or government-to-private-sector interaction without looking at both. The literature on international institutions introduces greater complexity to models of international politics while still assuming that states are unitary actors.[41]

Integration of the study of international institutions and theorizing about two-level games offers new insights into how international institutions lower transaction costs, not only at the international level but

[39] See Abbott and Snidal (2000), Simmons (2000), and Koremenos, Lipson, and Snidal (2001) for examples.

[40] See Bayard and Elliott (1994), Kherallah and Beghin (1998), and Zeng (2002) for studies of U.S. trade negotiations initiated under section 301 of U.S. trade law, which includes comparison of section 301 negotiations in GATT mediation with all other section 301 cases. GATT dispute cases are given separate treatment in analyses by Hudec (1993), Reinhardt (2001), Busch (2000), Maggi (1999), and Kovenock and Thursby (1992). U.S.-Japan bilateral talks are the focus of analyses by Yumiko Mikanagi (1996) and Leonard Schoppa (1997). For studies of the Tokyo Round, see Jackson, Louis, and Matsushita (1984) and Winham (1986). For a study of the Uruguay Round, see Croome (1995). Josling, Tangermann, and Warley (1996) give a historic overview of how GATT trade rounds have addressed agricultural issues. In one of the most comprehensive negotiation studies to date, John Odell (2000) examines ten negotiations in different negotiation contexts, presenting a framework to examine the effect of market conditions, culture and belief, and domestic politics on negotiation strategies and outcomes.

[41] See, for example, Keohane (1984), Fearon (1994), Bagwell and Staiger (1999), and Maggi (1999).

also at the domestic level. The literature on international institutions focuses on how international institutions correct for market imperfections that result from lack of certainty and enforcement of contracts in an anarchic world system.[42] Yet transaction costs are also incurred at the domestic level, and these may be harder to overcome than those at the international level (Moravcsik 1999, 301). Imperfections in political markets due to collective action problems and lack of information are often used to explain the rise of protection policies.[43] Even after an international institution has reduced international transaction costs, if obstacles to cooperation at the level of domestic politics remain, liberalization will be unlikely. Changing this domestic balance is a fundamental aspect of how international institutions promote cooperation. Governments must form a coalition to support a liberalization policy, and doing so requires committing to compensate some groups and convincing other politicians they will not be blamed for giving in to foreign demands. International institutions are important because they reduce transaction costs between states and also *within* states.

Overview of Argument

International institutions make liberalization more likely when they compensate for the collective action problems and segmented policy-making that support protection policies. Where trade politics are often dominated by narrow interests demanding protection and bureaucratic actors with a vested stake in the status quo, new negotiation stakes and information provided by an international institution can increase the lobbying for liberalization and break down the walls of bureaucratic jurisdiction. In particular, agricultural liberalization is most likely when the lobbying for protection by farmers and the policy autonomy of agriculture ministers is counterbalanced by a free-trade coalition and broad policy jurisdiction.

Two kinds of institutional arrangements for trade negotiations can help establish these conditions necessary for liberalization. The first negotiation structure links agricultural issues in a comprehensive negotiation package with other sectors. The second places the single policy within the legal framework of trade rules. While each represents a distinct causal mechanism and arises in a different kind of negotiation,

---

[42] In addition to Keohane (1984), examples of other studies that focus on transaction costs within anarchy to explain state cooperation include Yarbrough and Yarbrough (1992), Martin (1992a), Frieden (1994), and Weber (2000).

[43] See, for example, Simmons (1994) and Krueger (1996).

both rely upon the larger GATT institution to reinforce the credibility of the negotiation structure that places agricultural issues in a larger context of interests.

The study of issue linkage is prominent in both American politics and international relations. Cross-sector issue linkage is the focus of this book. When the agenda and procedures of a negotiation bind together negotiations for market opening across multiple sectors into a single package deal, this broadens the economic stakes of the negotiation. This kind of all-or-nothing approach forces a choice between preferences for protection of one sector and liberalization of another. Institutionalization of this negotiation structure increases the credibility of the linkage. Once there is a credible issue linkage, it motivates those who gain from free trade to lobby against those who prefer protection. The wide scope of the agenda also brings in more policy actors and reduces the autonomy of representatives for any single interest within decision making. Politicians can more easily accept an agreement that holds a balance of gains and losses for domestic interests.

In contrast to issue linkage, legal framing relies on narrowing the scope of the negotiation agenda. Evaluating a single policy issue in the context of international trade law introduces reputation and international obligation as additional factors. Adjudication of disputes publicly brands those who violate their commitments in terms of a specific policy measure. To the extent that countries fear that a bad reputation may reduce their ability to negotiate future liberalizing agreements or their leverage against discriminatory policies, this kind of negotiation will bring early settlements. A legal ruling against a policy legitimizes demands for liberalization, and this strengthens arguments favoring liberalization while placing opponents on the defensive. The normative pressure of international law has political utility to persuade domestic audiences. At the same time, the rules hold implications for material interests because of their role to promote trade. As the combination of these normative and trade interests, international obligation represents a new stake in favor of liberalization.

The political economy of agricultural trade in Japan and the EU represents the classic example of how a well-organized lobby and biased political system can produce high levels of protection. Liberalization of such sensitive policies requires broadening interests and lowering political costs. The negotiation structure can facilitate this process, although the relative effectiveness of different negotiation structures is conditioned on the domestic political context. The contention that the GATT/WTO institutions have promoted agricultural liberalization in trade rounds and dispute settlement proceedings over the protests of farm groups counters the argument that states will not cooperate on issues when they face opposition by powerful domestic interests. Indeed, linkage and law provide more leverage to open markets than do threats of retaliation.

Studying variation within and across trade institutions offers new insights into how institutions affect state behavior. First, the disaggregation of the number of issues, rules and norms, and the number of actors reveals the relative influence of distinct features in the negotiation structure. Second, the examination of the domestic level effects of international institutions demonstrates the causal mechanism by which international institutions promote cooperation.

Methodology and Organization

In the following chapters, a combination of quantitative analysis and comparative case studies is used to examine agricultural negotiations between the United States and Japan and Europe from 1970 to 1999. Over this period, U.S. advocacy of liberalization and foreign protectionist lobby resistance to liberalization of the agricultural sector have both remained fairly steady. Five hypotheses are compared in order to study the effect on negotiated policy liberalization resulting from two negotiation structures, cross-sector issue linkage and legal framing, and to consider the alternative influence from threats, domestic politics, and budget pressures. Focusing on negotiations where Japan and Europe are on the receiving side of U.S. demands for agricultural market liberalization facilitates analysis of variation in negotiation structure while partially controlling for the primary alternative explanations of trade policy: U.S. interest and power, on the one hand, and protectionist lobby interest and power, on the other. Moreover, evidence that institutional context influences negotiation outcomes even in such a least likely case for trade liberalization as the agricultural sector provides a strong test of institutional theories about international relations.[44]

First, the effect on liberalization from different negotiation features is evaluated in quantitative analysis of an original dataset, which includes over 250 products that were the subject of U.S. negotiations with Japan and Europe from 1970 to 1999. A negotiation on an agricultural trade barrier forms the unit of analysis. "Agricultural products" include fishery, tobacco, and alcoholic beverages in addition to raw and processed

---

[44] For an explanation of case study analysis and the use of least likely cases for testing theories, see Eckstein (1975).

foodstuffs.[45] Negotiations range widely in terms of agenda and procedures, including the following kinds of negotiations: GATT and WTO dispute settlement cases, which are legalistic proceedings initiated by a formal complaint; GATT trade rounds, which are comprehensive talks on rule making and tariff bargaining; ad hoc bilateral talks; and regional talks such as the APEC sectoral trade liberalization negotiation.

Then, comparative case studies are used to examine the process by which the institutional context of the negotiation influences the policy outcome. The goal is to explain whether issue linkage works through the connection with export interests and whether leaders perceive that accepting the authority of legalistic settlements holds legitimacy that will reduce their political costs. Attention is given to decisions that shape the negotiation agenda, rules, and procedures. How do interest groups respond to changes in the negotiation context? Which policymakers have the lead role and what do they say to justify their decisions? How well does the policy outcome fulfill different policy objectives? By answering these questions, we move closer to understanding the logic of liberalization. Supporting evidence is based on interviews with government and interest group officials and is supplemented by documents, media reports, and secondary materials.[46]

Some of the chapters examine a series of repeated negotiations on the same agricultural policy issue. These cases offer an opportunity to analyze the changes in domestic political behavior corresponding to different negotiation structures when the same agricultural issues are at stake. Other chapters compare different agricultural products in order to reflect the variation in political sensitivity even within the sector. Political sensitivity will vary according to the share in total agricultural production and labor, the political strength of the region where it is produced, and public interest in the issue. For example, rice holds a prominence in Japanese society that overshadows all other agricultural issues. By comparing cases of highly sensitive agricultural products, such as rice in

---

[45] Agricultural commodity refers to the definition typically used in trade negotiations to mean agricultural products: the harmonized system (HS) code chapters 1 to 24. This includes fish, alcohol products, and tobacco within the definition of agriculture. In addition, I include starch products and some other processed food products (HS chapter 35). Some negotiations, such as the Uruguay Round, may separate fish into a different negotiating group from other agricultural goods, but I include as *agricultural* all negotiations on fish trade issues. I do not include negotiations related to territorial boundaries and fishing rights.

[46] I conducted over one hundred interviews in Japan during August 1996, July 1997–July 1998, and January 2000, and in Europe during July 1999 and July 2000. I interviewed U.S. officials both in Washington, DC, and in the U.S. embassies in Tokyo, Brussels, and Geneva.

Japan, with relatively less sensitive products, such as fish, the qualitative analysis of the case chapters takes into account these political differences.

Negotiated Policy Liberalization

This study evaluates negotiation outcomes by the degree of policy change to lower trade barriers that is mandated in the terms of the negotiation settlement. In the long run, implementation policies and markets will determine the negotiation's economic impact. However, the most important political decisions revolve around the commitments written in the agreement, and this *negotiated policy liberalization* will most directly reflect government choices about the acceptable degree of market opening.

The focus on the policy agreement differs from other studies that use economic measures of liberalization, such as trade flows, import penetration ratios, and price differentials.[47] One drawback of these economic measures is the difficulty to distinguish between changes that result from national tastes, vagaries of weather conditions, and shifting world demand and supply, on the one hand, and changes that result from political decisions about trade policy. Furthermore, the interaction between prior trade levels and the policy decision to liberalize means that studying trade levels alone is inadequate.[48] Therefore, the empirical economics literature often examines policy variables for comparison of patterns of protection across sectors (Ray 1981; Ray and Marvel 1984; Lee and Swagel 1997). This requires a uniform policy measure of annual level of tariff and nontariff barriers for a given commodity group, which limits the available data. For this book, it is more important to match closely the specific negotiation topic with the direct policy outcome.

Negotiated policy liberalization is also distinct from success for U.S. exports. Some studies evaluate negotiation outcomes in terms of whether the United States achieved its negotiation objectives.[49] This ap-

---

[47] For studies with such measures in agricultural political economy, see, for example, Lindert (1991), Ames, Gunter, and Davis (1996), and Abbott (1998).

[48] In a model of endogenous protection, Trefler (1993) illustrates that the impact on imports is actually underestimated by ten times when considering only change in trade after the exogenous policy change.

[49] This is the approach adopted by Bayard and Elliott (1994, 59–64). A combination of interviews with U.S. negotiators and business representatives and analysis of U.S. market shares provides the evidence for Bayard and Elliott to judge whether the negotiation was a U.S. success. The authors admit that success may include a discriminatory deal favoring a

proach may underestimate liberalization because U.S. demands strategically call for more than could be expected and thereby produce a shortfall in the outcome from the initial objectives. Moreover, the absence of a rise in U.S. sales following a policy change does not necessarily mean that the negotiation outcome was insignificant—for example, exports of other countries may increase their market share or local producers may adapt to maintain their market share.[50] Therefore this book emphasizes the change in policy rather than the market outcome for the United States. While full implementation and improved market access are important, they are conditional upon first reaching the political agreement in the negotiation.

Chapter Overview

Part 1 presents the core of the argument about the importance of negotiation structure. Chapter 2 analyzes two kinds of negotiation structures that characterize the institutional context of negotiations: issue linkage and legal framing. It posits the causal mechanism by which these institutional variables in the negotiation structure promote liberalization by changing domestic level politics. After discussing expectations for liberalization in different kinds of negotiations, a final section of the chapter addresses the question of interests and the choice of negotiation structures.

Chapter 3 presents hypotheses and statistical evidence to support the importance of negotiation structure when controlling for alternative factors such as budget conditions, economic growth, political variables, and whether the United States issued a threat of retaliation.

Parts 2 and 3 present the case study analysis of U.S.-Japan and U.S.-EU negotiations. First, chapter 4 provides the background for understanding the protection policies and important domestic actors in Japan. The case studies of U.S.-Japan negotiations in chapter 5 are a sequential comparison of three negotiations on the same set of agricultural prod-

---

U.S. company and not fall under genuine liberalization. Leonard Schoppa's (1999) analysis of U.S.-Japan negotiations uses the same data.

[50] For example, a 1994 deal to allow the import into Japan of U.S. Red Delicious variety of apples brought American apples into Japanese grocery stores but failed to produce a substantial market increase for the United States because Japanese consumers rejected the product. Marketing failure by U.S. companies and a poor match between the product and Japanese consumer demand were cited as the causes of the failure (Kajikawa 1999, 112). New Zealand exporters were more successful, and Japanese producers maintained their niche for high-quality apples.

ucts in different negotiation contexts. The negotiations on beef and other products began in the Tokyo Round, were renewed in bilateral talks, and were finally resolved in a negotiation shaped by GATT dispute settlement proceedings. This offers a controlled comparison of how similar demands by the United States on the same set of domestic constituents in Japan led to different domestic political debate and negotiation outcomes depending on the negotiation context.

Chapter 6 addresses the most difficult agricultural negotiation for Japan — ending the ban against importing rice. Through examination of the different phases of the Uruguay Round trade negotiation, the case study shows that increases in the institutionalization of the issue linkage in the negotiation agenda led to increased mobilization by exporter industries and persuaded leaders that liberalization was necessary. Then, in a comparison with another cross-sector negotiation, this chapter discusses how the fishery and forestry lobbies were able to resist liberalization during a 1998 APEC trade negotiation because the voluntary nature of the institutions provided weak leverage for U.S. demands. Although rice farmers are much more politically influential than fishermen and foresters, a strong issue linkage in the Uruguay Round led to concessions on rice while the weak institutional linkage in APEC let fishermen and foresters resist any concession.

Shifting to the study of European agricultural policies in part 3, chapter 7 provides the background on the protection policies and interests for EU agricultural policy. Chapter 8 compares the failure of the Tokyo Round with the success of the Uruguay Round. While both were major GATT trade rounds with U.S. demands to reform CAP, the procedures differed in ways that had important implications for the conduct and eventual outcome of the negotiation.

The resistance of the EU to legalistic pressure is explored in chapter 9, which provides an overview of reasons for the tension between GATT and CAP. In a case study of a controversial failed negotiation, this chapter looks at the issue of hormone-treated beef, which united European consumers and farmers against American beef imports. The EU ban against this meat led to a U.S. complaint to the WTO and a ruling against the policy as a violation of EU commitments. The refusal to follow this ruling highlights the process by which EU institutions and norms prevent successful adjudication of agricultural policies.

Chapter 10 offers comparative perspectives on Japan and the EU reaction to different negotiation structures. In particular it extends the analysis of why Japan is more responsive to legalistic pressure than most countries and why the EU is more resistant. It concludes with suggestions of broader implications and future research.

This chapter introduced the puzzle that agriculture negotiations have brought widely different results, including some of the most dramatic negotiation failures as well as substantial concessions in an area of highly sensitive domestic policies. Against the background of consistently strong U.S. pressure and equally strong domestic resistance by farm lobbies in Japan and Europe, the major difference lies in how the negotiation structure frames the issue. The analysis of agricultural trade negotiations in the subsequent chapters will show how these differences in the context of the negotiation influence liberalization outcomes. By pointing to the domestic level effects of international institutions, the book integrates the international institutions literature with theorizing on two-level games. The results show that seemingly minor issues such as the agenda and procedures of a negotiation determine whether decision-makers listen to farmers protesting outside their doors or whether they weigh the broader interests of the economy and international obligation.

Part I

NEGOTIATION STRUCTURE AND TRADE LIBERALIZATION

2

Framework for Analysis of Negotiations

STATES INTERVENE in agricultural markets because farmers are an important political constituency whose role in society rallies the sympathy of the general population. To explain why liberalization occurs at all in sensitive agricultural markets, it is necessary to consider what conditions raise the overall costs of continued protection and lower the political costs of liberalizing farm support programs.

When U.S. officials have concerns about the policy of a trade partner, they often face a choice of multiple strategies for how to negotiate the issue. A legal strategy through GATT dispute mediation involves filing a formal GATT complaint and then relying on mediation by a panel of appointed diplomats and legal scholars. A more ad hoc approach is typical in bilateral negotiations where the United States relies on informal talks. Finally, there is a third option of pursuing the issue in the broader context of a negotiation including multiple sectors such as a regional trade forum or GATT trade round. In many cases a given trade barrier complaint could be raised in any of these negotiation fora. Given these many different kinds of negotiations, the question is whether the variation in the institutional context of the negotiation will change the outcome. Does it matter whether negotiators discuss one issue separately or combine several issues for joint discussion? Would negotiators reach the same agreement whether they meet alone in a room, or whether they present legal arguments and hear a judge's ruling?

Any negotiation will be characterized by its institutional context. For the purpose of comparison, this context can be thought of as the negotiation structure, which consists of *the agenda, rules, and procedures specific to the negotiation that regulate the interaction between states as they address a policy dispute.* The primary dimensions of variation are the issues on the agenda and their relation to each other, the rules that form the standard of evaluation, and the actors who participate. First, the agenda can range from a narrow focus on a single policy to a multisector negotiation. When there are multiple issues, the agenda may treat each issue separately or bind them all into a single package. Second, formal rules or international law provide a standard for judging different policies. In the absence of any formal rules, the immediate interests of the participants form the only standard of evaluation. Third, the actors who participate may be limited to officials from the two parties in the dispute, but sometimes a mediator or other states are also involved in the same negotiation.

This chapter presents a theoretical framework for understanding how the institutional context of a negotiation changes the aggregation of domestic interests to favor liberalization. It identifies two distinct negotiating strategies that promote liberalization: issue linkage and legal framing. Once established in the institutional context of the negotiation structure, both issue linkage and legal framing influence the mobilization of domestic interests and their access to the policy process. This draws attention to the possibility that variation at the international level of the negotiation has important implications for interests and political persuasion at the domestic level. When there is a close fit between the negotiation structure and the domestic political context, liberalization is more likely to result.

The next two sections present the central argument of this book about how institutions influence negotiation outcomes. The third section gives the expectations for liberalization created by different levels of issue linkage and legal framing and considers the factors that condition when issue linkage or legal framing will be more effective. The fourth section discusses the question of the endogeneity between interests and the choice of negotiation institutions.

Issue Linkage

Appreciation for the importance of issue linkage has a long tradition: writing in 1716, the French diplomat François de Callières proclaimed that "the great secret of negotiation is to bring out prominently the common advantage to both sides and to link these advantages that they may appear equally balanced to both parties" (Sebenius 1983, 282). This secret has not evaded the attention of scholars. The concept of issue linkage, broadly conceived as simultaneous discussion of several issues for joint settlement,[1] plays a central role in theories about international cooperation.

As captured in the words of Callières, issue linkage is one strategy to make mutually advantageous deals politically possible. Expanding the scope of an agreement changes the bargaining space between states, and

[1] Sebenius (1983, 287) offers the definition, "issues are said to be 'added,' combined, or linked when they are simultaneously discussed for joint settlement."

it also resolves internal divisions by providing incentives to gain the support of key groups within states (Tollison and Willett 1979; Mayer 1992). Those groups that would oppose an agreement because of one issue may be persuaded to support it by addition of another issue that promises offsetting gains. Alternatively, the addition of another issue may bring in new actors in favor of the agreement to counter the opposition by the first group. In either case, addition of another issue changes the balance for and against the expanded agreement.

Similar tactics operate in domestic politics, where issue linkage is commonly used to reach agreements in legislatures and cabinets. William Riker (1986, 89–102) discusses vote trading as one form of political manipulation whereby a different aggregation of interests leads to different outcomes. He gives the example of the Constitutional Convention of 1787, when a combination of decisions on navigation acts and slave trade created appeals for northern states from domestic shipbuilding lobbies and also generated lobbying pressure on southern states from slaveowners. Another well-known example is given in the classic account by Alexander Gerschenkron (1989) of the iron and rye coalition in Germany under Bismarck, which was an issue linkage for greater trade protection of agricultural and industrial interests. This same logic of combining issues to form a coalition of support in domestic politics also creates the potential for an issue linkage in an international negotiation to promote a domestic coalition of support for the international agreement.

The study of regimes in international relations highlights the utility of issue linkage as a means of building cooperation (Haas 1980, Krasner 1983a; Keohane 1984). Within the context of regimes, issue linkage is one mechanism that facilitates agreements in a comprehensive framework for a given policy area.[2] Joint agreements on related policies are useful given both the existence of overlapping issues and the need for side-payments to balance gains and losses. As different issues are addressed together within a regime, countries are able to pursue diffuse gains across issues and time, rather than requiring a one-to-one exchange of benefits. The added flexibility reduces the transaction costs for reaching cooperative agreements.

The notion of spillover describes the expectation that cooperating on some issues would lead to improved relations, new interests in continued cooperation, and further expansion of activities into new policy spheres. This neo-functionalist explanation of an automatic process of issue linkage was mostly applied to explain early European integration

[2] Regimes represent "principles, norms, rules, and decision-making procedures around which actors' expectations converge in a given area of international relations" (Krasner, 1983a, 2).

and was largely discredited by the failure of European Community until the 1990s to expand beyond commercial policy.[3] However, the possibility for strategic use of issue linkage has re-emerged in new debates over whether entrepreneurial leaders and judicial decisions have extended integration into areas beyond the original preferences of states (Pollack 1997; Sweet and Brunell 1998; Moravcsik 1999).

Although most studies of issue linkage discuss the strategy as one that takes advantage of different preferences among actors across issues, this is not a necessary precondition. Susanne Lohmann shows that there simply needs to be sufficient interest to cooperate on one issue to make it credible that both sides are better off cooperating on the linked issues than having a breakdown of cooperation on both issues and future interaction on those issues.[4] Furthermore, while some linkages open opportunities for both sides to improve their gains, in other cases the linkage constitutes *coercive cooperation* in which the gains from linkage accrue to only one party in the negotiation (Stein 1980; Martin 1992a). Foreign policy events like the OPEC oil embargo or the U.S. wheat embargo against the Soviet Union drew attention to coercive linkages between security and economic issues.[5] Economic sanctions represent a tool short of war by which states try to coerce others to withdraw from territories or improve their treatment of their own people. These measures rely upon linking unrelated issues, and their success depends on measures to convince both allies and the target that the linkage would be enforced.

Skeptics argue that issue linkages bring agreements only where there is not strong opposition to any individual components of the agreement. As James Sebenius (1983) points out, simply adding issues does not necessarily promote the likelihood of agreement. On the contrary, the addition of a nonnegotiable issue will cause the collapse of the entire negotiation. This is a necessary caveat against the utility of issue linkage in all situations but still allows that issue linkage can facilitate agreements in most cases. A more pessimistic view rejects the notion that linking issues could increase cooperation beyond the level possible on each separate issue given the preferences of different groups. For example, Andrew Moravcsik (1998, 65, 483) downplays the role of issue linkage in the process of European integration. He contends that when

---

[3] See Haas (1958) for an example of this argument.

[4] Lohmann (1997, 47) models a negotiation as a repeat prisoner's dilemma in which actors start with identical payoffs ex ante, and issue linkage promotes cooperation given intermediate levels of a time discount factor for future interaction. She explains that the "linkage 'pools' the incentive constraints across issues; the credibility surplus on one issue dimension works to reduce the credibility deficit on the other issue dimension."

[5] See, for example, Keohane and Nye (1977), Paarlberg (1985), and Kirshner (1995).

domestic losers were strong, they prevented the agreement, and linkages were present only when losers were diffusely organized, such as taxpayers who pay for financial sidepayments. This critique is particularly relevant because farmers both are highly organized and strongly oppose liberalization. Robert Paarlberg (1997) warns that linking agricultural issues to industrial issues slows down progress on both because of the political difficulty of making concessions on agricultural liberalization. To answer such critics, this book evaluates the role of issue linkage in the area of agricultural policy where there is strong domestic resistance in Japan and the EU against cooperation on agricultural liberalization.

DEFINITION

The presence of an issue linkage depends on the *degree to which the outcome of the negotiation for one issue is tied to the outcome for other issues included on the negotiation agenda.* The issue linkage is embedded within the negotiation structure when governments formally agree to jointly address a specified set of distinct issues. The issue linkage is observable in the public declaration of the agenda that starts the negotiation and later in the form of draft agreements. Howard Raiffa (1982) refers to the use of a "single negotiating text" as a bargaining device in both the Camp David peace talks and the Law of the Sea negotiations that combined multiple topics for negotiation. A strong linkage places all of the issues on the negotiation agenda as part of a single "package deal" that states must either accept or reject in entirety. Thus failure to reach agreement on one issue necessitates a failure on the other issues as well. In contrast, a weak linkage will bring together multiple issues for discussion but provide flexibility about whether any given issue will be in the agreement.

Although linkages between economic issues and security, environmental, or other kinds of nontrade concerns are important, they lie beyond the scope of this analysis. Here the focus is on issues that are jointly included on a trade negotiation agenda. Depending on the negotiation, they may range from service industry regulation to industrial tariffs and agricultural market policies or include rules for patent protection or labor and health standards. The issues are not substantively related insofar as discussions on the different issues could proceed to their conclusion in isolation.

Cross-sector issue linkages combine policies related to two or more of the sectors for primary goods, manufactured goods, or services. When agreement within an issue would provide only losses for one side, the inclusion of another area with potential gains can increase the likelihood of reaching an agreement (Tollison and Willett 1979; Hoekman

1989). In trade negotiations, the key factor is that the linked issues include both import and export interests for participating nations. Export sectors have an economic stake in the continued openness of the international economy and are likely to oppose protection of their home market (Milner 1988, 21). This provides potential for a bargain that balances exporter gains with importer losses. It has often been noted that politicians view trade in mercantilist terms where more exports are good and more imports are bad. Politically, a sense of fairness in opening markets reciprocally is necessary to maintain a free trade policy. Ratification depends upon gathering sufficient allies within a country who support the agreement. This kind of cross-sector linkage has been the focus of several studies of American trade policy that show how the strategy of reciprocal market access agreements led Congress to support liberalization measures because it tied market gains for exports with the lowering of domestic tariffs against imports (Gilligan 1997; Bailey, Goldstein, and Weingast 1997). Studies of European integration have also emphasized the role of broadening the scope of sectoral issues in order to bring greater involvement by more actors and avoid the veto of any one sector opposed to an agreement (Lieber 1970). In his study of U.S.-Japan trade negotiations, Leonard Schoppa (1997) emphasizes the importance of participation expansion as a necessary condition for Japan to change policies.

The tradeoff between conflicting sectoral interests for trade policy sets the stage so that liberalization is neither automatic nor impossible. On the one hand, if there was no opposition to liberalization for any of the sectors, then the policy changes would occur without an international negotiation. On the other hand, if the dominant interests across sectors all favor protection, then cooperation brings protection rather than liberalization. The classic example of such log-rolling behavior at the national level is the Smoot-Hawley tariff legislation of 1930. This bill, originally intended to raise duties on agricultural imports, passed Congress after "distribution of favors all around" increased duties on both manufactured and agricultural products (Taussig 1964, 495). To avoid this process of giving protection to everyone, the issue linkage must engage a sector favoring liberalization to counterbalance the sector favoring protection.

Institutions and Credibility

A credibility problem for a cross-sector issue linkage arises because all nations want special exceptions for their sensitive trade issues. Formalizing the linkage as a package negotiation helps to build its credibility by making defection more costly.

How can countries uphold the commitment to give a joint decision on both issues when they would rather defect from the linkage agreement? Issue linkage strategies rely on persuading states to compromise by making concessions on some issues for the sake of achieving gains on others. However, often the preferred outcome would be to take the gains without offering any concessions. Therefore one would expect states to challenge the agreement to link issues. This gives rise to a credibility problem for linkage.[6] It is especially difficult for countries to make a credible commitment to exchange concessions when there is strong opposition against the concessions in one area, such as agriculture.

A wide literature has addressed the role of institutions to promote credible commitments. Douglass North (1990, 58) states that "creating an institutional environment that induces credible commitment entails the complex institutional framework of formal rules, informal constraints, and enforcement that together make possible low-cost transacting." Through providing information about preferences and monitoring against defection, institutions shape beliefs and strategies. Firms, international organizations, international legal rules, and domestic legislatures are all examples of different institutional frameworks capable of increasing the credibility of commitment.[7]

The formal commitment by governments to an agenda embracing an issue linkage strategy enhances the credibility of the linkage by investing sunk costs and creating a focal point for the form of a cooperative agreement. Only through lengthy negotiations can countries reach a common agenda in the first place, and the risk that any single change will unravel the consensus makes all participants reluctant to change the agenda by dropping or adding issues. The high cost of renegotiating the whole agenda makes it more difficult to change the issues than if the negotiation began with an informal understanding or even just a broad slate of issues. When a negotiation agenda has been formalized, any government or domestic actor within a country that argues for a change must present a strong case to justify the exception.

---

[6] Eichengreen and Frieden (1993, 94) claim cooperation by means of issue linkage is more difficult than cooperation on a single issue, since it adds the linkage itself as an additional dimension requiring credible commitment. Morrow (1992) argues that offers to link issues in security crises are often unsuccessful because they are seen as a signal of weakness, which leads the opponent to make a more aggressive challenge rejecting the linkage.

[7] See, for example, Williamson (1985), Keohane (1984), Simmons (2000), and Martin (2000).

Enforcement of the linkage depends on subsequent behavior by participating nations that reinforces or undermines the issue linkage contained in the formal negotiation agenda. The effort to enforce the linkage becomes a game where the entire package and the negotiation process itself are held hostage. A state or group of states must refuse to continue negotiations unless other states show that they are negotiating in good faith for all of the issues. This leads to a correlation between the strength of the linkage and the interests of states. Only when there are major interests at stake would a state attempt to force an agreement on one issue even at the risk of losing a broad negotiation package. Richard Steinberg (2002) argues that this introduces a coercive element because powerful states can more easily threaten to exit the negotiation or the organization as a tactic to coerce weaker states to accept an agreement. However, consensus norms of GATT have also allowed developing nations to wield an exit threat and take actions to reinforce a linkage, as seen by the role of agriculture exporters among developing countries to push developed countries to accept more agricultural liberalization in the Uruguay Round (Ricupero 1998, 21–22).

In summary, formalizing a cross-sector linkage creates a credible commitment to make an agreement for broad liberalization. The importance of a credible issue linkage lies in how it changes the aggregation of domestic interests in the country that wants protection for one sector but generally favors free trade. The next two sections will discuss how the cross-sector linkage overcomes domestic obstacles to accepting agricultural trade liberalization.

Mobilization of Domestic Interests

Issue linkage is important because of its role in mobilizing new interests. More domestic actors become involved in the negotiation when the issue linkage broadens the stakes for each single part of the negotiation. Since deadlock on one topic will directly cause the failure of the entire negotiation, anyone with something to gain from the undertaking must press for progress on every issue being negotiated. Increasing participation has long been a tactic to overcome entrenched interests in domestic politics. E.E. Schattschneider (1935, 40) argues that by expanding the scope of conflict, losers try to "involve more and more people in the conflict until the balance of forces is changed." By the same logic, participation expansion can increase the range of potential agreement for international negotiations (Sebenius 1983). In particular, the two-level game framework highlights that domestic support in one country for the demands of another country will promote agreement (Putnam 1988; Bayell 1994). Using evidence from U.S.-Japan trade negotiations, Leonard Schoppa (1997, 41) argues that U.S. demands are more effective when they widen participation to include "latent supporters of the foreign demand." If there are interests that supported the need for liberalization before the negotiation, what happens during the negotiation to mobilize them? The answer lies in the nature of the specific interests raised by the issue linkage *and* the institutional context that makes the linkage credible to these new actors.

In negotiations with a cross-sector linkage that includes agricultural and industrial sectors, issue expansion dilutes the influence of entrenched farmers by forcing them to compete with other interest groups who join the debate on agricultural policy. Before a negotiation, export industries have only a passive concern for the affairs of local import-competing sectors. Certainly they have little reason to expend resources lobbying on agricultural issues. However, an issue linkage in the negotiation structure ties the fate of an agreement to expand exports in industrial goods or services with an agreement to open markets in other sectors, such as agriculture. This creates incentives for export industries and officials of trade ministries to advocate agricultural liberalization as part of their promotion of the entire package deal. As a result, large potential gains from one part of a package lead to pressure on all issues.

The credibility of the linkage changes its impact on domestic politics — the more credible the linkage, the more likely that representatives of export interests will enter the agricultural policy debate and advocate liberalization. If a government challenges the linkage by refusing to negotiate seriously on agricultural liberalization, two scenarios may result: trade partners will delink the issues and agree to liberalization of industrial goods even without liberalization of agricultural goods, or trade partners will insist on the linkage and refuse to negotiate any agreement without an agriculture deal. If the linkage does not seem credible, export interests expect the first scenario and have little reason to care about the progress of agricultural negotiations. However, if the linkage is credible they will expect the second scenario and lobby for agricultural liberalization in order to avoid negotiation breakdown. The formal agenda provides information about the issue linkage at the initial stage of the negotiation. Later efforts to delink issues provide additional information. Negotiation deadlock can actually be helpful in this situation because it acts as a clear signal that the linkage is credible and will encourage more mobilization by export industries.

In the absence of an institutionalized issue linkage, domestic interest groups are unlikely to mobilize for agricultural liberalization. Even if there are multiple sectors, both industry groups and officials are likely to focus exclusively on the negotiation group directly related to their area because they lack information that their interests may actually depend as much on progress on other issues as on the negotiation in their own industry group. Consequently, the farm lobby and agriculture ministries are the only ones to give attention to negotiations on agricultural issues alone. Without countervailing pressure, politicians are more likely to accede to the farmer demands.

Expanding the Policy Jurisdiction

By broadening the negotiation stake, a package negotiation structure compensates for a major policy obstacle to agricultural liberalization: the autonomy of agricultural interests over policy within their own policy sphere. Before the linkage, agricultural interests dominate the policy debate. After the linkage, agricultural interests must contend with opposition from other groups that will also join the decision-making process.

The cross-sector linkage influences the policy jurisdiction of ministries by how it defines the scope of the agreement. A negotiation on a single agricultural policy falls under the jurisdiction of the agriculture ministry. When agriculture is one item in a multisector package, though, more decisions are likely to rise to an interministerial process. Certainly, the technical aspects that often constitute the largest share of negotiation proposals remain in the hands of the experts in the agriculture ministry. Nevertheless, interministerial consultation forces early recognition that tradeoffs are necessary.

Expanding the policy jurisdiction is important because of differences between ministry interests. Ministries and political committees have their own priorities that influence their approach to any policy, such that one can say "each institutional venue is home to a different image of the same question" (Baumgartner and Jones 1993, 31). Graham Allison's (1971) classic study of bureaucracy's role in foreign policy highlighted the explanatory value gained by looking at government decision-making as having multiple actors, each with distinct interests. In the field of economics, studies of economic regulation have long pointed to occasions when an industry under the supervision of a ministry controls the agency's policies in ways that determine the supply of regulation policies (Stigler 1971). A vivid example of the importance of changes in which groups influence policy is given in Robert Lieber's (1970) analysis of pressure groups in Britain and its decision to join the European Common Market. Lieber says British leaders allowed pressure groups such as farmers and economic ministries to dictate Britain's demands during its first attempt to gain membership in the Common Market, only to have the application rejected. Later, the Foreign Office was given greater authority and political parties took direct involvement in policy-making so that narrow interests had less influence on the negotiation, which facilitated agreement on the terms for British membership. Theories of congressional institutions posit that the committee with final authority over legislation will determine the form of the policy agreement (Shepsle and Weingast 1995). This attention given to the structure of committee and bureaucratic jurisdiction at the domestic level points to the need to consider whether the international negotiation agenda changes which committees or bureaucracies have authority over the policy.

Attention to the bias of individual ministries is especially important for the study of agricultural policy. Agriculture is often given as an example of this kind of regulatory capture and described in terms of the iron triangle among interest group, agency, and legislative committees (Mulgan 2001; Sheingate 2001). Farm groups have such influence over the policies of the Ministry of Agriculture in most countries that the ministry supports farmer demands for protection as part of its bureaucratic mission. To the extent that agriculture ministries are granted autonomy over policy decisions, they are likely to take the side of farmers and favor protection.

However, studies on delegation have demonstrated that the nature of the policy issue will influence the degree of autonomy granted to a bureaucracy (Bendor, Taylor, and Van Gaalen 1987; Epstein and O'Halloran 1999; Martin 2000). Politicians make decisions to delegate according to the political interest in exercising direct control over outcomes relative to the efficiency gains of delegating to an agent that may have greater technical knowledge and independence to implement the desired policy. In this case, letting the agriculture ministry take the lead for agriculture negotiations is likely when both the political actors and the ministry share the same commitment to uphold status quo policies against foreign demands. However, when other issues are added to the negotiation, the logic of delegation changes. For decisions involving tradeoffs between agricultural and industrial interests, politicians may want more direct control. Those with a strong interest in industrial sector outcomes will favor delegation to the trade ministry. Issue linkage in the negotiation structure reduces the autonomy of the agriculture ministry when it brings political involvement by politicians outside of the agriculture policy committees and forces the agriculture ministry to make joint decisions with the trade ministry about the negotiation. The bargaining between bureaucracies and between politicians with diverse constituencies will likely produce a substantially different outcome than if one actor is granted sole decision authority — especially if that actor is a representative of agricultural interests.

The broader agreement also influences the approval procedures and is likely to bring greater legislative involvement at this final stage. For example, a negotiation to expand an agricultural import quota may be approved by the Japanese Ministry of Agriculture without any Diet vote, but a tariff reduction must receive Diet approval. Broad sectoral agreements address tariffs; moreover, as a treaty agreement, they require Diet approval.[8] Internal processes of the European Union are particularly prone to vary according to the scope of issues under discussion. An agreement on agricultural issues does not involve the European Parliament and would be addressed in the Agriculture Council with voting by qualified majority. In contrast, an agreement that includes service issues requires unanimity in the General Affairs Council, and an agreement establishing new measures for international trade cooperation, such as the Uruguay Round Agreement in 1994, requires the assent of the European Parliament (Bossche 1997; Elles 2000). These are just a few examples indicating that the nature of the negotiation agenda has direct impact on approval procedures for the prospective trade agreement.

The mobilization of interests created by the broad stakes of a package agreement will influence the position of the legislature as well. When considering treaty ratification, legislators want to maximize their ability to retain office, and they are also influenced by informed domestic groups that endorse the agreement (Milner 1997). Since a broad liberalization package promises large gains for the economy, it will enhance politicians' electoral prospects. The economic gains from the larger package and lobbying by industries will not assuage farmers or reduce their lobbying, but they do please some groups to offset any lost farm votes. A narrow agricultural liberalization agreement would not provide any potential electoral gain.

In sum, negotiation structure will vary in terms of whether it establishes a cross-sector linkage and how the formal agenda and behavior of states adds to the credibility of that linkage. The linkage is important because it signals that gains from liberalization in one sector depend upon losses in other sectors. Both industry lobbies and government officials take heed of these interests. Given broader stakes, they are more likely to favor liberalization of agriculture than if the decision only ad-

---

[8] Ministry of Agriculture official. Interview by author. Tokyo, 19 January 2000.

dressed agricultural issues. The broader scope of the agreement shifts decision making outside of the exclusive domain of agriculture interests. By increasing the mobilization of proliberalization interests and reducing the autonomy of agricultural interests in the policy process, the issue linkage changes the political balance to favor liberalization.

Legal Framing

A second type of institutional arrangement for the negotiation structure consists of framing the trade issue in a legal context. The previous section discussed the use of cross-sector linkages in comprehensive negotiations that involve bargaining over a wide range of trade issues. In contrast, legal framing occurs in negotiations over discrete policy issues and established trade rules.

A large number of trade disputes are addressed in the legalistic GATT dispute settlement procedures. This trend has grown rapidly since reforms strengthened the legal procedures of the GATT in 1989. The 1989 reforms and establishment of the WTO in 1995 increased the legalistic nature of the process by ending the defendant's right to veto the panel, building in a timetable for completion of each case, and establishing an appellate process with a panel of judges. In its first five years, 185 complaints were registered with the WTO, compared with less than 300 cases for the GATT since it was established in 1947 (Butler and Hauser 2000, 505).

The record of GATT dispute settlement cases is a strong indication that legalism influences state behavior even without the power of enforcement.[9] The GATT establishes a quasi-judicial process for settling disputes between parties in which a panel of three neutral diplomats hears formal legal argumentation and offers a ruling on a complaint. The legalistic framework shapes the kinds of arguments made in the negotiation.[10] For example, the United States may want to use its overall trade deficit to justify market-opening demands while Japan may want to point to its overall high level of agricultural imports to justify protection of one product, but neither argument has basis in GATT treaty law. The statements that would form the backbone of a bilateral discussion are irrelevant in a legalistic setting. Instead, negotiations within a GATT dispute settlement procedure quickly become very technical debates,

[9] See Busch and Reinhardt (2002) for a comprehensive review of the topic.

[10] Studies of the European Court of Justice show how the court procedures make countries adapt their position to fit within the bounds of what lawyers can argue for in court. This may lead to quite different outcomes (Burley and Mattli 1993).

and the final agreement is a document full of legal language interpreting how policies fit existing GATT law.

Nevertheless, while it is clear that the legalistic framework changes the nature of the debate, the important question is whether it also has an impact on policies. The trade law scholar Robert Hudec (1993, 353), argues that it does. He provides a comprehensive examination of the history of GATT dispute cases from 1945 to 1989 in which he shows that dispute settlement cases achieved a remarkable 88 percent success rate in dealing with trade problems. The WTO dispute settlement process has also performed well in its early years. Among the first eleven cases that were completed (with full information on implementation available) by the end of 1999, nine led to adoption of the recommendations in the ruling within the implementation period (Butler and Hauser 2000, 518). Given that the GATT/WTO dispute settlement proceedings appear to be quite effective at bringing policy changes, it is necessary to consider how legal framing characterizes these negotiations and why use of legal principles would influence trade policy decisions.

DEFINITION

As a dimension for the comparison of international institutions, legalization forms a continuum that varies according to precision of the rules, the obligation that states conduct their behavior according to the rules, and delegation to a third party of authority to interpret the rules (Abbott et al. 2000). Legal framing of a negotiation structure is defined as the degree to which *the negotiation occurs within the bounds of formal rules and appeals to third-party mediation.* The key distinction lies in the impartial standard to evaluate the policy according to rules accepted by all participants. The use of a policy process guided by legal reasoning confers a sense of legitimacy on the negotiation structure.[11]

Dispute resolution between states can range from ad hoc bargaining where there is no legal framing to a judicial settlement where there is complete legal framing of the decision. In ad hoc bargaining, the standard to evaluate the policies is how each side calculates the gains and losses for its own interests. Bilateral talks typically fit within this negotiation structure. States maintain complete autonomy to shape the form of the final agreement. In contrast, when they accept judicial settlement, states delegate to a third party the authority to shape the negotiation agreement. In a judicial settlement, disputes between states are settled

---

[11] See Finnemore and Toope (2001) and Franck (1990) for discussion of this notion of law as process.

according to the rules of international law where there is a "decision by a tribunal which, in virtue of its source of authority, composition, immunity from local jurisdiction, and powers of jurisdiction, is international rather than national" (Brownlie 1990, 713). GATT dispute settlement panels represent this kind of highly legalistic negotiation structure, and the changes created in the dispute procedures for the WTO are in the direction of greater legalization.

Between the low and high levels of legalization seen in bilateral bargaining and GATT disputes, some negotiations are partly characterized by legal framing without having any resemblance to court proceedings. In this kind of negotiation, participants may defer to a multinational committee or international secretariat to draft a common framework of principles for deciding outcomes. This would create a small degree of impartial mediation and delegation, even while states retain considerable control over both process and outcomes. The GATT trade rounds embody this kind of consultative process, where the negotiation produces a mix of ad hoc bargaining and legal framing.

How does this variation in the degree to which legal principles frame the negotiation structure shape the liberalization outcome? The next sections answer this question by examining reputation effects and the value in following the rules.

Raising Reputation Costs

The legal framework of the trade system uses concern about reputation to deter countries from cheating. Judicial settlement publicly brands those who violate agreed upon free trade rules. Many studies point to the information role of third-party mediation as a way to determine who violates the rules and to publicize that information.[12] When traders (including national governments and industry-level actors) lack strong interest in an issue, they are unlikely to undertake the costly act of investigating and publicizing violations. On the other hand, when a trader does have a strong interest in greater market access and will investigate and publicize unfair policies, its claims are biased. Bystanders (e.g., other governments and business actors not directly involved) are likely to dismiss such finger pointing about unfair policies. In contrast, a third-party ruling holds much greater credibility. The impartiality of the third party and the clarity of a judgment based on legal principles facili-

---

[12] See, for example, Milgrom, North, and Weingast (1990), Hungerford (1991), Staiger (1995), and Maggi (1999).

tate making a fair evaluation of who has a good reputation and who has a bad reputation. In this way, the legal framing of a negotiation amplifies the reputation effects of the negotiation outcome.

Governments care about their trade reputation because other states are less willing to make market liberalization agreements with a state that has a bad reputation. Not only will cheating reduce future cooperation between the two states in the dispute, but when an institution publicizes the defection from the rules, it allows *all* members of society thereafter to "selectively stigmatize" that state in their future trade policies (Lohmann 1997, 52). Although the GATT most-favored-nation principle, which requires that states extend trade concessions equally to all GATT members, reduces the ability to punish individual states, there are other ways that a bad reputation can matter. In particular, a record of cheating makes it more difficult to credibly commit to abide by future trade agreements. As a result, when dealing with a state that has a bad reputation, trade partners are likely to avoid negotiating free trade agreements (e.g., bilateral or regional association agreements for free-trade zones), and they will bargain harder to extract additional concessions as a risk premium for the uncertain compliance. In addition, a state with a bad reputation loses its ability to pressure others to liberalize. Conversely, a reputation for opening markets and complying with trade rules adds leverage behind requests that others should liberalize.[13]

For states that do not favor any liberalization, a bad trade reputation is not a problem. However, the advanced industrial nations benefit from liberalization in general even while they want to protect a few sensitive producer groups. When protection of such sensitive areas ruins their reputation, it sacrifices potential liberalization agreements on other issues that may be more important. Receiving a formal trade complaint against a policy signals to leaders that a particular protection policy will not be tolerated in silence by its trade partners. This triggers the reputation mechanism to force a government to face the tradeoff between its mixed preferences for liberalization and protection.

If negotiators want to protect their reputation, then they are better off to settle following the public complaint in order to avoid a lengthy, public dispute and possible violation ruling.[14] Anticipation of adjudica-

---

[13] One can also conceive of a less instrumental view of reputation. Policymakers, and even the nation as a whole, may be sensitive to "backpatting and shaming effects" because they participate in an ongoing interaction with others in the social environment created by an institution (Johnston 2001, 502).

[14] There are very few cases in which a country would have a high certainty of a non-

tion will lead defendants to make early concessions because they may be able to get a better deal and will avoid reputation losses (Butler and Hauser 2000; Reinhardt 2001). Indeed, three-fifths of GATT/WTO disputes end prior to a panel ruling (Busch and Reinhardt 2002, 468). Since immediate compliance after a ruling would forestall retaliation and normative costs, reputation costs emerge as the most important factor pushing for early settlement. A key corollary of this dynamic in favor of early settlement is that violation rulings will be subject to a selection effect for those hard cases where a country refuses to liberalize (Reinhardt 2001). Thus the consultation phase of the dispute may bring more liberalization than the higher level of legalism after a panel issues its ruling.

For negotiations with moderate legal framing such as trade rounds, reputation effects arise when a refusal to compromise on an issue by one state goes against the common framework others have agreed to follow. Blame for failure of the round would severely damage the trade reputation of the state, and other states would be less likely to pursue new liberalization agreements and would adopt tougher bargaining tactics in future demands on trade policies. Anticipation of such costs gives states incentives to accept liberalization.

The Value of Trade Rules for Political Persuasion

On another level, legal framing uses the value of trade rules to add a new stake, which can be referred to as international obligation.[15] The material and normative value accorded to rules by states forms the basis for this sense of international obligation. To the extent that trade rules help increase trade and rely on voluntary compliance, states will be reluctant to undermine them by refusing to change a policy that is declared a rule violation. In addition, the legitimacy conferred by legal framing persuades leaders and the domestic audience that liberalization is necessary.

---

violation ruling because the legal and diplomatic costs of initiating a complaint dictate against nuisance suits where there is no genuine legal problem with a policy. In the first five years of the WTO, only two out of forty-four panel decisions entirely dismissed the complaint at the first panel stage (Butler and Hauser 2000, 522).

[15] This term is widely used in the legal scholarship. Kovenock and Thursby (1992, 153) introduced it to the economics literature in a study of GATT dispute settlement that assumes there is an additional cost imposed for violating an explicit international agreement that is independent of whether the violation is punished.

Since both trade interests in the rules system and the normative respect for law promote liberalization and are likely to operate simultaneously, it is difficult to separate them for empirical testing. Consequently, for the analysis of this book, trade interests and respect for law are conceived to operate jointly as a double-sided pressure arising from legal framing at the highest level when there has been a violation ruling.

Let us first look at the economic interests served by following rules. To achieve reciprocal free trade gains, states need to know that their trade partners will follow trade commitments. This raises the classic dilemma of collective action; where a large number are cooperating to provide a public good such as free trade, there is temptation for each government to choose protectionist policies for sensitive industries. Governments established GATT as a solution to this problem. States benefit from the multilateral system of trade rules because it protects reciprocal exchanges and prevents the opportunism that otherwise would undermine trade (Maggi 1999; Bagwell and Staiger 1999). Without a system of multilateral rules, countries have incentives to seek special treatment through bilateral deals. However, this would reduce the ability to make a credible commitment to any one trade partner, since every deal would be subject to renegotiation. The repeated renegotiation of bilateral trade agreements raises considerable transaction costs.

The rules are meaningful only if states choose to follow them, and blatant disregard for the rules will erode general compliance. Hudec (1993, 177) refers to the "momentum and the institutional memory behind the dispute settlement process" that is built by successful cases settled on terms acceptable to the complainant. "If good results are achieved often enough, the cumulative weight of the positive results can be expected to make an impression on government expectations and, eventually, on government behavior as compliance becomes politically more acceptable back home" (ibid., 200). Conversely, if there are too many failures to achieve redress through the dispute resolution system, governments will lose respect for the rules. Failures may result from the legal incapacity of the dispute process to produce rulings. More often, they occur when governments refuse to follow a ruling. The outcome of each dispute strengthens or weakens the overall rule system. Therefore, one would expect countries to change policies that are designated as a violation in order to build the credibility of the trade system. The trade interest in the gains from a system of trade rules should discourage states from weakening that system by refusing to change a trade barrier.

Beyond economic interest, the international obligation associated with legal framing of a negotiation is also about respect for law. Perceptions about the nature of the process influence how people react to it. A judicial settlement transforms one government's demand for liberalization into an international obligation endowed with legitimate authority. This creates an additional cost from noncompliance, whether from embarrassment at being criticized by other governments and international press or from a more abstract discomfort with acting against accepted social norms.[16]

What is meant by legitimacy, and how is it created? Thomas Franck (1990, 16) defines legitimacy as "a property of a rule or rule-making institution which itself exerts a pull towards compliance on those addressed normatively." He argues that the normative force of international law depends in part on whether states comply and in part on how they perceive the legitimacy of the law (ibid., 46). One risks tautology by saying that legitimacy encourages compliance by definition and then showing that a legitimate demand brings compliance. Further specification of rule properties associated with legitimacy avoids this problem. In the context of trade negotiations, impartiality and consent are preconditions for legitimacy — the former ensures the fairness of the process, while the latter implies recognition of the proper jurisdiction.[17] Through reliance on a third party and common principles, legal framing of the negotiation structure adds legitimacy to the demand for liberalization.

A few examples illustrate the variation in legitimacy across negotiations. Trade negotiations conducted under GATT auspices have implicitly gained consent of all members, who accept its jurisdiction to provide the forum for regulating trade policies when they sign the agreement. A negotiation with strong legal framing, such as a GATT/WTO panel, offers high legitimacy because of the impartial nature of a panel of three neutral actors interpreting existing legal commitments. Mediation by the GATT Director-General in a trade round offers more moderate levels of legitimacy. On the other hand, a negotiation that takes place as ad hoc bargaining without a formal agenda will lack the persuasive value gained from the perception of liberalization as an international obligation.

Legitimacy changes the stakes of the domestic debate for opponents

---

[16] See Hurd (1999) for a study of the exercise of legitimate authority in international relations.

[17] See Finnemore and Toope (2001, 749) for fuller discussion of sources of legitimacy in law. They emphasize that law will be more legitimate if it "is viewed as necessary, involves in its construction those it binds, and adheres to internal legal values."

and advocates of liberalization. Rather than just being about weighing economic and political interests — farmers versus export industry — the decision to liberalize now includes compliance with international law. Senior politicians will be especially concerned to appear as leaders who can rise above local district interests. Not only do they interact with foreign leaders, but their leadership position within their party and before the electorate may be enhanced by their ability to conduct foreign policy. Even for interest groups, perceptions of legitimacy can be important. Because they depend upon support from wider society, interest groups want to present themselves as representing a sympathetic cause. Domestic supporters of liberalization, such as business groups and trade officials, prefer to frame their advocacy of agricultural liberalization as support of international rules rather than narrow self-interest. This same consideration of the wider public reaction puts farmers on the defensive when liberalization represents an international obligation — farmers are put in the position of condemning a respected international institution and asking for an exception for their interests. In contrast, when liberalization arises as a bilateral demand, the domestic audience is more likely to perceive it as bullying and groups can rally higher levels of opposition. Leonard Schoppa (1997, 36) argues that the effectiveness of threats will depend on whether they are perceived to be legitimate. The institutional context of the negotiation is an important factor to influence these perceptions of legitimacy.

Examples from Japan and Europe illustrate how legal framing can impact interest group activities and political debate. In Japan, when a business group advocates agricultural liberalization explicitly to reduce trade friction over the industrial goods trade surplus, it risks the threat of boycotts by agricultural cooperatives and gains a bad image among rural consumers. In 1984, during a U.S.-Japan bilateral negotiation on beef and citrus quota policies, several Japanese companies, including Sony Corporation, suffered from a boycott because their executives sat on a committee that issued a statement calling for reform of agricultural policies (Yoshimatsu 1998). The Japanese government pleaded with U.S. negotiators that politically it could not afford to end the quotas, and the United States accepted a partial compromise.[18] In the next negotiation on Japan's agricultural quota policies, the United States filed a formal complaint to GATT. Following the 1987 panel ruling against Japan, the business community and media editorials called on the government to accept the ruling. The prime minister intervened to tell Agri-

---

[18] Chapter 5 gives the details for both the 1984 and the 1987 negotiations that are related here in brief.

culture Ministry negotiators to settle the issue before his upcoming summit with President Reagan. In the different international context, the agriculture cooperatives could not mobilize a boycott against companies or massive demonstrations as they had during the prior negotiation (Nagao 1990, 94). The legitimacy of the liberalization demand forestalled such radical actions. An agricultural cooperative leader stated after the liberalization decision that "For this negotiation it was a talk among nations where we were no more than one group."[19] In the discussion of international law, farm groups lost their privileged status in domestic policy debate.

In the European context also, international obligation is used in domestic debate. When EU Trade Commissioner Pascal Lamy addressed the European Parliament Agriculture Committee in July 2000 to discuss changes in the banana import regime, which a WTO panel had ruled a violation in 1997, he repeatedly referred to the need for the EU to bring policies into conformity with WTO rules.[20] Not even representatives with close ties to agriculture questioned the need to follow international rules. One can readily imagine that their reaction would have been different had Lamy said that the EU must change its banana import regime because the U.S. multinational company, Chiquita, had filed a petition to the United States Trade Representative and on that basis the United States demanded liberalization of EU banana policies. In the WTO case, the EU still defied the ruling until April 2001 when it finally came into compliance.

Both normative pressure and trade interests provide additional reasons for states to take seriously a violation ruling against their policy. Although early settlement is also possible, normative pressure is strongest after the panel issues its ruling. As a result, one can distinguish between this trade-rule stake and the reputation stake discussed in the previous section. Both are causal mechanisms by which legal framing promotes liberalization, but reputation concerns encourage early settlement before a ruling, while the value of trade rules encourages liberalization *after* a violation ruling. If reputation is sufficient to explain liberalization, then governments will choose to avoid the public panel and get a better bilateral deal during the consultation phase of the dispute settlement procedures. When political opposition prevents early settlement, liberalization may still occur after the ruling if the high legal framing of the negotiation changes the domestic debate. In each nego-

---

[19] *Asahi shimbun*, 21 June 1988, cited in Nagao (1990, 94).
[20] European Parliament, Committee on Agriculture and Rural Development, Public Meeting on 10 July 2000, Brussels.

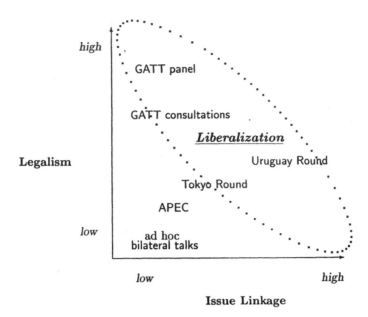

Figure 2.1: Expectation for Liberalization According to Negotiation Structure.

tiation, leaders must weigh their desire to keep the policy against the costs of being held in violation of their legal commitments.

Expectations for Liberalization

Figure 2.1 illustrates the variation in liberalization along the two dimensions of legalism and issue linkage. There is a continuum from negotiations with low legal framing, such as ad hoc bilateral talks during the 1984 U.S.-Japan beef citrus dispute, to those with high legal framing, such as the 1998 WTO panel on Japan's fruit quarantine policies. The consultation phase of dispute settlement proceedings represents a middle range of legal framing, in which the negotiation is settled after a formal complaint to GATT has been filed but before the establishment of a panel. Likewise, the strength of the issue linkage can range from a single-sector negotiation, a multisector negotiation like APEC where there is an informal commitment to make progress on multiple areas, or a package negotiation like the Uruguay Round that formally links issues in a single undertaking. The argument presented here proposes that liberalization is most likely to occur when there is either high legal framing or strong issue linkage, and liberalization is less likely when the negotiation context lacks both features. In figure 2.1, the dotted oval shows the range where liberalization is expected to be most likely. Within this sphere, there is further variation in the levels of liberalization, and the outer edge of the oval represents expectations of higher levels of liberalization.

While the combination of high legalism and strong issue linkage should bring the most liberalization, such a negotiation structure rarely exists. At their extremes, the two dimensions have an inverse relationship. Bargaining flexibility is necessary to make issue linkages, but this reduces the capacity for strict evaluation of right and wrong policies. On the other hand, for high legal framing, emphasis on judging the legality of a policy prevents connecting unrelated issues. Therefore, issue linkage and legal framing are two distinct sources of leverage. Each negotiation context provides a different mix of both.

Leverage from different negotiation structures counters domestic political problems that would otherwise render liberalization impossible. However, the nature of domestic politics will condition whether a cross-sector linkage or legal framing will have more impact on policies. Given the different political contexts in Japan and the EU, they may respond to the same mechanism differently. In particular, two characteristics of the domestic political context are important to explain a government's responsiveness to issue linkage and legal framing: *autonomy of the agricultural policy-making process*, and the *relative importance given to trade rules*.

In both Japan and the EU, agricultural policy autonomy over decision-making stands as a major obstacle to reforming the status quo.[21] Agricultural policy autonomy is the degree to which those who represent the agricultural sector make policy decisions affecting the sector independent of outside influence. A segmented political process with high autonomy for the agriculture ministry and agriculture political committees is the least likely to produce changes from status quo agricultural policies. In Japan, there is fragmentation over trade policy with divisions between the foreign ministry and the trade ministry. The weak prime minister's office fails to provide the central coordinating leadership to give overall direction to foreign policy and combat the "sectionalism" among ministries (Calder 1997, 15). In a process characterized as "decentralized bargained democracy," Japanese political actors debate issues at different decision points rather than through centralized examination of alternatives (Richardson 1997, 248). In this policy context, and with the strong backing of influential politicians, the

[21] See Sheingate (2001) and Keeler (1996).

agriculture ministry exercises a dominant role. The trade policy process in the EU varies considerably depending on whether the Council of Ministers grants a broad mandate giving autonomy to the Commission to conduct trade policy or whether the Agriculture Council takes a lead role (Meunier 2000). In the General Affairs Council, trade policy issues fall under the primary jurisdiction of the Trade Policy Committee, composed of national government trade officials.[22] However, often the national agriculture ministers in the Agriculture Council dominate agricultural trade decisions and override this trade committee (Keeler 1996, 103).

Issue linkage offsets the problem of agricultural sector policy autonomy. To the extent that it mobilizes other interests and opens access to agricultural policy decision making, issue linkage reduces the autonomy of agricultural interests. Given the similar problem faced in Japan and the EU in which agricultural interests dominate the policy process for agricultural trade negotiations, issue linkage is likely to be effective in both political settings. Even for the most sensitive political issues, when the entire negotiation package represents large economic interests, mobilization by export industries will counterbalance those seeking protection. In the public debate, media and policy elites will advocate accepting a broad package even if it means making some sacrifices. The decision by the Hosokawa administration to end Japan's rice import ban in 1993 represents one such example where overall gains from the agreement forced reluctant liberalization of a policy that had been considered political taboo; officials and Prime Minister Hosokawa repeatedly said both publicly and in private that Japan could not "wreck the Uruguay Round" over the rice issue, no matter how important rice was to Japan politically (Karube 1997, 104). In addition, issue linkage often brings reform through the small trades of concessions on less controversial issues that add up to bring important market opportunities.

Legal framing is less likely to resolve the particular political problems posed by an autonomous agricultural policy process because it has less impact on the scope of the policy process. Although the legal argumentation brings in new actors with legal expertise from other ministries, the narrow focus on the issue at hand means that the direct stakes are primarily for the agricultural interests.

The leverage from legal framing will influence policies of different

[22] The Committee on 133 is the name for this committee of trade officials from the national governments that advises the Council on trade issues in conjunction with the Commission Directorate on External Affairs. For more on EU trade policy process, see Smith (1996).

TABLE 2.1
Record of Dispute Settlement Activity by Japan and the European Union

		Complainant	Defendant
EU	GATT (1948–1989)	30	45
	WTO (1995–1998)	40	30
Japan	GATT (1948–1989)	4	19
	WTO (1995–1998)	10	12

Sources: Hudec (1993); "Overview of the State of Play of WTO Disputes" at www.wto.org.

Note: Cases include all issues in which Japan or the EC/EU were involved in a formal dispute. The two periods represent the GATT dispute settlement procedures until their reform in 1989 and the WTO dispute settlement procedures that began in 1995.

governments according to the degree to which they value the system of trade rules. Specifically, how much does the nation use the rules system, and to what degree does it benefit from the trade rules and hold respect for international institutions? These two questions help to distinguish the conditions likely to encourage negotiating behavior that prioritizes reputation or political persuasion.

First, a country that frequently uses the dispute settlement process will care more about its reputation because a better reputation will help pressure others to comply. As discussed earlier in this chapter, early settlement is advantageous to protect reputation and get a better deal, which leads one to expect that those using the rules the most will also tend to settle early before rulings. On this criterion, the EU should be more responsive to legal framing than Japan because it is a frequent user of the rules while Japan has only begun in recent years to actively engage in the dispute process as a complainant (see table 2.1). However, reputation will prevail only when the trade policy process is centralized in the hands of trade officials and the issue is not of high political sensitivity. If the agriculture ministry and others hostile to trade liberalization can dominate the policy process, the reputation mechanism will prove ineffective because these actors are unlikely to be influenced by the concern for trade reputation. For example, in the EU bananas dispute, because the necessary reform measures had to go through the Agriculture Council, the Agriculture Council could hold up EU implementation of the ruling against its banana import regime even while trade officials advocated changing the policy in order to comply with WTO rules.

Second, the perception of the legitimate authority exercised by the GATT/WTO and international organizations is greater in some national contexts than in others. This is readily apparent in a comparison of the United States, Japan, and the EU. While the internationalist policy elite in the United States supports the U.S. interest in multilateral cooperation, a vocal and not insubstantial minority on both the right and the left portray international organizations as threats to sovereignty. One does not need to look far for evidence of divisions within the United States on the legitimacy of existing international organizations: while serving as chair of the Senate Foreign Relations Committee, Jesse Helms threatened to withdraw U.S. support for the United Nations unless it became more cooperative with U.S. requests for reforms.[23] Nongovernmental organizations (NGOs) and the public turned out in huge numbers in Seattle in November 1999 to prevent the start of a new WTO trade round, and the consumer activist Ralph Nader vehemently opposed the mandate that the WTO should set the rules guiding globalization.[24]

However, in other countries there is support for rather than backlash against the authority of an international organization. Japan stands out as a country in which international organizations are widely respected. Officials still refer to the early postwar declaration that Japanese foreign policy should be UN-centered. In interviews, officials repeatedly mention that the constitution holds international law above domestic law. In a 1999 Prime Minister's Office poll, 49 percent responded that even if the ruling might go against Japan's interests, Japan should settle disputes based on international law in the WTO.[25] Because the legal principles of the entire institution are held as legitimate, very few question the idea that the WTO should guide the regulation of international trade.

The strong support for the GATT rules in Japan is built upon recognition of their tremendous importance to the Japanese economy. For Japan, the GATT rules are the primary guarantor of its access to foreign markets. In 1999 EU members sent 64 percent of their exports to other EU members, and the United States sent 36 percent of its exports to its NAFTA partners, Canada and Mexico.[26] In contrast, Japan has not pursued any free trade agreements, choosing instead to rely entirely on GATT rules to provide the basis for its trade relationships. In October 2001 Japan concluded its first bilateral free trade agreement — with Singapore — as an initial step to seek alternative institutional commit-

[23] *International Herald Tribune*, 26 January 2000.
[24] *International Herald Tribune*, 29 November 1999.
[25] See table 5.3 for full results of this survey, which was conducted by the Office of the Prime Minister.
[26] World Trade Organization Secretariat. "International Trade Statistics, 2000." (Geneva: WTO, 2000): 46, 62.

ments to free trade that would supplement its long reliance on the GATT. Canada's ambassador to Japan, Robert G. Wright, said, "For 40 years, Japanese were the strongest multilateralists on the block, then they suddenly felt very isolated, with free trade associations all around them."[27] An erosion of GATT rules would leave Japan particularly vulnerable because of its dependence on GATT to support free trade.

In Europe, the project of European integration complicates the question of legitimacy and international obligation. Preferential trade arrangements and the Common Agricultural Policy are central pillars of European integration. Yet these same policies create tension with the world trade rules (Farrell 1999, 22). On some trade issues related to these topics, European member nations must choose whether to give preference to European rules and the goal of European integration over international trade rules and the goal of free and fair trade. While EU treaty law recognizes the primacy of international law and the fact that GATT law is binding on EU institutions, a prominent decision by the European Court of Justice in 1993 cast doubt on the degree to which the EU international obligation requires it to bring policies into conformity with GATT rules.[28] The German government, supported by Belgium and the Netherlands, brought the action before the European Court of Justice regarding the banana import regulation of the Community. The German government argued that the regulation infringed on GATT provisions and was contrary to the intent to uphold international obligations. The court rejected this position and stated that the Community did not have to take into consideration GATT rules when evaluating the lawfulness of a regulation (Petersman 2000, 275). Not only are there questions of legal interpretation, the competing obligations within the EU represent different priorities over the goals for integration and the goals for freer trade. On many agricultural policy issues, normative pressure from obligation as a member of the EU competes with normative pressure from obligation as a member of the world trade system.

Taking into consideration both the use of the trade rules and the perceptions of international obligation, one expects that Europe would respond to reputation concerns and tend to choose early settlement, and Japan would respond to the value of the rules and make concessions after a violation ruling. The EU frequently takes the complainant position in GATT dispute cases whereas Japan has only in recent years be-

---

[27] *New York Times*, 9 November 2001.

[28] EC Treaty Provisions in articles 228 and 234 state the primacy of international law over secondary EC law (Petersmann 2000, 277).

gun to make active use of the trade rules. Consequently, the EU has more to gain from establishing a good reputation and encouraging early settlement of disputes by all countries. Japan has less reason to care about its leverage as a complainant than the EU, and its divided trade policy establishment delays concessions until a ruling adds new stakes. Once a ruling takes place, the high respect for international institutions and dependence on the GATT to maintain access to foreign markets make Japan more responsive. In the Japanese political context, there is neither the U.S. reaction against delegating trade policy regulation to an international authority, nor the EU dilemma of competing normative stakes with equivalent legitimacy. This makes Japan likely to be very responsive to legal framing. For the EU, legal framing is problematic when the trade issue relates closely to an important issue for European integration.

Choice of Negotiation Structure

The specific negotiation structure often is shaped by a series of decisions. Choices are made when states establish a regime such as the GATT and WTO, when they initiate a dispute in a particular negotiating forum, and when they determine the agenda and procedures of the negotiation. While this book focuses on how the institutional context of the negotiation structure influences outcomes, this final stage of the negotiation is not independent of the earlier phases. When an individual trade dispute arises, each state may choose the forum and shape the agenda, rules, and procedures in ways that will favor its own interests.

Critics of institutional theories contend that the apparent effect of an institution merely reflects the underlying interests of the countries that created it (Mearsheimer 1994–95; Strange 1982). Robert Keohane and Lisa Martin (1999) respond by pointing out that endogeneity is inherent within the logic of a functional theory of international regimes. States create institutions because they want to achieve desired outcomes and the institutions will advance their interests.

Indeed, when looking at international institutions such as the United Nations and GATT, there are many examples of rules and procedures tailored to fit the interests of strong states. The permanent membership and veto right of major powers in the UN Security Council are clear examples. In the area of trade, the weak enforcement measures of the original GATT 1947 rules allowed the defendant in a dispute panel proceeding to block adoption of a ruling against its policy. Downs and Rocke (1995) argue that this particular institutional design was chosen in an effort by states to pursue gains from free trade while also taking into account political needs that make protection desirable in some instances. The rules and dispute process accomplish this by discouraging most protection while weak enforcement or special escape clauses allow flexibility for protection when important domestic groups demand it.[29]

The concern is whether institutions have any effects at all. In this book, such questions about endogeneity are addressed in part by the focus on agricultural negotiations where the interests of the main actors are relatively stable — the United States wants agricultural liberalization by its trade partners, while Japan and the EU want to protect the sector. Agriculture represents a hard case for liberalization given strong interest group pressure and the history of high levels of protection. The evidence that variation of the negotiation structure influences outcomes for agricultural liberalization over the objections of the powerful farm lobbies of Japan and Europe counters the argument that institutions constrain state behavior only on easy issues. To consider variation in interests among agricultural negotiations, the statistical analysis in the next chapter looks at specific factors such as threats and the value of the product to the United States, as well as the economic and political conditions in Japan and the EU. Analysis also confirms that results are consistent when accounting for commodity effects. These steps attempt to control for interests in order to focus on how variation in the institutional context of a negotiation changes outcomes.

State preferences do not perfectly map onto institutions and predict outcomes because of intervening effects that arise when states create and use institutions to serve different functions. Three broad categories of arguments in the literature on international institutions offer explanations for why institutions could exercise influence independent of state interests: path-dependent processes, transaction costs, and agency slack. The first approach emphasizes path dependency, which refers to the observation that, once created, institutions tend to persist even after the underlying interests that motivated a particular setup have changed.[30] In some cases, interests adapt to deepen support. For example, establishment of GATT fostered economic interests favoring free trade, and these interests in turn maintained support for GATT.[31] A second, related

---

[29] Rosendorff and Milner (2001) make a similar argument to describe the decision by governments to include escape clauses in most trade agreements.

[30] See Krasner (1983b, 1999).

[31] Milner (1988) makes this argument in terms of domestic legislation that changed U.S. industrial interests. An example of the path dependency of institutions was already given in chapter 1; the United States proposed the lenient provisions for some forms of agricultural protection when it helped create the GATT in 1947. Later, when U.S. interests

argument points to high transaction costs that prevent creating new institutions every time interests shift. Because large institutions such as the GATT represent substantial investment in regime creation and have become a focal point as a legitimate forum in international affairs, governments are reluctant simply to start over to create new rules or major revisions (Keohane 1984). For most trade disputes, governments choose how to bargain from within existing international institutions rather than launch creation of a new institutional framework. The third approach conceives of states as principals that delegate authority to an international institution like the GATT to act as their agent. Delegation opens the possibility of slack between principal and agent, especially for judicial processes like GATT dispute panels.[32]

These arguments offer explanations for the influence of the broader framework of GATT rules but are less helpful for the more immediate decisions that shape the institutional context for a specific trade negotiation. There is not a clear formula for selecting the optimal strategy or venue for all trade issues. Rather, on a case-by-case basis, factors related to the political interests of both the United States and its trade partners, along with considerations of negotiation time and cost, could make one negotiation structure preferable over another. The legal strategy of the dispute settlement process offers the advantage of public attention that demonstrates to the domestic lobby that the government is taking its concern seriously. However, uncertainty about whether a GATT/WTO panel will support the U.S. complaint with a violation ruling and the costs in time and legal work discourage this strategy. Threats are appealing as a tactic that brings immediate relief, but this strategy risks harm to bilateral relations and possible counterretaliation. When there is concern about the political sensitivity of the issue for the trade partner, a trade round may be appealing because the multilateral context reduces the focus on U.S. demands, and the comprehensive scope presents offsetting gains and losses. The slow pace of trade rounds, which can take as long as eight years, may make it politically easier for

---

turned in favor of agricultural liberalization, it could not easily change these institutional provisions (Goldstein 1993).

[32] An extensive literature in political economy addresses the tradeoff between the loss of control and the efficiency gains that result when politicians delegate policy authority to bureaucrats. For some recent examples, see Bawn (1995), Aghion and Tirole (1997), Epstein and O'Halloran (1999), and Sloof (2000). Keohane and Martin (1999) suggest applying this framework to the delegation by states to international institutions. Research on the European Court of Justice illustrates how the court assumes an autonomous authority that could allow for rulings that were counter to the expectations of the member states when they first established the court institutions (Burley and Mattli 1993).

the trade partner eventually to agree to concessions. Yet such lengthy negotiations frustrate home lobby groups that must wait to see results. Similar to the trade rounds, negotiations in a regional trade association like APEC offer flexibility, while the limited set of actors and issues can avoid the deadlock that slows the trade round. These tradeoffs lead states to prefer different institutional venues under different circumstances.

The decision about which trade forum to use for a U.S.-Japan negotiation on rice illustrates how tradeoffs among interests under conditions of uncertainty may lead trade partners with different interests to agree on the same trade forum for the negotiation.[33] In 1986 the U.S. Rice Miller's Association launched a petition under section 301 of U.S. trade law. If the USTR had accepted the petition, it would have mandated that the United States investigate Japan's rice import ban and file a GATT complaint or issue retaliatory sanctions if Japan did not remedy the unfair trade barrier. U.S. and Japanese officials engaged in extensive discussions over whether to negotiate U.S. demands for access to Japan's rice market in a bilateral context, GATT dispute proceedings, or the Uruguay Round. Japanese leaders wanted to minimize rice liberalization, while U.S. officials wanted to achieve as much market access as possible, and both sides wanted to avoid negative spillover damaging the bilateral relationship. Despite divergent preferences for the negotiation outcome, both sides favored the same decision to negotiate the issue in the Uruguay Round. This choice reflected the uncertainty about the anticipated effect of the negotiation structure—Japan could hope rice would be ignored in the midst of a broad negotiation on many issues, while the United States could hope Japan would find it impossible to avoid the pressure to make a concession when all countries put their sensitive issues on the negotiation table.

Once the dispute is taken up in a particular institutional venue, other decisions shape the negotiation structure. In bilateral negotiations there is no need for a formal agenda or procedures for agreement—the negotiation structure is ad hoc bargaining without any delegation of authority to a third party or commitment to an agenda. The issues on the table and standard for evaluation may change fluidly as the negotiation progresses. For negotiations within the GATT framework, the institutional context of the negotiation forum already provides some constraints on the negotiation structure. In particular, for legal cases in dispute settlement proceedings, the rules and procedures are fixed in the GATT/WTO agreement: only the issue raised in the legal complaint is consid-

---

[33] See chapter 6 for a full case study analysis and references.

ered. Governments must decide whether to make an early concession
following the complaint, or to wait for a panel to meet and rule on the
policy. There is more room for negotiation of procedures in trade
rounds. Nevertheless, the existing consensus norms for GATT decisions
dictate that all participants must approve the agenda that launches the
round with a declaration of the topics and goals. In practice, from the
Kennedy Round launched in 1963 until the Doha round launched in
November 2002, gaining participation by many countries has required
including many issues on the agenda for a broad package that allows all
parties to believe they will gain from the negotiation (Steinberg 2002,
350). There are limits on the ability of any one state to stack the deck in
its favor. The choices that determine the venue and negotiation structure
are bounded by the existing GATT institutional framework, the influence of other actors, and conditions of uncertainty.

Since institutions such as the GATT are ultimately the result of state
choices, they can be challenged if states later withdraw their commitment. Governments may ignore a ruling against their policy, refuse to
discuss one part of the negotiation agenda, or, more drastically, withdraw from participation in the system of trade rules. Therefore, the
important question is whether the institution makes it easier for governments to maintain their commitment to the goals that led them to delegate to the institution in the first place. The effect of an institution depends upon what Peter Gourevitch (1996, 364) refers to as the "power
of the institution to produce a kind of politics that would not occur
without it." If successful, the institution reinforces state interests while
making possible outcomes that would not have been possible in the
absence of the institution.

Although the focus of this book is not to explain why a particular
institutional design was chosen, understanding the effects of different
institutional arrangements will inform analysis in future research on the
earlier stage of negotiations when actors design institutions and choose
the structure of a negotiation. Knowing the consequences of different
institutional choices is a step toward explaining why those choices were
made.

Conclusion

The institutions that regulate a negotiation influence the stakes that actors evaluate when deciding how to respond to a liberalization demand.
Not only does the negotiation structure lay out which issues will be
talked about, but it also frames the issues in ways that force tradeoffs

and privilege some actors and arguments over others. This can exert an important impact on decision making as lobbying of interest groups and policy jurisdiction adjust to the scope of issues defined in the negotiation structure.

This chapter examined two dimensions that shape the negotiation structure: issue linkage and legal framing. Both rely on increasing the consequences from refusal to cooperate with policy liberalization. Cross-sector issue linkage forces a tradeoff between the gains of a comprehensive liberalization package and the costs of liberalizing a weak sector. Legal framing brands protection a violation of international law and raises the obligation to support the trade system. Faced with these choices, states are more likely to accept liberalization.

Institutions make countries more likely to believe the tradeoff of interests is credible. Formalizing the issue linkage as an agenda to negotiate a package deal raises the costs against challenging the linkage. Trade rules establish the standard for evaluating the policy within a legal framework and help to publicize violations in a process that legitimizes the demand for liberalization.

To achieve liberalization, the negotiation structure must offset domestic political obstacles. Strong agricultural lobbying and the autonomy of agricultural interests in decision making have long upheld agricultural protection in spite of its internal and external costs. These factors may continue to prevent liberalization regardless of greater negotiation stakes. Policy change depends upon how the negotiation structure shifts the aggregation of domestic interests to make liberalization politically possible. A cross-sector linkage counters both domestic problems by mobilizing export interests to advocate agricultural liberalization and by expanding the jurisdiction of the policy process to give proliberalization interests greater access to decisions. Legal framing uses the legitimacy of the demand for a policy change to strengthen arguments in favor of liberalization.

The next chapter will use aggregate data to test the general claim that an institutionalized cross-sector linkage and high legal framing promote liberalization. Then, case study chapters will demonstrate how the causal mechanisms work through the domestic level.

3

Patterns of Agricultural Liberalization

THE PREVIOUS chapter proposed two pathways to liberalization: issue linkage and legal framing. In a comparison of Japanese and EU trade negotiations with those of the United States, this chapter uses statistical analysis to examine evidence from 268 cases of agricultural commodities that were the subject of negotiations during the period from 1970 to 1999. The focus on one sector and two trade partners evaluates how variation in the institutional context of the negotiation influences policy outcomes while controlling for political and economic factors that would be specific to the sector and region.

The findings confirm that for U.S. negotiations with both Japan and the EU, the likelihood of major liberalization is substantially increased when the negotiation structure includes an institutionalized cross-sector linkage. The similarity stops there, as differences emerge in how legal framing of the negotiation structure influences Japan and the EU. While a legal ruling against a policy is one of the most important factors to promote liberalization by Japan, it has no significant effect on Europe's decision on whether to liberalize a product. A legal complaint may lead the EU to make an early settlement, but violation rulings offer no additional leverage.

The analysis also compares the leverage from the negotiation structure with alternative sources of pressure for liberalization arising from budget constraints and threats of retaliatory trade sanctions. The evidence shows that these factors play a secondary role to features related to the institutions of negotiation structure.

Negotiation Structure Hypotheses

Negotiations come in many different forms, and variation in the structure of a negotiation holds significant consequences for how Japan and Europe respond to U.S. liberalization demands. This book makes the central claim that the institutional context of the negotiation makes liberalization more likely when it lowers the political cost of liberalizing farm support by means of issue linkage or legal framing. The negotiation structure directly determines which interests are at stake and which actors have a role in the domestic policy process. Liberalization is more likely when the negotiation structure broadens the stakes beyond the agricultural sector through engaging exporter interests or raising a sense of international obligation. The implication is that if the same policy dispute were raised in a different institutional context, there would be a different result. To evaluate the argument empirically, the first two hypotheses connect the logic of the theoretical argument about issue linkage and legal framing with specific features of negotiations.

Package Negotiations: Pressure from Cross-Sector Linkages

Cross-sector issue linkage promotes agricultural liberalization by bringing in new stakes to counterbalance agricultural interests. Broadening the negotiation agenda to include multiple sectors increases the potential to create a balance where both sides gain enough on some issues to accept sacrifices on other issues. Japan and the EU are asked to offer concessions in the agricultural sector, while both stand to gain from liberalization in the industrial and service sectors.

The focus here is on how the institutional context of a negotiation promotes cross-sector linkages through the establishment of a package negotiation structure. Package negotiations link distinct issues together for joint approval or rejection. A package deal for a trade negotiation consists of negotiations on multiple sectors (e.g., agricultural, industrial, and service sectors) that are combined in a comprehensive negotiation. Different levels of institutionalization form a weak or strong linkage between issues. In a negotiation with a weak linkage, the agenda includes multiple issues, but there is flexibility for concluding negotiations on each issue at its own pace. In contrast, a package negotiation with a strong linkage explicitly mandates that the negotiation shall conclude with an all-or-nothing approach that ties together separate negotiation deals and culminates in signing a single agreement. This formal commitment to the cross-sector linkage changes the stakes for domestic actors. By making it clear that specific gains for industry from an overall agreement depend on progress in negotiations about agriculture, a strong linkage increases the likelihood that business groups and trade officials will mobilize to advocate agricultural liberalization.

The combination of the formal agenda and the support for this agenda by at least some of the key participating states adds credibility to the cross-sector linkage. First, the formal agenda of the negotiation establishes whether talks will address multiple sectors and whether agreements on multiple issues will form a single package. Through this agenda, countries commit themselves at the outset of the negotiation to include all of the issues and strive to bring them to a joint conclusion. Second, subsequent behavior by states reinforces the linkage. By obstructing discussions in one negotiating group to match the deadlock in another negotiating group, a state can force parallel progress on different issues. Liberalization will be the most likely when the agenda endorses the linkage and some states make their participation contingent on the linkage approach.

The variation in trade negotiations facilitates testing the argument. GATT trade rounds are clear cases of negotiations that utilize cross-sector issue linkage. These negotiations encompass a broad negotiation agenda, including many sectors and other rules related to economic activities. Nevertheless, there are differences in the credibility of the cross-sector linkage even when comparing the two most recent trade rounds, the Tokyo Round (1973–1979) and the Uruguay Round (1986–1994).

There was a weak linkage between agricultural and industrial issues in the Tokyo Round. The negotiation culminated in ten agreements from which nations could pick and choose á la carte (Jackson 1997, 47). The agricultural group had a particularly weak linkage with the rest of the round. Subgroups for dairy, meat, and grains discussed separate commodity agreements rather than general principles for agricultural policy. Countries could choose whether to join the commodity agreements regardless of their position on other issues in the round (GATT 1979, 26). The United States tried to argue that it could not ratify the agreement without agricultural reforms.[1] However, the United States backed down to accept an agreement with less substantial agricultural liberalization because it had a greater interest in the overall gains from concluding the trade round. It had not been a credible threat for the United States alone to force the issue linkage, and this reduced the prospects for major agricultural liberalization.

In contrast, several conditions bolstered the credibility of the cross-sector linkage of the Uruguay Round. The agenda clearly established from the beginning that all negotiating groups were part of a "single undertaking" (Croome 1995, 34). The United States declared that it could not conclude an agreement without meaningful reforms in the agricultural talks and put its own sensitive agricultural items on the table.[2] Two later events strengthened the linkage credibility. First, the Latin American nations walked out of the 1990 Brussels meeting, say-

[1] See Winham (1986) for more on the Tokyo Round. In this book, chapters 5 and 8 provide more details.
[2] See Preeg (1995) for details on the U.S. approach to the Uruguay Round negotiation.

ing that they would not negotiate anything if the United States, the EU, and Japan would not agree to a substantive agriculture liberalization package. Then, in 1991 GATT Director-General Arthur Dunkel independently produced a draft agreement binding all parts of the negotiations into a single text. Given the credible cross-sector linkage of the Uruguay Round, one would expect more liberalization from the Uruguay Round than from the Tokyo Round.

Other negotiations have a less explicit package structure than either the Tokyo Round or the Uruguay Round. The APEC trade liberalization talks jointly address trade sectors ranging from agriculture to automobiles, but the principles of voluntarism and flexibility let countries set their own pace for accepting agreements on any or all of the negotiations.[3] This explicitly allows countries to delay liberalization of any particular sector. Ad hoc bilateral negotiations may also address multiple issues, but they do not bind them together with a formal agenda. For both APEC and comprehensive bilateral negotiations, tradeoffs across sectors in the negotiation are possible, but it is more difficult to signal to business lobbies that concessions in one area are necessary for gains in another area. The low level of institutionalization of a package approach in these comprehensive APEC and bilateral talks reduces the likelihood of domestic groups advocating agricultural liberalization.

Finally, many negotiations address only a single issue or sector and have no explicit linkage with other sectoral issues. For example, the U.S.-Japan talks on beef and citrus in the 1980s were never tied to talks on other trade issues, and the United States and Europe held consultations over wine trade issues during the 1990s in isolation from other trade problems. While these negotiations may have implications for other trade issues, there is not a formal cross-sector linkage in the negotiation structure. Leaders make broad connections among issues in all of their foreign policy decisions, but it is difficult to explain why concern for bilateral relations or separate negotiations would motivate a concession in one negotiation but not in another. The objective of this study is to compare different levels of institutionalized linkages, rather than informal connections among issues that arise in the daily conduct of diplomacy.

HYPOTHESIS 1: LINKAGE   *The more strongly the negotiation links multiple sectors in a single negotiation, the more likely the negotiation outcome will liberalize agricultural trade barriers.*

[3] See Funabashi (1995) for an overview of APEC.

The term "multilateralism" often refers to both multiple countries negotiating and the multilateral institutions that accompany such negotiations. This tendency to conflate features of the negotiation structure with the number of participants can interfere with analysis of the sources of cooperation. Studies about institutions and negotiations that address the question of whether more is better have concluded that it depends on the issue and the nature of the cooperation problem (Sebenius 1983; Martin 1992b; Kahler 1992). On the one hand, multiple countries making the same demand with the United States increases the pressure for liberalization and provides more options for different combinations of interests. On the other hand, one could argue that the United States will be more effective in a bilateral negotiation where it can take advantage of its greater power. Although both Europe and Japan are major economic powers, they may nevertheless be susceptible to U.S. unilateral pressure when singled out in bilateral talks. Therefore, it is necessary to disaggregate the number of participants from the institutional features that often accompany negotiations with many participants. The linkage hypothesis above emphasizes the importance of the latter institutional features, and the statistical analysis in this chapter will examine the effect of linkage while controlling for whether there are multiple participants.

Legalistic Negotiations: Reputation and Obligation

Legalistic procedures create leverage for liberalization through reputation concerns and the value accorded to the trade rules. When a country has a complaint filed against its policies under GATT dispute settlement proceedings, it faces the prospect that a third party will pass judgment on whether its policy is consistent with international trade law. This broadens the stakes for countries that refuse to cooperate because they are branded publicly. Insofar as reputation and support for the rules are jointly important, one expects to see the greatest liberalization from the dispute settlement cases that represent negotiations with high legal framing. However, reputation concerns and the importance of trade rules for political persuasion produce different expectations about which level of the dispute settlement process provides more pressure for liberalization. Two hypotheses distinguish between the causal mechanisms.

The legal framing of the negotiation establishes reputational stakes even before the most legalistic stage in which the appointed panel evaluates the policy. During the preliminary consultation phase following a complaint, the anticipation of a panel and possible violation ruling creates incentives to plea bargain (Butler and Hauser 2000; Reinhardt 2001). Indeed, 55 percent of all GATT/WTO disputes from 1948 to 1999 ended during the consultation phase (Busch and Reinhardt 2002, 467). This pattern reflects the fact that, by waiting for a panel to rule against a policy, the country suffers reputational damage from the adverse publicity and loses leverage to bargain the terms of the settlement. Moreover, a panel ruling will establish a precedent that holds general implications for similar policies.[4] Since 1995 the stronger WTO dispute process has added to the likelihood that refusal to follow a violation ruling will culminate in authorization of sanctions against the country as compensation for lost trade benefits. Eric Reinhardt (2001) shows that these factors in favor of early settlement create a selection process whereby most cases are settled early, and only the hardest cases go forward to a panel. The implication is that those cases that actually receive a violation ruling are likely to be on issues where the government simply cannot make a change regardless of the reputational consequences.

HYPOTHESIS 2A: LEGAL FRAMING   *The consultation level in the GATT dispute settlement process will have a positive effect on liberalization.*

Many GATT disputes do not end with an early settlement and instead proceed to a panel ruling. A violation ruling against a policy increases the level of legal framing.[5] While the concern for reputation should still dictate liberalization, the panel ruling also raises pressures related to international obligation that are distinct to this level of the dispute mediation.

Following a panel ruling against a policy, liberalization becomes an international obligation. Then both trade interest in the rules and normative pressure add to the negotiation stakes. The GATT rules maintain higher levels of trade than would be possible in the absence of such rules. However, since the rules are upheld only through voluntary compliance, widespread disregard will erode their credibility. Therefore, after a ruling, the decision to liberalize becomes a decision on whether to support international rules. In such a negotiation context, the country appears isolated against international norms if it upholds its protectionist policy. Internationalist elites and media are likely to criticize leaders who make the country a "criminal" in the view of the world, and

---

[4] Although GATT panels are not obligated to follow the precedent of prior rulings, related cases are taken into consideration by future complainants and panels.

[5] In cases where a nonviolation ruling occurs, one would not expect any change.

farmers will find it harder to argue that they deserve special treatment. These new political conditions make liberalization more likely.

HYPOTHESIS 2B: LEGAL FRAMING   *A violation ruling by a GATT dispute settlement panel will have a positive effect on liberalization.*

The hypotheses for legalistic negotiation context distinguish between the two posited causal mechanisms. The observable implication for each hypothesis points to a different level of negotiation. When reputation concerns are the primary source of leverage, states are likely to concede before a ruling. In that case, the dispute consultation process would have a positive effect on liberalization, but a violation ruling would not have a substantial effect. On the other hand, when the value of the trade rules and political persuasion is most important, then one expects that the largest liberalization will result from dispute settlement panel violation rulings.

In addition, the legal status of a policy influences the leverage provided by legal framing. For policies where GATT law is weak, such as export subsidies, one would expect less liberalization. This is especially important with regard to agricultural trade under the GATT 1947 treaty rules. The treaty has always fully applied to the agricultural sector, but special clauses, article 11:2c and article 16:3, exempted primary products from the prohibition against quantitative restrictions and export subsidies under special circumstances.[6] The conditions for granting the exemption are very specific about when quantitative restrictions are permissible, allowing quotas only when necessary for the function of a domestic supply reduction program.[7] Panel rulings on cases regarding quantitative restrictions have offered consistently strict interpretations of the rules (Hudec 1993). In contrast, GATT panels have proven unable to deal with export subsidies, in part because treaty law has been less specific about conditions necessary to justify use of export subsidies. For example, in a 1981 case between the United States and Europe over wheat flour export subsidies, the panel ruled that it could not

---

[6] When officials negotiated the original 1947 GATT rules, U.S. agricultural policy used price supports and supply controls such that many products could not compete with imports and could only be exported with the aid of subsidies. See Goldstein (1993) for a discussion of how U.S. preferences shaped the GATT institution.

[7] Some policies clearly did not fit those conditions. For example, in the 1980s the United States engaged in two negotiations over Japan's quota on beef, which was in clear violation of GATT rules because the government encouraged domestic beef production even while limiting imports.

reach a conclusion on whether Europe had taken more than its "equitable share of world trade" through use of export subsidies.[8] One would not expect a government to liberalize a policy when a panel fails to issue a ruling or declares that a policy is not a violation. Export subsidy cases will be less susceptible to pressure from most institutional variables given that a GATT panel virtually admitted its own incompetence to rule on the issue. The new WTO rules commit governments to reduce export subsidies, but not to eliminate them.

Although Japan has not used this as a policy tool, export subsidies form the linchpin for the European Common Agricultural Policy because of their role to aid in the disposal of the surpluses built up by price support policies. Moreover, since French farmers are among the largest beneficiaries of these subsidies, strong French opposition to any restraint of export subsidies also makes negotiations about export subsidies with the EU especially difficult. Since negotiations related to export subsidy policies form a significant number of EU trade conflicts with the United States, the weakness of GATT legal pressure on these policies may have a general negative effect on the likelihood of the EU to liberalize under legal framing.

Alternative Hypotheses

Several explanations exist for why a country chooses to liberalize. Threats, domestic politics, and budget constraints stand out as additional factors encouraging liberalization. To evaluate the relative importance of the above negotiation structure hypotheses, the statistical analysis compares the importance of negotiation structure variables with variables representing these alternative explanations for liberalization. Economic conditions and the number of negotiation participants are also important factors taken into consideration as control variables in the analysis.

U.S. Influence: Threats and Appeals

In the realm of economic negotiations, one way for the United States to exercise its power over other countries is by threatening to close off access to U.S. markets through retaliation. The United States can raise the costs of protection for Japan or the EU by targeting industries in these countries dependent on U.S. markets. The success of this strategy

---

[8] See Hudec (1993, 147–151) for analysis of the GATT law in this case.

depends upon the credibility of the U.S. threat, which is influenced by several factors. First, the United States must weigh the harm caused to itself by carrying out its own threat against the benefits if the other concedes (Stein 1980; McMillan 1990). One source of credibility for a threat is the domestic unity within the U.S. industry backing the demand for and use of a threat (Odell 1993). The high level of trade competition between the United States and Japan and the United States and the EU provides many potential targets for sanctions where the U.S. industry supports the extra protection that would result from carrying out the threatened retaliation (Zeng 2002). Unilateral liberalization of a policy in the United States will also generate demands on the U.S. government to pressure other governments to liberalize and level the playing field.[9] Since the U.S. government led the restructuring of the U.S. agricultural sector in the 1960s and has lowered some of its own subsidies and barriers to agricultural imports (although much protection remains), most of the sector strongly supports the government in its export promotion efforts. This establishes a foundation for the United States to issue credible threats in its agricultural trade negotiations with Japan and the EU.

Second, by making a public threat or drawing up a retaliation list, the United States signals its strong intention to follow through on the issue. In the realm of security politics, where credible threats underpin deterrence strategy, some studies discuss how public commitments are used to invoke audience costs against backing down (Fearon 1994; Schultz 1998). By publicly making a threat, the government raises its own costs of looking weak at home if it backs down. According to this logic, one could argue that section 301 investigations enhance the credibility of a threat by signaling that the issue is a high priority for the United States, and public threats — especially those giving a deadline and list of targets — are more effective. Publicizing the potential targets is intended to trigger lobbying by the targeted industries in the other country. Since U.S. retailers and consumers are also hurt by the sanctions, there are political costs from publicizing the list, so the U.S. government cannot lightly make specific retaliation threats.[10] Making the list public is a costly signal that the United States is serious. Therefore one would expect liberalization to be the most likely for section 301 cases and those negotiations where the United States issues a specific threat involving a deadline and target list.

---

[9] Elizabeth DeSombre (2000) develops this argument in the context of environmental regulation. She argues that U.S. industries joined environmentalists to push for international environmental regulation after the United States imposed strict regulations.

[10] Former USTR official. Interview by author. Washington, DC, 3 April 2000.

HYPOTHESIS 3: THREATS   *U.S. threats to close its markets will increase the likelihood of liberalization concessions in the negotiation. More explicit threats will have greater effect on the liberalization outcome.*

In addition to the use of threat tactics, the United States may use other sources of leverage to push harder for the liberalization of some issues over others. Economic and political considerations influence U.S. government priorities. Political importance fluctuates by subjective factors, such as when a senator from a state growing tobacco chairs the Foreign Relations Committee, or when the trader who controls rice exports is a major donor to the Democratic Party. While unable to measure such political maneuvering behind the scenes of a negotiation, those items of highest priority will often lead to threats and follow the logic of the hypothesis for threats. On the other hand, there are economic factors that generate more systematic expectations about U.S. priorities. In particular, the United States will most likely try to open markets in areas where it is strongly competitive. Items for which the United States already exports substantial amounts to the world will be the most likely to succeed in a new market. These are the products where the United States holds a large comparative advantage and potential to gain from trade. Moreover, from the perspective of balancing the U.S. trade deficit, higher-value exports will go further toward reducing the deficit. Therefore, one might expect a pattern favoring liberalization of the products that contribute most to U.S. export earnings.

The trade balance influences both the pressure from the United States to open markets and the domestic divisions for its trade partners. When the United States enjoys a larger surplus, there will be less political pressure to open foreign markets than when there is a growing deficit. Previous research has shown that a negative trade balance correlates with greater bargaining success for U.S. section 301 cases, and similar results have been found in GATT trade disputes.[11]

In particular, U.S.-Japan relations have long been characterized by tensions regarding the bilateral trade deficit, which accounted for one-third of the total U.S. trade deficit from the mid-1980s through the mid-1990s and was as much as seven times larger than the U.S. deficit with the EC in 1990.[12] While macroeconomic variables largely account

[11] Bayard and Elliott (1994, 89) find that the trade balance of the United States with the target has a negative correlation with the likelihood of the United States gaining concessions. Marc Busch (2000, 441) finds that the ratio of the trade dependence between the complainant and the defendant in the dispute has a negative correlation with the likelihood of concessions in GATT dispute cases. Both results are highly significant in the statistical analysis in both studies.

[12] In 1985 the United States had a total trade deficit of $86 billion. The bilateral trade

for the opposite paths of Japan's growing surplus in the 1980s and the United States' growing deficit, political attention focused on structural barriers and trade policies of the Japanese government (Bergsten and Noland 1993, 24). In efforts to reduce the deficit, successive U.S. administrations have pushed individual market access negotiations and called for broader reforms by Japan. The other side of the trade balance reflects the high dependence of Japanese exporters on U.S. markets. Japanese businesses that are worried that trade tensions will close off the vital U.S. market have pressured their own government to take liberalization measures to promote more imports from the United States. This illustrates how the trade balance can influence both U.S. demands and the response by its trade partners.

In sum, one would expect that threats, product value, and the trade balance will contribute to the variation in U.S. pressure across negotiations.

Domestic Politics Hypotheses for Japan and the European Union

The political dynamic that privileges the interests of farmers in domestic politics accounts for the high levels of protection in Japan and the EU and also complicates international negotiations. As Robert Putnam (1988) has put forth in his two-level game analogy, national leaders play at both international and domestic tables, and they can accept an agreement only if it satisfies key actors at both tables. A negotiator whose hands are tied by fierce domestic resistance will narrow the range of possible agreement. Thomas Schelling (1960, 22–28) makes this point when he posits that "the power to bind oneself" provides bargaining power — if one negotiator can convince the other side that it

---

deficit with Japan was $33 billion, and the bilateral trade deficit with the EC was $13 billion. In 1990 the total U.S. trade deficit had risen to $95 billion; the deficit with the EC had shrunk to $5 billion while the deficit with Japan remained fairly steady at $35 billion. By 1995 the U.S. deficit had doubled from its 1985 level to reach $174 billion, while the deficit with Japan had also nearly doubled to reach $59 billion. Meanwhile the relative share of the U.S. deficit held by Europe declined; in 1995 the U.S. trade deficit with the EU was only $8 billion. More recent trends show further increases in the U.S. trade deficit, which was $511 billion in 2000. However, the relative difference between the Japanese and EU share of the deficit has closed substantially. The deficit with Japan had grown to $92 billion, which was a relatively smaller share of the total. The deficit with the EU had grown relatively larger, to reach $62 billion. (Figures are for trade in goods, balance of payments basis, adjusted to 1995 prices. U.S. Census Bureau. www.census.gov/foreign-trade/balance/index.html. Accessed 7 July 2002. Adjusted to 1995 prices.)

faces a binding constraint against any concession, then it will be able to get closer to its own preferred outcome by forcing the other side to make concessions.[13] In this case, domestic political constraints in Japan or the EU may lead the United States to accept minor or no liberalization.

Therefore, political strength at home can translate into weakness at the bargaining table. When a government is firmly in power with a large parliamentary majority, it is more difficult to argue that it fears loss of elections if it angers its farm constituency. On the other hand, when the government has a weaker majority, politicians try to strengthen their base with farmers and can credibly argue that agricultural liberalization is politically impossible.

Japan provides an interesting case for testing the counterintuitive hypothesis that a stronger majority will make liberalization more likely even when the ruling party favors farm protection. In Japan all parties support agricultural protection, but farmers have formed one of the key support bases for the conservative Liberal Democratic Party (LDP).[14] Nevertheless, the fact that the other parties try to outbid the LDP in their passion for farm protection makes it possible for farmers to argue credibly that they would end their long-standing support for the incumbent LDP. Although the LDP held power for nearly the entire postwar period, there was still intense competition over district seats, and a continued majority was not a certainty.[15] In short, when the LDP majority is slim, the party leadership will find it difficult to persuade party members to consent to any kind of agreement that would inflict pain on an important constituency.[16] Under such conditions, LDP leaders can tell

[13] See Iida (1993) and Tarar (2001) for bargaining models of how domestic constraints can improve distributive outcomes for the constrained side. Milner (1997) uses an alternative bargaining model to argue that domestic divisions make cooperation more difficult rather than easier.

[14] For example, in the 1993 Lower House elections, the LDP won 60 percent of rural seats and only 26 percent of metropolitan seats (Mulgan 1997a, 889).

[15] In 1989 the LDP actually lost its majority in the Upper House. Following a split in the party in 1993, the LDP temporarily lost its position as ruling party and since then has had to forge a majority through formation of coalition governments. However, even prior to the 1989 and 1993 watershed years in Japanese politics, it was not unusual for the LDP majority to be quite slim, to the point where the conversion of independents to join the party was necessary to attain a complete majority (Curtis 1988).

[16] Aurelia George (1990, 133) makes this claim in her analysis of the prospects for rice liberalization. Timothy Curran (1982, 143) gives evidence that this connection between LDP weakness and farmer strength goes back to the 1970s; during the Tokyo Round, beef citrus negotiations stalled because the LDP held its majority by only eleven seats and felt that farmer dissatisfaction over the negotiations could jeopardize those seats and thereby

U.S. officials that agricultural liberalization would be politically too risky. Such statements carry weight with the U.S. government because the LDP has strongly supported the U.S.-Japan Security Treaty and military base hosting arrangements.

HYPOTHESIS 4A: JAPANESE DOMESTIC POLITICS *When the Liberal Democratic Party has a stronger majority in the Japanese Diet, liberalization will be more likely.*

In the case of the EU, both national- and European-level politics interact with the international level of trade negotiation. The aggregate analysis of this chapter simplifies this complex process by treating politics within the EU Council of Ministers, which includes representation by member governments, as the domestic politics of the EU. Approval by the Council is necessary both for the mandate that gives negotiating authority to the Commission at the start of a negotiation and for acceptance of the final negotiation agreement.

What determines political constraints in the Council? Certainly the electoral politics of each member nation influences its position in the Council. An upcoming election or weak political base of a member government can constrain its flexibility when voting on Council decisions. However, since the Council can vote by qualified majority for trade issues, it is difficult for EU negotiators to argue credibly that they have tied hands due to the electoral fortunes of one member.[17] Nevertheless, some members have more influence than others. In particular, the Council president has the authority to determine whether an issue is raised in the Agriculture Council, composed of agriculture ministers, or in the General Affairs Council, composed of trade and foreign ministers (Sherrington 2000, 41–42). Those opposing agricultural liberalization prefer to maintain control within the Agriculture Council, while those favoring liberalization try to push agricultural issues into the jurisdiction of the General Affairs Council.[18] Given the fixed rotation of the Council

---

threaten its majority. This complements the pattern described by Kent Calder (1988), whereby the LDP compensates key support groups during periods when its power is endangered and then engages in retrenchment during better times.

[17] The unofficial option of a veto (the result of the so-called Luxembourg Compromise) allows a member to dictate policy but is used only on rare occasions.

[18] Official of the German Federal Ministry of Food, Agriculture, and Forestry. Interview by author. Bonn, 20 July 1999. See Woolcock and Hodges (1996) for discussion of this issue as it related to the Uruguay Round negotiation.

presidency, there is no possibility for manipulation of this agenda-setting power as a negotiation tactic. When a member opposed to agricultural liberalization holds the presidency, an agreement for substantial liberalization will face more difficulty gaining a fair hearing in the Council than when a member with a more favorable position holds the presidency.

In the area of agricultural policy, France stands out as the strongest opponent to liberalization.[19] French President Jacques Chirac said, "France has led a permanent fight to maintain a certain idea of the CAP, while others want only to suppress it because they think it is too expensive and serves only our interests."[20] Although France and other anti-reform states will often be able to scuttle negotiations through backdoor opposition, France has a stronger role as agenda-setter to influence the negotiations when it holds the Council presidency.[21] However, France's ability to impose its agricultural preferences increases when it holds the presidency. Under these circumstances, negotiators of the Commission can more credibly argue that their hands are tied. Therefore, from the perspective of European level politics, one would expect less liberalization when France holds the influential post of Council president.

HYPOTHESIS 4B: EU INTERNAL POLITICS *Liberalization will be less likely if France holds the presidency of the Council during the key initial or final years of the negotiation.*

Budget Hypothesis

Liberalization could occur when a government decides it no longer can afford the costs of protection, in terms of both budget expenditures and inefficient use of economic resources. Robert Paarlberg (1997), in studies of the EU and U.S. agricultural reforms in the 1990s, cites cost-cutting as a major motivation behind moves toward lowering agricultural trade barriers.[22] Countries may liberalize protection policies for

[19] While Ireland, Greece, and other nations have larger agricultural sectors relative to the national economy, France has both the agricultural interests and the political weight. According to the voting rules governing the European Council after the Single European Act of 1987, France's vote is weighted by ten compared with three for Ireland and five for Greece.

[20] *International Herald Tribune*, 26 June 2002.

[21] For studies that attribute an agenda-setting role to the president of the council, see Wallace and Wallace (1996); Smith (2001); Sherrington (2000).

[22] See also Orden, Paarberg, and Rose (1999).

internal budgetary reasons and then seek credit on the international stage by making the policy changes in the context of a negotiation.

European officials openly discuss the need to reform policies in order to reduce expenditures. The EU devotes over half of the total budget expenditures to agriculture-related programs, making agricultural reforms an important way to reduce budget costs.[23] In particular, if budget savings motivate liberalization, export subsidy policies would be an obvious choice for making changes. Export subsidies are one of the most distortionary forms of expenditure in the CAP because they involve a high budget cost, amounting to nearly a third of total spending for agriculture, which in effect lowers prices for world commodity markets while keeping domestic prices high (Munk and Thomson 1994). When the United States demands changes of these policies that undercut U.S. agricultural export sales to third markets, some within the EU may also favor reforms of these policies to reduce their cost.

It seems less likely that budget reforms motivate liberalization policies in Japan, where spending on agriculture constitutes a smaller share of the national budget. The Japanese Ministry of Agriculture share of total budget expenditures fell from 13 percent in 1970 to 4 percent in 1997, as the role for direct government spending was reduced and protection was achieved through a combination of high consumer prices and import barriers.[24] Moreover, unlike the EU, the Japanese government has not used export subsidies as a policy measure.

If the costs of protection are the force behind liberalization, then one expects liberalization to occur during periods of belt tightening when there is reduction in budget expenditures. Spending on agriculture alone is less informative because of its endogenous relationship with agricultural policies. Looking at general budget trends provides a better indicator of when there are financial constraints on the amount of resources available. However, this makes several assumptions about the connection among overall budget spending, agricultural spending, and trade protection. One could also argue that during years with rising budget expenditures, governments want to start cutting programs and

[23] The European Agricultural Guidance and Guarantee Fund includes both guarantee funds for market and price policy support and guidance funds for agricultural structures policy. The total of both kinds of expenditures on agricultural policies was 88.5 percent of the 1970 budget, 70.5 percent of the 1980 budget, and 51 percent of the 1999 budget (EC 1999).

[24] Ministry of Finance official. Interview by author. Tokyo, 14 January 1999. For budget figures, see *The Statistical Yearbook of the Ministry of Agriculture, Forestry and Fisheries* (Tokyo: Statistics and Information Department, Ministry of Agriculture, Forestry and Fisheries, selected years).

would be more, rather than less, likely to reform agricultural policies. Therefore there can only be a weak expectation that budget growth will reduce pressure for liberalization and budget reduction will increase pressure for liberalization.

HYPOTHESIS 5: BUDGET CONSTRAINTS   *Total government spending will have a negative relationship with agricultural liberalization, such that liberalization is more likely when spending declines than during periods of budget growth.*

Agricultural Trade Negotiation Data

The evidence for statistical analysis is based on an original data set of agricultural trade negotiations. The dataset includes 154 negotiations between the United States and Japan and 114 negotiations between the United States and the EU, over the period from 1970 to 1999. A negotiation on an agricultural trade barrier forms the unit of analysis. Trade barriers are any government measure that obstructs trade, including tariff and nontariff barriers, and policies related to health and sanitary regulations that could be seen to act as a trade barrier. A negotiation consists of an exchange between two or more countries that begins with a demand for policy reform and concludes when there is either an agreement or a decision to indefinitely halt talks on the issue.

The length of negotiations varies from seven years for the Uruguay Round cases to a few months for some bilateral talks. Since a long negotiation and a short negotiation are treated equally, the focus of the analysis is on the policy outcome rather than bargaining efficiency. A different approach could evaluate which strategies achieve quicker results, but that is not the goal of this study.[25]

To maximize the variation in the kinds of negotiations, cases are coded to a high degree of specificity. Each case is a single commodity or commodity group among those negotiated. Hence there are multiple cases in a large negotiation such as the Uruguay Round, while another negotiation will focus exclusively on a single commodity. There is considerable variation within negotiations that would be hidden by aggregation of products. This is clearly demonstrated by the 1987 GATT dispute settlement panel, which addressed a set of twelve different agricultural commodities for which Japan restricted imports by means of

---

[25] The results presented in this chapter remain consistent when including an explanatory variable that records the total months duration of the negotiation.

import quotas. The final panel rulings varied for each commodity and the outcomes ranged from no change to complete liberalization. Although other studies might treat this as a single negotiation, for the analysis here it counts as twelve cases in order to reflect variation in negotiation context and outcomes. In addition, disaggregation allows inclusion of commodity specific features, such as the economic importance of each product to the United States.

Negotiations are coded as separate cases for instances where a single commodity has been the topic of multiple negotiations, as long as there is a clear initiation and end to one negotiation and a second initiation for the next negotiation. For example, there was a U.S.-Japan negotiation on beef in 1978 carried out in the context of the multilateral and cross-sector negotiation structure of the Tokyo Round, and when that agreement expired there was a second negotiation with a bilateral negotiation structure. These are treated as two separate cases. Table 3.1 shows examples of the negotiations on beef, which have been among the most numerous and controversial for both Japan and Europe. In the statistical analysis, a count variable was introduced to take into account the possibility that such repeated talks on the same issue have a special nature. However, there was no significant relationship between the number of the particular negotiation in the sequence of negotiations and the degree of liberalization. These repeated negotiations offer some of the best cases for qualitative analysis tracing how the process changes in each respective negotiation.

To fairly compare the GATT panel cases with trade rounds and bilateral negotiations, cases include only negotiations on policies that are specific and legally actionable under GATT rules. First, the negotiation must address a particular policy that is identified by name rather than as a general class of policy problems. Second, the trade policy in question must be of the nature that it could be accused as a potential violation of a GATT rule under the existing trade system, such that the case could stand as a candidate issue for a dispute panel in addition to being fair game for bilateral talks and discussion in a round negotiation.[26] Therefore, not all tariff reduction cases are relevant since there are many routine small cuts that occur in a trade round that would not be raised in other negotiations. Instead, the sample includes negotiations over quotas, high tariffs, subsidies, and other regulations.

---

[26] Assuming a broad interpretation of GATT law, any quantitative restriction could potentially have been addressed in a GATT panel even when a formal GATT complaint was never made. Likewise, complaints against export subsidies and variable levies indicate that the entire network of Europe's Common Agricultural Policies were potential GATT violations even if countries chose to address such issues in rounds instead of panels (Hudec 1993, 331, 491).

TABLE 3.1
Ten Cases of Beef Negotiations

	Trade Arena	Outcome	Liberalization
U.S.-Japan beef negotiations			
9/71–12/71	bilateral	expand quota	minor
9/77–12/78	Tokyo Round	expand quota	minor
10/81–4/84	bilateral	expand quota	minor
4/87–6/88	GATT DSP	end quota	major
9/86–4/94	Uruguay Round	lower tariff	minor
U.S.-EU beef negotiations			
9/73–4/79	Tokyo Round	modify tariff category	minor
1/87–9/87	GATT DSP	ban hormone-treated beef imports	none
9/86–4/94	Uruguay Round	38 percent export subsidy cut	major
1/89–12/95	bilateral	refuse to end ban	none
1/96–5/99	WTO DSP	refuse to end ban	none

The primary source material for coding negotiation cases consists of the annual yearbook *Nōrinsho nenpo* (MAFF annual report), published by the Japanese Ministry of Agriculture, the *Agriculture Situation in the Community Annual Report*, published by the European Commission, and the *National Trade Estimate Report on Foreign Trade Barriers*, published by the Office of the U.S. Trade Representative. In addition, secondary sources provide details on the cases and information on cases not mentioned elsewhere.[27]

The data include a comprehensive survey of the agricultural trade negotiations of the United States with Japan and the EU. Table 3.2 gives a description of the kinds of negotiations. The Tokyo Round (1973–1979) and Uruguay Round (1986–1994) represent two comprehensive GATT trade rounds. Each involved over one hundred countries and fif-

---

[27] Among secondary material, Aurelia George Mulgan's study (1997b) on Japanese agricultural trade negotiations and the Anania, Carter, and McCalla study (1994) on U.S.-EU agriculture trade conflicts were important sources of information. I used the section 301 cases in the Bayard and Elliott appendix (1994) and the GATT dispute cases in the Hudec appendix (1993), while updating the more recent cases with the data available on the USTR and WTO websites. Finally, I have searched the *New York Times*, *Financial Times*, *Asahi shimbun*, and selected archival files of the *Nihon nōgyō shimbun* (Japan agricultural newspaper).

TABLE 3.2
Negotiation Context: Kinds of Trade Arenas Included in the Dataset

Trade Arena	Japan	EU
Tokyo Round	18.8%	10.5%
Uruguay Round	12.3	22.8
GATT DSP	29.9	36.9
Bilateral	34.4	29.8
APEC	4.6	—

Note: The Japan data include 154 cases; the EU data, 114 cases.

teen negotiating groups on issues ranging from industrial tariffs and agriculture to rules for subsidies. The Uruguay Round brought in new issues such as services, investment, and sanitary regulations. GATT DSP refers to cases addressed at any level of the formal dispute settlement procedures of the WTO as well as the GATT.[28] Bilateral cases are those ad hoc negotiations outside of the GATT multilateral framework. For Japan, a final category exists for the regional trade organization, Asia–Pacific Economic Cooperation (APEC), which has addressed fish and forestry trade issues along with other sectoral issues.[29]

Operationalization of Hypotheses

This section outlines the coding of variables to test the above hypotheses against evidence from the dataset on agricultural trade negotiation cases (see the appendix for descriptive statistics). The explanatory variables below form the base model for statistical analysis and are summarized in table 3.3.

NEGOTIATED POLICY LIBERALIZATION

This is the outcome variable explained by the analysis, and it is defined as the reduction of explicit trade barriers through agreement in negotia-

[28] Later analysis will distinguish between the levels of GATT DSP mediation, but for the purposes of table 3.2, a case is categorized as GATT DSP whether agreement was reached after consultations or following a final panel ruling.

[29] The APEC cases are from the Kuala Lumpur Ministerial of November 1998 when APEC talks began to address trade issues with sufficient specificity to count as cases for this dataset.

TABLE 3.3
Base Model for Estimating Policy Liberalization

Variable	Hypothesis	Predicted Result	Japan Result	EU Result	Operationalization (Measure)
Linkage	1	+	+	+	strength of cross-sector linkage (0–3)
Legalism	2a	+		+	GATT dispute consultation (0–1)
	2b	+	+		GATT panel violation ruling (0–1)
Threat	3	+	+	+	specificity of threat (0–3)
Trade balance		−	−	+	bilateral trade balance (U.S. bn. $)
Product value		+	−		product share in U.S. ag. exports (%)
Politics	4a	+	+	NA	LDP share of Lower House seats (%)
	4b	−	NA	−	French presidency of Council (0–2)
Budget	5	−		−	annual budget growth (%)
Growth		+		+	annual growth of per capita GDP (%)
Multi		+	−		multiple country demand (0–1)
Export		−	NA	−	case about export subsidy (0–1)

Note: Variables represent those used to evaluate the respective hypotheses and additional control variables. The third column gives the predicted direction of the variable's influence on liberalization outcomes. The result columns summarize the direction of influence for statistically significant regression estimates. NA indicates a variable that is not applicable.

tion. The variable categorizes negotiation outcomes into three levels of liberalization for none, minor, or major degree of policy change. Negotiation outcomes were coded according to the following categories:

1. No liberalization: status quo or nominal change
2. Minor liberalization: partial change in the size of quota category, modification in the use of quarantine standards, moderate reduction in tariffs or subsidy levels
3. Major liberalization: tariffication of quantitative restriction, change in the nature of quarantine restriction, large reduction in tariff or subsidy levels

CROSS-SECTOR LINKAGE

A four-level ordinal scale measures the strength of cross-sector linkage. While any negotiation that addresses both industry and/or service goods issues together with agricultural issues qualifies as a cross-sector linkage, there are different levels in the institutionalization of the linkage. The highest cross-sector linkage value of 3 represents cases drawn from either the Uruguay Round or GATT dispute settlement cases that involve industrial and agricultural issues in a single complaint. The Tokyo Round receives the next level of cross-sector linkage strength, coded as 2. Finally, the value is 1 for all loosely tied multisector negotiations, such as the APEC talks or bilateral talks. Negotiations on agricultural issues alone are coded 0. This variable tests the hypothesis that the strength of the linkage between sectors in a negotiation will influence liberalization in agriculture.

LEGAL FRAMING

Two dichotomous variables measure the level of GATT dispute mediation. The first variable represents cases that involve a formal GATT complaint and reach settlement during the consultation process that precedes a panel. The argument about reputation predicts a strong positive effect from this variable. The second variable measures whether there was a GATT violation ruling on the policy. These are the cases that continued through the entire dispute settlement process until the panel delivered a violation verdict. If the value of trade rules influences decisions, one would expect violation rulings to have a positive effect on liberalization. This is critical for the evaluation of the argument that normative pressure, in terms of both respect for law and interest in maintenance of the trade rules promotes liberalization.

THREAT

A four-level ordinal scale measures the degree of specific and public commitment behind the threat of retaliation issued by the United States during a negotiation. It is coded 0 when there is no public record of officials in the U.S. executive branch or Congress making a threat in connection with the negotiation. Cases with general threats are coded 1 and include cases when the U.S. government initiates a section 301 investigation or an official of the executive branch or Congress claims that a concession on the specific issue is necessary to forestall rising protectionism in Congress. The variable is coded as 2 for specific threats when the U.S. government issues a deadline and target list or retaliation amount. Finally, the strongest threats, which are coded 3, represent cases for which the threat is carried out with implementation of sanctions in retaliation for a given trade protection policy.[30]

TRADE BALANCE

This variable is the bilateral trade balance for trade in goods measured in billions of U.S. dollars at 1995 prices.[31] The figures for the EU represent the aggregate trade of the current fifteen members with the United States. For consistency, this aggregated figure is used for the full period rather than adjusting for the changes in EU membership.

MAJOR U.S. AGRICULTURAL EXPORT

The significance of a product to U.S. interests is measured by that product groups' share in the total value of U.S. agricultural exports.[32] Using shares on a world export basis reduces the risk of endogeneity between existing protection and level of exports in the bilateral trade relationship. The ratio for the product share in total exports is one measure of

[30] For Europe there are not the general "trade deficit" and congressional protection complaints seen so frequently in U.S.-Japan relations, while on the Japan side there are no cases where an agriculture dispute led to implementation of sanctions.

[31] The data are from IMF, *Direction of Trade Statistics Yearbook* (Washington, DC, assorted years).

[32] There is some overaggregation given that U.S. trade data are subdivided into commodity categories. For example, the negotiation case may be about oranges, but it will be aggregated in a category as citrus fruit. The data are from USDA, "U.S. Foreign Agricultural Trade Statistical Report, Calendar Year," in *Foreign Agricultural Trade of the United States*, selected years. I thank Carol Whitton of the Economic Research Service, U.S. Department of Agriculture, for providing me with the data.

its importance to the United States and tests whether priority items to the United States gain more liberalization.

LDP STRENGTH

The ratio of the share of LDP seats relative to total seats in the Lower House of Parliament measures the strength of the LDP. This provides an indicator of when unpopular policy changes are likely to be especially difficult for the domestic political situation. In times of a narrow majority, party members and leadership are likely to be more cautious and fear taking risks, which would correspond with a lower likelihood of liberalization.

FRENCH COUNCIL PRESIDENCY

The variable for the authority of France within the Council of Ministers is a count variable for the number of times that France held the presidency during the initial year and the final year of the negotiation. Because France could at most hold the seat once during each of these two critical years, the value ranges from 0 to 2. Alternation of the presidency occurs by automatic rotation among EU members. When a strong opponent to agricultural reform like France holds this position in the Council of Ministers, agricultural liberalization faces powerful political opposition.

BUDGET

This variable measures the annual growth in total budget expenditures for the year in which the negotiation ended. For the European cases, the expenditures are those of total EU expenditures rather than national government budgets.[33] The growth of budget expenditures influences whether budget constraints add pressure for liberalization.

GROWTH

This is the most basic indicator of whether the negotiation takes place during good times or hard times and serves as an important control variable. Growth is measured by the rate of growth in per capita GDP

---

[33] The original data for Community expenditures are reported in 1998 prices in *The Community Budget: The Facts in Figures 1999*, published by the European Commission. For Japan, the expenditures are general account expenditures of the national budget as reported in *Financial Statistics of Japan 1999*, published by the Ministry of Finance.

during the final year of the negotiation.[34] For the sake of continuity, the EU data are the aggregation of the fifteen membership grouping over the full period. Generally one would expect that during periods of higher economic growth countries would be more open to liberalization.

MULTIPLE COUNTRIES

This is an indicator variable that represents whether the liberalization demand is made by the United States alone or by multiple countries. It includes multilateral trade rounds, dispute settlement cases with multiple complainants, or any negotiation in which countries in addition to the United States played an active role pushing for liberalization during the negotiation. Inclusion of this variable allows evaluation of yet another feature of the negotiation context—the number of countries involved.

EXPORT SUBSIDIES

This is an indicator variable for the U.S.-EU model reflecting the special nature of export subsidies in agricultural trade. The importance of this policy to CAP and the strong French opposition to changing it makes the variable another proxy for strong domestic political opposition to reform. Moreover, GATT law has been weak regarding export subsidies for primary goods. These reasons make one expect less liberalization for cases dealing with export subsidy policies. On the other hand, the budget hypothesis implies that these expensive policies should be a priority for reforms, in which case one would expect more liberalization. Since Japan does not apply any export subsidies, this variable is not used for the U.S.-Japan negotiations.

Statistical Analysis of Policy Liberalization

This section evaluates these hypotheses with statistical analysis of U.S.-Japan negotiations and U.S.-EU negotiations. Rather than combining all of the negotiations, separate analysis is conducted for U.S negotiations with Japan and with the EU. Since the variables in the model are unable to capture all differences between Japan and the EU, pooling these two datasets would produce misleading inferences about the negotiations. An advantage of conducting parallel analysis of two datasets is that this

[34] The data, which are reported in 1995 prices and exchange rates, are from the OECD Statistical Compendium CD-ROM, series E15CO059, JPNCO059.

approach allows for the possibility that the same variables may have different effects in each political context. For example, budget constraints may be more important for the EU given that over half of spending by the Community goes to the agricultural sector. The separate analysis also facilitates inclusion of some variables distinct to one or the other dataset, such as the LDP share of Diet seats and the presidency of the EU Council of Ministers.

For both the U.S.-Japan data and the U.S.-EU data, two models with different sets of explanatory variables are used to estimate the probability of liberalization. The alternative hypotheses for legal framing require two models: one model evaluates whether legal framing promotes liberalization at an early stage during GATT dispute consultations, and a second model evaluates whether legal framing promotes liberalization at a later stage during the GATT dispute proceedings after a violation ruling.

Given that the dependent variable measures policy liberalization with three ordered categories (none, minor, and major liberalization), ordered probit regression is an appropriate statistical model. Using this model assumes that there is an underlying continuum of policy liberalization that has a standard normal distribution. The unobserved liberalization scale has an order, but the categories may not occur in fixed intervals (i.e., the distance between none and minor liberalization may be smaller than the distance between minor and major liberalization). This is desirable given the nature of the dependent variable. Interpretation of statistical estimates is done through simulation by examining how a shift in the level of one variable will affect the probability of low, minor, and major liberalization while all other variables are held constant.[35] Use of simulation techniques generates these predictions while taking into account estimation uncertainty (King, Tomz, and Wittenberg 2000).[36]

The findings were robust to different specifications.[37] Two tests were undertaken to check the models presented in this chapter. First, the results were consistent when estimated as a probit model with a dichotomous coding of the dependent variable that collapsed the top two categories of major and minor liberalization. Second, as a test for omitted

[35] Holding other variables constant involves setting variables to their mean levels.

[36] The simulation technique used here involves a thousand random draws of coefficients and threshold parameters from their asymptotic sampling distribution, which is a multivariate normal distribution. I then calculate one thousand sets of predicted probabilities using each simulated set of parameters. These resulting predictions incorporate estimation uncertainty.

[37] Using Huber/White estimator of variance to calculate robust standard errors yielded consistent findings.

variables related to the different agricultural products, a fixed effects model of commodity groups was estimated as an attempt to control for product-specific effects.[38] The key variables for cross-sector linkage and legal framing retain significance for both the Japan and EU models in these two different tests of the models' robustness.

U.S.-Japan Agricultural Trade Negotiations

This section presents the statistical analysis of 154 cases of agricultural products addressed in negotiations between the United States and Japan. The results from the models reported in table 3.4 confirm the legalism and cross-sector linkage hypotheses by showing that a strong cross-sector linkage and a GATT violation ruling have a significant positive relationship with liberalization. The analysis also shows that threats and growth in the bilateral trade deficit increases the probability of liberalization while political weakness for the LDP reduces the probability of liberalization. However, the impact of threats and the LDP role appears small when compared with the influence of the negotiation structure. Moreover, the evidence indicates that the strength of multilateralism arises from the institutions that structure a negotiation rather than the number of countries.

The cross-sector linkage hypothesis finds strong support. Negotiations that linked agricultural and nonagricultural issues were more likely to produce substantial agricultural liberalization than negotiations that focused on agriculture only, and more institutionalized linkages had greater effect. To show the effect of a cross-sector linkage, two scenarios are compared with all other variables held constant while the value for the cross-sector linkage variable is changed. The first scenario sets the cross-sector linkage variable to the highest level, which represents a strongly institutionalized cross-sector linkage such as seen in the Uruguay Round negotiation. The second scenario sets the cross-sector linkage at its lowest value, which represents a negotiation where there is no cross-sector linkage. The beef-citrus negotiation in 1984 provides an example of such a negotiation that exclusively focused on agricultural issues. Table 3.5 shows that the shift in the linkage variable from 0 to 3 causes an average 82 percentage point increase (from 0.12 to 0.94) in the predicted probability of major liberalization.[39] A smaller shift of the

---

[38] Following the OECD Agricultural Accounts commodity categories, I classified the 154 Japanese cases into 19 commodity groups and the 114 EU cases into 13 commodity groups.

[39] The 82 percentage point increase is the difference between the 94 percent probability

TABLE 3.4
Ordered Probit Regression: Japanese Agricultural Liberalization

Variable Name	Model 1	Model 2
Cross-sector linkage	0.52**	0.94**
	(0.15)	(0.18)
GATT dispute consultation	0.43	
	(0.35)	
GATT dispute violation ruling		2.29**
		(0.47)
Threat	0.30*	0.42**
	(0.13)	(0.13)
Trade balance	−2.92**	−1.03
	(0.82)	(0.83)
U.S. export priority	−5.43*	−4.55
	(2.73)	(2.86)
Budget growth	0.04	−0.002
	(0.03)	(0.02)
Economic growth	0.05	−0.005
	(0.06)	(0.07)
LDP strength	12.89**	10.25**
	(3.13)	(3.02)
Multicountry demand	−0.75**	−1.54**
	(0.27)	0.32
First threshold	8.43**	6.75**
	(1.76)	(1.62)
Second threshold	9.44**	7.87**
	(1.79)	(1.64)
log-likelihood	−138.46	−126.50
gamma statistic	0.74	0.74
	(0.07)	(0.06)

Note: The number of observations is 154. Standard errors are in parentheses. The intercept is set to zero and two thresholds are estimated.
*Significant at the 5 percent level. **Significant at the 1 percent level.

linkage variable, from 0 to 1, such as in a hypothetical comparison of a single–sector negotiation and multi-sector negotiation with a weak linkage, causes an average 28 percentage point increase in the probability of major liberalization.

The results for both scenarios are graphically displayed together in

of major liberalization with a strong linkage (e.g., the variable is set to its highest value of 3) and the 12 percent probability of major liberalization predicted when there is no linkage. Table 3.5 reports this difference in the predicted probability for the top category of the dependent variable.

TABLE 3.5
Effect of Key Variables on Predicted Liberalization (U.S.-Japan)

Variable	Shift	Change in Probability of Major Liberalization	
Strong linkage	0 → 3	0.82	(0.63, 0.93)
Violation ruling	0 → 1	0.67	(0.49, 0.79)
Strong threat	0 → 3	0.46	(0.20, 0.68)
LDP strength	49% → 59%	0.39	(0.18, 0.58)
Budget growth	0% → 20%	−0.01	(−0.35, 0.35)
Multicountry	0 → 1	−0.54	(−0.71, −0.33)

Note: The table shows the predicted probability of major liberalization when changing the variable of interest and holding all other variables constant at their mean. Results are based on 1,000 simulations using the parameter estimates from model 2 of table 3.4. The 95 percent confident interval is given in parentheses.

the left triangle in figure 3.1.[40] The vertices of the triangle represent the three categories of the dependent variable and provide coordinates for the points inside the triangle that represent a simulated prediction of a negotiation outcome. Points located closer to the upper vertex of the

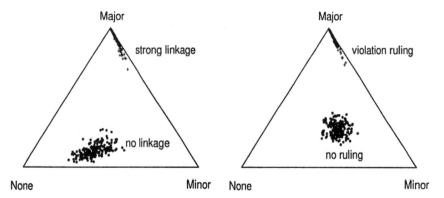

Figure 3.1: Negotiation Structure Effects on Predictions of Liberalization (U.S.-Japan). The figure shows the predictions for negotiation outcomes based on 200 simulations, using the estimates from model 2 in table 3.4. The predictions compare two scenarios by changing the variable of interest while holding all other variables constant at their mean. Each point represents one prediction of liberalization under the specified scenario.

[40] The parameters from the regression estimates shown in table 3.4 form the basis for simulating predictions of liberalization outcomes in each of the two scenarios. This kind of figure is called a "ternary plot" and has been suggested as a way to display results for a three-category dependent variable (King, Tomz, and Wittenberg 2000).

triangle indicate predictions for a negotiation with a high probability of major liberalization, points closer to the lower left vertex indicate a high probability of no liberalization, and points in the center of the triangle indicate an equal probability for all three categories of liberalization. Within the triangle, predictions for each scenario appear as a cluster of points. Dark circles represent the null category scenario with no linkage, and plus signs represent the high category scenario with a strong linkage. The spread of each cluster indicates the variation in predictions for each scenario that results from uncertainty of estimation.

In the left triangle, predictions for no linkage negotiations lie between none and minor liberalization, and predictions for strong linkage negotiations lie in the upper vertex, indicating a high probability of major liberalization. The gap between the clusters and the tight grouping of points illustrate the highly significant effect of adding a strong linkage to a negotiation. Without a linkage, the negotiation is likely to end with none or minor liberalization, while adding a strong cross-sector linkage makes it probable that the negotiation will end with major liberalization.

The comparison of the consultation phase and violation ruling in legalistic dispute settlement cases tests the implications for the different causal mechanisms by which legal framing exerts leverage. Model 1 in table 3.4 reports that the early consultation phase of GATT legal mediation does not have a significant influence on policy outcomes, which leads to the rejection of legal framing hypothesis 2a. In contrast, model 2 shows a significant positive impact from a violation ruling, in confirmation of legal framing hypothesis 2b. This pattern of negotiations indicates that GATT mediation influences Japanese policy by means of the ruling rather than consultation. The implication is that concern about protecting reputation and getting the best settlement is insufficient to bring liberalization. Early settlement during consultations would meet those goals, but Japan has been reluctant to plea bargain a settlement before a ruling. Of the forty-six cases of agricultural products involved in complaints filed by the United States, Japan reached a settlement before establishment of a panel in eighteen — 39 percent of the total. For the majority of cases, political opposition is too strong to allow for a plea bargain.

The beef and citrus negotiations in 1988 (discussed in greater detail in chapter 5) are illustrative of the political pressure against early settlement even when there was high certainty that the policy would be ruled a violation. When the Japanese government considered whether to reach early settlement with the United States after the complaint was filed, several LDP politicians requested that the government wait for a panel ruling. According to newspaper reports, many within the LDP thought that the ruling would make it politically easier to accept concessions, although it was recognized that the early settlement allowed for smaller and more gradual policy changes than would be possible after a panel ruling.[41] In the end the government chose to settle early, and in the next election, several agricultural district politicians involved in that decision lost their seats in what was seen as punishment by angry farmer constituents.[42] Perhaps reflecting on this experience, in a 1997 WTO case regarding a fruit quarantine policy, a senior Foreign Ministry official reported that the LDP and Ministry of Agriculture insisted that the government must not make any concession until the final ruling took place and every legal appeal had been exhausted.[43] Although many factors contribute to the political cost of liberalizing farm goods, this case shows that politicians in Japan fear that they will suffer greater political damage from early settlement than from following a violation ruling. This logic would explain the pattern observed in the data that Japan does not settle early for as many cases and on average agrees to less liberalization for cases when it accepts an agreement before a panel ruling than for cases after a violation ruling.[44]

The pressure arising after a ruling is necessary to make agricultural liberalization politically possible in Japan. The need to uphold the rules system by compliance with rulings has brought a concession in eighteen of the twenty cases ruled a violation, with sixteen cases resulting in major liberalization.[45] When controlling for other factors, a violation ruling is one of the strongest predictors of a liberalization outcome. Comparison of two hypothetical scenarios — where all factors relating to negotiations are identical and there is a violation ruling for one negotiation but not for the other — reveals the large effect on predicted liberalization outcomes. Table 3.5 shows that a violation ruling increases the predicted probability of major liberalization by 67 percentage points on average when compared with the scenario of a negotiation without a violation ruling. This difference in predictions is illustrated in the triangle on the right in figure

---

[41] *Financial Times*, 6 May 1988; *New York Times*, 21 June 1988; *Nihon nōgyō shimbun*, 24 June 1988.

[42] LDP Diet member Tokuichirō Tamazawa. Interview by author. Tokyo, 8 March 1999.

[43] The dispute was initiated by a U.S. complaint in October 1997, which resulted in the elimination of a particular varietal testing requirement for fruit and nuts in December 1999 after a panel ruling (WT/DS76/R) and Appellate Body ruling concurred that the policy represented a violation of Japan's commitments under WTO agreements. Ministry of Foreign Affairs official. Interview by author. Tokyo, 14 May 1999.

[44] The mean liberalization for eighteen cases settled during consultations is 1.9, compared with 2.7 for the twenty cases settled after a violation ruling. Note that liberalization ranges from 1 to 3, with a 2.01 mean for all cases.

[45] Two cases were ruled nonviolation, and some were settled after a panel was established but before a ruling was issued.

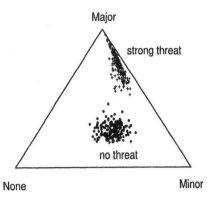

Figure 3.2: Threat Effect on Predictions of Liberalization (U.S.-Japan). The figure shows the predictions for negotiation outcomes based on 200 simulations using the estimates from model 2 in table 3.4. The predictions compare two scenarios when there is presence/absence of a strong threat and all other variables are held constant at their mean. Each point represents one prediction of liberalization under the specified scenario.

3.1. The scenario with no violation ruling has a cluster of predictions of minor liberalization, while the scenario with a violation ruling shows predictions tightly grouped with a high probability of major liberalization. The violation ruling shifts the expected outcome of the negotiation from minor liberalization to major liberalization.

In addition to linkage and legal framing, the empirical evidence shows that threats are also effective in U.S. negotiations with Japan. As hypothesized, threats have a positive effect on liberalization, and more specific threats have greater impact. Figure 3.2 compares the predictions of liberalization for a scenario of negotiations where there is no threat with a scenario of negotiations that have a threat of the highest level. The points representing the predictions for the no threat scenario fall into the central area, showing that any level of liberalization may be equally likely to occur. For cases with a strong threat, predictions have a higher probability of major liberalization.

However, the effect of a strong cross-sector linkage or a violation ruling is greater than that of a threat. Changing the linkage and ruling variables from low to high levels produced, respectively, an 82 and 67 percentage point increase in the likelihood of major liberalization, while changing the threat variable from low to high levels produces only a 38 percentage point increase in the likelihood of major liberalization (see table 3.5).[46] Comparison of figures 3.1 and 3.2 shows the greater cer-

[46] Shifting the threat variable from 0 to 1 yields an average 15 percentage point increase

tainty for the prediction that a linkage or a violation ruling will increase liberalization relative to the uncertainty surrounding the predicted effect of threats. The two negotiation structure variables fixed at their highest level produce a tight clustering of predictions for a high probability of major liberalization. In contrast, for the threat variable at its highest level, predictions are spread out across the major liberalization category. This indicates there is both a lower probability and less certainty that a threat would bring major liberalization.

The importance of the controversial U.S.-Japan trade balance is another component of U.S. pressure. The negative coefficient for the trade balance estimate means that the size of the U.S. trade surplus with Japan has a negative correlation with liberalization; negotiations that take place during years in which there is a larger U.S. deficit are more likely to result in liberalization. The trade deficit puts political pressure on Japan to liberalize its agricultural markets, in terms of both demands from the United States and urging from Japan's export industries that worry about trade tensions harming their interests.

The United States does not appear to use its leverage effectively to favor its big export items.[47] On the contrary, products that are leading U.S. agricultural export items are, if anything, less likely to be liberalized. This is counter to the expectation that Japan would give concessions to the items most important to the United States out of deference to the relationship or because the United States put more pressure on these issues.[48]

The statistical analysis confirms that domestic political constraints can help a government reach an international agreement closer to its own preferences. The variable for the LDP share of the total seats in the Lower House of the Diet is positive and highly significant: LDP strength makes liberalization by Japan more likely. This seems odd at first given the strong opposition to liberalization by the LDP, which has its electoral base in rural districts. However, the evidence fits the conjecture that having tied hands provides greater bargaining leverage. When the LDP is weak it faces political constraints, and this allows it to resist U.S. demands with claims that it is politically unable to risk hurting a key constituency. Comparing the scenario of the LDP holding 49 percent of

---

in the predicted probability of major liberalization, compared to the 28 percentage point increase from the same shift of the linkage variable.

[47] While the share of a product in the value of U.S. agricultural exports provides an indicator of the comparative advantage for the product relative to other agricultural items, it may be that U.S. government priorities are not related to this economic measure.

[48] However, for some important U.S. export crops, such as soy and feedgrains, the needs of Japanese livestock farmers motivated early liberalization prior to 1970, and subsequent negotiations were about smaller changes in the remaining trade barriers.

the Lower House seats with the scenario of the LDP holding 59 percent of the seats yields a 39 percentage point increase of the predicted probability for major liberalization. This is a substantial change, although it is smaller than the predicted increase in the probability of major liberalization that resulted from a strong linkage or a violation ruling.

Moreover, it is interesting to note evidence of an interaction between LDP strength and the role of threats in a negotiation.[49] When the LDP is strong, threats have an even greater impact; conversely, when the LDP is weak threats have less effect on negotiation outcomes.[50] Only from a position of political strength can the LDP adopt the unpopular policy of agricultural liberalization under bullying by the United States.

Budget constraints do not emerge as an important variable to explain liberalization by Japan. While increased spending may free up resources for the expense of protection policies and austerity may push for cutbacks, there is no evidence that this logic works in Japan. The variable measuring growth in government spending is not significant and it has a positive sign.[51] Table 3.4 shows that the budget variable has no effect on outcomes. These results are too weak to support any conclusions, but it appears that sometimes Japan is more likely to liberalize when the budget is growing. This may reflect the need for high compensation payments to make it politically possible to accept liberalization. For example, the Japanese government passed a 6 trillion yen (50 billion dollar) spending package for rural areas in conjunction with ratification of the Uruguay Round Agriculture Agreement. Expensive liberalization packages such as this contradict the notion that budget constraints explain the trade policy reforms.

Although theories about multilateralism often assume that having more countries will improve the likelihood of cooperation, the evidence here disputes this notion — multiple countries making demands reduces the likelihood of liberalization by Japan. This suggests that the United States may be able to leverage additional pressure from the special relationship in a bilateral negotiation. When comparing the scenario of multiple countries making demands with the scenario of the United States acting alone, results show that the former scenario reduces the probability of major liberalization by 54 percentage points. In other words, all else being equal, the United States has a better chance to gain

[49] See Davis (2001) for an analysis of this relationship.

[50] There may also be a selection effect in which the United States makes stronger demands when the LDP majority is secure and refrains from pushing hard when the LDP is weak.

[51] Moreover, the budget and economic growth variable are jointly insignificant. A likelihood-ratio test for omitting both the growth and budget variables from model 1 yields a Pearson $\chi^2 = 3.35$, p-value $= 0.19$.

major liberalization when it acts alone than if there are other countries making the same demand. This lends support to the idea of U.S. influence through its position of power. However, while the effect is significant, it is still smaller in magnitude than the negotiation structure variables. One implication of this finding is that the power of multilateralism is not because multiple countries make demands during a negotiation to apply greater peer pressure. Rather, multilateralism is important through the institutions that often accompany negotiations involving many countries.

In summary, the statistical analysis of U.S.-Japan negotiations shows that when controlling for threats, economic and budget variables, and the electoral position of the ruling party, issue linkage and violation rulings stand out as the most important predictors of agricultural liberalization. The disaggregation of negotiation structure variables provides insights into which specific features of the negotiation structure promote liberalization. The importance of violation rulings relative to a weak effect for the consultation phase of dispute proceedings distinguishes between the two posited mechanisms for legal framing. For Japan, the value of rules rather than concern about reputation provides the persuasive power for legal framing.

U.S.-EU Agricultural Trade Negotiations

The evidence from the U.S.-EU data for 114 negotiations corroborates the finding in U.S.-Japan negotiations that cross-sector issue linkage plays a prominent role in any explanation of liberalization. GATT legal procedures hold weaker influence relative to issue linkage in the European context and relative to the influence of these same institutional features in Japan. Hence, whereas there were two pathways to liberalization in Japan, for Europe there is only one negotiation structure with strong prospects for substantial liberalization — an institutionalized cross-sector linkage. Threats and budget constraints also promote liberalization, while the political constraints arising when France holds the presidency of the Council of Ministers restrict bargaining options and help the EU resist liberalization.

The two models estimating liberalization in U.S.-EU negotiations are presented in table 3.6. The significant positive coefficient for cross-sector linkage confirms the issue linkage hypothesis. Linking agricultural issues to other sectoral negotiations increases the probability for more liberalization in Europe, and more institutionalized linkages have greater effect. When comparing the scenario of a single-sector negotiation with a negotiation that is otherwise identical but has a strong

TABLE 3.6
Ordered Probit Regression: EU Agricultural Liberalization

Variable Name	Model 1	Model 2
Cross-sector linkage	0.37*	0.44*
	(0.18)	(0.19)
GATT dispute consultation	0.87*	
	(0.38)	
GATT dispute violation ruling		0.76
		(0.67)
Threat	0.26*	0.18
	(0.12)	(0.11)
Trade balance	3.72**	3.67**
	(1.19)	(1.24)
U.S. export priority	1.86	1.46
	(1.65)	(1.64)
Budget growth	−3.09**	−2.38*
	(1.18)	(1.12)
Economic growth	0.38*	0.38*
	(0.16)	(0.16)
French Council presidency	−1.02**	−0.84**
	(0.31)	(0.30)
Export subsidy case	−1.23**	−1.19**
	(0.27)	(0.27)
Multicountry demand	−0.40	−0.78
	(0.45)	(0.51)
First threshold	−0.62	−0.66
	(0.60)	(0.59)
Second threshold	0.55	0.49
	(0.60)	(0.59)
log-likelihood	−99.68	−101.59
gamma statistic	0.67	0.65
	(0.08)	(0.09)

Note: The number of observations is 114. Standard errors are in parentheses. The intercept is set to zero and two thresholds are estimated.
*Significant at the 5 percent level. **Significant at the 1 percent level.

cross-sector linkage (shifting the variable from 0 to 3), the predicted probability of major liberalization increases by 39 percentage points on average (see table 3.7). A smaller shift from no linkage to a weak linkage (shifting the variable from 0 to 1) causes an average 11 percentage point increase. The triangle shown on the left in figure 3.3 illustrates the effect of adding a strong linkage. The cluster of circles representing the predictions for no linkage cases lies between the categories predicting

TABLE 3.7
Effect of Key Variables on Predicted Liberalization (U.S.-EU)

Variable	Shift	Change in Probability of Major Liberalization	
Strong linkage	0 → 3	0.39	(0.01, 0.71)
Dispute consultation	0 → 1	0.31	(0.02, 0.58)
Strong threat	0 → 3	0.29	(0.04, 0.55)
French Council	0 → 1	−0.31	(−0.46, −0.14)
Budget growth	0% → 20%	−0.19	(−0.32, −0.07)
Export subsidy	0 → 1	−0.38	(−0.52, −0.24)

Note: The table shows the predicted probability of major liberalization when changing the variable of interest and holding all other variables constant at their mean. Results are based on 1,000 simulations using the parameter estimates from model 1 of table 3.6. The 95 percent confident interval is given in parentheses.

either none or minor liberalization, while the cluster of plus symbols in the upper category of major liberalization represents the predictions for the second scenario when there is an institutionalized cross-sector linkage. The spread of predictions for each scenario indicates that there is greater uncertainty for predictions of the outcome of U.S.-EU negotiations relative to those for Japan (see figure 3.1), which reflects the weaker fit of the model to the data. Nevertheless, the substantive effect

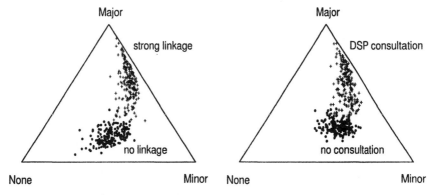

Figure 3.3: Negotiation Structure Effects on Predictions of Liberalization (U.S.-EU). The figure shows the predictions for negotiation outcomes based on 200 simulations using the estimates from model 1 in table 3.6. The predictions compare two scenarios by changing the variable of interest while holding all other variables constant at their mean. Each point represents one prediction of liberalization under the specified scenario.

is large—adding a strong linkage to the negotiation structure increases the predicted outcome of the negotiation to major liberalization.

Unlike Japan, the EU has displayed intransigence in the face of violation rulings but has frequently made concessions during the earlier stage of consultations under GATT mediation. The specification of model 1 in table 3.6 shows that there is a significant positive effect for the consultation phase of the dispute settlement procedures, which supports legal framing hypothesis 2a. Table 3.7 shows that a change in this variable increases the probability of major liberalization by 31 percentage points. The right graph of figure 3.3 displays predictions from the scenario of negotiations that culminate in the consultation phase of GATT dispute mediation and a base category including all other negotiations. The predictions from the consultation scenario have a higher probability of major liberalization than other negotiations, all else being equal. Although predictions are widely spread out, which indicates higher uncertainty, the EU response to consultations is still sufficient to produce an expectation that the negotiation will bring major liberalization.

Consultations form a less legalistic negotiation structure than a GATT panel, but nevertheless, the negotiation context takes on some characteristics of legal framing. The consultations begin with a formal complaint based on interpretation of GATT law, and the talks are premised on the fact that consultations may proceed to panel mediation.[52] The importance of consultations demonstrates that legal framing influences European policy at a different level of legalization than Japan. This evidence supports the argument that concern for reputation leads the EU to avoid rulings, and it also highlights the ability of the Commission to push through a decision to settle early for a better deal that will bring less harm to reputation.

On the controversial cases, the EU has entirely disregarded both the reputational harm and international obligation arising from violation rulings. The specification of model 2 in table 3.6 shows that a violation ruling is a weak predictor for EU trade liberalization. This contrasts with the evidence from the data for U.S.-Japan negotiations and goes against the expectations of legal framing hypothesis 2b regarding the pressure from a GATT ruling. Nevertheless, it corroborates evidence from two recent dispute cases in which the EU refused to comply with

---

[52] Under GATT 1947 rules it was possible for a country to block the panel, and the EC took advantage of this on several occasions. Since establishment of the WTO in 1995, the option to block a panel ended. Empirical examination of this rule change reveals little impact on the pattern of dispute initiation or outcomes (Busch 2000; Goldstein and Martin 2000).

violation rulings. The case by the United States against the EU banana import regime produced a WTO ruling against the EU policy in April 1997, and when the EU had not complied two years later, the WTO authorized the United States to impose sanctions. It took another two years before the EU changed its policy in a settlement satisfactory to the United States in April 2001. In the second case, the EU refused to change its ban against imports of hormone-treated beef after a negative WTO ruling in 1998. Neither the ruling nor subsequent U.S. retaliatory sanctions have overcome EU resistance to changing the policy. Chapter 9 will examine more closely why legal framing has less impact within the EU political context as a result of conflict between the obligations of the GATT with the goals of European integration.

In an issue related to the impact of legal framing on EU policy, the difficulty of negotiating liberalization of export subsidy cases is readily apparent. The variable for negotiations involving export subsidies as the trade barrier is highly significant in both EU models with a large negative effect on liberalization. The United States made strong demands for restraint of these subsidies that were undercutting U.S. agricultural exports, and in 1985 Congress initiated a new export subsidy program to retaliate against European subsidies (Yeutter 1998). However, the GATT exceptions allowing export subsidies for primary goods reduced the ability of the United States to use leverage from international trade law against the export subsidy policies of the EU. The negative finding for export subsidy cases proves the ability of the EU to resist reform of a policy strongly backed by France, even when it is a policy that both is a priority to the United States and raises budget expenses.

Threats also promote liberalization in Europe. Model 1 in table 3.6 shows a positive and significant coefficient for the threat variable. However, the variable does not reach significance in model 2, which indicates that it is less robust when including the violation ruling variable. The addition of a strong threat (shifting the variable from 0 to 3) causes an average 29 percentage point increase of the predicted probability for major liberalization.[53] This is less than the impact of linkage and about the same as the impact of low-level legal framing, and it is much less than the impact of threats on Japan. One problem reducing the effect of sanctions may be that the amount of sanctions is spread across multiple countries, which diffuses the pressure against the obstinate governments, any one of which can block a policy change.

Although threats positively relate to liberalization as hypothesized, two important cases show that some issues are impervious to threats. In

[53] The smaller shift from 0 to 1 causes a 9 percentage point increase on average.

the disputes over Europe's ban on hormone beef and its preferential import arrangements for bananas, U.S. threats and retaliatory sanctions of 100 percent import duties on 300 million dollar value of EU exports brought no change in the policies when retaliatory duties went into effect in spring 1999. A frustrated Congress proposed a rotating product list for sanctions, thereby increasing the total number of targeted industries that faced the threat of U.S. sanctions. After Congress passed this "carousel retaliation" in section 407 of the Trade and Development Act of 2000, European officials claimed this would only worsen the dispute and threatened to initiate their own dispute against the policy at the WTO.[54] The EU eventually agreed to reform its banana import policy to comply with the WTO ruling, but it continues to defy both rulings and sanctions in order to maintain its ban against hormone-treated beef.

The more balanced structure of trade between the EU and United States changes the effect of the trade balance. The statistical analysis reveals a puzzling positive relationship between the trade balance and liberalization. It is difficult to explain why a high U.S. trade surplus with the EU would promote European agricultural liberalization in specific negotiations. It may be a reversal of the pressure argument as U.S. businesses interested in the EU export market restrain U.S. demands on the more controversial agricultural cases. More research is necessary to explain this finding further.

As expected, France holding the position of president in the EU Council of Ministers blocks liberalization. The estimate for the coefficient is significant and in the predicted negative direction. This confirms the EU internal politics hypothesis 4b that liberalization is less likely when an antiliberalization government like France acts as agenda-setter for Council policy-making. The model predicts that in a hypothetical negotiation when France holds the presidency during the initial or final year of the negotiation, there will be a 35 percentage point increase in the chance of deadlock and a 31 percentage point decrease in the probability of major liberalization when compared to a negotiation where France is simply one among many in the Council room (see table 3.7). Figure 3.4 shows a clear pattern. The scenario of French Council presidency has predictions spread across the lower left vertex of the triangle, showing the expectation that such conditions will not produce any liberalization. The wide spread of points across the category reflects the considerable uncertainty surrounding the estimation of the effect of the French presidency. As Council president, the French government can protect the policy autonomy of agriculture. In contrast, when a different

[54] *Agra-Europe*, June 2000; Sek (2002).

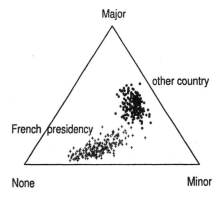

Figure 3.4: French Council Presidency Effect on Predictions of Liberalization. The figure shows the predictions for negotiation outcomes based on 200 simulations using the estimates from model 1 in table 3.6. The predictions compare two scenarios where France does/does not hold the EU Council presidency during either the initial or the final year of the negotiation.

nation is Council president, it may encourage more involvement of trade ministers in Council decision making and prevent the Agriculture Council from acting as a veto player. The implications of this finding are significant for understanding both trade negotiation outcomes and the policy process in the EU.

Although the United States does not appear to receive any advantage from bargaining alone with the EU, neither do multiple countries add leverage. The insignificant coefficient of the variable for multiple country cases indicates that the EU has not been pressured by having many countries join the United States to request market opening. This provides further support that while negotiations with an issue linkage often involve many countries, it is not the number of countries alone that explains those liberalization outcomes.

As expected, budget constraints are an important factor for EU agricultural policy. The highly significant negative coefficient for the budget growth variable supports the logic of the budget constraints hypothesis 5; the EU is more likely to liberalize during periods of budget contraction than when there is budget growth. Budget-cutting concerns may help back U.S. demands for policy changes that also reduce spending for agricultural protection.[55] Yet the marginal effect of budget growth

[55] My aggregation of EU budget expenditures does not address how budget constraints affect national government policies. It is possible that when Germany or Britain are

on a negotiation is smaller than for either negotiation structure or threats. Table 3.7 shows that a 20 percent change in budget spending shifts the expectation of major liberalization by only 19 percentage points. There may be cuts in agricultural spending outside of negotiations that are not being captured in this model of negotiated policy liberalization. It is quite possible that budget constraints push for broad-based reforms on an internal level rather than discrete trade policies addressed in negotiations. The evidence presented here supports the conclusion that budget constraints are important but do not fully account for the variation in negotiation outcomes.

In summary, a credible issue linkage broadening the negotiation stakes can bring Europe to accept substantial agricultural liberalization. EU institutions isolate agricultural decision making, and this autonomy of agriculture interests over agricultural policy makes reform unlikely. Liberalization is most difficult when France holds the presidency of the Council and can reinforce the policy autonomy of agricultural interests within the Council of Ministers. An issue linkage broadens the policy arena because the additional economic stakes from an issue linkage lead industry groups and trade officials to take interest in agricultural talks. This makes issue linkage an especially effective solution to the obstacle facing agricultural reform in the EU. On the other hand, legal framing of the negotiation structure at best brings an early settlement prior to the actual onset of panel proceedings. Unlike Japan, a legal ruling against a policy has no effect on the EU. The features of the institutional context of the negotiation are important for understanding when liberalization is more likely. However, they also interact with the nature of the issue and the EU domestic political context.

Conclusion

This chapter has presented evidence against the explanation that U.S. coercion opened Japanese agricultural markets while financial constraints forced Europe to reform the Common Agricultural Policy. Observers have been too quick to dismiss the GATT as ineffectual against agricultural trade protection. Disaggregating the means by which institutions facilitate liberalization provides a more nuanced understanding of how the negotiation context affects state behavior.

Analysis of over 260 cases of negotiated agricultural trade barriers

launching austerity programs at home, they also try to restrain EU spending policies that are supported by their large membership contributions.

reveals that variables in the negotiation structure significantly improve the likelihood of liberalization across negotiation cases when controlling for the use of threats, domestic political constraints, and budget trends. While threats promote liberalization by Japan and the EU, they are not necessarily the best tool for opening sensitive agricultural markets. A strong cross-sector issue linkage causes a greater increase in the likelihood of liberalization than a strong threat.

Liberalization was less likely when Japan and the EU faced strong domestic political constraints. A narrow political majority for the LDP reduced the probability that Japan would accept liberalization. The proxy variable for tied hands in EU politics also influenced predictions of negotiation outcomes — France holding the presidency of the Council of Ministers during the negotiation substantially reduced the probability of EU liberalization. This evidence that domestic constraints helped Japan and the EU to negotiate agreements closer to their preference for less agricultural liberalization confirms the bargaining logic of two-level games discussed by Schelling and Putnam.

In addition, the variation in negotiation outcomes challenges simple explanations that budget constraints explain the pattern of liberalization. Reduction of overall spending levels appears to create pressure for reducing agricultural spending and predicts liberalization by the EU. However, comparison of thirty years of negotiations reveals that the rise and decline of budgetary conditions exerts less influence on negotiations than factors directly related to strategies, such as linkage, legal framing, or threats. In addition, the evidence of the EU's reluctance to accept liberalization in negotiations about its expensive export subsidy policies goes against the logic of budget cutting. In Japan, the frequent use of generous compensation packages to soften the burden of agricultural liberalization casts doubt on the view that the Japanese government has liberalized policies in order to reduce costs.

The evidence shows that legal framing is an effective strategy to promote liberalization. However, the leverage of legal framing interacts with domestic interests and institutions as seen by the different reaction of Japan and the EU to the GATT adjudication process. A GATT violation ruling was one of the strongest factors to persuade Japan to liberalize its agricultural markets. In Europe, these same violation rulings had no impact on policy outcomes. Only at lower-level consultations during the GATT dispute settlement process did legal framing exert positive pressure on EU liberalization.

The central finding presented in this chapter is the strong support for the cross-sector linkage hypothesis. Statistical analysis showed that a strong cross-sector issue linkage improved the likelihood of major liberalization in Japan by 82 percentage points and in the EU by 39 percentage points, on average. In comparison, a threat increased the likelihood of major liberalization in Japan by only 46 percentage points and in the EU by only 29 percentage points. In negotiations with both Japan and the EU, an agenda that links together agricultural and industrial issues made major liberalization the likely outcome, whereas under the same conditions but in the absence of a linkage, the negotiation was likely to result in none or minor liberalization. This significant finding for the ordered scale measuring the institutionalization of the linkage confirms that it is important not only for the negotiation structure to include multiple sectors on the agenda, but also for institutions to reinforce this linkage.

On the other hand, having more countries join the United States to issue liberalization demands does not increase the likelihood of liberalization. The analysis showed that multiple countries making a demand reduced the probability that Japan would agree to major liberalization, and had no effect on the EU. Often multilateralism is used as a term to refer both to cooperation among multiple countries and to the institutions that accompany such negotiations. The findings here suggest that different aspects of negotiation structure should not be conflated. An institutional context creating a strong linkage is essential for an effective multilateral negotiation.

Part II

U.S.-JAPAN TRADE NEGOTIATIONS

4

Farm Politics in Japan

PURSUIT OF economic efficiency would dictate against a land-scarce and highly industrialized country like Japan devoting resources to sustain its agricultural sector. However, economic efficiency alone rarely determines policy. There are many other social goals, such as support of rural society and a valued social tradition, that justify the choice of Japanese policymakers to protect the agricultural sector. Politics also intrudes on decision making. Mancur Olson's (1965) argument about collective action explains that those societal interests with the strongest incentives and capacity to organize will form effective pressure groups, and Gary Becker (1983) modeled how competition among pressure groups results in policies that favor the politically powerful. This perspective accounts for protection as the result of the willingness of government actors to supply protection in response to farmer demands. Building on this framework, this chapter examines the actors and interests that explain the preference of the Japanese government for agricultural protection.

Industrial growth turned Japan into a leading economic power that could afford to guarantee high living standards for its people, and farmers continued to hold a special place in Japanese society and politics even while their economic role declined. Low productivity and inability to compete in free markets motivate Japanese farmers to seek protection. Their high level of organization in agricultural cooperatives and electoral rules favoring rural areas help farmers gain political allies to support their demands. Farmers form the core constituency of the dominant Liberal Democratic Party and are also courted by *all* opposition parties. This political influence for agricultural interests enhances the bureaucratic power of the Ministry of Agriculture, Forestry, and Fisheries (MAFF) vis-à-vis other ministries. In addition to the political strength of farmers and their allies, weak opposition from other groups, such as consumers, the food industry, and big business interests, has permitted the buildup of high levels of agricultural protection in Japan. In a land of dense population where crowded cities are the reality for most, people cling to their heritage as a farming nation, and the public has readily accepted arguments that farming preserves rural culture and environment. Despite recommendations by economists of the potential welfare gains from liberalization, the political economy of agricultural policy in Japan creates a strong expectation for protection of this sector (Honma 1994; Hayami 1988).

The base expectation for high protection of farmers in Japan makes it surprising to observe liberalization resulting from international trade negotiations. The previous chapter showed through statistical analysis that Japan has liberalized policies during some negotiations, and that it was more likely to liberalize a policy that was subject to a GATT violation ruling or a strong cross-sector issue linkage. However, the statistical analysis only established the general pattern without explaining how the strong domestic opposition to liberalization was overcome during the negotiation. Closer examination of the domestic political context is necessary to understand the strength of domestic opposition to liberalization and highlight how the international negotiation influences this balance. This chapter has three tasks: first, to present an overview of protection policies; second, to examine the interests of key actors and show why liberalization is an unexpected outcome from the perspective of domestic politics; and third, to discuss the kind of evidence from case studies that would support different hypotheses for liberalization. Subsequent chapters will build on this foundation and use evidence from the policy process to explain the outcomes of key negotiations.

Agricultural Protection

Both limited land and policy-induced constraints shape the structure of agricultural production in Japan. First, there is the inescapable fact of a large population relative to a small amount of arable land. The United States has about eighty times the amount of agricultural land of Japan, and even France and Germany have, respectively, five and three times more land than Japan.[1] When considering the amount of land used for farming on a per capita basis, the United States has 1.49 hectares for every person in comparison with only 0.04 hectares per person in Japan. Although Japan has less arable land available, it has a greater share of the population still engaged in agricultural production, with 4.5 percent of the Japanese population engaged in farming compared with only 2.3 percent in the United States.[2] Land reform laws bestowed on Japan by

---

[1] See table 1.1.

[2] For the sake of cross-national comparison, these figures, which are reported in table

the U.S. Occupation brought greater social equality through distributing land to small owner farmers, but thereby laid the basis for inefficient land usage. Farmers have held onto their land even as nonagricultural income sources have come to exceed farm income for the majority of Japanese farm households.[3] Government policies to encourage higher productivity have made little progress to shift land to large-scale farms with greater commercial viability. Both social traditions and inheritance laws encourage farmers to retain their farmland even when they retire or take on additional employment, and consequently the scale of agriculture has increased much more slowly in Japan than in either Europe or the United States (Moore 1990, 205). The resulting pattern of small-scale and part-time farming holds down agricultural productivity gains. Different land endowments render it impossible for the Japanese agricultural sector to compete with the U.S. agricultural sector, and social and policy constraints have delayed structural adjustment of the sector.

In the 1960s, as economic growth gained momentum and Prime Minister Hayato Ikeda pursued the goal to double the income of all Japanese in a decade, the government also launched new policies to broaden the safety net for the declining agricultural sector. The 1961 Agricultural Basic Law established the principles that guided Japanese agricultural policies until Diet passage of the 1999 Food, Agriculture, and Rural Areas Basic Law. The main objective of the 1961 law stated that "agricultural productivity should increase in such a way as to reduce the disparity in productivity between agriculture and other industries."[4]

1.1, rely on the UN Food and Agricultural Organization figures, with a common definition of agricultural population as those actively engaged in farming, forestry, or fishery and their dependents. Often the Japanese government will cite a larger agricultural population figure that includes part-time farmers. For example, the *73rd Statitistical Yearbook of the Ministry of Agriculture, Forestry and Fisheries Japan 1996–1997*, indicates that the farm population, including those who engaged in farming for less than 29 working days in a year, amounted to 7,013,430 persons in 1997. The number of farmers is a much smaller 3,533,000 when including those who worked over 60 days and falls to 2,518,880 when including those who worked over 100 days. The FAO figures report the economically active population in agriculture for 1997 as 3,246,000 (note the numbers are not directly comparable because the FAO figure aggregates for farming, fisheries, and forestries while the MAFF figure includes only those engaged in farming).

[3] In 1997, out of the total 2,567,990 farm households listed by the Japanese Ministry of Agriculture, 1,722,060 (or 67 percent) earned their main income from jobs other than farming (MAFF 1997, 17).

[4] *Nōgyō kihon hō* of 1961, cited in Moore (1990, 291). Several amendments and additional laws modified the means for achieving this goal, but the Agricultural Basic Law continued to provide the overall framework.

TABLE 4.1
Japan: OECD Estimates of Support to Agriculture

Year	1986–88	1997–99
Producer support estimate (all crops)	67%	61%
PSE (rice)	85	83
PSE (milk)	84	78
PSE (beef)	44	33
Consumer support estimate	58	50
Total support as percent of GDP	2.6	1.7

Source: OECD (2000a, 217–218).
Note: The percentage producer support estimate measures the monetary value of transfers to agricultural producers relative to the total value of farm production. The percentage consumer support estimate measures the tax on consumption associated with agricultural policies relative to total consumption of food commodities (negative values are
listed in positive terms). The percentage total support estimate measures the share of all
agricultural support in the GDP.

Toward this purpose, the government provided income support for
farmers through administered prices, supply management, and trade
barriers such as quotas and tariffs. Spending for infrastructure, insurance, and research were other aspects of government support.

These policies have produced high levels of protection. Japan's nominal rate of protection (measured as the percentage by which domestic
prices exceed border prices when averaged across common agricultural
commodities) rose from 44 percent above international prices in the late
1950s to 151 percent in the early 1980s (Hayami and Anderson 1986,
22). By 1988 the price differential had reached as high as 241 percent,
which meant that Japanese consumers spent almost two and a half
times more for their food than they would have spent making their
purchases at international prices.[5] Table 4.1 shows that over 60 percent
of the value of farm production has resulted directly from government
policies, and over 50 percent of total consumer expenditure on food
consisted of a consumer tax. In total, these wealth transfers to agriculture represented 2.6 percent of GDP in 1986–1988. While protection
has declined in the past decade, government policies remain central to
agricultural production in Japan.

Japan's spending for agricultural protection created a budget burden

[5] The OECD reports the consumer nominal assistance coefficient for Japan over the
period 1986–88 as 2.41, which means domestic prices exceeded international prices by
241 percent (OECD 2000a, 219).

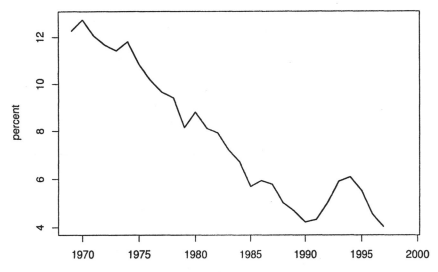

Figure 4.1: Trend in Agricultural Budget Expenditures by Japan. The figure shows expenditures of the Ministry of Agriculture, Forestry, and Fisheries as percent of total government expenditures based on fiscal year general accounts budget, 1969–1997. *Source*: MAFF, The *Statistical Yearbook of the Ministry of Agriculture, Forestry, and Fisheries.*

that forced some policy reforms, but spending remains high. Budget expenditures for agricultural support policies totaled nearly 14.9 billion U.S. dollars in 1998 (OECD 2000a, 188). Nevertheless, this represents a much smaller share of government spending than past levels. The decline was in large part due to a transfer of the cost of protection from government budgets to consumers. In a system dating back to the Food Control Act of 1942, the government had purchased rice at a high price from producers and sold it at a lower price to consumers while the budget absorbed the difference (Moore 1990, 288). Following a policy shift in 1976 to pass the burden of high producer prices directly on to consumers, the ratio between the government's purchase price and the consumer's price shrank dramatically, from 35.8 percent in July 1976 to 7.2 percent in 1977 (Terasawa 1984, 23). In addition, while unable to muster the political backing to reduce rice prices, over the years the government has made efforts to reduce the rate of the annual increase. As a result of such changes, agriculture's share of the total budget has steadily fallen from a high of 13 percent in 1970 to a low of 4 percent in recent years (see figure 4.1).

Actors and Interests

The negotiators for Japan during agricultural trade negotiations argu-ably have the toughest job imaginable, since they are caught between the demands of Japan's best ally abroad and the protests of its most favored constituency at home. However, from a bargaining perspective, domestic opposition may increase a negotiator's leverage if it convinces the United States that making a concession would result in unacceptable costs to the Japanese government.[6] Japanese negotiators may be able to extract from their trade partners better deals for less agricultural liberal-ization because they can credibly argue that agricultural liberalization is politically impossible.

This section provides background on the politics of agricultural pro-tection. Showing the basis of farmer power in Japan will demonstrate why any liberalization is unlikely and even modest changes of agri-cultural trade policies represent substantial concessions for international cooperation by Japan.

Politicians and the Rural Vote

Electoral bias and the power of organization form the root of farmers' influence. In spite of the steady decline in the number of farmers in Japan, they have remained among the most politically influential voting groups. Aurelia George Mulgan (1997a) suggests that the overweighting of rural districts in the allocation of Diet representation is a large part of farmers' voting power.[7] Demographic and employment changes re-duced the size of the agricultural electorate from 25.4 percent of na-tional electorate in 1969 to 10.7 percent in 1993 (ibid., 878). However, through a combination of inertia and deliberate political strategy, elec-toral districts did not adjust to compensate for the rapid urbanization of the postwar period. In consequence, prior to reforms in 1994, a single rural voter held almost three times the weight of a single urban voter in his or her representation in the House of Representatives and almost

---

[6] Schelling (1960, 37) examines this bargaining strategy from the perspective of making a credible commitment to take a particular action (in this case, refusal to concede in a trade negotiation) so as to give the other party (the U.S. negotiators) the "last clear chance" to avoid cooperation failure. Studies of two-level games have further developed how domestic politics can influence the capacity of a state to use such bargaining strate-gies (Evans, Jacobson, and Putnam 1993).

[7] See also Mulgan (2000) for more analysis of the sources of the farm lobby's political influence.

seven times the weight in the House of Councilors; reform in 1994 reduced the vote differential in the Lower House to a 2:1 gap.[8]

This rural bias works to the advantage of the long-ruling LDP. Farmers are now well established as a core LDP constituency, but conservative government assiduously courted farmer's support during the early postwar years, when strong leftist sentiment existed in both rural and urban districts. During the 1949 to 1953 period of crisis for conservative government, spending to support farmers' interests and policies to encourage the centralization of agricultural cooperatives helped the LDP to establish a strong rural base (Calder 1988, 257–261). Local chapters of the cooperatives followed central directives and provided an extensive network that could exchange promises to support the LDP in return for continued government largesse. The conservative politics and personalized campaign strategies of the LDP were more amenable to rural than urban constituencies, and LDP support in these districts grew even when its support in urban districts declined.

The bias in the electoral system is not the only factor enhancing farmer's voting weight. The share of "pro-agriculture" voters is larger than the number of farmers because there is wider identification with agricultural interests by extended family and nonfarmer residents in rural districts. Moreover, strong community solidarity and social hierarchies in rural districts have produced higher voter turnout than in cities and more predictable voting patterns because local leaders can direct the vote to favor particular candidates (Curtis 1999, 221).

Rural electoral success has been the key to the LDP maintaining its nearly unbroken status as ruling party. In the LDP electoral setback in the 1976 general election, even though it won only one-quarter of the vote in urban districts, the LDP held onto power by virtue of its hold on rural seats. A study by the *Asahi shimbun* following the 1976 election showed that under a hypothetical redistricting to narrow the rural-urban seat differential to 2:1, the LDP would have failed to gain a majority in the election (Hemmi 1982). The decline in the number of farmers has led to parallel declines in LDP vote shares (ibid., 221–222). The urban-rural divide was apparent in the 2000 Lower House election, when the LDP lost nearly all of the seats in major urban constituencies but maintained its status as ruling party by winning seats in rural dis-

[8] Mulgan (1997a, 882–883) calculates that the House of Councilors prefectural constituencies held a ratio in 1993 of 6.7:1, and the House of Representatives constituencies held a ratio of 2.84:1. Following the 1994 reforms, the most extreme gap stood at 2.137:1. The ratio represents the differential between the most densely populated constituency and the least densely populated constituency.

tricts and forming a coalition with an urban party. Regardless of the decline of rural population and reform of electoral districts, the LDP can still be called "the party of the farmers" (Mulgan 2001, 15).

Few issues unite Japanese politicians as strongly as the desire to help farmers. While farmers have voted in large numbers for the LDP, opposition parties also try to win their favor by supporting higher producer prices and opposing liberalization (Rothacher 1989, 116).[9] There are few signs of campaigning based on urban-rural cleavages in which politicians appeal to urban interests by criticizing generous government policies for farm areas. Indeed, the Communist Party, which has a largely urban constituency, often makes the most radical statements for increasing agricultural protection and supported the rice import ban both because of ideological support for what are seen as disadvantaged farmers and because the party is affiliated with the Food Agency's unions (Kuo and Yanagisawa 1992, 24).[10]

Resolutions favoring agricultural protection passed in the Diet with unanimous support in 1980, 1984, and again in 1988. The first resolution expressed concern about overdependence on foreign imports of food supply, and the latter two resolutions reaffirmed the need to increase self-sufficiency and specifically emphasized opposition to importing rice.[11] Through these highly visible acts, politicians attempt at once to show farmers that they are supporting them and to strengthen the hand of negotiators against foreign pressure. Even politicians without strong agricultural connections voted in favor of the resolutions, thereby committing themselves to oppose liberalization.

There have been some differences among parties in their degree of hostility to liberalization and their willingness to consider partial liberalization as a necessary compromise. One exception to political unanimity in support of agricultural policies has been Kōmeitō, which has an almost entirely urban constituency drawn from members of a Buddhist religious group. This party has expressed concerns about the costs

[9] In interviews with Diet members representing the Japan Socialist Party, Shinshintō, and Communist Party in July 1996, all expressed support for farm protection policies.

[10] See, for example, its strong statement against the Uruguay Round Agriculture Agreement. Syūgiin nōrinsuisan iinkai chōsashitsu (Lower House Agriculture Committee Research Section, Gatto uruguai raundo nōgyō kōshō kankei shiryo (Documents regarding the GATT Uruguay Round agriculture negotiation) (January 1994): 53–63.

[11] *Shokuryo jikyūryoku kyōka ni kan suru ketsugi* (Resolution on the strengthening of food supply capacity). 8 April 1980 (91st Diet Session, Lower House Resolution); *Kome no jukyū antei ni kan suru ketsugi* (Resolution on the stable supply of rice). 20 July 1984 (101st Diet Session, Lower House Resolution); *Kome no jiyūka hantai ni kan suru ketsugi* (Resolution against the liberalization of rice). 20 September 1988 (113th Diet Session, Lower House Resolution).

of agricultural protection in terms of high prices, and it supported the need for some agricultural policy reforms, including partial liberalization. However, the party has not taken a strong position against protection: Kōmeitō politicians concur that the government must help small-scale farmers and that Japan should not be overly dependent on imports.[12] Similarly, the Jiyūtō (Liberal Party), led by Ichirō Ozawa, has been more open to view agricultural liberalization as part of broader deregulation of the Japanese economy. However, the party suggests proposals to strengthen Japanese agriculture through structural reforms.[13] While there are some voices for reform, the goal to maintain self-sufficiency levels in agriculture receives unanimous support.

Farmer Cooperatives as a Powerful Vote Machine

Strong organization by farmers in agricultural cooperatives magnifies their political influence. The cooperatives, called Nōkyō (Nōgyō Kyōdō Kumiai), have a central organization, Zenchū (Zenkoku Nōgyō Kyōdō Kumiai Chūōkai), and a political organization, Zenkoku Nōseikyō (National Council of Farmers' Agricultural Policy Campaign Organization). Holding near universal farm membership across all regions of Japan, the cooperatives dominate rural life as a central channel for the distribution and retail of agricultural products and inputs such as fertilizer, while also serving as the primary farmer financial institution that holds their savings and provides insurance policies (Goto and Imamura 1993, 19). The path to political activism for young men in rural society often begins with the local cooperative youth league and proceeds through municipal and prefectural office.

For local and national elections, the cooperative forms an essential electoral base. As one politician commented in an interview, it is not only that farmers will offer their own vote, but they also have the time and the influence to canvass the neighborhood during campaigns.[14] In Japan, where campaign activity is based on local networks through a personal vote machine (called Kōenkai), the support of members like Nōkyō elites is invaluable. An Upper House politician commented, "Nōkyō is the most active group in electoral districts. It works by mak-

---

[12] Kōmeitō member of the House of Representatives. Interview by author. Tokyo, 2 February 1999.

[13] Liberal Party Member of the House of Councilors. Interview by author. Tokyo, March 1999.

[14] Kōsuke Hori, LDP member of House of Representatives. Interview by author. Tokyo, 11 January 2000.

ing demands and returning the favor by doing election activities. Politicians cannot ignore Nōkyō."[15] Surveys of politicians indicate that they feel support from agricultural cooperatives plays a positive role in their election campaigns, and endorsement by the local agricultural cooperative is highly sought after (Mulgan 1997a, 884).

A key source of farm power is the fact that farmers can credibly threaten to shift their vote if politicians do not deliver on promises. The agricultural cooperatives make it possible to deliver—or not deliver— farm votes. Prior to elections the Zenkoku Nōseikyō polls politicians on their views, thereby extracting promises to oppose liberalization and support price increases for agriculture.[16] Since all political parties in Japan support agricultural protection, it is credible for farmers to threaten a change of allegiance.

On some occasions, farmers have punished politicians when they are seen as having served farmers poorly. One example arose regarding a domestic policy, the annual setting of the government purchase price for rice, which was a decision that long represented the biggest political issue for agriculture in Japan. In 1971, as the government faced a large surplus supply of rice and growing budget costs, then Prime Minister Eisaku Satō called for a freeze in the government-set price for rice, which led local Nōkyō groups to lobby in favor of opposition candidates. Ultimately, the LDP granted a small increase in the rice price and got away with a slap by farmers—some LDP prefectural candidates lost against opposition candidates who received farmer support, and several rural Diet seats that should have been sure wins were lost (Hemmi 1982, 237). One Nōkyō leader said in a newspaper interview at the time, "Many of us in Nōkyō feel that we should enter our own rival candidates in the Upper House election, to teach the LDP a lesson" (ibid., 236). Another example, discussed in the next chapter, centers on the liberalization of beef and citrus products in negotiations with the United States in 1988. During the watershed election of 1989, the LDP lost its majority in the Upper House for the first time since gaining power in 1955. Along with a corruption scandal and unpopular tax increase, agricultural trade liberalization was often cited as a cause for the LDP defeat because some Nōkyō members had campaigned for opposition candidates, and the LDP lost six out of seven seats in beef- and orange-producing districts (George 1990, 117). Such painful lessons reinforce the power of farmer threats.

[15] Liberal Party member of the House of Councilors. Interview by author. Tokyo, March 1999.

[16] This phenomenon was widely cited in interviews by the author with Nōkyō officials and politicians and has also been referred to in other studies, such as Mulgan (1997a) and Hemmi (1982).

Politicians clearly believe that agricultural liberalization carries substantial political risks. When asked in early 1989 to describe the electoral impact for the LDP in the case that the LDP "takes a different position from that of the [Nōkyō] federations" on the question of agricultural liberalization, 139 Lower House politicians gave the following responses: 47 percent said they expected that LDP electoral support would greatly decrease, 24 percent expected a partial decrease, and 21 percent expected only a slight decrease (Romana 1991, 18). It is said that while Nōkyō votes alone are not enough to win an election, losing Nōkyō support could easily result in election defeat.

The Ministry of Agriculture

The Ministry of Agriculture, Forestry, and Fisheries holds a dual mandate to provide for the welfare of those employed in farming, fishing, and forestry and to provide for the secure supply of food to the general population.[17] The role of MAFF extends deep into rural society, as its policies guide not only farm prices and land use but also the structural improvement projects for rural areas (Goto and Imamura 1993).

MAFF advocates some reforms to improve the efficiency of Japanese agriculture, but it has opposed trade liberalization. Within MAFF, the Food Agency has a large interest in trade policy given its role until 1996 as the purchaser, importer, and distributor of staple grains (rice and wheat), and its close cooperation with Nōkyō in the management of these policies.[18] To the extent that liberalization of trade and internal deregulation threatened the role of the Food Agency and its eleven thousand employees, MAFF long held a strong vested interest in maintaining the status quo food management and trade policies (Domon 1994, 133). MAFF officials comment only half-jokingly that if Japan continues liberalizing its agricultural trade barriers, Japanese farming will disappear along with the ministry itself.

The formal policy process gives jurisdiction for agricultural affairs to MAFF, trade policy to the Ministry of International Trade and Industry (MITI), and coordination of foreign economic affairs and diplomacy to

[17] Chapter 1, article 3, of the 1949 Law Establishing the Ministry of Agriculture, Forestry and Fisheries.

[18] This role was based on the 1942 Food Control Law, which was replaced in 1995 by the new Staple Food Law. The change took place in the context of domestic deregulation and in order to adjust to liberalization following the Uruguay Round negotiation. Under the new law, farmers can directly sell their product to consumers and there is competition along the entire distribution chain. However, the Food Agency continues its operations for stabilization of rice and wheat markets by means of its authority over price, storage, and trade policies.

the Ministry of Foreign Affairs (MOFA). In practice, MAFF takes the lead role for agricultural trade negotiations. Only MAFF possesses the knowledge and the political connections necessary to navigate this sensitive area, and it represents a politically powerful opponent within bureaucratic turf rivalries. While MOFA and MITI generally favor agricultural liberalization, they do not try to interfere with agricultural policy unless the negotiation raises serious implications for foreign and trade affairs.[19]

MAFF gains influence from its relationship with the LDP. The relations between the LDP and MAFF bureaucrats, on the one hand, and between both MAFF and the LDP with Nōkyō, on the other, create a corporatist structure—an "iron triangle" based on the "mutual exchange of favors" (Mulgan 2001, 4). The power to distribute generous subsidy allocations endows the post of MAFF minister with "great clout in LDP faction politics" (Rothacher 1989, 120). Moreover, many former MAFF bureaucrats have become politicians and are active in agricultural policy committees. While these political connections strengthen MAFF vis-à-vis other ministries, they also constrain it. Any decision of significance draws attention from politicians and requires their approval. During negotiations, officials constantly visit key LDP and opposition politicians. They cannot go forward without a "go-ahead signal" from politicians, and they know that angering politicians could lead to interference on other ministry business in the future or even damage their professional careers (Fukui 1978, 111, 140). Hence MAFF officials enter negotiations under close political supervision with little negotiating flexibility.

The position of MAFF in Japan finds parallels with that of European agriculture ministries. As will be discussed in chapter 7, French and German agriculture ministries as well as the EU-level Directorate General for Agriculture similarly back entrenched protection policies and enjoy corporatist ties for cooperation between the government and agricultural interest groups (Keeler 1996; Sato and Schmitt 1993). The form of the policy process differs, but the autonomy of agricultural interests and their stake in the status quo are similar in both settings.

Consumer Groups and Public Opinion

Little countervailing pressure opposes farmer demands. Although consumers stand as major beneficiaries from liberalization, they have not

---

[19] MITI official. Interview by author. Tokyo, 3 June 1999.

lobbied for liberalization. The reason lies with consumer group preferences as well as the fact that consumer organizations lack the political weight of farm organizations. According to a 1997 Japanese government survey comparing prices in Tokyo and New York, Japanese consumers pay nearly 20 percent more on average for food products than Americans, and they pay double the price for rice, which is still an improvement from 1988 when Tokyo residents paid six times more for rice than New Yorkers.[20] While these figures lead one to expect that consumers would oppose the cost of agricultural protection, Steven Vogel (1999) shows across a range of areas, including agricultural policies, that consumers in Japan do not always follow the expectation to prioritize their preferences by price. Instead, consumer groups advocate tough regulatory standards that may hinder trade and oppose agricultural liberalization.

Food safety and quality rather than price dominates the concerns of Japanese consumers. One of the largest consumer organizations, Shufuren (Housewives Association), often coordinates activities with the agricultural cooperatives and is an outspoken opponent of further agricultural liberalization.[21] The Japanese Consumers' Cooperative Union also publicly argues that its opposition to import liberalization serves the public interest (Rothacher 1989, 119).

There is little indication that consumers care about gaining access to less expensive and more diverse food choices through greater liberalization. In a 2000 poll by the Prime Minister's Office, 82 percent of respondents indicated they would buy domestic over imported food, largely due to their concern over safety.[22] A 1994 Jiji Press survey on Japan's high import dependency for its food supply showed that 79 percent favored current or higher levels of self-sufficiency while only 13.8 percent favored an increase of cheaper imports regardless of whether this increased Japan's import dependency.[23] Hence it is ques-

---

[20] Volatile exchange rates complicate such international price comparison. According to a 1997 MAFF price survey (1999, 41), in a comparison for the year 1997 at the exchange rate of 126 yen/dollar, the price ratio for New York and Tokyo would be 46:100 for rice and 87:100 for a representative sample of different food products. Using different methods to measure the consumer burden from agricultural support policies, the OECD (200a, 217) estimates that for the period 1997–1999, Japanese consumers spent double the amount they would have spent making their same purchases at world market prices (a consumer nominal assistance coefficient of 2.02). The figure on rice prices in the 1980s is from a 1988 study by Nikkeiren and Rengo cited in the *Los Angeles Times*, 6 July 1988.

[21] Shufuren representative. Interview by the author. Tokyo, 9 August 1996.

[22] *Japan Times*, 8 October 2000.

[23] This figure aggregates two categories of responses: 36.6 percent favored increasing self-sufficiency and 42.4 percent favored current levels. See *Yoron chōsa nenkan* (Opinion survey yearbook) (Tokyo: Ministry of Finance Publishing Office, 1994), 495, question 16.

tionable whether consumers even form a latent support group for foreign demands to liberalize agricultural markets.

U.S. negotiators have on many occasions tried to justify demands for Japanese agricultural liberalization by saying this would be in the interests of Japan's consumers. However, the Japanese government has just as readily countered that Japanese consumers do not want liberalization. Opinion polls show mixed support for liberalization, depending on the wording and timing of the poll. A 1994 poll by the Prime Minister's Office showed that 77.4 percent favored domestic production of agricultural goods even if the cost was higher than imported food.[24] Nevertheless, a 1994 NHK survey demonstrated that partial liberalization gained support by 60 percent of respondents.[25] In an earlier poll in 1981, the *Yomiuri shimbun* reported that 61 percent of respondents favored liberalization as long as it did not influence domestic agriculture, while 15.5 percent favored increasing imports for the sake of cheaper prices and richer diet, and 11 percent said they opposed any liberalization because it would harm domestic agriculture.[26] In short, consumer opinion was prone to manipulation to support either side of the debate.

Big Business

While the LDP relies on farmers for votes, it cannot ignore the views of its corporate supporters. Big business and the food industry provide another potential source of countervailing pressure against farmers. Keidanren, the Japan Federation of Economic Organizations,[27] acts as the principal voice for business; the chairman is called the "prime minister of *zaikai* "business world" and holds considerable authority to speak on issues of importance to the Keidanren membership as well as

[24] This figure combines two categories: 44.7 percent favored domestic production at least for rice and basic foodstuffs, and 32.7 percent favored domestic production for foodstuffs in general. *Yoron Chōsa Nenkan* (1995, 97).

[25] The poll asked respondents to choose whether (1) Japan should absolutely not open the market, (2) partial liberalization cannot be avoided, but Japan should put efforts into supporting farmers, or (3) for the advancement of free trade, Japan should actively pursue market opening. Respectively, 14.1 percent, 60.1 percent, and 21.3 percent of respondents chose each of the three choices (4.5 percent did not answer). *Yoron Chōsa Nenkan* (1995, 535).

[26] *Yomiuri shimbun*, 6 July 1981.

[27] Beginning in April 2002, Keidanren merged with Nikkeiren to form a single organization named Nippon Keidanren (Japan Business Federation). This book uses the former names of the two organizations.

broader questions regarding the direction of the economy (Yoshimatsu 1998, 329). Its 2001 membership included 1,003 of Japan's leading corporations, as well as 117 industry-wide groups representing such sectors as manufacturing, trade, distribution, finance, and energy.[28] Keidanren has stood as an advocate of the liberalization and deregulation of the Japanese economy, although forming a consensus among diverse industry interests sometimes complicates its support for liberal economic policies. This organization has multifaceted roles as an executive council for all of the main trade associations, a think tank, a lobby organization for economic policy, and a formal consultant with government ministries participating in the policy process through various advisory councils. Its influence has also arisen through informal contacts with bureaucrats and politicians, and until 1994 it acted as the central coordinator for distributing political contributions from corporations to LDP campaign funds (ibid., 330). Alongside Keidanren, Nikkeiren (Federation of Employers' Associations), Keizai Doyūkai (Japan Association of Corporate Executives), and Nishō (Japan Chamber of Commerce and Industry) regularly issue recommendations about economic policies and occasionally enter policy debates on agricultural policy.

From the perspective of business interests, agricultural liberalization represents a way to both reduce trade tensions and the internal costs of protection. The high cost of food, inflated land prices, and government expenditures all represent internal costs resulting from agricultural protection policies. Meanwhile, the increase of Japan's trade surplus has caused trade friction with the United States and led to worries among export industries about the prospect of protection measures against Japanese goods. Although agricultural protection policies are not a major factor behind the trade imbalance between Japan and the United States, both American government officials and Japanese business leaders have seen agricultural liberalization as one way to reduce trade tensions over Japanese industrial exports to the United States. Beginning in the 1980s, when trade tensions escalated, Keidanren issued reports advocating agricultural reform, and officials warned that refusing U.S. demands would increase the movement toward protectionism in the United States (Keidanren 1999, 426). In 1987 Toshikuni Yahiro, vice-president of Keidanren and a member of the working group on reducing U.S.-Japan trade friction, said that "unless Japan does something like liberalizing its rice market, trade friction will be hard to solve."[29]

The food industry holds an even more direct interest in agricultural

[28] Figures for 2001 membership. See www.keidanren.or.jp.
[29] *Asahi shimbun*, 16 October 1987.

liberalization. Japanese food-processing companies lose international competitiveness when they pay high input costs to purchase domestic raw materials such as wheat for noodles, and barley or rice for beer and sake. At the same time, they must compete in the domestic market with imports of processed foods (Saito 1997, 28). The continued reduction of tariffs on imports of processed goods only worsened the situation for Japanese companies. Beginning in 1980 Keidanren initiated discussions about agricultural protection and the loss of international competitiveness of Japan's food industry (Keidanren 1999, 426). As an industry, it is not inconsequential — in 1994 the food industry employed 1.23 million people and accounted for 11 percent of Japan's industrial production.[30] Furthermore, the food industry has connections with the broader business community. Many firms belong to the dominant enterprise groups such as Mitsubushi and Mitsui, and the food industry is represented within Keidanren on the Food Industry Policy Subcommittee of its Agricultural Policy Committee.

However, there are also reasons for companies and business associations to be reluctant to voice their preference for agricultural liberalization. Some businesses hold a stake in continued agricultural protection. For trade companies, those lucky few to hold import licenses have a vested interest in protection for the sake of large quota rents. The licenses guarantee that they can sell cheap imported goods at high prices in the regulated domestic market and earn profit windfalls. For example, the marketing margin for sales of grapefruits was 145 yen/kg, until the abolition of the import quota in June 1971 reduced the margin to 34 yen/kg (Hayami 1988, 54). Many processing companies and distributors are also reluctant to increase imports because of their fear that Japanese consumers' concern about food safety of imported goods will limit demand. In a 1997 poll by the Ministry of Agriculture that asked officials from food-processing and distribution-related industries about policies toward agricultural imports, only 17.2 percent favored increasing imports, while 52 percent favored maintenance of current policies, and 16 percent favored reduction of imports. Of the latter, most cited food safety as a reason alongside freshness and quality for their reluctance to have more imports (MAFF 1999, 114). Thus in a typical negotiation over quota issues, trade firms and food processing companies would be lined up on both sides of the dispute.

For large firms in the food processing industry, an exit option to

[30] See Keidanren (1996), *Shyokuhin kōgyō hakusho* (Food industry white paper). Report no. 12. The employment and share of industry production remain at similar levels as those reported in 1982 (Rothacher 1989, 65).

move operations overseas relieves pressure from high domestic prices and hence reduces the need for them to lobby for changes in domestic agricultural policies. There has been a growing number of firms such as Ajinomoto or Kirin Beer that have established overseas production factories (Saito 1997). Discussions by food industry and trade company executives in colloquia sponsored by Keidanren raise the prospect of the hollowing out of Japan's food industry as companies shift to rely on overseas production (Keidanren 1999, 607).[31]

In addition, business leaders give higher priority to general economic issues related to tax or deregulation policies than to agricultural policy. Since advocacy of agricultural liberalization hinders progress on these other priorities, this discourages lobbying on agricultural policy. Politicians from rural districts do not hesitate to tell industry association officials that they will be unable to support their requests on economic policy if the industry association says too much about agricultural liberalization. For example, during one meeting about tax policy, a politician spent the entire time criticizing a business representative for the position his organization had taken on agricultural policy and refused to discuss the corporate tax issue at hand.[32] Given that lobbying on agricultural issues would take resources and attention away from lobbying for core goals of business associations, under most circumstances these groups would choose not to take any strong position on sensitive agricultural trade policies.

The long partnership between big business and the LDP forces business leaders to take into consideration the political sensitivities of politicians — all are aware that farmers are an important constituency for the LDP, and business leaders know that any request they make for agricultural liberalization represents a highly controversial demand. Not only do business groups prioritize other specific issues, but they also share a concern for the continued electoral victories of the LDP.

Finally, business groups are reluctant to publicly advocate agricultural liberalization because doing so risks backlash from farm supporters. The farm cooperatives closely watch who criticizes their position and can coordinate punishment against specific targets. Boycotts by farmers form a lingering threat. An example frequently cited by industry officials in interviews occurred in 1984 when Hokkaido farm cooperatives

---

[31] See discussions in following issues of the Keidanren monthly newsletter: "Shokuhin sangyō no hassō to nōsei no arikata o kangaeru" (Thinking about the food industry and the ways of agricultural politics), *Keidanren geppō* (1988) 6:2–29; "Nihon nōgyō, uchinaru kaikaku, sotonaru kaizen" (Japanese agriculture, reform from within and improvement from without), *Keidanren geppō* (1991) 6:10–27.

[32] Industry association official. Interview by author. Tokyo, 20 April 1999.

led a boycott against the products of Sony, Daiei supermarket, and the leading food-maker Ajinomoto because their executives were members of a Keidanren committee that had issued calls for reform of agricultural policies (Keidanren 1999, 428).[33] The boycott was called off after the executives apologized to farmers and quit the committee. Even if farmers are a small share of the national consumer market, their protests draw bad publicity, especially in rural regions. This incident made Keidanren officials reluctant to speak out on agricultural liberalization thereafter (Yasuhara 1985, 144). In another such incident, Mitsubishi Kōgyō Cement suffered from a Nōkyō boycott because an executive of the company belonged to a Nikkeiren committee that called for reforms of agricultural policy. Since then it has been difficult for Nikkeiren officials to find executives willing to serve on that committee.[34] Stories of these incidents reverberate through business circles.[35] In a survey of food industry officials views on rice liberalization, 51 percent refused comment, saying the topic was a taboo subject in the food industry.[36] Criticizing agricultural protection risks reducing leverage on national economic policies and losing customers in rural areas.

In short, from the perspective of domestic politics in Japan, the prospects for liberalization appear extremely unlikely. Farmers and their political allies vehemently oppose liberalization while consumers and business groups hold mixed preferences on liberalization and are reluctant to oppose the farmers even if they favor liberalization.

Drawing Implications

Against the odds, some negotiations have brought liberalization. Closely examining the process of negotiation cases will offer clues to which factors overcame the strong domestic resistance. Three categories of evidence are particularly useful for gaining insights into the negotiation process. First, the timing of the shifts in the position of domestic actors during the different stages of the negotiation process offers insights into which factors have influenced outcomes. Second, public state-

[33] Keidanren officials. Interviews by author. Tokyo, 9 August 1996, 20 April 1999. See also Yoshimatsu (1998).

[34] Nikkeiren official. Interview by author. Tokyo, 13 January 1999.

[35] For example, a business executive for an electronics firm who wrote an article on agricultural liberalization said he did not list his company affiliation given the concern that Nōkyō would stop buying their products (Company executive. Interview by author. 8 January 1999).

[36] *Mainichi Daily News*, 26 March 1991, cited in Mulgan (forthcoming).

ments and interview comments from negotiators, politicians, and others with a stake in the negotiations reveal how these actors perceive the choices they face, and how they explain their decisions to the public. Third, the form of the policy outcome may be more complementary with some policy goals than others. Even along the continuum from protection to liberalization, there are many different means of protecting internal markets — quotas, subsidies, and tariffs are some of these policy tools. One can infer policy priorities from the choice of one form of liberalization over another. Each hypothesis for a causal mechanism generates observable implications for the likely sequence of events, rationalization of the decision, and form of agreement.

When will industry groups cast aside their cautious approach to openly advocate agricultural liberalization? The issue linkage hypothesis leads one to expect that measures to strengthen the issue linkage will make export interests lobby more for agricultural liberalization. For example, when the package negotiation as a whole stalls over agricultural talks, then there should be public statements from exporter organizations urging compromise on agricultural issues for the sake of a favorable conclusion of the negotiation. Informal contacts are a major component of business lobbying, but the shift from relying on informal contacts and low-profile positions to public advocacy of controversial liberalization policies represents a significant increase in the intensity of business pressure. In addition to business groups, one would also expect politicians to point to the larger interests of the national economy as justification of a concession on agricultural trade. For an issue linkage to promote agricultural liberalization, the form of agreement must involve a balance of gains in other sectors to offset liberalization in agriculture.

The legalism hypothesis raises the expectation that the initiation of a complaint to GATT or a violation ruling by a panel will bring liberalization of the specified policy. Leaders are likely to justify the decision as a matter of compliance with international law. Finally, the form of the policy change provides evidence for the role of legalism. States that are trying to comply with international trade law will change policies that are not compatible with GATT rules, such as quantitative restrictions or export subsidies, and replace them with GATT-compatible tariffs. On the other hand, policy changes like the expansion in size of a quota may represent a concession granting greater market access to the United States but remain in violation of GATT principles. Such forms of policy liberalization suggest that other pressures outside of the legal framework motivate the policy change.

Alternative explanations for liberalization include threats, domestic politics, and budget constraints. If threats are behind liberalization, then one would expect compromise agreements immediately after the publication of a target list. According to the expectations of the U.S. influence hypothesis, exporter mobilization would focus on the problem of trade friction rather than on the gains from a successful negotiation deal. As for the policy outcome, evidence that the form of policy change grants discriminatory access favoring U.S. products would indicate that factors related to U.S. influence had a larger role than those related to international law, which emphasizes nondiscrimination.

Domestic politics filter reactions and decisions in a negotiation. The importance of the farm vote produces an expectation that there would be a toughening of the government position against liberalization when the ruling party is politically weak. The prospect of a close electoral campaign pushes the party to favor policies that cater to domestic constituents rather than foreign demands. The domestic politics hypothesis implies that during the negotiation, governments will try to use domestic opposition for negotiation advantage by emphasizing their political vulnerability.

The budget hypothesis states that financial constraints motivate liberalization. If true, one would expect that moves toward budget austerity would produce liberalization regardless of the timing and events of the negotiation. The rationalization of the policy reforms should emphasize the need to reduce growing budgets. Finally, the clear expectation is that the form of policy changes will reduce the total budgetary cost. For example, a shift from quantitative restriction or price support to a direct income subsidy that raises the budget cost discredits a budget-cutting explanation for the policy. On the other hand, reducing price support subsidies in favor of tariffs will produce both a reduction in expenditure and an increase of revenue from the tariffs.

In this chapter, analysis of the actors and interests inside Japan has explained why we observe high levels of protection. Understanding changes in these policies requires looking at external actors and interests. The next two chapters will examine how foreign pressure played a major role to overcome the domestic obstacles against liberalization. However, a satisfactory explanation must go beyond generalizations about foreign pressure. Why did the domestic actors change their strategies in response to one kind of foreign pressure and not another? The following chapters will analyze the policy process in key negotiation cases and show the influence of different negotiation structures on the domestic balance of interests.

5

Legal Framing and Quota Policies

THIS CHAPTER examines an interconnected series of negotiations on agricultural products under quota protection. Spanning two decades and fifteen commodities, the negotiations occupied a central place in U.S.-Japan agricultural talks. The United States tried every tool in the arsenal of trade policies against Japan. Over the course of the negotiations, talks broke down repeatedly, the media speculated on harm to the bilateral relationship, and some Japanese politicians lost office over the issue. Ultimately, achievements in the talks pushed forward the Tokyo Round, yielded a panel ruling that set a major precedent for GATT rules on quota restrictions, and created momentum toward liberalization measures in the Uruguay Round agricultural agreement. A participant in the negotiations for Japan called the 1988 negotiation a watershed for Japanese agricultural policy.[1] Heralded as a success for liberalization, the outcome also brought considerable pain for Japanese farmers.

The United States began demanding liberalization of beef and citrus in the early 1970s in bilateral talks and then made this a priority negotiating demand in the Tokyo Round. The expiration of the agreement reached in the Tokyo Round set the stage for the second major negotiation in 1984, which returned to bilateral negotiation structure. The decisive turning point came during the third negotiation in 1988, when bilateral talks entered formal GATT dispute adjudication. Table 5.1 shows the chronology of related negotiations on commodities under quota policies.

The agricultural quota negotiations offer an ideal case study for testing the role of negotiation structure because negotiations about the same policy and commodities took place across such a range of negotiation types. In particular, there is wide variation along the dimension of legalization. Negotiation structure was characterized by low legal framing in the first phase, the absence of legal framing in the second phase, and high legal framing in the final phase. On the other hand, issue linkage was less relevant for the negotiations on the quota policies. Only the first negotiation had a negotiation structure with an issue linkage, and it was a weakly institutionalized linkage. Therefore, the analysis

[1] Ministry of Agriculture official. Interview by author. Tokyo, 29 June 2001.

TABLE 5.1
Chronology of Three Sets of Quota Negotiations

	Product	Trade Arena	Legal Framing	Liberalization
Phase 1				
9/73–4/79	22 quota items	Tokyo Round	low	minor
9/77–12/78	beef/citrus	Tokyo Round	low	minor
Phase 2				
10/81–4/84	beef/citrus	bilateral	none	minor
7/83–4/84	13 quota items	GATT consulta- tions	none	minor
Phase 3				
7/86–2/88	12 quota items	GATT DSP panel	very high	major
4/87–6/88	beef/citrus	bilateral/GATT DSP	high	major

in this chapter will give less attention to the issue linkage hypothesis and focus more on the effect of the variation in legal framing on each phase of the negotiation.

This chapter will demonstrate how the negotiation structure increased the credibility of the U.S. demand for liberalization of the quotas during the third negotiation. In the first negotiation, U.S. efforts to link its request for an end to the quotas with the success of the Tokyo Round lacked credibility because agricultural talks had already been separated from the overall negotiation in the agenda and procedures. In the second negotiation, the United States threatened that refusal to end the quotas would lead to protectionist legislation, but it backed down when faced with the argument that it was politically impossible for the Japanese government to end the quotas. By the time of the third negotiation, the United States had to demonstrate that, unlike in the past, this time it would not accept a partial change. Legal framing of the negotiation through the dispute settlement procedures of GATT added leverage to U.S. demands so that both government leaders and agriculture groups in Japan realized that partial reform was not an option. In addition to shaping the credibility of U.S. demands, high legal framing changed the domestic political balance. The dispute settlement process reduced the access to negotiations by agricultural interest groups and increased the involvement of senior politicians who were more inclined to accept

TABLE 5.2
Fifteen Agricultural Import Quota Products

Beef — Citrus Negotiations
  Beef
  Oranges
  Orange juice

GATT 12 Negotiations
  Milk and cream, preserved (skim milk powder)
  Processed cheese
  Dried leguminous vegetables (peas and beans)
  Starch and inulin
  Groundnuts (e.g., peanuts)
  Beef preparations
  Nonsucrose sugars and syrups
  Fruit purees and pastes
  Canned pineapple and fruit pulps
  Noncitrus fruit and vegetable juices
  Tomato juice, ketchup, and sauce
  Miscellaneous food preparations

---

liberalization for the sake of Japan's trade interests and responsibilities to GATT.

Quotas for Beef, Oranges, Peanuts, etc.

The quota policy commodities represent a wide range of products subject to a similar form of trade regulation. A subset of fifteen of these quota products became the topic of the series of negotiations between the United States and Japan from 1973 to 1988. Table 5.2 lists the fifteen commodity categories. The statistical analysis presented in chapter 3 treated each product and each phase of the negotiation as a distinct case in order to take into consideration variation in trade values for the United States and important differences among the products in terms of their treatment in the negotiation and the liberalization outcomes. For example, beef held greater political and economic significance than nuts for both Japan and the United States; the beef quota was clearly against GATT law while the peanut quota was ruled to fit within the GATT guidelines for permissible quotas, and the final outcome brought substantial liberalization of beef and little change for nuts.

The variation in the nature of the commodities encompasses products with expanding domestic demand and others facing oversupply problems, products with broad regional distribution and others with high regional concentration, and primary goods as well as processed goods. Despite the difference among products, the outcomes for all of the quota items occurred roughly in parallel in terms of the timing and the degree of change. This is a first indication that the negotiation context had greater influence than the product-specific characteristics. In addition, the commentary of the media and other observers referred to the quota products as a single policy problem. Therefore, after a brief overview of the different products, the rest of the chapter will generally refer to the set of products and analyze each phase as one negotiation, while giving attention to the variation among products when relevant.

The two most prominent quota products were beef and citrus. The problem of beef and orange market access became a prolonged controversy in U.S.-Japan relations that assumed a significance far beyond its economic share of the bilateral trade relationship. In 1978 U.S. exports of beef and citrus products to Japan were valued at only 141 million dollars, compared with total U.S. agricultural exports to Japan of 4.5 billion dollars (U.S. FAS basis). Even after liberalization in 1991, beef and citrus trade continued to represent a small share of U.S.-Japan agricultural trade. For the U.S. government, however, beef and citrus industries were important to strategic political districts in the Midwest, California, and Florida, and the commodity associations engaged in active lobbying (Porges 1994, 243–244). Moreover, as the U.S. trade deficit with Japan more than doubled from 1981 to 1984, beef and oranges became the symbols of the kind of all-American products that Japan should buy.[2] Japanese beef cost three times the price of American beef and four times the price of Australian beef, while a pound of oranges cost two dollars more in Japan than in the United States.[3] The issue became a lightening rod for all frustrations over the U.S.-Japan trade imbalance. As an egregious trade barrier at the border, the agricultural quotas provided an easier target for U.S. negotiators than the complex structural impediments that many viewed as the trade barrier keeping U.S. industrial goods out of Japanese markets.

There was tremendous diversity in the economic and political characteristics of the products. The market for beef experienced a sharp rise in demand as Japanese dietary habits shifted toward higher meat con-

---

[2] The U.S.-Japan bilateral trade balance, adjusted to 1995 prices, was 11 billion dollars in 1981 and 25 billion dollars in 1984 (IMF, *Direction of Trade Statistics Yearbook*).
[3] *Washington Post*, 21 November 1982.

sumption.[4] These conditions made imports seem less threatening. In contrast, existing supply reduction policies for oranges and milk in Japan made acceptance of imports particularly difficult.

Regional concentration also varied. More dispersed producers, such as dairy farmers, held a wider political base, while those concentrated in a single region, such as orange producers, could appeal that their collapse would devastate the region.[5] Each quota had its own strong political backing, whether it was the quota for devil's tongue (konyaku), produced primarily in Prime Minister Takeo Fukuda's district, or the quota for oranges, fiercely defended by the active orange growers' cooperative association. Geography had special significance for the case of Japanese pineapples, which are grown only in Okinawa. There it provides the major industry for several economically depressed regions that had already suffered under the liberalization of fresh pineapples. The concentration of U.S. military bases in Okinawa made this an especially sensitive issue — indeed, Okinawan farmers and politicians filed a petition with the U.S. embassy stating that pineapple liberalization would increase resentment of the U.S. bases among the local population (Yaguchi 1988, 6).

In addition, some producers had corporate allies. Several of the commodities, such as juices and tomato products, were first-stage processed goods. For these products, both the farmers and the companies involved in processing them had a stake in continued protection. In particular, orange liberalization faced opposition from trading firms that held existing import licenses and benefited from quota rents (Kusano 1983, 55). These companies lobbied energetically to preserve their vested interest in the existing protection regime. On the other hand, food industry firms strongly called for liberalization of products that were major inputs for processed goods, such as starch, sugar, and dairy products.

Although there were differences in the economic and political charac-

---

[4] Between 1970 and 1997, the share of beef in the daily per capita calorie supply of Japanese people grew by a factor of 3.5, while the total consumption of domestic and imported beef grew from 312 thousand metric tons to 1373 thousand metric tons (FAO 2001).

[5] Over one-fourth of all beef-producing farms are located in one prefecture. Orange production occurs primarily in the southern islands of Shikoku and Kyūshyū. Dairy farmers are more widely distributed, although nearly one-fourth of all dairy farmers are in Hokkaido. In Japan a specific kind of potato provides the raw material for starch, and the production of this product is highly concentrated. In 1974, at the start of the negotiations, over 50 percent of all farm households producing potatoes and other minor cereals (not including rice, wheat, or barley) lived in either Hokkaido or Kagoshima Prefecture (MAFF 1997).

teristics of each product, all were protected by quantitative restrictions that limited imports. Such import quotas long formed the foremost trade barrier against agricultural imports into Japan. These policies originated as part of a much wider set of quota policies.[6] When Japan joined GATT in 1955, the government justified its quotas under the GATT treaty's article 12, which grants exceptions for quotas necessary for protection of international balance of payments. However, this justification ended in 1963, when the government formally withdrew its GATT exception for balance of payments quotas and designated the quotas as "residual import restrictions" (*zanson yūnyū seigen hinmoku*). Thereafter, the quotas stood in a grey area of questionable legality under GATT rules. In article 11, the GATT provisions explicitly condemn "prohibitions or restrictions, other than duties, taxes, or other charges, whether made effective through quotas, import or export licenses, or other measures." In subsequent liberalization packages, the government eliminated many of the quotas to reduce their number from 103 in April 1964 to 58 by the end of 1970 (Murata 1995, 20).[7] Further reduction to 5 remaining quotas in 2000 has been the outcome of repeated negotiations that will be central to this study of U.S.-Japan agricultural trade negotiations.

Economic and political features of an industry or commodity are important to explain the demand and supply of protection. However, for these agricultural products, neither the similar form of protection nor the timing of liberalization can be adequately explained by the features describing each commodity. Therefore, the subsequent analysis turns to how international negotiations influence changes in the form and level of protection.

Phase 1: Bilateral and Multilateral Talks

The first negotiation on the quota items began in a bilateral context and was restarted as part of the Tokyo Round multilateral trade negotiation. This section analyzes the negotiation process and argues that a weak issue linkage made it easier for Japan to resist U.S. pressure to get an agreement with only moderate liberalization.

The initial demands for liberalization of Japan's agricultural quotas arose in U.S.-Japan bilateral talks in the early 1970s. In July 1972 the

---

[6] Cabinet order designates certain products as quota items. These products then require advance import authorization through the acquisition of importer licenses as stipulated in the Foreign Exchange and Foreign Trade Control Law.

[7] A quota item consists of a CCCN four-digit commodity category.

U.S. government issued a report calling for Japan to increase market access for agricultural goods and, in particular, calling for the complete liberalization of its beef market. Subsequently, the major frontal assault on the quota policies occurred in U.S.-Japan bilateral talks conducted in parallel with the Tokyo Round. The United States demanded the full end to all quotas, but the final policy outcome was the elimination of some of the smaller quotas and the expansion of the quota amount for most of the items.

The negotiation occurred in a period of economic distress for the world economy and the United States in particular. Restructuring of the postwar economic order had taken on a new urgency in the 1970s against the backdrop of the 1971 Nixon shocks.[8] The U.S. government singled out unfair practices by trade partners as one source of the U.S. economic problems. A 1971 report by an expert commission appointed by the Nixon administration recommended starting a multilateral trade negotiation as one way to achieve the needed liberalization and turn around the U.S. economic problems (Winham 1986, 75). The trade round got underway in September 1973, but the 1973 oil shocks added a new crisis followed by a period during which the developed economies experienced stagnating economic growth and rising prices. Such serious economic problems distracted governments from giving attention to the trade round and made it difficult to propose reducing protection (ibid., 8). In the end, the U.S. Congress did not grant negotiating authority to the president until the end of 1974, and only in 1977 did the United States again focus on restarting the negotiations as a way to help address the problems in the global economy. Ultimately it took seven years of negotiations before the round drew to a close in April 1979.

For Japan, the trade round was both an opportunity and a challenge for its trade policy. The seventh GATT round of trade talks took the name "Tokyo Round" because of the Japanese role to advocate starting a new round and to host the GATT ministerial meeting that launched the round. The government of Eisaku Satō strongly called for a new round at the April 1971 GATT Council session, even before the United States and EC showed any interest in a new round (Fukui 1978, 76). Japanese leaders knew that other countries held high expectations for large Japanese concessions on trade, given that in the 1970s Japan had switched from being a country with a trade deficit to one with a trade surplus at the same time as the United States encountered increasing

---

[8] The Nixon administration allowed the dollar to float and imposed a 10 percent import surcharge as a stopgap measure against the soaring balance-of-payments deficit.

economic difficulties.[9] A Japanese official who worked in the GATT organization during the Tokyo Round later wrote, "The world expected that now that Japan was doing so well it could stand in the U.S. place as the engine to push forward liberalization with tariff cuts, abolition of quotas, and deregulation" (Takase 1997, 9).[10]

U.S. pressure on Japan to take the lead through a major liberalization package in the Tokyo Round was highlighted at the London summit meeting of industrial nations in May 1977. The United States and Europe urged Japan to spur its economy through domestic growth and reduction of its trade surplus. The Carter administration argued that Germany and Japan alongside the United States had responsibility for global recovery and must switch from surplus nations to deficit nations to restore balance to the international economy.[11] U.S. expectations for Japan to make concessions in the round targeted the agricultural sector.

Although budget constraints typically encourage liberalization, in this case, U.S. demands for liberalization of commodities protected by quotas went directly against Japanese government efforts to reduce the costs of agricultural protection by diversifying its agricultural sector. Japanese expenditures for agriculture represented nearly 12 percent of total budget expenditures in 1974.[12] This burden motivated reforms in domestic policies to reduce the budget costs. The main budget problem lay with the cost of supporting high rice-producer prices and disposing of the surpluses generated by these policies. A policy shift in 1976 reduced the government payments to support the high producer prices and increased the price paid by consumers, which provided immediate relief for the budget problems by the next year (Terasawa 1984, 23). These policy reforms occurred independently of the trade policy discussions of the Tokyo Round. However, as the government tried to reduce the rice production that was creating annual surpluses, it encouraged farmers to shift into production of other commodities, such as beef, citrus, and vegetables. Since quotas were necessary to keep out imports and maintain high domestic prices for these products, their liberalization would undermine the entire program of agricultural restructuring.

The Ministry of Agriculture and politicians united to oppose liberalization of any quotas. At the beginning of the Tokyo Round in 1973,

---

[9] The U.S. trade deficit with Japan in 1972 stood at 4.2 billion dollars in contrast to a deficit of 165 million dollars with the European Economic Community (*New York Times*, 15 April 1973).

[10] Author's translation.

[11] *Washington Post*, 24 April 1977.

[12] MAFF, *The 56th Statistical Yearbook of the Ministry of Agriculture, Forestry and Fisheries, 1979–80*.

the agriculture minister and MAFF vice-minister told the Cabinet and Diet that any liberalization was impossible (Fukui 1978, 110).

The Tokyo Round and a Weak Linkage

The Tokyo Round called for a package negotiation on a range of issues. The Tokyo Declaration established the agenda for the new round with a call for the liberalization of tariff and nontariff barriers. Specific mention was made that negotiations on different sectors and aspects of the rules were all part of a package; the declaration stated that "The negotiation shall be considered one undertaking, the various elements of which shall move forward together."[13] Six main negotiating groups were established in 1975 to address tropical products, tariffs, nontariff measures, sectoral negotiations, safeguards, and agriculture. The following year, countries established a seventh group on improvements in the GATT framework. The United States strongly backed the inclusion of agriculture within this larger package. Special Trade Representative Robert Strauss said that "without a good agricultural settlement there is no Tokyo Round."[14] However, the Tokyo Declaration weakened the linkage of agriculture by stating that the approach to agricultural negotiations "should take account of the special characteristics and problems in this sector."[15]

The choices of the United States, EC, and Japan shaped the negotiation structure. All sides felt that the decision on how to structure the talks would greatly shape the outcome. The key point was the separation of agriculture for special treatment within the negotiation, in terms of both negotiating groups and bargaining standards. Progress during the initial years of the Tokyo Round stalled over this largely procedural debate between the United States against Europe and Japan on the treatment of agriculture. The Preparatory Committee for the round reported in 1973 that "it was suggested by some delegations that a distinction should be made in the negotiations between agricultural and industrial products and this will have to be defined. . . . On the other

---

[13] Text of the Tokyo Declaration issued at the end of the ministerial meeting held in Tokyo, 12–14 September 1973, in Winham (1986, 415).

[14] 1978 statement by Robert Strauss cited in Curran (1982, 124) This comment by Strauss reflects the pressures he was under. The Department of Agriculture, in a report before the round, urged Congress that agricultural liberalization should be the minimum requirement for a satisfactory settlement and that withdrawal from GATT and tariff increases should be held as the threat to help reach such an agreement.

[15] Text of the Tokyo Declaration in Winham (1986, 414).

hand, other delegations considered that no distinction should be made between agricultural and industrial products" (GATT 1979, 18). Agriculture groups in the United States feared that a deal on industrial issues alone would leave behind their interests in an agricultural deal. They pushed to have the 1974 Trade Act explicitly call for holding agricultural talks in the same room with industrial talks.[16]

Finally, the breakthrough occurred in a July 1977 agreement between the United States and EC.[17] In a major concession to restart the negotiations, the United States agreed to have separate agriculture and industry negotiation groups. The agreement also laid out a timetable for the completion of the round that included parallel deadlines for directives on treatment of agriculture and tariff cuts (Curran 1982; GATT 1979). This set the stage for agricultural negotiations to be treated separately from the formula for industrial goods tariff reduction while remaining loosely within the framework of the overall negotiation. The United States had backed down on its demand for a strong linkage but still indicated that agricultural liberalization would be a necessary part of an agreement.[18]

Although Japan shared the EC preference for the weak issue linkage, the final settlement occurred as the result of meetings between U.S. and European officials. A U.S. negotiator said, "Japan hid behind any shrub that would provide cover, and Europe provided it."[19] While the adamant resistance to any reform of the Common Agricultural Policy by EC leaders blocked progress in the agriculture group negotiations, Japan faced less pressure. After the July 1977 breakthrough, Japan was under renewed demands from the United States. However, the decision on procedures reached between the U.S. and EC negotiators determined the negotiation structure for all participants, and thereafter a weak issue linkage characterized the Tokyo Round. Japan could no longer hide behind the EC, but the negotiation context was more favorable now for all countries that opposed major agricultural liberalization.

After this first decision was made to separate the negotiating groups, the Agriculture Group adopted a "request-offer" procedure for the bar-

[16] Former official of U.S. Special Trade Representative Office delegation to the Tokyo Round. Interview by author. Washington, DC, 5 April 2000.

[17] See chapter 8 for more analysis of this decision.

[18] The report to Congress on the negotiation described the decision as follows: "[U.S. negotiators] agreed to drop the U.S. insistence that agriculture be negotiated along with industry on the condition that there would be a 'substantial result for agriculture' in the MTN [multilateral trade negotiation]." (U.S. Senate 1979b, 15)

[19] Former official of U.S. Special Trade Representative Office delegation to the Tokyo Round. Interview by author. Washington, DC, 5 April 2000.

gaining over reduction of agricultural tariff and nontariff measures (Winham 1986, 166). Request-offer negotiations would involve the primary supplier issuing its requests on each item of importance and the importer giving their offer of a cut in the tariff rate. In practice, bargaining occurred on discrete items as well as the overall balance of a bilateral trade profile. This stood in contrast with the formula approach for cutting industrial goods tariffs, which involved bargaining on a general principle for how to cut tariffs across all products taken together.

The division of dairy, grains, and meat into three subgroups contributed to the isolation of talks on these major agricultural commodity issues from the talks on other agricultural goods and the overall trade round. The commodity agreements for dairy and meat formed separate agreements that governments could choose to accept or reject independent of the other agreements of the Tokyo Round.[20] Although a grains subgroup existed in the Tokyo Round, grains issues were also being addressed outside of the Tokyo Round in the framework of the International Wheat Council (IWC) in London, which began discussions in 1975 on a new International Wheat Agreement (Winham 1986, 252). Discussions within the Tokyo Round grains subgroup halted in 1977, pending progress in the IWC talks. In a final meeting in 1979, the grains subgroup decided it could not do anything useful without further progress in the international grains negotiations of the IWC (GATT 79, 26). The separate treatment of the major commodities eroded the connection of agricultural talks with the other areas of the Tokyo Round negotiation.

As a result, while the negotiation structure consisted of a multilateral negotiation on a comprehensive package of issues, agriculture fit only loosely within this package. Several factors contributed to the isolation of agricultural issues: the agenda for the round emphasized that agricultural issues should be given special treatment; the agricultural talks were conducted in their own group, which rejected the tariff cut formula approach; and there was fragmentation within the agricultural commodities talks as some core products were discussed outside of the agriculture negotiating group.

Consequently, considerable uncertainty remained about which issues were the necessary components for a final package. Near the end of the negotiation in the summer of 1978, Nobuhiko Ushiba, who was a Foreign Ministry diplomat appointed to lead the Tokyo Round negotiations for Japan as the minister for external economic affairs, stated at a press

---

[20] The two agreements created were the Arrangement Regarding Bovine Meat and the International Dairy Arrangement.

conference that a major question of the negotiation was the size of the package deal.[21] The fact that the size of the package was still not defined this late in the negotiation indicated the low credibility of the linkage among all of the negotiation groups included on the agenda. In particular, it was unclear whether agriculture was an integral part of the overall negotiation that would affect the prospects for agreement in other areas.

U.S.-Japan Agricultural Negotiations

The first phase of the U.S.-Japan agricultural quota negotiations was a hybrid case of an ad hoc bilateral talk and a GATT-institutionalized negotiation. The United States raised the beef quota issue in bilateral talks in 1971 in the context of the joint Japan-U.S. Commission on Trade and Economic Affairs.[22] The Japanese government agreed to expand the quota size as a partial concession, and the issue was set aside. The new Carter administration decided that beef and citrus liberalization by Japan would help to counter protectionist sentiment in Congress about the growing U.S.-Japan trade imbalance and would provide an important lever to gain congressional support of the Tokyo Round agreement (Fukushima 1992, 297). During his February 1977 visit to Tokyo, Vice-President Walter Mondale initiated a new high-level negotiation when he renewed requests for beef and citrus liberalization and urged Japan to abolish its GATT-illegal quantitative restrictions on agricultural products. In meetings to discuss the multilateral trade negotiation, a delegation from the U.S. Special Trade Representative urged Japan again on the importance of reaching agreement on agricultural market access in general and the beef and citrus case in particular (Sato and Curran 1982, 129).

However, talks remained primarily bilateral in the early stages. The first temporary agreement, in January 1978, represented a bilateral package deal with several issues regarding U.S.-Japan economic relations and including a compromise on the beef and citrus negotiation (Fukushima 1992, 298). Thereafter, talks continued among U.S. and Japanese negotiators for the Tokyo Round. A U.S. negotiator said the

[21] *Nihon nōgyō shimbun,* 21 July 1978.

[22] "Gatto kankei nenpyo: Nihon nōsanbutsu yūnyū jiyūka no kei" (GATT chronology: The record of Japan's agricultural liberalization), *Nōgyō to Keizai* (Agriculture and economics), (Tokyo: Mainichi shimbun, 1994) 49.

talks were carried out "in parallel with the Tokyo Round, but not in the round."[23]

The distinction of whether the locus of negotiations was bilateral or multilateral held important consequences for bureaucratic procedures. As long as the negotiation remained on the bilateral level, it gave the dominant role to the ministry with primary jurisdiction, which in this case meant MAFF. In contrast, the Tokyo Round decision making relied upon an interministry process among the division chiefs of MAFF, MITI, MOFA, and the Economic Planning Agency (EPA). They met on a weekly basis, and MOFA drew up the initial position paper and coordinated among all members. A unanimity rule guided this bargaining among equals. Fukui (1978) argues that the Foreign Ministry influence is greater for multilateral negotiations while the domestic ministries, such as the Ministry of Agriculture, have more influence for bilateral negotiations on narrow issues. In the multilateral negotiation, MAFF retained its veto role over agricultural liberalization, but these meetings formalized the interministry decision process in a way that forced MAFF to take into account the concerns of other ministries about Japan's foreign relations and gains from a successful Tokyo Round agreement. Keeping talks at the bilateral level in the early years helped MAFF to resist U.S. demands effectively.

Exporter mobilization in the first four years of the Tokyo Round was supportive of the negotiation, but big business did not unite to lobby strongly for trade liberalization. The Japan Foreign Trade Council actively lobbied for the Tokyo Round. Representing a group of trading companies, it had a clear interest in liberalization, for, with the exception of those few traders holding import licenses for protected items, these companies would benefit from greater market opening (Curran 1982, 68). Keidanren also advocated the start of the Tokyo Round and continued support throughout the negotiation. In February 1973, in a meeting with high-level MITI officials, Keidanren leaders requested faster trade liberalization in Japan (Fukui 1978, 99). Later in 1975, the president of Keidanren and the Japanese Chamber of Commerce and Industry met with Prime Minister Takeo Miki to urge him to push forward the Tokyo Round negotiations in the upcoming summit meeting (ibid.). However, policy advocacy by the organization was limited by the fact that its membership included both strong and weak industrial sectors with opposing interests in liberalization. In a review of different industry trade association statements and periodicals, Curran (1982,

69–70) describes a general passivity by industry groups toward the round, even where one would have expected strong support by associations of industries dependent on export markets, such as the Japan Automobile Association.

MITI was basically in favor of free trade and closely listened to the concerns of big business about protectionism against Japanese exports. It especially favored agricultural liberalization, mostly from the perspective that concessions on agriculture would provide bargaining chips useful in negotiations on other issues in the Tokyo Round. From this perspective, MITI hoped to make linkages between agricultural and industrial goods in spite of the formal separation of the negotiating groups. However, coal, leather, and textiles were industries where MITI favored increased protection. Whenever MITI tried to pressure MAFF to make more concessions on agricultural issues, MAFF officials would mention these sensitive items, and MITI would withdraw its demands (Fukui 1978, 136). In the end, while MITI favored liberalization through a successful Tokyo Round agreement, its advocacy of the round was held back by the perception that Japan's strong industries would make only small gains from an agreement while the weak industries would have to make large concessions (Curran 1982, 73).

The status quo seemed to offer as much as the gains from the round without the cuts. This reflects that officials in business and MITI still felt the status quo was an option. The talks had failed to convince these groups that the round could fail and that such a failure would damage the GATT system and lead to the closure of markets.

Toward Forward Movement: 1977–1979

The increase in trade conflict and restart of Tokyo Round negotiations in 1977 increased the concern of the business community about agricultural issues. Rising friction indicated that failure to liberalize in the Tokyo Round would result in growing protectionism rather than a return to the status quo. In March 1978 a joint House and Senate committee of the U.S. Congress threatened unilateral import surcharges against Japan if it did not take measures to address its trade surplus. Earlier talks in Congress had singled out agricultural issues, and the beef and citrus quotas in particular, as problem areas.[24] Although U.S. government negotiators did not issue public threats, the congressional

---

[24] *Nihon nōgyō shimbun,* 13 May 1978.

hearings on the trade imbalance were constantly in the background as an indirect threat.[25]

The increasing attention to Japan's trade surplus and accompanying pressure from the United States changed the stakes of the trade round for Japanese business. Now exporters hoped that increasing imports by Japan in other sectors, such as agriculture, would reduce Japan's trade surplus and thereby alleviate the soaring value of the yen (Curran 1982, 94). The main economic ministries (MITI, MOF, EPA), as well as business associations voiced concerns that the lack of progress in the agricultural negotiations would endanger the interests of the industrial sector.[26] Agricultural groups complained that they faced divisions within the government. Nevertheless, while U.S. trade pressures and veiled threats helped to convince Japan's business community and some leaders to favor agricultural reform, domestic opposition continued to prevent major concessions in the bilateral negotiations.

Bilateral deadlock motivated both sides to shift talks into the forum of the Tokyo Round. In the fall of 1977, the United States applied increasing pressure on Japan in a series of bilateral meetings. In January 1978 the two countries reached a provisional agreement for expanding agricultural import quotas, but this agreement unraveled and negotiations again broke down. Thereafter, U.S. and Japanese officials agreed to move talks to Geneva, where the Tokyo Round multilateral trade negotiation was centered. Japanese officials often favor the multilateral context for volatile issues because they think that the broader context will allow more "give-and-take" (Fukui 1978, 150). In this case, they hoped that the U.S. demands for agricultural liberalization would become more moderate and that the United States would accept the other trade-opening measures that Japan made in the Tokyo Round as compensation for doing less on agricultural issues. On the other hand, the U.S. government hoped to apply additional pressure on the Japanese government through the leverage of the broader stakes of the Tokyo Round. This indicates that while the choice of negotiation venue was shaped by the expectations and preferences of both sides, they held different expectations about the influence a particular negotiation context would hold for the outcome.

As a consequence of the shift, in Japan, all of the agricultural trade issues were now placed in the interministry decision process for the Tokyo Round. This broader jurisdiction created more pressure for a

---

[25] Former official of USTR delegation to the Tokyo Round. Interview by author, Washington DC, 5 April 2000.

[26] *Nihon nōgyō shimbun*, 12 May 1978.

compromise by MAFF. The new negotiation venue also provided some political cover for politicians hoping to avoid blame for sacrificing Japanese farmers for U.S. interests. Japanese leaders believed that whereas the public would see a concession in a bilateral forum as capitulation to the United States, the public would view a concession in a multilateral forum as a compromise for "world opinion."[27]

The United States pushed to establish a linkage between the beef and citrus agreement and the overall Tokyo Round. In meetings in May, U.S. Special Trade Representative Robert Strauss told Prime Minister Takeo Fukuda that Japan should eliminate its beef and citrus quotas and argued that conclusion of the Tokyo Round negotiations was necessary to stop the protectionist trend in Congress; later the same month he told Japanese officials that conclusion of the Tokyo Round depended on settlement of the agricultural problems (Sato and Curran 1982, 148).

However, the linkage imposed by the United States lacked credibility. The United States could not argue that this issue would cause the collapse of the round as a matter of principle, for two reasons. First, the Tokyo Declaration had not created a strong mandate to demand substantial agricultural liberalization, and the 1977 procedural decisions further separated agricultural issues from the overall round. Second, under the request-offer bargaining standard, no country had an obligation to make a specific policy change on any given agricultural product. Therefore, while Japanese officials admitted the informal pressure from the U.S. effort to link the beef and citrus negotiation with the overall Tokyo Round, there was not any public acknowledgment.[28] The formal negotiation structure did not support the U.S. claim that beef and citrus liberalization was necessary for the round, and no Japanese official or politician wanted to argue that the political requirements of Congress meant that Japan must liberalize sensitive products.

In spite of the U.S. pressure on the issue, the Japanese government continued to refuse to end the quotas. Japanese Minister of Agriculture Ichirō Nakagawa told U.S. negotiators in the final month of the negotiation in December 1978, "I am about to be fired and can't do anything more. There would be no agreement unless you took back your demand for liberalization [of the orange import quota]" (Sato and Curran 1982, 171). The Japanese government would agree to concessions

---

[27] Interviews cited in Curran (1982, 58). Fukui (1978, 150) also cites interviews indicating that the prevalent view among bureaucrats at the time held that the Japanese public would more favorably perceive concessions in multilateral negotiations.

[28] Former MAFF official who participated in the Tokyo Round negotiation. Interview by author. Tokyo, 18 March 1999.

only in terms of expanding the quota. Even on this point, the government resisted expanding the quota to the degree demanded by the United States.

When the U.S. position tied an agricultural agreement to the need for a Tokyo Round agreement, this also pushed U.S. officials to weigh the consequences of a failure to reach agreement. Following the refusal by Nakagawa to end the quotas, U.S. officials consulted and agreed that rejecting the quota expansion settlement as it stood would delay and potentially disrupt the multilateral trade negotiation (ibid.). U.S. Ambassador Michael Mansfield decided to tell the administration to accept the deal. In the tradeoff between the stakes of the round and the agricultural issues, both Japan and the United States faced a decision on how much they would risk to defend their position.

Final Agreement: Partial Liberalization

In the end, both sides compromised to accept partial liberalization. In the Nakagawa-Mansfield Agreement reached in December 1978, Japan offered additional concessions, increasing the size of the quotas, and the United States accepted a compromise short of its original demand for elimination of the quotas. This bilateral agreement was formally appended to the Tokyo Round agreement as an addendum. It called for expanding the quota for beef, oranges, orange juice, and grapefruits over the next four years and specified that the governments would again discuss the question of eliminating the quotas in 1983.[29] The agreement also modified some of the other agricultural quotas with an increase of import allocation for some quotas, and elimination of eleven quotas (two additional quotas were partially eliminated). Senior LDP leaders and the interministerial process reached this decision and allocated to each ministry a fixed number of quotas to eliminate. To fulfill its share of quota elimination, MAFF officials selected those products where it anticipated the least domestic damage (e.g., products like nonedible seaweed, molasses, malt, and beef offal).[30] There were some substantial increases in market access, but the total agreement represented minor

---

[29] The agreement increased the high-quality beef quota from 16,000 tons to 30,000 tons over the four-year implementation period from 1979 to 1983. The orange quota increased from 4,500 to 8,200 tons over the four years. There were also substantial quota increases for orange juice and grapefruit juice (Fukushima 1992, 298).

[30] Former MAFF official who participated in the Tokyo Round. Interview by author. Tokyo, 18 March 1999.

liberalization because most of the quotas would continue as GATT-illegal barriers restricting imports.

Overall, the Tokyo Round included only modest changes in agriculture relative to other sectors. On average, countries reduced tariffs by 7 percent for agricultural goods, compared with 39 percent average reduction of tariffs on finished manufactured goods (GATT 1979, 122). Moreover, only one-third of agricultural trade products were covered by tariffs at the time, and many of the nontariff barriers remained intact. For Japan, its offer on industrial goods covered 2,600 items with an approximate import value of 247 billion dollars (1976 prices), while the offer on agricultural goods covered just 226 items with an approximate value of 34 billion dollars.[31] Across all agricultural items raised in the Tokyo Round, the United States issued requests to Japan on 130 items, and Japan made some form of concession on 108 of these items, including tariff changes and quota adjustments. Japan's agriculture offer included a zero tariff binding for soybeans and large tariff reductions for nuts, chocolates, and biscuits/cookies. U.S. negotiators reported satisfaction with the results of the U.S.-Japan agreement even while hoping to achieve an end to the quotas in the future.[32] The *Wall Street Journal* (6 December 1978) aptly summed up the agreement as "a farm-trade agreement that neither side is fully satisfied with but one that both can live with" (Reich and Endo 1983, 85).

The negotiation outcome did not fundamentally change Japan's agricultural policies. Many of Japan's agricultural quotas were maintained without tariffication and remained GATT illegal. Japan did not have to modify the nature of its domestic regulations because it changed only the level of the access provided by the quantitative restrictions.

In addition, the form of the concessions catered to U.S. interests. By creating categories for "hotel-grade beef" and "seasonal citrus," the quota increases were specifically designed to fit U.S. market needs. A former Ministry of Agriculture official involved in the negotiation said, "If we had to accept the intrusion of beef imports, the goal was to give maximum satisfaction to the United States."[33] The bias in market access was achieved because of the structure of the U.S. beef industry. The United States imports inexpensive, grass-fed beef while it exports the higher-quality, grain-fed beef (nicknamed "hotel-grade" although it was

[31] *Nihon nōgyō shimbun,* 28 July 1979.
[32] Former official of USTR delegation to the Tokyo Round. Interview by author, Washington, DC, 5 April 2000.
[33] Former MAFF official. Interview by author. Tokyo, Japan, 12 April 1999.

not restricted from retail sales outside of hotels), and at that time the United States was the only exporter of this kind of beef (Sato and Curran 1982, 122). General liberalization of Japanese beef trade would have allowed market share gains by Australian grass-fed beef over the U.S. beef exports, whereas restricting the quota increases to hotel-grade beef privileged the U.S. market access. With regards to citrus, the agreement established seasonal differentiation in quotas as a way to balance the different growing schedules in the United States and Japan. This arrangement would reduce competition with the Japanese growers and ensure that both Florida and California growers could benefit from the quota increases (ibid.).

This kind of arrangement to narrow and target the benefits of liberalization reflected the bilateral origins of the negotiation. During the bilateral talks, both Japan and the United States had the flexibility to reach this kind of agreement. Because the Tokyo Round agriculture group did not produce a general formula that would further constrain the form of policy change, no change was necessary when talks shifted from the bilateral context into the multilateral trade negotiation or when the agreement was appended to the final Tokyo Round agreement.

The negotiation never engaged in a legal framing approach, so the case does not provide a strong test of the legal framing hypothesis. During the bilateral negotiation phase, talks went forward without any GATT mediation. Although the United States officials emphasized that the quota policies were contrary to GATT rules, there was no specific mention of appealing to a GATT panel for a ruling on the issue. When the negotiation shifted to the Tokyo Round, the GATT context offered some enhanced legitimacy. Nevertheless, legal framing remained low. U.S. and Japanese officials negotiated separately without any mediation by the GATT Director-General. Furthermore, the request-offer bargaining process emphasized the balance of benefits between the two countries rather than require fitting the policy in a general framework of rules. Consequently, absent third-party mediation or a legalistic principle as the baseline for bargaining, the procedural and normative pressures of legal framing did not arise.

During this first phase of the quota negotiations, U.S. bilateral pressure in combination with the broader stakes of the round helped to bring about some liberalization. In the early years of the negotiation, bilateral pressure in isolation proved insufficient to produce agreement. Even before the Tokyo Round, the United States clearly stated demands for the full end of the quotas, and the Nixon administration import surcharge and statements from Congress set the stage for strong U.S.

pressure on Japan to increase its imports. However, these talks and their continuation at the bilateral level during the early years of the trade round ended in standstill. Moving talks to Geneva and into the Tokyo Round context helped to break the deadlock. Escalating U.S. bilateral pressure and the stakes of the round worked together to offset the fierce domestic opposition in Japan.

Two factors allowed Japan to strike a narrow deal for minor rather than major liberalization. First, the Tokyo Round negotiation did not apply a strongly institutionalized cross-sector linkage in the agenda. The United States hinted that the ratification of the Tokyo Round by Congress depended on a good agricultural deal with Japan, but the formal negotiation agenda left uncertainty and room for flexibility regarding the linkage between agriculture and other parts of the negotiation. Given the weakly institutionalized linkage, it was not credible that the United States would unilaterally force the failure of the entire round in order to get more concessions on agricultural items from Japan.

Second, the request-offer procedures for agricultural talks and the bilateral nature of such bargaining made it easier for Japan to make partial concessions for the minimum satisfaction of the United States. A formula approach forces general liberalization across products and leaves the decision on the formula to upper-level political and bureaucratic leadership. In contrast, the request-offer approach allows countries to narrow the scope of their offer according to the circumstances of each commodity and trade partner. The level of jurisdiction also resides with the ministry section directly responsible for the commodity, which tends to make liberalization more difficult. In other words, the mechanism by which a linkage forms — broadening sectoral interests and bureaucratic jurisdiction — operates more effectively under a formula negotiation approach rather than a request-offer approach.

The case of the Tokyo Round holds important implications for understanding both the establishment of negotiation structure and its effect. Clearly the negotiation structure itself is the product of an informal negotiation among nations. The resistance of Europe and Japan was partly responsible for the separation of agriculture into its own negotiation group, choice of the request-offer procedure, and the further subdivision into commodity agreement negotiations. No other countries or GATT authority came to the aid of the United States to urge a stronger linkage, and the United States backed down to accept a weak linkage. This weak linkage helped provide some leverage to the United States to get more concessions within the Tokyo Round context than had been possible when talks were only at the bilateral level. Yet it was insufficient to bring major liberalization.

Phase 2: Bilateral Talks

The next negotiation took place from late 1981 to 1984 and addressed the same policy question — the U.S. demand that Japan end its quota policies for beef, citrus, and thirteen other agricultural items. However, in contrast to the Tokyo Round negotiation, the second phase was a negotiation conducted entirely by an ad hoc bilateral approach. The agenda focused exclusively on the agricultural issues. In spite of strong U.S. demands backed by threats, Japan again refused to end the quota policies, and the United States again accepted a partial liberalization measure for quota expansion.

As the U.S. trade deficit and the Japanese surplus both continued to grow during the early 1980s, overall trade tensions intensified. From 1980 to 1984, the U.S. trade deficit quadrupled from 26 billion dollars to 113 billion dollars, and Japan's trade surplus grew from 2 billion dollars to 44 billion dollars (Bergsten and Noland 1993, 34). This was a period when the trade deficit between Japan and the United States became a high-profile political issue, and appeals from U.S. industry for protection such as local content bills emerged. Congress was considering a 10 percent surcharge on imports from Japan.

Against this background, the United States raised again the issue of Japan's agricultural quotas. The U.S. demands began with the U.S.-Japan consultation on agricultural trade in December 1981.[34] Talks went forward at the bilateral level in the U.S.-Japan working group on agricultural product import restrictions, but they broke down in April 1982. Two months later, Japan offered a wide range of tariff cuts, including seventeen agricultural products as part of a comprehensive package offered to appease U.S. and European complaints about Japan's trade surplus.[35] However, Japan resisted changes on the quota policies, and the series of bilateral talks continued. Later, in October 1982, talks in Honolulu ended in acrimony as the Japanese side stated there would be no liberalization of the quotas and the U.S. negotiators walked out of the meeting and called off talks one day early.

U.S. threats escalated as the negotiations dragged on. The talks continued through repeated meetings in 1982 and 1983, and U.S. officials

[34] Reich, Endo, and Timmer (1986) provide a full account of the negotiations that is drawn on for the factual narrative given here.

[35] Indeed, the package was offered in a timely fashion immediately preceding the Paris Summit of Industrial nations. The package achieved the desired effect, for Prime Minister Zenko Suzuki bragged afterward that at the summit "no country criticized Japan's trade policies." Cited in Ishikura (1988, 131).

warned that failure to achieve a beef and citrus agreement would result in congressional protectionist legislation. USTR William Brock told Japanese officials that without substantial increases in the beef and citrus quotas, the United States would restrict imports of Japanese goods.[36] On the day that the Japanese agriculture minister arrived for a final set of negotiations in April 1984, the Senate Finance Committee Trade Subcommittee issued statements calling for sanctions against Japanese industrial goods if agricultural liberalization was not forthcoming (Ishikura 1988, 138). The rising pitch of U.S. threats supported the government strategy to convince the Japanese government that there would be wider consequences for the Japanese economy if the government refused to open its agricultural markets.

In part, the U.S. retaliatory threats spurred domestic groups in Japan to back liberalization. In November 1982 a leading Japanese economic magazine came out with a special issue urging Japan to liberalize beef and orange markets, and a policy forum composed of academics urged liberalization of other quota items as well as the beef and citrus quotas (ibid., 140, 147). Fearing U.S. protectionism against Japanese exports, Japan's industrial interests began advocating agricultural liberalization as a means of appeasing U.S. trade complaints (Reich, Endo, and Timmer 1986, 176). Organizations of big business such as the Keizai Dōyūkai issued statements backing comprehensive liberalization in late 1982. The Keidanren Food Industry Committee issued a report in September 1983 that urged ending the quotas restricting the import of products used as inputs for the food processing industry. The report gave the following rationale: "Japan's agricultural policy is geared toward protecting farmers, while it ignores industrial users and individual consumers of farm products. This situation not only makes the people's lives more difficult but also hinders Japan's food industry from becoming as competitive as its foreign counterparts."[37]

The following week, the Keidanren Commerce Committee released a policy statement about the importance of supporting the free-trade system and called on Japan to liberalize all of the agricultural items under quota with the exception of rice and wheat.[38] Keidanren presented its reports in meetings with LDP officials, such as an October meeting between the Keidanren Food Industry Committee Chairman Bunzo Wa-

---

[36] *Washington Post*, 15 April 1984.

[37] Keidanren report quoted in Rothacher (1989, 118).

[38] Keidanren. "Jiyū bōeki taisei no iji/kyōka ni kan suru kenkai to teigen" (An opinion and proposal regarding the support and strengthening of the free trade system). Report by Commerce Committee, 27 September 1983.

tanabe and LDP Agriculture Committee Chairman Kōichi Katō (Keidanren 1999, 427).

Reasons for business groups to oppose agricultural protection had existed for years, but they had not been singled out as policy priorities. The added concern of escalating trade friction with the United States and potential retaliatory threats gave Keidanren and Keizai Dōyūkai the incentive to advocate reform. In a press conference in June 1983, the Keidanren chairman said, in reference to U.S.-Japan trade tensions and the problem of agricultural liberalization, "It is coming to the time when we must either accept America's demands or reject them. . . . If we reject them, the movement toward protectionism in the United States will heighten. If that does not matter, then we can continue to reject [their demands]" (Keidanren 1999, 426).[39]

On the other hand, U.S. pressure hardened domestic opposition in Japan. The Japanese Central Agriculture Cooperative threatened to reduce purchases of U.S. grains and soybeans, thousands of farmers protested in Tokyo, and the media and public opinion were highly critical of the U.S. negotiating position (Reich, Endo, and Timmer 1986). The lobbying by the agricultural cooperatives was very active. In November 1982 the agricultural cooperatives political organization Zenchū jointly sponsored with consumer organizations several symposia across the major cities in Japan to publicize the harmful impact of liberalization on Japanese lifestyle (Ishikura 1988, 147). In 1983 opposition parties issued declarations against quota enlargement at their party meetings and vowed support for the agricultural cooperatives petition drive (ibid.).

The actions of the farm groups dampened the advocacy of agricultural liberalization by industry groups. For example, when the Keidanren Food Industry Committee was preparing its 1983 report, it toned down the advocacy of liberalization after meetings with farm groups and MAFF (Keidanren 1999, 427). The committee faced further problems when, in March 1984, agricultural cooperatives in Hokkaido launched a boycott against the products of several companies whose executives served on the committee. Watanabe resigned as committee chairman, and thereafter business groups were reluctant to speak out actively in favor of agricultural liberalization (Keidanren 1999, 428; Yasuhara 1985, 144).

The strong domestic resistance helped the Japanese government argue that it was politically impossible for it to accept quota liberalization. One of MAFF's chief negotiators for the beef and citrus negotiation, Hiroya Sano, said that U.S. negotiators were persuaded only by the

---

[39] Author's translation.

realization that the political process in Japan made the government *politically incapable* of ending the quota policies.[40] The decision to end the quota policies would require approval by the agriculture affairs committees of the LDP Policy Affairs Research Council, which are dominated by rural district politicians. Moreover, the prime minister at the time, Yasuhiro Nakasone, was from a weak political faction and depended on several powerful farm district politicians from other factions to maintain his position in power. U.S. officials eventually became convinced that the Japanese government would not be able to end the quotas, and the United States agreed to move to a compromise position for quota expansion (Reich and Endo 1983, 93).

However, even quota expansion proved difficult. From late 1983 through early 1984, talks remained bogged down over the degree of market opening.[41] As a tactic to shift momentum in the negotiation, in July 1983 the United States formally filed a GATT complaint against thirteen of the agricultural quota policies. Although the U.S. officials did not file a complaint on beef and citrus products, the policies were similar. This step framed the quota policy issue in a legalistic context. Even while consultations on the thirteen quota items moved forward in the early stages of the GATT dispute settlement procedures, the beef and citrus talks remained at an impasse. The Tokyo Round agreement expired in March 1984 without a new agreement. The April meeting of the Japanese agriculture minister in Washington, DC, led to another breakdown. Strong political resistance in Japan prevented conclusion of any agreement.

Only when the United States further increased the GATT stakes did Japan moderate its position. The day after the USTR instructed the staff to begin preparations for submitting the beef and citrus case to GATT, the Japanese agriculture minister agreed to concessions allowing a larger quota increase (Porges 1994, 236). Early settlement would forestall more comprehensive reforms and further acrimony in Japan's trade relations with the United States were foreseen to result if the case continued to a GATT panel. Although officials announced the formal agreement later, the compromise at this time was the underpinning of the final conclusion of the negotiation. The United States pledged not to file a GATT complaint on the beef and citrus policies and to put on

---

[40] Interview by author. Tokyo, 12 April 1999. See also articles by Sano (1987; 1988).

[41] During talks in January 1984 the two sides remained far apart—the U.S. negotiator proposed an annual increase of 10,000 tons of high quality beef, and the Japanese negotiator responded with a proposal for a 4,200-ton annual increase. Agreement on oranges and other quota policies also remained distant (Reich, Endo, and Timmer 1986).

hold for two years its complaint on the thirteen other agricultural products. While the agreement occurred before any panel had been established, Japan's concession came in anticipation that a GATT panel ruling might require the elimination of the quotas.

The outcome of the second phase of negotiations resembled the outcome of the first phase. Japan agreed to quota expansion that would nearly double the size of the quotas over four years. The final agreement called for a 6,900-ton annual increase in high-quality beef imports as well as increases in quota sizes for other products and phased elimination of the quota for grapefruit juice. The evaluation of the agreement by the executive director of Zenchū, Iwao Yamaguchi, shows how the outcome reflected a partial victory for all sides: "We were able to prevent liberalization of beef and oranges . . . but we were not able to apply a brake on the increasing of import quotas" (Reich, Endo, and Timmer 1986, 179).

The agreement continued to reflect the flexibility of the bilateral framework for fixing an agreement to favor U.S. exports by means of the hotel-grade beef and seasonal citrus categories. Although Australia subsequently reached its own beef quota expansion agreement with Japan in November 1984, the quota expansion still favored the grain-fed beef exported by the United States over the grass-fed Australian beef. Trends in beef trade flows indicate the distinct biases resulting from the bilateral agreement. U.S. market share increased as a result of the 1978 and 1984 quota expansion for hotel-grade beef imports. Australia's ambassador to the GATT reported that the U.S. share of total Japanese beef imports increased from 13 percent in 1976 to 39 percent in 1987, while Australia's share fell from 74 percent to 41 percent.[42] The fact that the final agreement gave narrow concessions to the United States supports the expectations of the hypothesis that U.S. coercion forced the concessions. Although the United States did not achieve its demand for an end to the quotas, quota enlargement helped to boost both total U.S. exports to Japan as well as its relative market share.

However, retaliatory threats alone did not suffice to yield an agreement. Japan had continued to refuse larger quota expansion even when threats by U.S. negotiators and congressional activities indicated there was a strong prospect of restrictions against Japanese industrial exports. Industrial groups in Japan advocated liberalization concessions, but agriculture group lobbying also increased. Moreover, the policy process within Japan remained locked within the framework of the LDP Policy Affairs Research Council where rural district politicians had veto

[42] *Journal of Commerce*, 5 May 1988.

power. Therefore, even following the repeated breakdown of talks, escalation in bilateral trade tensions, and Keidanren reports favoring liberalization, the government resisted concessions. While threats broadened the economic stakes for Japan, they did not overcome the political threshold to make compromise possible.

Two factors helped push the United States and Japan to compromise on their earlier positions and accept minor liberalization. First, Japan used its political weakness to persuade the United States to accept a more modest agreement. At the same time, Japan could offer the United States increases in quota categories that were tailored to boost U.S. market shares. Second, the prospect of a change in the negotiation context convinced Japan it needed to make some concessions or face greater pressure later. The prospect of a GATT legal case framed Japan's choices so that it preferred the partial settlement with the United States that left the quota and distribution systems intact.

This second phase of the negotiation demonstrates the limits of U.S. threats on politically sensitive issues. While the threats mobilized domestic business interests in a way similar to issue-linkage pressure, they also increased domestic opposition. Even though there was considerable concern in Japan about Congress passing protectionist legislation, this did not prevent it from resisting for years of contentious negotiations and a partial settlement.

Phase 3: GATT Mediation

In 1988 Japan agreed to eliminate its quotas on beef, citrus, and several other agricultural items. This outcome represented the culmination of the long history of negotiations. In part, the momentum from prior negotiations pushed forward the agreement for major liberalization in this third negotiation. On the other hand, the past record, where the United States twice demanded quota elimination and twice accepted partial changes, reduced the credibility of U.S. threats for this final negotiation. The fact that separate negotiations on agricultural issues were taking place in the Uruguay Round trade negotiations at the same time also gave Japan the easy option of trying to defer discussion pending the outcome of the larger trade round.[43] Therefore, it was by no means certain that the third negotiation would end any differently from the previous two.

[43] The Uruguay Round began in 1986 and was scheduled to end in 1990, although it ultimately continued for another three years. The next chapter discusses this negotiation case.

High legal framing sets this negotiation apart. The United States again raised the same demand for the end of the quotas, but this time the trade arena was the GATT dispute settlement process. The legal framing of the third negotiation played a critical role in increasing the credibility of the U.S. demands while diffusing political opposition within Japan.

The Panel on Twelve Agricultural Items

The United States moved quickly to initiate GATT dispute proceedings in spite of Japan's reluctance. In late 1985, U.S. Agriculture Secretary Clayton Yeutter again called for the end of Japan's quota policies. Japan favored bilateral settlement but refused to agree to end the quotas. Faced with Japanese government resistance, the United States issued a formal complaint to GATT against the twelve less politically sensitive quotas in July 1986.[44] U.S. officials hoped to use the precedent from a GATT case on these smaller items as leverage for the bigger target of Japan's beef and citrus quotas.[45] Filing the complaint initiated a process that would lead to a panel of third-country representatives (typically diplomats or legal scholars) passing judgment on the GATT legality of the policies subject to complaint.

Initially, Japan resisted establishment of the panel.[46] However, international opinion against Japan's delaying tactics grew, and given its stake in the GATT system, Japan found it difficult to oppose the GATT adjudication process. At the second GATT Council meeting, the Japanese delegation consented to establishment of a panel. Disagreement on terms and panel membership further delayed establishment of the panel until March 1987.

The negotiation from this point onward became highly legalistic in nature. Both countries sent representatives to argue the legal technicalities of whether Japan's domestic policies fit the provisions of GATT article 11:2(c), which grants an exception to allow quantitative import restrictions for primary products when necessary for the implementa-

[44] For a full analysis of this case and its political and legal background, see Eichmann (1990).

[45] USTR official. Interview by author. Washington, DC, 3 April 2000.

[46] Resistance was possible because under GATT procedures at the time, all GATT Council members had to consent to the establishment of a panel. The establishment of the WTO in 1995 changed the dispute settlement procedures to end this right of the defendant to block a panel. Under the new rules, cases proceed automatically to a panel unless a consensus of all members opposes the panel.

tion of domestic supply control policies.[47] MOFA and MAFF jointly represented Japan and designed the legal argumentation. The discussion was bounded by the legal framework — Japan could not use political sensitivity to justify trade barriers, and the United States could not use its trade deficit with Japan as leverage for changing Japan's quota policies. One of the members of the Japanese negotiating team said, "There was no way to present nontrade argumentation — generally the GATT twelve argument was based on article 11:2(c) of the GATT Agreement." [48] After hearing both sides and receiving advice from advisors of the GATT legal office, the panel members issued their ruling in November 1987. The ruling declared that Japan's quota policies for ten of the twelve items violated GATT rules.[49] Only the quotas for peanuts and beans were ruled to conform with the GATT rules.

At first the Japanese government thought it could again achieve a settlement for partial liberalization. The Japanese ambassador to the United States made efforts to reach a compromise settlement with a promise to liberalize some but not all of the items among the quotas found illegal by the GATT panel report (Eichmann 1990, 42). At the December meeting of the GATT Council, the Japanese delegation tried to partially accept the agreement. The rulings against the quotas for starch and skim milk powder were especially problematic for MAFF negotiators because these products are important commodities that are produced in the districts of influential politicians. Japanese officials also disagreed with several aspects of the legal interpretation of the panel.[50] The restrictive interpretation by the panel concerning the applicability of the GATT exception for agricultural quotas rendered most of Japan's quota policies illegal. Moreover, the legal principles articulated in the rulings against quota items under state trading such as starch were identical to those that would face Japan's policies on beef and even rice. Fearful of a precedent with implications that could undermine the foundation of Japan's agricultural protection system, negotiators refused to

[47] Article 11 is about the general elimination of quantitative restrictions, but article 11:2(c) allows for import restrictions on primary products as part of a program to reduce supply of a product or like product in the domestic market. In this case, some of the legal debate centered around whether skim milk powder represented a like product with raw milk such that the production controls in place on milk justified the quota for skim milk powder.

[48] Former Ministry of Agriculture official. Interview by author. Tokyo, 8 December 1998.

[49] *Japan — Restrictions on Imports of Certain Agricultural Products*, GATT Doc. L/6253 (18 November 1987).

[50] Former MAFF official. Interview by author. Tokyo, 7 May 1999.

accept the full panel report during the December meeting even in the face of complete isolation as country after country joined the United States to call on Japan to accept the report (Sakuma 1988, 5).

However, the legal ruling changed the stakes for Japan. Two months later, the government accepted the panel report in full.[51] The following comments from two high-level officials involved in the negotiations explain the change in position:

> In December we said to go to the end resisting. But then it became a choice of leave GATT or follow the ruling—only two options.[52] In the end of course we had to follow the rules. Then we could use the budget for a domestic adjustment policy. Japan has to operate within GATT rules, unless it were some policy where we would all lose the next election and then maybe we would not be able to accept.[53]

> Japan rejected the panel in the first GATT Council meeting, but then the government was criticized by other countries and by the media and Japanese society. The criticism was along the lines that Japan as a GATT member should support the GATT rulings. Companies were also concerned about not raising the risk of retaliation. Generally, though, it was support for the panel process of GATT rather than retaliation fears that motivated the decision. The feeling was that Japan should respect the GATT.[54]

In short, the legal ruling had changed the domestic and international political pressures for liberalization. Japanese policymakers were uncomfortable with Japan standing in opposition to international law, and countries used the ruling to claim that Japan was obligated to open its agricultural markets.

The favorable public opinion toward using international law to settle trade disputes is evident in a 1999 poll. Although this survey question was not asked during the period of the negotiation in 1988, it is relevant since it was conducted after a WTO panel had ruled against Japan in a case related to agricultural trade.[55] Table 5.3 shows that the impor-

---

[51] While the government noted its difficulty implementing the ruling on starch and dairy products, in legal terms, this note was not a reservation of legal rights, and Japan had fully accepted the panel ruling.

[52] GATT rules actually do not call for expelling members, but this exaggeration by the official may reflect the feeling that rejecting the ruling would have been tantamount to isolation within the trade system.

[53] Official of LDP Policy Affairs Research Council. Interview by author. Tokyo, 10 May 1999.

[54] MAFF official. Interview by author. Tokyo, 8 December 1998.

[55] The United States complained that Japan's administration of quarantine bans for varietal testing of apples and other products was not justified on a scientific basis. A WTO

TABLE 5.3
Public Support for Settling Trade Disputes by International Law

Should Japan resolve trade disputes in WTO Dispute Settlement Proceedings?	
Yes, because it is important to settle disputes according to international law.	48.9%
Yes, because rulings in favor of Japan will bring favorable settlement.	12.3
No, because it is important to have flexible process that takes into consideration bilateral relations.	10.0
No, because Japan would have to follow negative rulings.	7.8
Do not know (or other).	21.0

Source: *Yoron chōsa nenkan* (Opinion Survey Yearbook) (Tokyo, 1999), 102.
Note: Responses to 1999 Prime Minister's Office Survey asking the following question: The number of trade disputes brought to the WTO is increasing. Among the following statements, which most closely reflects your thinking about resolving trade disputes related to Japan in the WTO?

tance of following international law was the most frequently given reason for supporting resolution of trade disputes in the formal dispute settlement proceedings.

There is a strong political consensus that Japan should follow its international commitments. Politicians did not publicly dispute the fact that Japan would have to comply with the ruling. The concern that Japan act as a good international citizen reflects both public sentiment and the diplomatic sensitivities of a country that has a negative historical legacy to overcome. Yet even right-wing politicians who make controversial statements about Japan's war history do not direct their conservative rhetoric to advocate that Japan should withdraw from its international commitments to the UN, GATT, or other multilateral institutions.

On several occasions during interviews, politicians and officials mentioned that the Japanese Constitution subordinates domestic law to international law. They were referring to chapter 10, article 98, which states, "The treaties concluded by Japan and established laws of nations shall be faithfully observed." The preamble to the constitution also reconciles the concepts of national sovereignty and international rules in

---

panel was established at U.S. request on November 18, 1997. On October 27, 1998, the panel issued its report on the case, "Japan—Measures Affecting Agricultural Products" (WT/DS76/R), which found that Japan had acted inconsistently with the SPS Agreement in its bans related to plant quarantine policies. Japan appealed the ruling but accepted the final violation ruling by the Appellate Body issued February 22, 1999 (WT/DS76/AB/R).

the statement: "We believe that no nation is responsible to itself alone, but that laws of political morality are universal; and that obedience to such laws is incumbent upon all nations who would sustain their own sovereignty and justify their sovereign relationship with other nations."

Both the sense of international obligation and Japan's trade interests in the system of rules made politicians reluctant to disregard GATT rulings. Typical is the view expressed by a senior politician and former minister of agriculture, Masami Tanabu. He supported the government decision to follow the GATT 12 panel ruling and a more recent 1999 WTO ruling regarding apple imports even though his district of Aomori-ken has a heavy concentration of apple growers who would suffer under the GATT 12 panel recommendation for liberalization of apple juice and the WTO panel recommendation to end the ban on fresh apple imports. In spite of his constituency interests against liberalization, he said that he supported changing the policies because "Japan is an economic power and must follow the rules. Just like with sports, we must all play by the same rules."[56]

The GATT Panels and Beef and Citrus Liberalization

The beef and citrus talks had been on hold, but now the United States used the GATT dispute process to signal it would not negotiate on the basis of quota expansion. The United States filed a GATT complaint on beef and citrus quotas in March 1988, immediately after Japan had accepted the ruling on the other quota policy items. U.S. Agriculture Secretary Lyng said at the time, "We are firm in our position that the import quotas on beef and citrus products and related measures that restrict consumer access to imports be removed. Both Ambassador Yeutter and I have repeatedly told the Japanese that we will not negotiate a new agreement that does not provide for complete liberalization."[57] Placing the negotiation in the GATT process framed the issue as the GATT legal status of the domestic program itself and not just the level of U.S. imports. This made it impossible for Japan to begin negotiations with proposals of quota expansion. The subsequent submission of independent GATT complaints against Japan's beef quota by Australia and New Zealand further reduced the prospect for Japan to cut side deals to avoid comprehensive reform.

The result of the GATT case on twelve agricultural commodities ap-

---

[56] Interview by author. Tokyo, 3 February 1999.
[57] *Los Angeles Times*, 5 May 1988.

plied considerable leverage on Japan to force a settlement on the beef-
orange case (Sakuma 1988, 94). Given the similarity of the legal issues,
the ruling on the GATT case for the twelve agricultural commodities
removed any doubt that Japan's quantitative restrictions on beef and
citrus would also be ruled GATT illegal. A USTR negotiator for the case
later remarked that when they won the GATT 12 case, U.S. negotiators
knew that Japan's protection policies for beef and even rice were now
vulnerable.[58] In Japan, LDP leaders, farm group representatives, and
newspaper reports all expressed the belief that the GATT 12 report
meant that Japan's beef and citrus policies were also in violation of
GATT.[59] In this case, the GATT dispute settlement process gave clear
information that Japan would eventually face the choice of either accepting full reform as recommended by the panel or rejecting a GATT
ruling against its policies backed by wide international opinion. By
shaping the perceived alternative to a negotiated settlement on the beef
and citrus negotiation, the GATT 12 case made Japanese negotiators
more willing to compromise.[60]

Both reputational and normative stakes dictated against ignoring the
expected negative ruling. The government would find it hard to veto a
ruling given Japan's status as one of the primary beneficiaries of the
GATT rules, which maintain market access for Japanese exports. Media
reports linked Japan's decision on this case with future criticism of Japan and its need to set an example given its potential to influence other
countries.[61] An editorial by a major daily newspaper said, "It is a matter
of course that one changes protection policies that violate international
rules."[62] LDP Secretary General Shintarō Abe issued a statement in
March that there was little question Japan would have to follow a rul-

[58] USTR official. Interview by author. Washington, DC, 3 April 2000.

[59] LDP Secretary General Shintarō Abe acknowledged that because Japanese government policies stimulated domestic production of beef, it would be difficult to win a case
before a GATT panel (*Asahi shimbun*, 25 March 1988). This policy clearly conflicted with
the GATT requirement that quotas are permissible only when necessary because of government policies to reduce domestic production. An agriculture cooperative official later
wrote about the negotiation that "once the GATT 12 recommendation came out, it deep-
ened the belief that beef and citrus were also in violation of GATT" (Ishikura 1988, 222).
The Japanese media reported that the panel would surely rule against Japan, and this
would mandate liberalization within two years (*Asahi shimbun*, 5 May 1988).

[60] Odell (2000, 155) makes this point in his discussion of this negotiation. Porges
(1994) also emphasizes the interconnectedness of U.S. strategy for the GATT 12 and beef
and citrus negotiations.

[61] *Asahi shimbun*, 25 May 1988.

[62] *Asahi shimbun*, 27 May 1988.

ing.[63] One MAFF negotiator said in an interview, "Japan has to accept panel decisions. Japan also starts its own panels with complaints against others, and so it cannot disregard rulings itself and then demand that other countries follow rulings."[64] These statements reflect both the pressure of international obligation and concern that refusal to follow a ruling would damage Japan's trade reputation.

Japanese officials first tried to delay the establishment of a panel on the beef and citrus issue by blocking the U.S. request for a panel in April.[65] However, harsh criticism from the United States, other GATT members, and within Japan led the government to accept the panel at the next GATT Council meeting in early May 1988. If Japan blocked a panel or later ignored a GATT ruling against its programs, U.S. retaliation was a certainty and would have more legitimacy with the backing of a GATT ruling against Japan's policy. U.S. Trade Representative Clayton Yeutter stated in a press briefing, "We will be a lot harder to deal with when we have a GATT panel report."[66] U.S. officials said that if Japan continued to refuse to end the quotas, they would consider retaliation against Japanese products valued at more than 1.5 billion dollars in trade a year.[67]

Industry groups in Japan focused on agricultural issues more during this period and lobbied for liberalization. In early 1988 Nikkeiren, the Japan Federation of Employers' Associations, issued a report calling for agricultural liberalization as a means of reducing food costs and providing an alternative to wage increases. Keidanren also pushed for agricultural liberalization and warned in its 1988 *White Paper on the Food Industry* that protection "cost jobs and tax revenues by forcing the Japanese food-processing industry to go offshore."[68] Sanctions by the United States against Japan's industrial exports were perceived as a certainty if Japan opposed a ruling.[69] Given that the U.S. market was the largest single destination for Japanese exports, the prospect of retaliation gave rise to serious concern among export firms, who had the most

[63] *Asahi shimbun*, 25 March 1988.

[64] Former MAFF official. Interview by author. Tokyo, 21 January 1999.

[65] This resistance may have been in part a show of resolve for the sake of an important election that month to be held in the orange-producing district in Saga-ken, a prefecture where nearly one-third of all voters are farmers and where the opposition was holding up agriculture as a major voting issue (Nagao 1990, 93).

[66] *Chicago Tribune*, 5 May 1988.

[67] *Washington Post*, 4 May 1988.

[68] Keidanren report as summarized in Porges (1994, 242).

[69] *Asahi shimbun*, 24 March 1988.

to fear from the escalation of trade friction that would result from a refusal to settle the GATT dispute.

In contrast to earlier negotiations, the legal framing of the negotiation structure this time made it more difficult for Japanese agricultural groups to mobilize their influence against liberalization. The GATT panels shut out interest groups through closing off information during the panel arguments and framing the issues in terms of legality rather than interests. An official from Zenchū complained about this lack of transparency, saying that the GATT panel procedures represent a process that is like a court except that it is a strange court where information is not made public — MAFF and MOFA officials from Japan participate in panel sessions, but they are not allowed to discuss the proceedings. He cited the problem that for panel cases, "the panel participants are not agriculture experts and instead they are lawyers arguing and thinking about law."[70]

This process is difficult for interest groups to penetrate. They could still lobby the Japanese government directly, but the only way to influence the panel outcome was the legal argumentation by the Japanese representatives who spoke to the panel. The government formed a common position to present to the panel in a process of consultation among politicians and officials from different ministries and within the Ministry of Agriculture. However, Zenchū was not consulted at this stage. A high-level Agriculture Ministry official involved in the negotiation commented that while in other negotiations he frequently consulted with the main farm lobby, Zenchū, during the GATT 12 panel negotiation he had no contact with interest groups.[71] In the GATT 12 case, he said contacts with farm groups were limited to those at a lower level, such as between the Livestock Bureau of MAFF and the Dairy Council. The official went on to explain the lack of more extensive consultations, saying that "It was too technical . . . this is the nature of the GATT process." Following the beef-citrus liberalization, the director of Zenchū, Iwao Yamaguchi, explained that the agriculture groups had not been able to protest as strongly against liberalization during this third phase of the negotiations compared with prior talks. He said, "This negotiation was a talk between nations. We were no more than one group" (Nagao 1990, 94). By transforming the negotiation into a dis-

[70] Official of Zenchū. Interviews by author. Tokyo, 30 October 1998, and 28 May 1999 (follow-up interview).

[71] The official specifically referred to the Uruguay Round as an example of a negotiation that involved such frequent consultations with Zenchū. Ministry of Agriculture official. Interview by author. Tokyo, 7 May 1999.

cussion of legal principles and international politics, the GATT panel reduced the lobbying influence of the agricultural groups.

Arguments about political sensitivity carried little weight in the legal context of the negotiation. During the earlier negotiations in the 1980s, the Diet had passed two unanimous resolutions against liberalization. As the United States took the beef and citrus case to GATT, the LDP policy committee for agriculture passed a resolution against liberalization.[72] Timing was particularly risky for the LDP because the agreement came in the year before an election and at a time when the LDP was trying to pass a politically unpopular consumption tax. Yet these political problems had no bearing on the legal discussions of the GATT DSP negotiation. The MAFF negotiator, Hiroya Sano (1988, 9–10), said that while the government could argue that it was politically unable to end the quotas in 1984, this argument was not possible in 1988.

The move to the GATT panel process increased the input from other ministries and high-level politicians who favored concessions on agricultural liberalization. Within the GATT process, MAFF had to rely on MOFA and even MITI for advice on how to shape its arguments (Eichmann 1990, 38). Then during the final decision-making stage, senior politicians were involved and the prime minister intervened at critical junctures.[73] On the one hand, the technical nature of discussions and third-party mediation during the panel depoliticizes issues, and it reduces the influence of interest groups. On the other hand, in government policy circles, going before a quasi-court as a nation elevates the negotiation above the bureaucratic level of annual U.S.-Japan agricultural negotiations. MAFF remained the key ministry for actual policy questions on the agricultural issues, but it had less autonomy.

In Japan, intervention by senior politicians tends to favor liberalization. Higher-level politicians are concerned about maintaining good relations with the United States and appearing as a national leader, and also with earning the support of big business. It is politicization at the lower levels of rank-and-file members where there is danger that politicians will only consider their district's farm interests. A former MAFF negotiator explained that the senior politicians are secure in their electoral district, so they focus on building their broader political reputation and fundraising capability, while junior politicians must still curry favor from farm groups to maintain their seat.[74]

The political debate at the time reveals the perception that a GATT

---

[72] *Asahi shimbun*, 28 March 1988.
[73] Former MAFF official. Interview by author. Tokyo, 18 March 1999.
[74] Former MAFF official. Interview by author. Tokyo, 17 January 1999.

ruling would lower domestic political costs. Many politicians favored letting both the GATT 12 and also the beef-citrus negotiations go before a GATT panel because they felt that it would be politically easier to explain a liberalization decision to farmers when there was a ruling that the policy violated international law.[75] Politicians would have less fear of backlash from farmers if the ruling legitimated the need for liberalization and reduced the accountability of any one politician for the outcome. One former MAFF official with long experience in U.S.-Japan agricultural trade negotiations said WTO/GATT panels were preferable to bilateral negotiations even when Japan faced the same pressure from the United States. He explained:

> For domestic persuasion it is better to discuss the issue in a multilateral setting. If the decision is made by a neutral panel, then people think that there is nothing for it but to follow.[76] Although the United States is sponsoring the issue, the U.S. face is not seen. Domestically, people want a more equal relationship. For apples [the 1998 quarantine case] it was better for the United States to bring it to the WTO.

For Japanese officials and the public, change mandated by "international consensus" as determined by a GATT panel was more legitimate than unilateral U.S. demands.

The assumption that Japan would eventually follow a ruling if one were forthcoming — no matter how harsh its consequences — shaped the decision to liberalize beef and citrus quotas before the panel made a ruling. It led the government to choose a third option — early settlement. The GATT process allows for parties to reach a bilateral deal at any time during the dispute mediation process in what resembles an out-of-court settlement. There are several advantages to such a deal. Settlement before a panel ruling against the policy allows greater flexibility for attaching conditions to the agreement and also avoids a high-profile trade dispute and legal precedent. The Japanese media, Ministry of Agriculture officials, and LDP politicians discussed the pros and cons of waiting for a ruling or making an early settlement.[77] In the end, it was decided that by concluding the negotiation bilaterally before the GATT

---

[75] Newspaper reports (see, for example, *Financial Times*, 6 May 1988, and *New York Times*, 21 June 1988) and interviews with negotiators and politicians all referred to this perception.

[76] The official said "*shikatta ga nai*" (Japan must follow) to explain the Japanese public's attitude. This phrase carries a sense of resignation to something inevitable and is common in Japanese.

[77] *Nihon nōgyō shimbun*, 9 June 1988.

ruling, they could gain more adjustment time for farmers.[78] In consideration of the large number of Japanese farmers producing beef and oranges, the government felt it had to get the best terms possible. Koichi Katō, a leading LDP politician who had been closely involved in the decision, explained afterward in a newspaper interview that given the expectation of a harsh ruling against Japan's policy by the panel, it was better to reach an early compromise.[79]

Japan's negotiators were able to use their bargaining leverage from early settlement to gain transition measures. The final settlement called for full liberalization of the Japanese beef and citrus markets to be phased in through raising the quota ceilings annually for three years, replacing the quotas with tariffs in 1991, and then reducing the tariff rates thereafter. A GATT recommendation would likely have mandated ending the quotas in two years. Under the shadow of the forthcoming ruling, the government chose to end the quotas while seeking to reduce the shock to Japan's farmers.

The speed of reaching the agreement reflected political intervention by Prime Minister Noboru Takeshita. After the establishment of the GATT panel in May, a settlement was made in June, before the panel even met for its first session. Following the London Summit meeting in early June, the prime minister instructed negotiators to make an agreement before the G7 Summit Meeting in Toronto on June 20. He wanted a quick agreement so that he could demonstrate his leadership skills on the international stage.[80] On the night before the summit, Japanese negotiators reached agreement with the United States.

The outcome represented major liberalization, even when taking into consideration the transitional period conditions attached to the agreement.[81] First, Japan agreed to end the quotas. Equally important were changes in domestic marketing requirements. The government ended both the domestic content mixing requirements for orange juice and price-setting in the beef market by the quasi-governmental Livestock

---

[78] Former MAFF official. Interview by author. Tokyo, 21 January 1999.

[79] *Nihon nōgyō shimbun*, 24 June 1988.

[80] *Asahi shimbun*, 9 June 1988; former Ministry of Agriculture official. Interview by author. Tokyo, 18 March 1999.

[81] In practice, the phased-in transition meant that while some quotas were ended in 1988, other quotas were expanded in size in a transition schedule leading up to their elimination in 1990 or 1991. Following quota elimination, the government could use 70 percent tariffs, which would decrease incrementally each subsequent year. In some of the categories, such as dairy and starch, there were minor measures fully liberalizing some products while extending quota protection on other products for several years of transition. By 1994 the last of these quotas was eliminated. See Masuda (1998, 220).

Industry Promotion Corporation. The agreement would allow imports to directly enter the Japanese market. American officials were reported to be fully satisfied with the agreement at the time.[82] A report by the American Chamber of Commerce in Japan (ACCJ 1997, 115) gave a very positive assessment of the outcome. On a scale of 1 to 10 (with 10 being the best evaluation), beef exporters gave the agreement a perfect rating, while evaluations by citrus exporters ranged from 7 to 10.

Regarding the agreement on twelve agricultural items for which there had been a GATT ruling, the degree of policy change for each item varied according to both the specific ruling on the item by GATT and the political sensitivities in Japan. Among the ten items ruled as a violation, the milk products quota and starch quota were the most politically controversial for the Japanese government because of the anticipated impact on the large dairy and potato (starch) industries and because of the legal precedent.[83] Japan delayed ending these two quotas for five years in order to liberalize the quota in the context of the Uruguay Round negotiation. However, beginning in 1988, the government granted expanded quota access and liberalized other items within the quota categories such as ice cream, which led the ACCJ report to give the dairy agreement a rating of 7 (ibid., 119). A lower rating of 4 to 5 was given to the agreement on dried beans, which was one of the two policies where the GATT panel ruled that Japan's policy was not GATT illegal and hence the quota remained unchanged. On the question of pineapple products, which were especially sensitive because pineapple production is entirely in Okinawa, where U.S. military bases are the source of political tensions, the United States accepted a modest reform to end the quota while allowing other measures to guarantee continued production for Japanese pineapple growers.[84]

Real market changes were apparent. The share of imports in the total domestic beef market rose from 31 percent in 1986 to 55 percent in 1995, while imports of orange juice quadrupled, and imports of apple juice (one of the ten items in the GATT 12 panel) tripled (ibid.; Jussaume 1994). There was no clear evidence of bias favoring the United States. Indeed, Brazil captured much of the orange market increase, and EC exports gained most of the expanded market for dry

[82] *New York Times*, 21 June 1988.

[83] MAFF official. Interview by author. Tokyo, 7 May 1999.

[84] In an unusual new arrangement, imported pineapple products would be duty free when mixed at a fixed rate with Japanese pineapples, but the imports would face a high tariff when not mixed with Japanese products. MAFF officials were quoted stating that their repeated emphasis of the base problem during the negotiation led the U.S. negotiators to accept this measure (*Nihon nōgyō shimbun* 22 July 1988).

TABLE 5.4
Growth in Imports Following 1988 Agreement

	Legal Ruling	Imports, 1988–1996 (percent increase)
Beef	none	130%
Oranges	none	34
Tomato juice	violation	890
Apple juice	violation	1,941
Milk	violation	201
Pineapples	violation	174
Peanuts	nonviolation	−19
Dried beans	nonviolation	−19

Source: FAO (2001).

Note: Increase in total quantity of imports comparing annual imports in 1988 with annual imports in 1996.

milk. Australia and New Zealand were satisfied with the Japanese offer on beef and dropped their GATT complaints.

Table 5.4 shows the import growth following the agreement. Growth is measured from the base year of 1988, which gives the quantity of imports when the quotas remained intact, and the final year of 1996, when the reforms were fully implemented.[85] Among the GATT 12 products, the items that were ruled illegal by the panel experienced high import growth—imports of apple juice, for example, increased by 19 times the original import quantity. On the other hand, for beef and citrus products, Japan made a settlement with the United States before the panel ruled, and they experienced more modest import growth. Beef imports more than doubled in total import quantity while orange imports grew by a third. The only reduction in imports occurred for the two products that received a compliance ruling from the GATT panel. Other factors related to demand and supply are not taken into consideration here, so these figures represent only a simple measure of the effect of the agreement on market changes.

As MAFF announced the agreement, it also entered discussions with the Ministry of Finance regarding compensation to help ease the income loss for Japanese farmers. Months later, the Diet approved a $616 mil-

[85] Some of the Uruguay Round implementation is also conflated in these figures since the two agreements overlap in time period of implementation. The table shows the import quantities for canned pineapples, ground nuts, and evaporated milk products. These were the specific items under quota considered by the GATT 12 panel.

lion supplemental budget for immediate agricultural adjustment measures, which included a subsidy of 9,064 dollars per acre of orange production land converted for production of alternative crops.[86] All tariff receipts from liberalization were also designated for use as agricultural adjustment funding.

The political costs from this agreement were high: the LDP lost its majority in the Upper House election in 1989. Although a major corruption scandal and introduction of an unpopular consumption tax hurt the LDP in this election, anger in rural areas over the liberalization decision was often given along with these other reasons as a major factor in the electoral defeat (Kobayashi 1991, Yamaji and Ito 1993). Particularly noteworthy was the LDP loss of votes in rural areas (Kobayashi 1991, 93). Several incumbent politicians were selectively punished for the liberalization agreements, as witnessed by the fact that Nōkyō members campaigned for opposition candidates and the LDP lost six out of seven seats in beef- and orange-producing districts (George 1990, 117). One LDP politician who lost his seat, Tokuichirō Tamazawa, said in an interview that farmer anger over the beef liberalization agreement cost him the election.[87] Farmers were also angry over the 1987 decision by the Nakasone government to cut the producers' rice price set by the government.

Public opinion polls showed that the sharpest drop in LDP support over the period from 1986 to 1989 was among farmers, who recorded a 15 percent reduction of their support for the LDP, while at the same time LDP popularity among all groups declined by 11 percent (Curtis 1999). One poll showed that only 54 percent of farmers voted for LDP candidates in the 1989 Upper House election, whereas 77 percent of farmers had voted for the LDP in the 1986 election (ibid., 48). The downward trend for the LDP continued, and the LDP number of seats won in the Lower House election dropped from 300 in 1986 to 275 in the 1990 election.[88] The weakness in rural districts was particularly alarming for a party where rural strength was the source of its power base.

The electoral punishment appeared to focus on the beef-district politicians. A former MAFF negotiator said that agriculture groups did not blame any politician for the liberalization of other quota items that

---

[86] Porges (1994, 256) reports the budget as 104.4 billion yen. This converts to 616 million dollars given the 1988 exchange rate of 169.36 yen/dollar.

[87] Interview by author. Tokyo, 8 March 1999.

[88] *Asahi shimbun, Japan Almanac 1998* (Tokyo: Asahi Shimbun) 64.

were eliminated following the panel ruling.[89] He said that given the panel ruling, nobody could be blamed since Japan had ratified GATT rules and could not evade its legal obligations. The agreement for beef and citrus was greeted with more domestic backlash because of its large impact on domestic agriculture as well as the early settlement before a panel ruling. Agriculture groups were reported to be angry at the appearance that the government had surrendered without resistance (Asano 1988, 10). There had been strong resistance to making a concession prior to a summit meeting.[90] Therefore, the fact that, despite these objections, the agreement was timed around the summit may have worsened the political perception that Japan had given in to the United States in the beef and citrus agreement.

In summary, the legal framing of negotiations in the GATT dispute settlement procedures changed the domestic debate in three ways: first, it added credibility to the U.S. demand and shaped the negotiation options; second, the legitimacy of the GATT ruling made it easier for Japan to accept liberalization as necessary for both its trade interests and its obligation to international society; and third, the legalistic nature of the negotiation made it more difficult for agriculture interest groups and MAFF officials to dominate the policy process. The credible U.S. threat raised the costs of refusing to end the quotas, while the normative pressure and policy process diffused the domestic political opposition.

Conclusions from Three Phases of Negotiations

Over the three sets of negotiations on agricultural quotas, the U.S. demanded full liberalization while Japan tried to grant only minor reform. Evidence is strong that farmers continued to wield considerable political influence over the Japanese government position. Generous compensation accompanied liberalization, indicating that budget constraints were not the primary concern. Indeed, liberalizing these commodities while not reforming rice policy only hindered efforts to restructure Japan's agricultural sector.

Broadening the stakes created pressure for liberalization. In the first negotiation, the simultaneous bilateral and multilateral negotiations led the United States to enlarge the stakes on the beef and citrus issue by stating that a beef and citrus agreement was critical for the success of

[89] Former MAFF official. Interview by author. Tokyo, 17 January 1999.
[90] *Nihon nōgyō shimbun*, 8 June 1988.

the Tokyo Round. Nevertheless, the weakly institutionalized issue linkage between agricultural talks and the other parts of the trade round reduced the credibility of the U.S. claim that elimination of agricultural quota policies by Japan was necessary for the completion of the round. Business and MITI favored completion of the Tokyo Round, but they did not push hard on agricultural issues in particular. MAFF negotiators were able to limit the amount of reform to narrow concessions favoring the United States and leave intact many of the GATT-illegal quotas.

However, threats alone fail to account for outcomes. In the second set of negotiations in the early 1980s, the United States threatened that without beef and citrus reform, protectionist sentiment in Congress would lead directly to legislation blocking Japanese-manufactured imports. This mobilized industrial groups in Japan to lobby for agricultural reform, but at the same time it also raised domestic opposition. Boycotts by farm groups brought a quick end to business group statements on agricultural trade policy. Retaliatory threats failed to bring negotiations to conclusion for two years, and it was the prospect of a GATT complaint and request for mediation that pushed Japan to make a settlement in 1984.

The GATT dispute settlement process added new leverage in addition to U.S. threats by providing a credible alternative scenario of pressure for comprehensive reform backed by a legitimate authority. In the second phase negotiation in 1984, GATT dispute settlement as the alternative to no agreement persuaded Japan to cut another bilateral deal for quota expansion. In the third set of negotiations in 1988, using the GATT dispute process moved the question from the level of protection to the means of protection. Adding reputational and normative stakes increased the costs of noncooperation for Japan. By thus reshaping the choices available and clarifying the standards of evaluation, the institution made the cooperative outcome for quota elimination the best choice for Japan. In doing so, it forestalled either a partial outcome of quota expansion or the U.S. implementation of trade sanctions.

The context of the negotiation also altered the domestic policy process. In comparison with the bilateral negotiation in the early 1980s, in the 1988 negotiations with high legal framing, agricultural groups encountered greater difficulty to lobby against liberalization, and the Ministry of Agriculture had less autonomy. Business groups voiced their concerns, and intervention by senior politicians dictated a broader set of priorities.

In light of strong support for the GATT system and international law in Japan, there was wide consensus that Japan could not ignore a negative ruling against its policies. This shaped the decision in the GATT 12 case, where there was a violation ruling, and in the beef and citrus case, where both sides anticipated that a panel would rule against Japan's quota policies. In both disputes, by creating a sense of international obligation and signaling about negotiation outcomes, legal framing brought liberalization.

6

Linkages in Comprehensive Negotiations

In 1990 THE GATT system seemed on the verge of disaster as differences over agricultural issues threatened to cause the collapse of the Uruguay Round. Stubbornly refusing to consider importing even a grain of rice, Japan stood among the culprits responsible for the problems of the negotiation. At the same time, regional trade areas flourished. Japan along with Australia had taken the lead to establish the Asia-Pacific Economic Cooperation forum as a new model for an informal regional association. However, four years later the Uruguay Round was heralded as a success after having produced broad liberalization across sectors, including agriculture. Overturning the predictions of many, Japan agreed to import 4 to 8 percent of its domestic rice consumption. On the other hand, the APEC talks had failed to produce substantial liberalization. In a showdown with the United States in 1998, Japan refused to modify its fishery and forestry trade policies. Cooperation proved more difficult for the APEC negotiation than for the Uruguay Round, in spite of the fact that fishermen wield less domestic political clout than rice farmers. Given that both negotiations involved multiple countries and multiple sectors with large potential for mutual gains, what accounts for the different outcomes?

In the context of Japanese politics, the agreement for partial opening of the rice market represented a major political step. The import of rice required the overhaul of the entire food control system and large budget outlays for compensation payment to rural regions. The deal transformed Japan from a closed market into the top U.S. rice export market, and other rice-exporting states, such as Thailand, Australia, and China, also benefited. In contrast, even as Japan replaced its rice import quota with tariffs in 1998, it continued to uphold quotas for some fish products as the last remaining GATT-illegal quantitative restrictions.

This chapter examines the two negotiations in terms of the institutionalization of the cross-sector linkage and the normative pressure from the agenda. Whereas the Uruguay Round represented a negotiation with a strongly institutionalized linkage and moderate legal framing, APEC provides an example of a weakly institutionalized linkage with a low degree of legal framing. The analysis of this chapter will show how these differences in the negotiation structure help explain why liberalization of politically sensitive items was possible in the Uruguay Round, but not in APEC. Since both negotiations involved less legal framing than the GATT dispute cases discussed in the previous chapter, the case study analysis here focuses primarily on the variation along the dimension of the institutionalization of the issue linkage in a comprehensive negotiation.

The Uruguay Round: Ending the Rice Import Ban

No sooner had the implementation of the Tokyo Round agreements concluded than calls for a new trade round began. Dissatisfaction with agricultural trade affairs gave rise to some of the urgency for another round. The GATT ministerial meeting in 1982 stated in its final document that efforts must be made "to bring agriculture more fully into the multilateral trading system by improving the effectiveness of GATT rules and to seek to improve terms of access to markets and to bring export competition under greater discipline" (Fitchett 1987, 168). At that meeting, the United States first proposed launching the eighth GATT negotiation round. Thereafter, momentum grew for a comprehensive effort to address problems in the trade system, such as agricultural trade friction, and to extend the rules to new areas, such as services and intellectual property rights. By 1986 preparations had begun to lay the groundwork for beginning the negotiation and establishing an agenda.

Japan had high expectations that it would benefit from a Uruguay Round agreement restraining U.S. unilateral trade measures, opening industrial goods markets, and providing guidelines for services and investment. As a trade-dependent country, Japan had the most to fear from the growing trend toward protectionism and the aggressive bilateral trade policy of the United States. Officials hoped the new round would satisfy some of the U.S. trade concerns and lead to the elimination of the U.S. section 301 policy.[1] The government actively participated in the service negotiations and had objectives to make gains for Japan's interests in the area of new rules for antidumping policies, a common trade barrier used against Japanese exports, as well as intellectual property right protection, which was important for a country with Japan's strength in technology development (Mizoguchi and Matsuō 1994, 210). Nevertheless, agriculture was the Achilles heel for Japan. Leaders faced the dilemma that any talk about negotiating rice policy

[1] Former MITI official. Interview by author. Tokyo, 3 June 1999.

would raise controversy at home, but other countries would agree to the new round only if agriculture was included on the agenda.

The United States insisted that there could not be any trade agreement without progress in agricultural liberalization, and the newly formed Cairns Group (fourteen agricultural exporting nations) issued a paper threatening to walk out of the negotiations if their goal for agricultural liberalization was not achieved (Preeg 1995, 58). Developing nations, which were reluctant to include liberalization of services on the agenda, viewed agricultural liberalization as a critical area for potential gains. Japan and the EC reluctantly agreed to include agriculture on the negotiation agenda. The Punta del Este Ministerial Declaration, which launched the Uruguay Round in September 1986, gave a broad mandate for the agriculture negotiation group with the following statement: "Negotiations shall aim to achieve greater liberalization of trade in agriculture and bring all measures affecting import access and export competition under strengthened and more operationally effective GATT rules and disciplines" (Croome 1995, 387).

From the start, the Uruguay Round set a broad agenda that lay the foundation for cross-sector linkage. Fifteen negotiation groups would address topics ranging from traditional issues like tariffs for trade in goods to new issues such as services and investment rules.[2] The Punta del Este Declaration linked these fifteen negotiation groups with the statement that "the launching, the conduct and the implementation of the outcome of the negotiations shall be treated as parts of a single undertaking" (ibid., 383). At the ministerial meeting, nations agreed that failure of any negotiation group would stop the entire negotiation. The oft-repeated refrain, "nothing is agreed until everything is agreed," reflected an effort to maintain fairness and avoid neglecting the interests of any group through a partial agreement (ibid., 34). Countries favoring agricultural liberalization wanted to use the linkage to push for more agricultural reforms. On the other hand, countries like Japan hoped that addressing agricultural issues within a broader context would divert attention away from the area and lead others to accept modest agricultural reforms in a compromise for the sake of the larger package. From these contradictory expectations came the agreement to negotiate agriculture as one negotiating group linked with other groups by a com-

---

[2] The fifteen groups were as follows: tariffs, nontariff measures, natural resource base products, textiles, agriculture, tropical products, subsidies, safeguards, GATT articles, dispute settlement, multilateral trade negotiation arrangements, functioning of the GATT system, trade-related aspects of intellectual property, trade-related investment procedures, and services. For an overview of the Uruguay Round, see Preeg (1995) or Croome (1995).

mitment to pursue joint agreement in all groups. Thereafter, the resolve of the United States and the Cairns Group to achieve substantial agricultural liberalization and the actions of the GATT director-general reinforced the cross-sector linkage.

The Uruguay Round incorporated a limited degree of legal framing, which is the negotiation structure dimension describing whether a negotiation occurs within the bounds of established rules and third-party mediation. Some topics in the round could have been raised as a discrete legal issue in a GATT panel, and Japan's rice import ban was a prime candidate for a complaint to a GATT panel.[3] Other topics, however, were new issues within the GATT system, such as service-sector negotiations, or talks over how to restructure the GATT rules themselves. Consequently, negotiators were not trying to judge the legal status of policies, and the negotiation did not resemble adjudication. Rather, negotiators sought an overall agreement that all participants could accept, and negotiations went forward as loosely structured bargaining. Some informal meetings took place between negotiators from only two states, while other meetings brought together ministers from all 117 participants. Third-party mediation occurred when the GATT director-general helped to coordinate positions and create a consensus position among participants. However, for the most part, issue linkage proved to be the driving force behind the negotiation. These aspects of legal framing, the potential for legal adjudication of some of the issues, and the mediation from the director-general, were effective because they increased momentum to pursue the negotiation as a single undertaking.

Putting Rice on the Negotiation Table

For Japan, it was difficult to consider talking about rice policy in an international forum. In the 1980s a common refrain by politicians declared that Japan should not import a single grain of rice. The Diet had passed unanimous resolutions in 1980 and 1984 calling for greater self-sufficiency in agriculture and opposing liberalization, particularly of rice. As the staple food in Japanese daily food consumption, rice accounts for 25 percent of the average Japanese individual's daily calorie

---

[3] Since no GATT panel explicitly made a ruling on the rice policy, its legal status was not certain. Later the 1988 GATT panel ruling against other Japanese agricultural quota policies made it reasonable to expect a complaint and violation ruling against the rice quota as well. A Japanese official of the GATT secretariat, Tamotsu Takase (1997, 11), refers to the rice policy as having been a violation of GATT rules.

intake (MAFF 1999, 83). More than half of all Japanese farm households are engaged in rice farming.[4] Consequently, agricultural cooperatives and rural politicians give top priority to the interests of rice farmers.
As the Uruguay Round got underway, the likelihood for rice liberalization appeared extremely low. Writing in 1988 and citing public statements by top political leaders in Japan, a leading scholar of Japanese
agricultural politics wrote that "rice is in a category of its own — a 'nonnegotiable' — and there are no indications that in the near future liberalization will be contemplated" (George 1988, 55).

Few voices in Japan advocated liberalization of agriculture, especially
not rice. Although the Ministry of Foreign Affairs generally takes a
more liberal position on economic policy and viewed compromise on
agriculture as a necessary step for Japan's foreign relations, one official
said that many thought it was "politically dangerous to touch upon
rice."[5] The Ministry of Agriculture and all political parties opposed reform. Consumer groups actively opposed liberalization, mostly because
of food safety concerns. In November 1986 a meeting of national consumer organizations passed a resolution against rice imports.[6] Even
public opinion polls showed little support for liberalization. In a poll by
the *Yomiuri shimbun* (1 December 1986), 65 percent of respondents
said they did not want to try eating imported Californian rice. More
specifically on the question of trade policy, a poll by the *Yomiuri shimbun* (9 February 1987) showed that 53.4 percent opposed rice liberalization while 37.4 percent were in favor.

Although many food industry companies and exporter associations
had an interest in agricultural liberalization, they avoided making proliberalization statements that could anger farmers and politicians. In a
January 1987 policy statement, Keidanren (1991, 16) took a cautious,
proreform position on agricultural policy; the statement focused on the
need for liberalization of inputs used in food processing and deregulation of the domestic retail process for rice, but it did not advocate ending the rice import restrictions. Agricultural reform was a lower priority
than other trade issues being brought up in the Uruguay Round, and a
Keidanren official said the organization was reluctant to risk angering
Nōkyō over the issue. Moreover, he said that the food industry subcommittee of Keidanren had less concern for rice liberalization because rice
is not a major raw material for processed food.[7] There are exceptions,

[4] In 1997, of a total of 2.47 million farm households (counting those with 3 hectares of
land or sales of at least 500,000 yen), 1.37 million households engaged in rice farming
(MAFF 1997).

[5] MOFA official. Interview by author. Tokyo, 27 May 1999.

[6] *Asahi shimbun*, 30 March 1987.

[7] Keidanren official. Interview by author. Tokyo, 9 August 1996.

such as the sake (rice wine) and sembei (rice cracker) industries, but for the most part, rice is consumed directly. This contrasts with sugar or dairy products, which are major inputs for the food industry such that high domestic prices undermined the competitiveness of Japan's food industry.

Japanese officials agreed to discuss rice policy in the Uruguay Round when faced with the alternative of a bilateral negotiation. The U.S. Rice Millers' Association (RMA) submitted a section 301 petition in 1986, thereby raising the prospect of a bilateral negotiation or a U.S. request to initiate GATT dispute settlement proceedings. Threats of unilateral sanctions were also a strong possibility given the political support for the RMA in Congress. The entire California congressional delegation urged the USTR to accept the case, and House agriculture subcommittee hearings also expressed support.[8] Japanese leaders strongly requested that the U.S. government not approve the petition. After meetings with top officials from Japan, USTR Clayton Yeutter decided to reject it while making a strong public announcement that in return, he expected the Japanese government to take positive steps to address the rice issue in the context of the Uruguay Round. By April 1987 the Japanese government publicly announced it would consider the U.S. demand for rice liberalization as part of the agricultural reform talks of the Uruguay Round.[9] The RMA submitted a second section 301 petition in 1988, but the same pattern repeated itself. Prime Minister Noboru Takeshita and 390 Diet members signed a letter to President Ronald Reagan urging him to reject the petition.[10] Yeutter accommodated those requests by once again turning down the petition while saying better results would be possible in the Uruguay Round.

The broad agenda helped persuade Japanese leaders to discuss rice policy since Japan would not be alone in addressing sensitive topics. Tsutomu Hata, who served as minister of agriculture at the time, later said that "when even the United States was putting its dairy, sugar, and peanuts on the table and others like France had difficulties, it was hardly conceivable that Japan could get an exception." He used this to explain to farm groups that Japan must discuss agriculture because others were also putting everything on the table.[11]

The multilateral setting promised to defuse the domestic backlash against the United States. An LDP policy statement on 14 September

---

[8] *Inside U.S. Trade*, 3 October 1986.

[9] *Asahi shimbun*, 24 October 1986; 9 April 1987.

[10] *Inside U.S. Trade*, 14 October 1988.

[11] Tsutomu Hata. Minshutō member of the House of Representatives and former minister of agriculture in two LDP cabinets. Interview by author. Tokyo, 9 June 1999.

1988, at the time of the second RMA petition, said that it would be a major political problem if the rice problem was discussed in any negotiation forum except for the Uruguay Round.[12] A leading LDP politician, Kōichi Katō, warned the United States that a demand to open the rice market would rouse anti-American feelings in the public.[13] Heeding such concerns, the U.S. State Department cautioned against bilateral talks on the rice issue. Cables from the Tokyo embassy reported that addressing rice through a section 301 petition would substantially harm diplomatic relations between the two countries. Later in 1988 Secretary of State George Schultz was alleged to have privately promised the Japanese that the United States would "never tackle the rice issue."[14] Given that congressional pressure made it impossible to drop the matter, both sides agreed that the broad context of the Uruguay Round would make it politically easier to discuss the issue. A USTR official said, "If Section 301 made the focal point on rice, the Japanese would feel picked upon and forced to resist doing anything. We had an informal understanding that they would do something [on rice] in the Uruguay Round."[15] Later Yeutter wrote about his decision to reject the two petitions by the rice industry:

> I was criticized for that here in the United States but rejecting those petitions made it possible to avoid major strains in U.S.-Japan relationships and also directed the focus of this issue to the Uruguay Round where it belongs. If there are to be significant changes in the agricultural policies of Japan, the United States, and other major trading nations, the proper forum is the Uruguay Round where we can all go down the reform road together.[16]

Uncertainty about the outcome made it politically easier to commit to negotiate about rice in the Uruguay Round. A broad agenda with many participants added new pressures, but it also left room to doubt whether any major reforms would emerge. The fact that the Tokyo Round had ended without significant agricultural liberalization reduced expectations that this round would be any different. An official from one of the agricultural interest groups said that his organization did not oppose the government promise to discuss rice liberalization in the Uruguay

[12] Liberal Democratic Party, "Kome no shijō kaihō ni tsuite no beikoku seimai gyōsha kyōkai (RMA) ni yoru shintsūshōhō dai301 jō teiso ni tsuite" (Remarks about the RMA Section 301 petition for rice market opening), duplicate of manuscript for remarks by LDP chief secretary, 14 September 1988.

[13] *Christian Science Monitor*, 20 May 1988.

[14] *Inside U.S. Trade*, 14 October 1988, 6; 5 December 1986.

[15] Former USTR official. Interview by author. Washington, DC, 4 April 2000.

[16] *Inside U.S. Trade*, 25 May 1990.

Round because they hoped to get support from France and other countries and thought the talks would go better than if Japan faced the United States alone in bilateral talks.[17] A MAFF official said that once Yeutter rejected the RMA petition, there was a sense of relief in the government, and not much attention was given to the prospect of negotiating rice policy in the Uruguay Round. In hindsight, they realized that had been "easy thinking."[18] Yet even if reforms were necessary, the negotiation would take at least four years, so politicians could temporarily delay hard choices.

On the other hand, by 1987 it was clear that Japan's rice policy would be very vulnerable on legal grounds if taken before a GATT panel. The GATT panel ruling against Japan's quota policies for twelve agricultural items in 1987 held strong implications for the rice import ban. A USTR negotiator of the case said, "When we won on GATT 12, we knew their defense on rice was lost."[19] Masami Tanabu, the minister of agriculture for an LDP cabinet during the Uruguay Round, concurred that "the GATT 12 panel ruling made it clear that rice also violated GATT."[20] If the rice policy had been brought before a GATT panel and found in violation, Japan would have faced the choice of full liberalization of rice or violation of GATT rules. In comparison, talking about rice policy in the uncertainty of the Uruguay Round seemed much more promising to Japanese leaders.

Once negotiations began, the Japanese government tried to keep a low profile in the agriculture negotiation group. At the time of the December 1988 mid-term meeting in Montreal, the United States hoped for a Japanese concession to break the stalemate. Reagan reportedly sent Takeshita a letter urging Japan to show "significant and recognizable developments in the reform of Japanese agricultural policy" (Sato 1996, 85). The letter reflected the U.S. expectation for Japan to deliver on its earlier promise to address rice opening in the Uruguay Round by announcing at this time that Japan would consider an agreement for partial opening. In response, Takeshita insisted that the negotiation had to include reforms by other nations before Japan would make its own concessions (ibid., 86). The Japanese position at the Montreal meeting called for clarifying existing GATT laws to authorize quantitative restrictions for basic food products such as rice. Only on the issue of export subsidies, which Japan does not use, did Japan's proposal advo-

---

[17] Former official of Zennōrin. Interview by author. Tokyo, 26 October 1998.
[18] Former MAFF official. Interview by author. Tokyo, 8 December 1998.
[19] Former USTR official. Interview by author. Washington, DC, 4 April 2000.
[20] Interview by author. Tokyo, 3 February 1999.

cate major changes. In this way, MAFF negotiators stalled while the United States and EC stood as the obstinate parties blocking agreement. Three months before the meeting, the Diet had passed by unanimous vote a resolution against liberalization of rice, and this had effectively eliminated any flexibility for Japan's negotiators on the issue.[21]

Strengthening the Single Undertaking Approach

The Brussels ministerial meeting in December 1990 was a turning point for the Uruguay Round. While the meeting itself ended in failure, this setback reinforced the credibility of the cross-sector linkage by showing that some nations were willing to risk the entire negotiation for the sake of achieving substantial agricultural liberalization. The meeting had been scheduled as the concluding session for the Uruguay Round. However, since deputy-level preparatory work had not made progress, a breakthrough was necessary at the ministerial level. In high-level talks in Geneva prior to the official meeting, U.S. officials demanded rice market opening. Clayton Yeutter insisted that a concession by Japan at this time was important to get the EC to compromise on export subsidies and to address concerns of developing nations that export rice.[22]

However, those who had hoped that senior political leaders would intervene to save the Uruguay Round were disappointed. Japanese officials refused either to make a concession on rice or to put forward new proposals for substantial reforms on other agricultural issues. When the negotiation group on agriculture was at a standstill and Agriculture Minister Tomio Yamamoto was told there were thirty minutes left for submission of revised negotiating proposals, he said that "no matter how much time passes, our position will not change."[23] When the chairman of the agriculture committee, Mats Hellström, put forward a proposal at the final session of the agriculture meeting, Japan was among

[21] "Kome no jiyūka hantai ni kan suru ketsugi" (Resolution against rice liberalization), passed by the Lower and Upper House in the 113rd Diet session on 20–21 September 1988. A Cabinet legal advisor told Diet members that such resolutions did not have legally binding force, but Diet members urged that in a Parliamentary system the cabinet should be held responsible to act on the expressed unanimous will of the Diet. Agriculture Minister Tomio Yamamoto responded that he agreed with the Diet members and felt responsibility to follow the resolution. *Shūgiin nōrinsuisan iinkai chōsashitsu* (Lower House Agriculture Committee Research Section), *Gatto uruguai raundo nōgyō kōshō kankei shiryo* (Documents regarding the GATT Uruguay Round agriculture negotiation) (January 1994): 107–109.

[22] *Nihon nōgyō shimbun*, 4 December 1990.

[23] *Nihon nōgyō shimbun*, 8 December 1990.

the first nations to voice its objections.[24] Yamamoto criticized the proposal for not reflecting Japan's position on basic food security and did not relent when Hellström asked in a private meeting with him that Japan consider just a small opening to rice imports. After Japan, Korea, and the EC said that they could not accept the proposal as a basis for negotiations, the Latin American agriculture export nations walked out, thereby ending the meeting without an agriculture agreement (Stewart 1993, 204).

The other negotiation groups had for the most part made sufficient progress to reach agreements within a few days.[25] However, these groups stalled to wait for progress in the agriculture negotiation group, and then the collapse of the agricultural talks led to suspension of the entire conference. The Brussels meeting demonstrated to everyone that lack of progress in agriculture negotiations would lead to failure of the entire round.

Japan's negotiation stance at the Brussels meeting clearly rejected U.S. requests that Japan show leadership to help break the stalemate. This is surprising given the timing at a sensitive moment in U.S.-Japan alliance relations. After Iraq's invasion of Kuwait, governments were absorbed by the unfolding Gulf crisis even while they were working toward a conclusion of the Uruguay Round. As Japan came under criticism for its refusal to commit troops in support, one might have expected that Japanese leaders would want to make trade concessions to avoid trade friction adding further strain to relations. In contrast, the Japanese government refused to make any concessions on agriculture. Carla Hills said that many members of Congress knew that Japan had failed to contribute to the Uruguay Round and was the first to object to the agriculture proposal during the final session of the Brussels agriculture group meeting in December 1990. She warned that their anger at Japan being a free-rider would likely spill over to affect other areas in the U.S.-Japan relationship.[26] When Japan's foreign minister visited the United States later in January 1991 to discuss the Gulf conflict, he also found himself being urged by President Bush to show more leadership in the agricultural negotiations of the round.[27] In spite of this high-level pressure from the United States, for another year the Japanese government re-

---

[24] The proposal consisted of a memo suggesting that negotiations start on the basis of a five-year plan for 30 percent reduction of domestic support, reduction of trade barriers to allow 5 percent minimum access, and 30 percent reduction of export subsidies.

[25] Preeg (1995,121); *Asahi shimbun*, 8 December 1990.

[26] *Asahi shimbun*, 5 January 1991.

[27] *Asahi shimbun*, 17 January 1991.

fused to modify its position, continuing to oppose any rice liberalization.

In a second key development for the Uruguay Round, GATT Director-General Arthur Dunkel took measures to strengthen the linkage
among different negotiating groups. When negotiations reconvened in
1991, he assumed the chair of the agriculture negotiation group in order to push forward this problem area. Then, at the end of the year, he
produced the "Draft Final Act Embodying the Results of the Uruguay
Round of Multilateral Trade Negotiations," later known as the Dunkel
Draft. This document gave an outline of a final agreement on all negotiation groups, including agriculture.[28] The draft called for tariffication,
which meant the conversion of all nontariff barriers into tariff-quotas.
In effect, this modified the agenda of the negotiation by setting the principle of comprehensive tariffication without exception as the baseline
for negotiations. In addition, a procedural step backed up the concept
of a single undertaking: the final agreement texts would form a single
charter for a new trade organization such that accepting all agreements
was a condition of membership (Hudec 1993, 193).

The document placed the burden on countries like Japan to justify
why they deserved an exception for their sensitive agricultural policies.
With over one hundred participants in the Uruguay Round, any exception risked unraveling the entire consensus. Negotiators could not simply make a deal for special arrangements with one or two principal
suppliers as had been common practice in past negotiations. Japanese
diplomats reported that this development caused them great difficulties
(Akao 1994, 47). Dunkel, as well as U.S. and EC officials, criticized
Japanese appeals for special treatment of rice by saying that granting one
country an exception would lead to all countries seeking exceptions.[29]

For Japan, the message was strong that rice reform was linked to the
fate of the round. Yeutter, now serving as U.S. secretary of agriculture,
said there was "no way" to conclude the Uruguay Round without reform by Japan. He declared that "the Japanese rice market must
open. . . . They better get the word concession into their vocabulary."[30]
Following the Brussels meeting and emergence of the Dunkel Draft as a
new focal point for agreement, pressures for a rice concession increasingly connected the single issue to wider consequences. Both Dunkel

[28] The draft agreement called for a reduction of export subsidies by 36 percent in value,
tariffication of all nontariff barriers with minimum access of 3–5 percent, reduction of
tariffs on average by 36 percent, and reduction of domestic subsidies by 20 percent from
1986 levels (Croome 1995, 296).

[29] *Asahi shimbun*, 22 November 1991.

[30] *Inside U.S. Trade*, 8 June 1990.

and his successor Peter Sutherland pressured all sides on the need to make concessions in the agriculture group for the sake of an overall agreement. USTR Carla Hills adopted a tough position in her meeting with the Japanese agriculture minister in November 1991. She emphasized that even the United States was including its sensitive products in the comprehensive tariffication framework, and it was unreasonable for Japan to seek exceptions on rice.[31] She warned that if the round failed, the blame would fall on Japan. Sources within the Japanese government expressed their concern about this scenario in which Japan refused concessions on rice and the Uruguay Round collapsed with everyone placing the responsibility on Japan.[32]

Rising Proliberalization Voices within Japan

During the progress of the Uruguay Round negotiations, a change occurred in the dynamic of interest group pressures as it became clear that concessions on agriculture were necessary to save the Uruguay Round. In July 1990 Keidanren issued a letter to the government on trade matters that stated:

> The government should reduce or eliminate restrictions on agricultural imports, while taking measures to minimize damage to Japan's farmers. . . . Japan should not try to protect any domestic product or service from foreign competition (to successfully conclude the Uruguay Round). Rather, the nation should play a leading role in the multilateral forum to eliminate world trade barriers.[33]

As the negotiation stalemate continued, policy recommendations from business groups became more frequent and specific. In October 1990 the chair of the Keidanren rice issue committee, Seizō Yamazaki, stated explicitly that Japan should provide "minimum access" to foreign rice imports in order to contribute to the successful conclusion of the Uruguay Round.[34] During the Brussels ministerial meeting in December 1990, top business officials said Japan must support GATT and accept liberalization without exceptions.[35] The chairman of Keidanren, Seiki Tōzaki, in January 1991 publicly called on the government to open the rice market to imports. He said this difficult step was necessary to revi-

---

[31] *Asahi shimbun*, 16–17 November 1991.
[32] *Asahi shimbun*, 22 November 1991.
[33] *Daily Yomiuri*, 2 July 1990.
[34] *Daily Yomiuri*, 24 October, 1990.
[35] *Nihon nōgyō shimbun*, 6 December 1990.

talize the Uruguay Round and that Japan "owes GATT" since it has benefited so much from the free-trade system.[36] Such statements were risky given the potential for backlash from farmers and rural politicians.

The actions of Dunkel to restart the round in 1991 were a catalyst for further business lobbying on agricultural liberalization. Throwing aside its earlier fears that advocating rice liberalization would lead to farm boycotts against member companies, a general meeting of Keidanren in May 1991 passed a resolution urging the government to show leadership in the round and specifically calling for rice market opening.[37] Nikkeiren and Keizairen shortly followed with similar statements to show a strong front from the major Japanese business organizations calling for Japan to take a more flexible position on rice. Upon publication of the Dunkel Draft, Keidanren immediately endorsed the draft in its entirety. This angered MAFF negotiators, who felt the draft ignored every point in their arguments about special treatment for agriculture. Jirō Shiwaku (1994, 15), the lead MAFF negotiator in the Uruguay Round, complained that such irresponsible behavior undermined Japan's position in the negotiations. Disregarding the anger of agricultural interests, the business groups continued their lobbying. In 1992 Keidanren issued a report titled "A Call for Decisive Action to Ensure the Success of the Uruguay Round." In addition, companies in rural areas asked employees and local politicians to support liberalization, although always through informal networks so that nothing would be in writing.[38]

At the same time, farmer interest groups were finding it more difficult to lobby against liberalization. Certainly, farm groups were active publicizing their opposition. However, there was concern among the leadership that they risked losing the wider support of society if they pushed too hard against issues with broad popularity. An official of Zenchū said that "Zenchū cannot just say all that we want. We need the support of people and must avoid making them angry."[39] Increasingly, media editorials urged the government to exercise a leadership role within the Uruguay Round because the Japanese economy was the leading beneficiary of the GATT system of trade rules and had the most to lose from a failure of the negotiation and the turn toward protectionism that would follow.[40] Against this background, farm groups found it difficult

[36] *Journal of Commerce*, 28 January 1991.
[37] *Asahi shimbun*, 30 May 1991.
[38] Zenchū official. Interview by author. Tokyo, 1 December 1998.
[39] Zenchū official. Interview by author. Tokyo, 30 October 1998.
[40] *Asahi shimbun*, 9 December 1990.

to attack the GATT institution or the liberalization agenda of the negotiation. One Zenchū official active in coordinating their position toward international negotiations said, "Because Japan's interest is in trade, it is hard to argue for why only agriculture should get an exception. Not only Keidanren, but many groups think this. Politicians also can't just talk about agriculture and must represent their district."[41]

Consequently, farm groups protested against agricultural liberalization but not against companies urging compromise for the round. Whereas Keidanren had previously shied away from proliberalization statements from fear of provoking the wrath of the agriculture community, Yamazaki explained that "this kind of reaction is most unlikely this time, because the leaders of agriculture organizations have come to the conclusion that such protection would be useless today. In fact, we have not received any pressure from farming organizations."[42] Even during the half year following the collapse of the Brussels meeting, the agricultural group protests against Keidanren for its advocacy of rice liberalization had declined noticeably.[43] Although reportedly some agricultural groups considered launching a boycott against companies as had happened in 1984, such actions never materialized.

Public opinion began showing more support for a limited degree of rice liberalization. The *Asahi shimbun* conducted polls in May 1990 and December 1991 in which they asked respondents which of the following three options they supported: a limited quantity of imports, complete liberalization, or the current policy banning imports.[44] In the 1990 survey, which occurred prior to the Brussels meeting, 44 percent favored limited imports. In the 1991 survey, 50 percent favored limited imports. Although this represents a small change, it reflected movement toward more support for at least some liberalization.

The wider implications for the Uruguay Round made it easier for proliberalization interests within the government to play a role in the decisions for agricultural trade policy. For example, MITI would normally not become involved in agricultural policy, but because of the issue linkage, agriculture negotiations influenced other areas of the Uruguay Round under MITI jurisdiction. This gave MITI both motivation and an opening to encourage agricultural liberalization indirectly through its pressure for a successful conclusion of the overall negotiation. One senior official said, "Agriculture is a MAFF area. We cannot

---

[41] Zenchū official. Interview by author. Tokyo, 1 December 1998.
[42] *Daily Yomiuri*, 24 October, 1990.
[43] *Asahi shimbun*, 30 May 1991.
[44] *Asahi shimbun*, 12 December 1991.

tell MAFF that it should liberalize rice. However, we could say that there is a need for saving the Uruguay Round. . . . Politically it is not tolerable to have the negotiation collapse, and most politicians recognize this. Japan is a trading state and cannot go forward alone."[45] The venues for voicing concerns about the need for compromise on agriculture positions were both informal channels and monthly consultation meetings about the Uruguay Round among division heads from MITI, MAFF, MOFA, and the EPA. At these meetings, officials discussed the situation in each negotiation group and the progress of the overall round. Taking this opportunity, MITI and MOFA urged MAFF to put forward more cooperative positions in the agriculture negotiating group.

In 1990 senior LDP politicians began making statements about the need for a flexible position on rice. They typically prefaced their comments by talking about the broader gains from the Uruguay Round and saying that even if it meant making a concession on rice, Japan should take leadership in the negotiation.[46] Japan had strong motivation to see the round concluded both for the direct economic gains and to strengthen the GATT. Takeshita alluded in 1990 to the ultimate dilemma facing Japan; "it would be impractical if Japan had to leave GATT to keep its rice import ban" (Sato 1996, 89).

The release of the Dunkel Draft in the fall of 1991 prompted the Japanese government to rethink its position on rice. When hearing earlier versions in discussions with the GATT director-general, there had been rising concern that Japan's negotiation points were not reflected in the document. The draft did not allow flexibility for agricultural exceptions, and the single undertaking made it essential to reach some kind of agreement on agriculture. A senior politician, Ichirō Ozawa, said in a public statement that refusing tariffication would risk isolation. He declared that Japan must begin negotiating on the assumption of tariffication and focus more on gaining the best terms within that framework (as set forth in the Dunkel Draft).[47] Shin Kanemaru, one of the most influential LDP politicians at the time, stated publicly that if Japan wanted to sell its cars abroad, it would need to buy some American rice.[48]

Meeting in Tokyo in December, top negotiators and politicians discussed how to adjust their strategy in light of the Dunkel Draft. The chair of the LDP Policy Affairs Research Council, Yoshiro Mori (who later became prime minister), reported that the government was consid-

---

[45] Former MITI official. Interview by author. Tokyo, 3 June 1999.
[46] *Asahi shimbun*, 20 May 1991.
[47] *Asahi shimbun*, 18 November 1991.
[48] *Asahi shimbun*, 18 November 1991.

ering many proposals, and that nobody talked anymore about the declaration that Japan would not allow *a single grain of imported rice* into Japan.[49] Thereafter, the government accepted the possibility of partial liberalization. The proposal circulated in MAFF and LDP circles consisted of a two-step process in which Japan would import a fixed amount of 3 to 5 percent of consumption for five years and then accept tariffication (Koizumi 1994, 26–27). This was still far from what the Dunkel Draft demanded because the government continued to oppose immediate tariffication and insist on the need for an exception to allow Japan to have an import quota operated under the food control system. Nevertheless, the new position represented a compromise to allow some market opening, which was a significant retreat from the existing import ban. Indeed, it foreshadowed the final agreement to allow partial liberalization by means of an import quota.

After the United States and the EU finally settled their outstanding differences over agriculture in the Blair House agreement of November 1992, attention shifted to Japan. The government had been asking for special treatment for agriculture in a common position with European countries, and officials had also been able to conveniently say that U.S.-EU conflict — not Japan's rice policy — was the main obstacle in the negotiation. Prime Minister Kaifu said in May 1991 that Japan would not change its policies until after the United States and the EU made concessions.[50] Once the EU accepted tariffication as part of the Blair House agreement, it was even more difficult for Japan to request an exception. Now pressure against Japan came from not only the United States, but also from Europe. In the weeks after the Blair House agreement, EU negotiators accused Japan of shirking its trade responsibilities and declared that now it was Japan's turn to make concessions on nontariff barriers, including the rice quota system.[51] Japan was the last major obstacle to an agreement.

At first many in Japan thought they could gain understanding for its desire to maintain self-sufficiency in rice. However, the import ban contradicted the Dunkel Draft plan for comprehensive tariffication, and it became clear that any action to block a part of the agreement would attract the ire of other nations with a stake in successful conclusion of the Uruguay Round. Political pressure from Congress and the RMA made it impossible for the U.S. administration to allow the rice issue to fade from view, and other governments were also disinclined to recog-

---

[49] *Asahi shimbun*, 2 December 1991; 5 December 1991.
[50] *Asahi shimbun*, 20 May 1991.
[51] *Journal of Commerce*, 7 December 1992; Karube (1997, 140).

nize the Japanese request. The leader of a Japanese group of LDP Diet members in charge of agricultural policy visited Geneva to explain why Japan needed a special exception for rice. On his return to Japan, he said that other countries expressed understanding for Japan's difficulties but said that the Uruguay Round must go forward according to common principles among many nations, and he concluded that Japan could not be optimistic about gaining special exceptions.[52] Fear of isolation persuaded many to advocate that Japan must make a concession on rice, and this was a common theme in Japanese media reports and editorials (Karube 1997, 53).

As negotiations neared their end in 1993, voices for liberalization grew louder. In February 1993 a group of 113 former bureaucrats, scholars, and journalists issued a declaration recommending that Japan should accept tariffication of rice and focus on helping farmers achieve competitiveness after liberalization (ibid., 50). Public opinion turned to favor a concession, and business pressures continued to escalate. In a 1993 opinion poll by NHK, 65.2 percent favored partial liberalization while only 20.6 percent said they opposed any form of market opening measure.[53] In August 1993, Nikkeiren released a report calling for gradual opening of the domestic rice market and changes in the rice-pricing system.[54] Shortly thereafter, Keidanren released a report listing thirty items where reform was necessary to help boost Japan's ailing economy, and agricultural reform appeared among the major requests.[55] However, on the other side of the debate, agricultural groups continued to hold protests, and Diet members talked of passing yet another Diet resolution against liberalization.[56]

One aspect of sectoral weakness complicated the government's negotiating stance — the weather. The cool summer of 1993 brought a terrible rice harvest that forced the government to import emergency rice supplies to meet domestic demand. While Prime Minister Hosokawa said emergency imports and the issue of market opening in the negotiations were separate, the need to import rice in the summer of 1993

---

[52] *Asahi shimbun*, 16 June 1990.

[53] *Yoron Chōsa Nenkan* 1994 (Opinion Survey Yearbook 1994), "Seiji ishiki 1993 ni kan suru yoron chōsa" (Opinion poll regarding views of politics in 1993) (Tokyo, 1999), 530. The question (no. 28) asked whether respondents favored full opening under tariffication, partial opening with conditions, or no opening measures at all.

[54] *Daily Yomiuri*, 18 August 1993.

[55] The report called for lowering subsidies on various agriculture goods and reforming the distribution system for rice and grain production (*Daily Yomiuri*, 2 September 1993).

[56] *Nihon nōgyō shimbun*, 22 October 1993; 27 October 1993.

made arguments against allowing any rice imports seem even more unrealistic.

The political climate also brought dramatic change during the critical
summer of 1993. Scandals, recession, and the defection of party members dealt a crushing defeat to the LDP in the Lower House election in
July. The LDP lost its majority and was replaced by a coalition government made up of an assortment of former LDP politicians and opposition parties. While one should not underestimate the significance of the
change in ruling party, it had only marginal impact on the settlement of
the agriculture negotiation.[57] First, farm groups did not lose their political influence when the LDP fell from power. In fact, the reverse was
true. Political uncertainty and narrow electoral margins gave incentives
for politicians from all parties to make appeals to farmers. Second,
there was little difference between the LDP and the new coalition regarding their position toward the Uruguay Round. The three unanimous Diet resolutions calling for self-sufficiency in rice put all parties
on record against liberalization. In its first months in office, the new
coalition government continued to argue against comprehensive tariffication of agricultural goods. Not only were policies similar, but some
of the same key leaders remained involved in the negotiation, just under
the name of a different party. Indeed, the foreign minister of the new
coalition administration, Tsutomu Hata, was a former LDP member
who had twice served as minister of agriculture for LDP cabinets and
who had been a long-time leader of the agriculture committees within
the party.

While the LDP had been a strong farm group ally, it is unlikely that it
would have been any more resistant to the pressures for liberalization
than the coalition government. As early as December 1991, the LDP
and MAFF had drawn up detailed plans for a partial liberalization proposal that was remarkably similar to the final agreement. In the year
prior to the LDP fall from power, Prime Minister Kiichi Miyazawa was
reported to have been preparing for how to time the announcement of a
compromise agreement for partial liberalization of rice.[58] Furthermore,
the LDP was not shut out of the final decision making. Even in the last
months of the negotiation, when the LDP was an opposition party, negotiators continued to consult on an informal basis with some party
members.[59] Nevertheless, the fact that the party was temporarily out of

[57] The top MAFF negotiator, Jirō Shiwaku (1994, 16), has written that the change in the
Japanese administration had little impact on the outcome.

[58] *Daily Yomiuri*, 29 December 1992.

[59] Former MAFF officials. Interviews by author. Tokyo, 24 July 1996; 29 June 2001.

office made it easier for the LDP power-brokers consulting with MAFF to consent tacitly to a compromise while publicly insisting they objected. For the LDP, it was simply fortuitous timing that the decision came while they were out of power. Given the options presented to Japan in the negotiation, any party would have chosen to make a similar compromise on rice.

Ending the Ban

Agreement was reached in the last weeks before the December 15 deadline. Formally, the rice-opening agreement was the product of a compromise proposal submitted by the GATT official heading the agriculture negotiating group.[60] Prime Minister Hosokawa dramatized the issue by making a public announcement at a midnight press conference on December 7 that the government was considering a new compromise proposal. He called for Japan to endure sacrifices in difficult areas such as agriculture for the sake of the future of the world's free-trade system and bringing a successful conclusion to the Uruguay Round (Akao 1994, 47). Prior to making the decision to accept rice imports, Hosokawa told his associates that "Japan cannot become the criminal that wrecks the Uruguay Round" (Karube 1997, 104).

During internal political debates as well, the government used the broader gains of the agreement and the requirements of multilateral negotiations to explain why Japan had to accept the GATT proposal. The following exchange during a Diet committee meeting on 8 December 1993 is illustrative: a senior LDP politician, Kōsuke Hori, argued that even partial liberalization would violate the Diet resolutions for complete self-sufficiency and urged the government to renegotiate the proposal with a tougher position. Hosokawa responded that it was necessary to evaluate the Uruguay Round negotiation as a whole, and that in a multilateral negotiation it was unreasonable for Japan to insist that it could not import even a grain of rice.[61]

On December 13, just two days before the final meeting of the Uruguay Round, the government announced it would accept the compro-

---

[60] Many reported that the United States and Japan reached an unofficial understanding in negotiations in October and November 1993, and that for political reasons in Japan, this agreement had to be kept secret and the appearance upheld that the proposal originated with the GATT officials (Karube 1997, 106). However, Japan's negotiators continue to deny this story.

[61] 128th Session of the Lower House of the Diet, Budget Committee Meeting Records, 8 December 1993.

mise proposal for partial liberalization. The final agreement ended Japan's ban on rice imports and represented a major policy adjustment. However, this concession fell short of full liberalization. Despite the calls for tariffication without exceptions, a special category was created for minimum access agreements on commodities meeting specified criteria.[62] Japan agreed to import 4 percent of consumption starting in 1995, with gradual increase of minimum access imports scheduled to reach 8 percent of consumption in 2000. This contrasted with tariffication, which would have replaced the import ban with high tariff barriers and mandated minimum access imports of 3 to 5 percent of consumption.[63] To gain an exception to the general rule of tariffication, Japan agreed to import more. Many officials and politicians admit privately that it would have been better for Japan to accept tariffication from the beginning, and indeed five years later the government changed the policy.

However, politically the minimum access compromise was preferable since it guaranteed stability from market fluctuations and involved the least change in domestic programs so it would appear that the Diet resolutions had been respected. Masami Tanabu, the agriculture minister in the Miyazawa cabinet, said that during cabinet discussions of the minimum access versus tariffication decision earlier in 1991, he favored tariffication but others raised the fear that more rice would enter unexpectedly under tariffication due to fluctuation in markets and exchange rates. The three Diet resolutions made it difficult to accept tariffication.[64] From the perspective of MAFF, the minimum access agreement preserved the role of the Food Control Agency that regulated domestic rice production and distribution. Tariffication would have meant the end of this system and threatened the jobs of thousands of affiliated employees (Domon 1994, 133).[65]

From the U.S. perspective, the maintenance of the quota system through minimum access contained its own advantages. Under market management by the Japanese bureaucracy, U.S. rice could gain a larger market

---

[62] The Agreement on Agriculture in article 4:2 mandates conversion of trade barriers into ordinary customs duties, that is, tariffication. Special Treatment under annex 5 of the agreement allows for an exception from this clause for an agricultural product, subject to the following three criteria: imports composed less than 3 percent of domestic consumption in the base period of 1986–1988, no export subsidies have been provided since that period, and production restrictions are in effect.

[63] *Nihon nōgyō shimbun*, 11 December 1993.

[64] Interview by author. Tokyo, 3 February 1999.

[65] This was also confirmed in interviews with MAFF officials, who said it was one factor among many that were taken into account (interviews by author. Tokyo, 8 August 1996; 30 June 2001).

share than it would through competition with low-cost producers under a less regulated tariffication policy.[66] It was reported that as a condition for accepting this special treatment, U.S. negotiators received a promise for preferential purchasing of California rice by the Japanese government (Domon 1993, 40). In 1999 U.S. rice exports received 48 percent of the total minimum access imports of Japan, with its largest share coming from the government purchase market. Thailand and Australia received, respectively, 22 percent and 16 percent.[67]

Table 6.1 shows the degree of market opening in terms of policy change, increased imports, and reduction in monetary transfers. In terms of actual trade flows, the agreement turned Japan from a closed market into the top market for U.S. rice exports. In 1999 U.S. rice exports to Japan had a value of 145 million dollars, which constituted 15 percent of all U.S. rice exports.[68] This represented a tiny share of total U.S. agricultural product exports to Japan of 8.9 billion dollars, but from the beginning, this negotiation had more symbolic importance to the United States than actual trade significance. Japanese compliance with the letter of the agreement is remarkable given the domestic surplus conditions for rice production. The government must use subsidies to induce Japanese farmers to reduce domestic production. At the same time, the Food Agency purchases foreign rice imports that it then sells for a loss while also paying high storage costs. U.S. officials express discontent that much of the imported rice is used for emergency supply storage, processing industries, or foreign aid and little reaches the supermarket shelves to compete with domestic rice, but they admit that Japan fully imports the amount that it has committed to import in the agreement.[69]

While the rice problem dominated Japanese media and political attention in the Uruguay Round, the agriculture agreement included liberal-

[66] Official of U.S. Embassy to Japan. Interview by author. Tokyo, 30 March 1999; LDP member of the House of Representatives. Interview by author. Tokyo, 26 April 1999.

[67] China won 11.7 percent of total Japanese rice imports. However, when looking at the share of imports allocated by the free-market bidding system (simultaneous buy and sell), China won 52.2 percent of these imports relative to the U.S. share of 30.7 percent. In the government purchase market (ordinary minimum access tenders), China won 2.6 percent relative to the U.S. share of 51.8 percent. Market differences in the quality and price of rice and end-use account for some of the disparity between the two markets, but there is also room for government discretion when it offers contracts. Data from USDA Foreign Agricultural Service, "Grain Report," no. JA0006. 24 January 2000.

[68] USDA, "U.S. Exports of Rice, Calendar Years." Online database available at www.fas.usda.gov/scriptsw/bico/bico.frm.asp.

[69] Foreign Agriculture Service officer of the USDA working at the U.S. Embassy in Japan. Interview by author. Tokyo, 2 December 1998.

TABLE 6.1
Japanese Rice Market Liberalization

	1986–88	1997–99
Policy measure	import ban	tariff quota
Import quantity	17.9	577.4
(thousand metric tons)		
Import dependency	0.2%	5.6%
(import share of total supply)		
Producer subsidy estimate	85%	83%
(percentage PSE)		

Sources: FAO (2001); OECD (2000b).

Note: Four measures for the change in market access when comparing the average over the base years of 1986 to 1988 with the average over three years of the implementation period from 1997 to 1999. Imports are the total from all countries. Some imports were allowed under the ban for limited processing purposes. Percentage PSE calculates the value of monetary transfers from policies targeted to rice production as a share of the value of rice production.

ization on other agricultural items as well. It called for a 20 percent reduction of domestic subsidies, tariffication of nontariff barriers (such as quotas), and a 36 percent reduction of export subsidies. All measures were for the six-year period starting in 1995. The subsidy reduction would require that Japan reduce its aggregate spending for agricultural support from 5 trillion yen in the base period 1986–1988 to 4 trillion yen in 2000.[70] Since such subsidy reductions were modest and Japan did not have export subsidy policies, the most significant changes for Japan resulted from the tariffication of all remaining agricultural quota policies.[71] The agreement stipulated that, on average, tariff rates must be reduced by 36 percent over six years, with a minimum reduction of 15 percent. In Japan, implementation required the overhaul of food control policies with four separate major pieces of legislation.

The government explained the decision as a necessary sacrifice for the

[70] The category of subsidies excluded income support, infrastructure investment, or other policies that would not distort trade. Figures reported are from Japan's national schedule submitted to the Uruguay Round. *Shūgiin nōrinsuisan iinkai chyōsashitsu, Gatto uruguai raundo nōgyō kōshō kankei shiryo*: 27.

[71] The agreement converted the remaining fixed quotas into tariff-quota protection for the following agricultural products: wheat, barley, dairy products, starch, mixed beans, groundnuts, konnyaku (devil's tongue), raw silk, and pork. Note that fishery goods were addressed as part of the general tariff negotiating group rather than the agriculture group. Japan committed to reduce its fishery tariffs by 33 percent on average and did not have to make commitments to change subsidy or quota policies for fishery goods.

sake of the success of the Uruguay Round. In his press conference speech on 14 December 1993, Prime Minister Hosokawa raised the specter of what would have happened if he had not accepted the compromise in agriculture.[72] He said that the failure of the Uruguay Round when other countries had accepted the agreement and Japan had refused would have led to harsh criticism of Japan and deepening protectionism that would have threatened the foundations of Japan's economy. He further added that Japan owed an immeasurable debt to the framework of free-trade rules supported by GATT and therefore could not cause the failure of the Uruguay Round.

The official statements from different political parties reflected variations on the same theme. Kōmeitō justified acceptance of the decision in terms of Japan's contribution to the Uruguay Round and to upholding the free trade system. The Japan Socialist Party made it clear that it disliked the agreement and could only accept it for the sake of the Uruguay Round and because the party felt obligated to support the cabinet as a member of the new ruling coalition. Meanwhile, from its opposition status, the LDP criticized the specific agriculture agreement while at the same time saying it could not evaluate the agricultural deal independent of the entire Uruguay Round agreement, and that the party recognized the importance of supporting the international trade system. Only the Japan Communist Party urged rejection of the decision. Statements by individual Diet members generally reflected the position that the agriculture agreement was in the national interest given that there was no other option for concluding the Uruguay Round.[73]

Perceptions of the Uruguay Round agreement in Japan were mixed. Business groups were generally satisfied that the Uruguay Round had concluded with substantial progress for liberalization across different sectors. The Keidanren evaluation of the round praised the inclusion of agriculture in the GATT framework while it criticized Japan's lack of leadership and effort to avoid tariffication of rice.[74]

On the other hand, agricultural interest groups said the outcome on the rice issue was worse than they had hoped for, referring to it as a disaster and disappointment.[75] One representative of the cooperatives said that the anger over the agreement could be seen by the fact that

---

[72] *Shūgiin nōrinsuisan iinkai chyōsashitsu, gatto uruguai raundo nōgyō kōshō kankei shiryo*: 27.

[73] Ibid., 53–63.

[74] Keidanren, "Evaluation of the Uruguay Round Agreement, Future Tasks and Recommendations," 19 April 1994.

[75] Zennōrin official. Interview by author. Tokyo, 26 October 1998; Zenchū official. Interview by author. Tokyo, 30 October 1998.

several of the top personnel of the agricultural cooperatives were either transferred from their positions or forced into early retirement.[76] While unhappy with the agreement, it was difficult for farmers to punish politicians in the next election. Because a coalition of former opposition parties made the final decision to accept the agreement, those parties were seen as culpable. The LDP was not in office then, but after the LDP regained power in 1994, it led the ratification process. In short, all of the major parties were on record having backed the agreement at some point. Farmers were left with no outlet for venting their sense of betrayal.

The large compensation spending that accompanied liberalization appeased farmers and demonstrated that budget constraints were not an important factor in the decision process. The subsidy reductions called for were modest and exempted rice supply adjustment expenses. When the various proposals for agricultural trade proposals were under consideration, negotiators did not even consult with the Ministry of Finance over the cost of the different options.[77] Ministry of Finance officials had input only on agricultural trade issues with regard to putting together a compensation package to help farmers adjust to the liberalization measures. From the early stages of the negotiation, MAFF had one group of officials addressing the trade policy proposals of the negotiation and another group addressing the need to raise a compensation package for farmers to go along with any policy changes.[78] Closely following the announcement of the Uruguay Round agreement, the Diet passed a 6 trillion yen (U.S. $50 billion) package of subsidies and rural public works projects. When Ministry of Finance officials tried to draw this sum from within existing regular budget allocations for the Ministry of Agriculture, political intervention forced them to make the allocation as a separate extra-budget compensation figure. Kōsuke Hori, who led the ratification effort as chair of the LDP Policy Affairs Research Council in 1994, said that "the importance of the money was justified as building efficiency of farming to help them compete better, but in truth it was straight compensation. It was necessary for approval."[79] Clearly farmers retained considerable political backing and could gain large financial transfers from the state even while they could not prevent the liberalization agreement.

[76] Zenchū official. Interview by author. Tokyo, 1 December 1998.

[77] Ministry of Finance official of the Budget Division. Interview by author. Tokyo, 14 January 1999.

[78] MAFF official. Interview by author. Tokyo, 30 April 1998.

[79] Kōsuke Hori, LDP member of the House of Representatives. Interview by author. Tokyo, January 1999.

Concluding Remarks on the Uruguay Round

This discussion of the Uruguay Round began with the observation that in 1986 the political consensus favored the existing rice import ban. By 1993 business groups, the media, public opinion, and even senior LDP leaders indicated support for some opening of the rice market. When the government accepted a compromise proposal for partial liberalization, the political consensus supported that decision.

U.S. pressure on Japan to open its rice market forced the issue to prominence on the negotiation agenda. The section 301 petitions by the RMA raised the specter of bilateral pressure, which made Japan commit to reach some kind of agreement in the multilateral setting. However, after four years of negotiations and during a sensitive period for the U.S.-Japan alliance, in December 1990, Japan continued steadfastly to resist U.S. pressure. Only the combination of U.S. threats and the stakes created by the negotiation structure were sufficient to produce the concession on the rice issue.

The sequence of events and evidence of domestic mobilization for liberalization supports the logic of the cross-sector linkage hypothesis. The cross-sector linkage enabled the United States and the Cairns Group to signal at the Brussels meeting in 1990 how much they were willing to risk for the sake of meaningful agricultural reform. The intervention of the GATT director-general reinforced the cross-sector linkage by establishing procedures in support of the single-undertaking approach. Thereafter, export groups in Japan became increasingly vocal in their demand that flexibility on rice imports was necessary for the sake of the larger negotiation stakes. The shift in the government's position to consider partial liberalization options occurred at the end of 1991 following these two events.

There was also evidence that interest groups and politicians believed that appeals to the GATT and broader economic interests would persuade the domestic audience to accept liberalization. Business groups used rhetoric supporting the trade system in their calls for concessions on agriculture. Once the final compromise proposal had been accepted, politicians referred to the larger gains of the round and Japan's obligation to the GATT system when they explained their decision to end the import ban.

Over the long term, the cross-sector linkage negotiation structure made liberalization more likely at less political cost than if the United States had tried to open Japan's rice market through bilateral pressure. Even in the most politically sensitive case, a strong cross-sector linkage with some legal framing promoted substantial liberalization. The institutionalization of the linkage helped to signal to domestic interest groups the wider stakes of the negotiation and encourage their mobilization for liberalization of agriculture. Against the background of this changed domestic debate, the potential gains from the package deal and the legitimacy of the institution helped to persuade leaders. The next case will show that when the negotiation structure did not promote this change in the political balance, liberalization did not occur despite U.S. pressure and Japanese exporter interests.

APEC: Victory for Fishers and Foresters

Why would Japan undermine its own regional cooperation project? After years of effort to develop the Asia-Pacific Economic Cooperation forum, Japan had much at stake in the diplomatic process as well as a strong interest in the potential economic gains from regional trade liberalization and facilitation measures. Yet in 1998 at the Kuala Lumpur ministerial meeting, Japan refused to commit to tariff reductions in forestry and fishery sectors, thereby blocking agreement on early voluntary liberalization of nine priority sectors, including industrial goods. Harsh criticism met this decision as foreign leaders, especially U.S. officials, blamed Japan for turning APEC into a meaningless talk shop. The fact that shortly thereafter Japan agreed to accept tariffication of its most politically sensitive issue, rice imports, only makes it more puzzling why it resisted strong U.S. demands on forestry and fishery issues during APEC talks. This case of failed foreign pressure presents an opportunity to test which factors determine Japanese decisions about whether and when to liberalize sensitive markets.

Different explanations of the driving force in Japanese trade policy decisions produce divergent predictions for this negotiation. In light of strong U.S. pressure, arguments about the importance of U.S. power and coercion as well as portrayals of Japan as a state that is particularly reactive to foreign pressure support predictions that Japan would offer at least some concessions for liberalization (Calder 1988; Mikanagi 1996; Lincoln 1999). Because APEC addresses cross-sector trade liberalization, the presence of proliberalization interests within Japan formed another source of pressure for liberalization. Consequently, the negotiation meets the conditions under which two-level models of foreign pressure predict liberalization: multilateralism, broad participation by ministries including advocates of liberalization, and economic gains for Japan's export industries (Schoppa 1997; Mulgan 1997b). The failure to achieve any liberalization therefore serves as a cautionary note against arguments that U.S. pressure at the international level or divided interests at the domestic level are sufficient to bring about liberalization.

In contrast to these positive expectations for liberalization, the negotiation structure hypotheses presented in this book predict that APEC would encounter difficulties achieving liberalization. APEC is widely viewed as a negotiation forum with low levels of institutionalization (Kahler 2000; Aggarwal and Morrison 1998). The principle of voluntarism weakens the cross-sector linkage for trade liberalization, while the lack of any kind of dispute mediation or binding principles lowers the level of legal framing.

Fishery and Forestry Trade in Japan

In contrast with the weak position of Japan in world agricultural production, historically Japan has been among the top fishing nations and now ranks third in world fishery production. In addition to the less efficient coastal fisheries, there are also offshore and distant water fisheries, many of which are large-scale corporate operations that also export production. The fishing industry also includes processing businesses that demand cheaper inputs, whether imported or domestic. Therefore, within the sector there are mixed preferences for trade policy. Nevertheless, similar to the agricultural sector, the fishery sector lacks comparative advantage relative to industrial sectors and has experienced a rapid decline in population.[80] Just as limited land constrains agricultural productivity in Japan, restricted access to foreign waters constrain Japanese fisheries.[81]

The political organization of fisheries parallels those of farmers insofar as both sectors fall under the jurisdiction of MAFF. In the LDP Policy Research Affairs Council, there is considerable overlap among the politicians who participate in the Agriculture Committee and those who participate in the Fishery Committee.[82] The fishery associations also have a central organization, Zengyōren (National Federation

[80] The population of those engaged in fishing declined by 37 percent, from 469,680 in 1976 to 287,380 in 1996. Calculated from figures in MAFF, *The Statistical Yearbook of the Ministry of Agriculture, Forestry and Fisheries*, selected years.

[81] See Imamura (1995) and *Shyokuryō hakusho (heisei jyūichi nenban): aratana gyōgyō chitsujo e no taidō* (Food white paper 1999: Movement toward a new fisheries order) (Tokyo: Food and Agriculture Policy Research Center, 1999) 25–29.

[82] LDP Policy Research Affairs Council official. Interview by author. Tokyo, 21 January 2000.

of Fisheries Cooperative Associations), which lobbies the government against liberalization. The fact that fisheries are spread throughout many prefectures and impact local economies amplifies their voice, but fishermen lack the political influence of farmers (Bergin and Howard 1996, 60–62). Farmers outnumber those employed in fishing by nearly seventeen to one.[83]

Fishery markets retain the last remaining formal quantitative restrictions among traded goods in Japan. Nine categories of fish, including herring, cod, and pollock, are subject to import quotas. These products account for one-fourth of total U.S. fishery exports to Japan.[84] The average tariff rate for fish products was 4.6 percent in 1998. As part of the Uruguay Round market-access negotiations, Japan reduced tariffs on fishery items by 30 percent on average. However, unlike the agriculture group negotiations of the Uruguay Round, the market-access negotiations did not address changes in quota policies, and the Japanese government refused U.S. requests to end the quotas in the Uruguay Round.

Japan's trade in forestry products is characterized by high import dependence — Japan imports 80 percent of domestic demand.[85] The average tariff for forestry products was only 1.7 percent in 1997. However, the United States complained about high tariff rates on value-added wood products in addition to testing methods and standards that form an obstacle to trade.[86] Like the fisheries sector, forestry has a small number of people actively engaged in the sector but benefits from high levels of political organization and the support of rural district politicians. Both forestry and lumber-processing industry associations coordinate activities during negotiations and are capable of bringing politicians to back their cause (Mikanagi 1996). While in 1995 there were only 860,000 people directly engaged in forestry work, 2.5 million households are classified to have forestry interests in terms of their employment or private assets.[87]

A key political dynamic is the joint action by farm, forestry, and fishery constituencies in terms of joint demonstrations sponsored by the

[83] In 1996 there were 287,380 workers engaged in fishing and 4,780,300 farmers when including those who worked in each sector more than thirty days of the year. Calculated from figures in MAFF (1997, 24, 313).

[84] Office of the U.S. Trade Representative, *The 1998 National Trade Estimate Report on Foreign Trade Barriers*, 205, at www.ustr.org. The nine categories fall into five import quotas.

[85] Asahi Shimbun, *Japan Almanac 1998*, 144.

[86] Office of the U.S. Trade Representative, *The 1999 National Trade Estimate Report on Foreign Trade Barriers*, 212, accessed at www.ustr.org.

[87] Asahi Shimbun, *Japan Almanac 1998*, 143.

cooperatives and shared political backing by politicians. Coordination
of the three sectors was typical in past U.S.-Japan negotiations and the
APEC talks.[88] All three primary sectors are in decline but have well-
organized political lobbying power. Japan is the largest importer of agriculture, forestry, and fishery products, and the United States is its top
source for these imports.

The Negotiation Structure of APEC

The project for a new intergovernmental economic institution for the
Asian region originated as a joint Japanese and Australian project in
1988. APEC began as a forum for gathering the foreign and trade ministers of seventeen nations and held its first meeting in 1989. MITI
helped to develop the original proposal and to shape early developments in cooperation with the Australian government.[89] Japan had multiple interests in this new forum. Asia had displaced the United States as
Japan's largest trade partner by the late 1980s, and facilitating further
trade and investment in the region was crucial to Japan's own economic
growth. In addition, APEC was an effort by Japan to integrate China
and the United States in the Asia-Pacific community while also building
Japan's global political power through its role as a regional leader (Funabashi 1995, 195).

The specific tasks that were outlined for APEC rest on three pillars:
liberalization of trade and investment, facilitation of trade and investment, and economic and technical cooperation. There were different
views of the larger purpose of the organization. Charles Morrison (1998)
describes APEC as a combination of three models of cooperation with
the following goals: community building, intergovernmental coordination to identify economic problems, and trade liberalization. Tensions
among these goals arise in both the preferences of members and the
kind of institutional development necessary, with the United States emphasizing the third goal and the consequent need for formal institutions,
while Malaysia and others emphasize the first goal and resist institutionalization.

From the outset, APEC has been a voluntary organization without
legal authority. The principle of voluntarism means that commitments
are not obligatory or binding and have tended to be imprecise in form

---

[88] All three representative interest groups for forestry, fishery, and agriculture met together with party and government for trilateral meetings before the APEC 1998 meeting.
(LDP Policy Affairs Research Council official. Interview by author. Tokyo, 21 January
2000.)

[89] MITI official. Interview by author. Tokyo, 22 January 2000.

(Kahler 2000; Janow 1996/97). The role of informal advisory councils such as the Eminent Persons Group and the rejection of any dispute settlement process mean that APEC involves very little delegation to third-party mediation. This contrasts with the more legalistic nature of the GATT/WTO trade system in which countries ratify new trade rules and tariff schedules and take their complaints over violations to formal dispute panels.

The low legal framing of APEC represents a choice by the participating nations. Some have attributed an Asian cultural resistance to legalism as the cause for the general pattern of low legal framing of institutions for international cooperation in East Asia (Aggarwal and Morrison 1998). However, as Miles Kahler (2000, 562) points out, the willingness of Asian nations to use Western legal procedures in the WTO indicates that there is something more strategic than cultural behind the choice of an informal setting. He argues that the developing-country members feared that the relative weight of Japan and the United States would dominate the agenda-setting, and that the United States would pursue unilateral enforcement. As a result, they would consent only to an informal institution. One of the Japanese Foreign Ministry officials closely involved in the APEC negotiations during the late 1980s wrote the following statement describing the choice of institutional design:

> Right from the outset of APEC, "voluntarism" has been, ironically, the source of strength as well as weakness gripping the APEC regime. If APEC had been conceived and predicated upon an institution of legally binding authority, it would not have seen the light of day in the first place in my opinion. ASEAN, China, or Korea would have refused to join the forum. "Voluntarism" is the glue that brought them together, however loose or ineffective the glue might have been.[90]

However, it is not that the institution was established to do nothing. The reluctance of participating nations to delegate authority to a third party reflects their insistence that they maintain close control over the conduct of negotiations even while trying to achieve liberalization. APEC has grown from a consultation group into a decision-making body that sets the agenda for concrete economic goals. In Bogor, Indonesia, in 1994, APEC leaders declared they would achieve "free and open trade and investment in the region by 2020," with developed nations pledging to meet an earlier target of 2010.

The 1995 APEC ministerial meeting in Osaka confronted the task of implementing the ambitious goal of the Bogor Declaration. Given the principle of voluntarism, leadership by example formed one of the ways

---

[90] MOFA official. Written correspondence to the author, 9 March 2000.

to pressure others to liberalize. Indonesia had set an example by uni-laterally adopting a wide range of tariff cuts and liberalization measures before its debut as host of the Bogor meeting. However, concerns about angering farm constituencies prevented Japan's officials from putting forward any similar bold measure as host nation (Funabashi 1995, 216). With Japan already having low tariffs on most industrial goods, any major liberalization package by Japan would have to bring cuts in primary sectors.

The Osaka meeting represented a crucial event determining the na-ture of the rule framework that would guide the APEC process of liber-alization. Earlier discussions in APEC had called for comprehensive lib-eralization, and the United States had insisted that a comprehensive package was essential for the United States to participate. Criticism came from all sides when the Japanese draft proposal for a meeting of senior officials in May called for special treatment for sectors where liberalization would be especially difficult (i.e., agriculture, forestry, and fisheries for Japan). Only Korea and China backed the Japanese posi-tion. A leading Japanese newspaper derisively described Japan as the only holdout against the tide of liberalization in Asia.[91] In a compro-mise, the leaders' declaration included in the liberalization section a "comprehensiveness" clause to satisfy the United States and Australia and also a "flexibility" clause to satisfy Japanese concerns about special treatment. The two relevant clauses from the Osaka Action Agenda are as follows:

Clause 1. The APEC liberalization and facilitation process will be comprehen-sive, addressing all impediments to achieving the long-term goal of free and open trade and investment.

Clause 8. Considering the different levels of economic development among the APEC economies and the diverse circumstances in each economy, flex-ibility will be available in dealing with issues arising from such circumstances in the liberalization and facilitation process.[92]

This artful diplomacy saved the Osaka meeting from embarrassing failure. Comprehensiveness meant that the agenda would address multi-ple sectors. However, promises of flexibility and voluntarism under-mined an all-or-nothing package approach. As a consequence of the Osaka compromise, there was a weakly institutionalized cross-sector linkage in subsequent APEC talks.

In the next step toward specific trade liberalization commitments,

[91] *Nikkei shimbun*, 21 November 1995.
[92] The text of the Osaka Action Agenda is available at www.apecsec.org.sg.

member countries selected sectors for early voluntary sectoral liberalization (EVSL) at the 1997 APEC ministerial meeting in Vancouver, Canada. As an informal institution, APEC's procedural rules developed in an ad hoc manner. This was especially apparent regarding the criteria for selecting sectors. Member nations were asked to submit a list of sectors to the Canadian hosts, from which the top fifteen were selected. Generally, the cutoff line was support by eleven countries for a candidate sector to be included.

The EVSL plan for liberalization across fifteen sectors addressed a broad range of goods in order to balance the interests of the diverse membership, but it did not reflect Japan's preferences. Japan nominated the following sectors: film, pharmaceuticals, transportation equipment, investment regulations, gum/rubber products, fertilizer, and environmental equipment.[93] Among these, environmental goods and telecommunications were chosen as two of the nine priority sectors.[94] Other sectors with potential gains for Japanese industry, such as autos and rubber, were among six secondary priority sectors.[95]

For Japan, the selection of forestry, fisheries, and food products as three of the fifteen sectors posed a political problem. Nevertheless, in the expectation that the flexibility clause would avert the need for cuts, Japan accepted the EVSL agenda produced by the Vancouver meeting, which mandated that fishery and forestry liberalization would come up for discussion at the 1998 ministerial meeting as priority sectors and food products would be addressed later among the second tier of liberalization items. Reflecting the voluntary nature of APEC commitments, Japanese officials announced following the meeting that its commitments were not binding.[96]

The EVSL process of selecting sectors failed to increase leverage to mobilize a broad coalition of export interests in Japan. The ad hoc procedures undermined the legitimacy of the EVSL agenda within the Japanese government. Officials voiced discontent with the choice of sectors and complained that U.S. and Canadian officials determined the selection criteria behind the scenes.[97] Consequently, liberalization across the fifteen sectors appeared as a one-sided demand rather than an interna-

[93] *Nihon keizai shimbun*, 25 October 1997, cited in Krauss (forthcoming).

[94] The nine priority sectors were forestry, fisheries, environmental goods, toys, gems and jewelry, chemicals, medical equipment, energy, and telecommunication.

[95] The six sectors in the secondary priority category for EVSL liberalization were oilseeds and products, food, rubber, fertilizer, autos, and civil aircraft.

[96] MITI official. Interview by author. Tokyo, 22 January 2000.

[97] MOFA official. Interview by author. Tokyo, 14 May 1999; MITI official. Interview by author. Tokyo, 22 January 2000.

tional obligation to which all nations had committed themselves. The duties of chair were given to the nation that took the lead to nominate the sector for inclusion in EVSL. Japan's role as chair of one of the fifteen sectoral negotiations is notably minor compared to the United States and Canada, each of which was chosen to chair four of the sectoral negotiation groups.[98] Moreover, several of the sectors that were of most interest to Japanese industry were slated for the second stage of liberalization. Those industries therefore were not engaged during the first stage of priority liberalization. Hence the selection of sectors reduced both the economic and normative pressure on Japan to make concessions on forestry and fishery issues.

The 1998 APEC Ministerial Meeting in Kuala Lumpur

Meeting in the Malaysian capital of Kuala Lumpur in November 1998, the leaders' goal was to reach an agreement on commitments for liberalization of the nine priority sectors, and then to negotiate the liberalization of the remaining six sectors in 1999. The plan to achieve zero for zero tariff reduction called for eliminating tariffs across all sectors, although the timetable would vary by country and sector. According to the U.S. coordinator for APEC in the State Department, the nine sectors involved annual trade of about 1.5 trillion U.S. dollars, and the significance of an agreement could extend far beyond this since APEC agreements have in the past influenced policies beyond the member nations.[99] Indeed, the United States hoped to use an APEC deal to build momentum for WTO talks scheduled to begin a year later in November 1999. As nations in Asia still reeled from the Southeast Asian financial crisis, many also hoped APEC could contribute to the recovery of the region.

The formal agenda of APEC continued to reflect the Osaka declaration, which promised the dual commitment to pursue comprehensiveness and flexibility in liberalization negotiations. This led to different interpretations over whether it was necessary to agree to liberalization on all sectors. U.S. officials insisted that the agreement represented a balanced package in which "everyone gets a little, everyone gives a little," and urged Japan that its participation in an agreement on all nine sectors, including forestry and fisheries, was necessary.[100] Deputy U.S. Trade Representative Richard Fisher announced before the meeting that "If Japan did not participate in these two sectors, then the ministerial

---

[98] MAFF official. Interview by author. Tokyo, 14 January 2000.
[99] *New Straits Times*, 7 December 1998.
[100] *Asahi Evening News*, 4 November 1998.

and heads of state and leaders meeting would be a failure and Japan would be responsible."[101] On the other hand, Japanese officials insisted that since APEC consisted of voluntary commitments, it had no obligation to agree to any particular liberalization measure.

Even before the meeting began, the Japanese government announced that it would not join the tariff reduction plan for forestry and fisheries, although it would contribute with technical cooperation in the two sectors and with tariff reductions on the other seven sectors.[102] Officials from Australia and New Zealand said no package would be credible without Japanese participation, and U.S. Trade Representative Charlene Barshefsky condemned Japan for playing "a destructive role" by holding up the trade deal in Kuala Lumpur.[103] China and South Korea at first showed support for Japan's request to allow special treatment of some sectors, but with China's focus on gaining WTO entry and President Kim Dae Jung's status as a reformer and urban constituency representative, they did not strongly back Japan's position.[104] Trying to gain support, Japanese officials resorted to hard politics: the Malaysian trade minister complained that Japan linked its promised economic aid package with the outcome of the forestry and fishery issue.[105] Overall, Japan was isolated in its request for special treatment.

Despite such isolation and strong U.S. pressure, divisions within the Japanese government were resolved in favor of the Ministry of Agriculture position. Officials from MITI and the Foreign Ministry suggested making a small tariff concession so that the package could move forward.[106] However, the Ministry of Agriculture, which could not obtain the political backing for any tariff concession on the two sectors, adamantly refused. According to one top official, the Foreign Ministry in the end supported the Agriculture Ministry's refusal to make any concession because of the feeling that the United States was trying to force tariff concessions on Japan in a way that countered the voluntary nature of APEC.[107] Furthermore, he said the nine sectors had been poorly chosen during the Vancouver meeting and Japan had only agreed to accept the package out of the understanding that the voluntary nature of APEC liberalization would obviate the need to make any unwanted

---

[101] *New Straits Times* (Malaysia), 12 November 1998.
[102] MAFF official. Interview by author. Tokyo, 14 January 2000.
[103] *Yomiuri shimbun*, 16 November 1998.
[104] MAFF official. Interview by author. Tokyo, 14 January 2000.
[105] *New Straits Times*, 14 November 1998.
[106] Interviews by author in Tokyo: MOFA official, 14 May 1999; MAFF official, 18 March 1999; MITI official, 22 January 2000.
[107] MOFA official. Interview by author. Tokyo, 14 May 1999.

cuts. No politicians broke ranks to urge compromise for the sake of the success of the negotiation. The top bureaucrat who serves as advisor to the cabinet (*naikaku kanbō fukuchōkan*) mediated the dispute between the different ministries. At this level the decision was made to take the hard position that there would be no climbing down from the refusal on tariff cuts.

Thereafter, officials from all three ministries and politicians consistently upheld the government position that APEC was not a place for tariff negotiations. The common refrain stated that the appropriate forum for discussing tariffs was the WTO, where binding commitments could be made, and not APEC.[108] Politicians from the agriculture, forestry, and fisheries committees of the LDP went to Kuala Lumpur as part of an "APEC Action Corps" to urge the foreign minister and trade minister not to make any compromise.[109] MITI officials had no choice but to assent. Nevertheless, they must have keenly felt the awkwardness of being put in the position of refusing liberalization in the APEC forum that MITI had originally promoted. MITI Minister Kaoru Yosano reportedly complained that conflicting interests at home had forced him to act in a "disgraceful manner."[110]

Business groups called on Japan to contribute to the EVSL liberalization, but they did not oppose the concept of voluntarism. Prior to the Kuala Lumpur meeting, Keidanren stated that Japan should participate in liberalization of the fifteen sectors, including forestry and fisheries, and urged Japan to show leadership for implementing the EVSL proposal. However, it also included the caution that "work must proceed in a manner consistent with the principle of voluntarism."[111] An earlier report had expressed concern that the non-binding principles of APEC would delay liberalization but admitted that the voluntary approach should continue given the diverse economic and cultural situation among members.[112] With low expectations for concrete gains from trade liberalization, Keidanren instead emphasized the importance of projects to promote infrastructure in the region and to develop intellectual property rights protection. At the APEC meeting in Kuala Lumpur, the meeting of business leaders focused on policies to deal with the financial

[108] *Yomiuri shimbun*, 16 November 1998.
[109] *Nihon nōgyō shimbun*, 15 November 1998.
[110] *Yomiuri shimbun*, 9 December 1998.
[111] Keidanren, "Proposals and Expectations toward APEC Activities," 20 October 1998. Policy report available at www.keidanren.or.jp/english/policy/pol089.html.
[112] Keidanren, "Toward the Development of APEC," 16 September 1997. Policy report available at www.keidanren.or.jp/english/policy/pol065.html.

crisis. After difficulties reaching a consensus on the trade issues, the business advisory council passed a resolution in favor of liberalization of the fifteen sectors. Low levels of participation by senior business leaders from Japan, the United States, and others in the region showed a lack of interest in the meeting.[113] This rather tepid support by business for the EVSL agenda was insufficient to overcome the strong opposition in Japan to concessions.

In the end, the Japanese government prevented agreement to begin early liberalization on the nine sectors. Other nations would not accept an agreement in which Japan refused to join some parts, but Japan would not offer any concession toward liberalizing the forestry and fisheries sectors. Although the agenda had not institutionalized an all-or-nothing approach, in fact, the choice came down to moving forward on the package as a whole or not at all. In addition to the United States, other APEC members such as Indonesia and Thailand had considerable interest in Japanese liberalization of the forestry and fisheries sectors, where they were major exporters. Without agreement for liberalization of those sectors, these countries could not agree to concessions in other sectors.[114]

Ending the deadlock, the APEC trade ministers agreed to forward the entire package for EVSL to the WTO. While nations were welcome voluntarily to begin tariff cuts before such WTO talks began, they did not sign an APEC agreement. The Japanese Foreign Ministry spokesperson welcomed the outcome—saying that EVSL should be implemented according to the principle of voluntarism and "The WTO is a far more appropriate body to reach a binding trade agreement. We are ready to put these two sectors on the WTO negotiating table."[115]

Criticism for the failure of the Kuala Lumpur meeting was directed at Japan. Newspaper headlines declared "Asia summit yielded little fruit" and reported that the outcome reinforced the APEC reputation for talk rather than action.[116] The Japanese media also criticized Japan's lack of leadership.[117] U.S. officials were very dissatisfied; it was reported that when meeting with Trade Minister Yosano, Charlene Barshefsky was so furious over Japan's refusal to liberalize forestry and fisheries that "she

[113] *The Australian*, 20 November 1998.

[114] I thank Ellis Krauss for sharing this important point with me in correspondence about the case. See Krauss (forthcoming).

[115] *New Straits Times*, 16 November 1998.

[116] *Wall Street Journal*, 19 November 1998.

[117] *Yomiuri shimbun*, 9 December 1998.

would have pounded the desk if there had been one."[118] She told Foreign Minister Kōmura that it was meaningless to defer the issue. The 1999 *U.S. Trade Estimates Report* on Japan clearly placed the onus of responsibility on Japan for preventing an EVSL deal in APEC:

> As the world's second largest economy, Japan's full participation in these [EVSL priority sector] initiatives was regarded as vital to ensuring their successful completion in 1998 as directed by APEC leaders. Facing strong domestic pressure, Japan refused to participate in tariff reductions in the fisheries and forestry products sectors at the November 1998 APEC Leaders' Meeting, thereby blocking APEC's adoption of the policy package.[119]

Ultimately Japan's strategy successfully ended trade talks on forestry and fishery issues and indefinitely delayed talks on food products. Along with other disagreements that resulted in the collapse of the WTO ministerial meeting at Seattle in December 1999, EVSL was quietly dismissed. There was inadequate support for a sectoral approach to liberalization, and the meeting failed to launch a new comprehensive trade round. The Japanese government has upheld its position that it will discuss forestry and fishery issues only in the context of a comprehensive WTO trade round.

Comparing APEC with Liberalization of Rice

Comparison of the decision by Japan to refuse tariff cuts on forestry and fishery issues in 1998 and the decision to accept the tariffication of rice illustrates how negotiation context can be more important than the size and influence of the protection lobby. While rice represents the hardest case for liberalization in Japan, the government made concessions first in 1993 to end the import ban and allow minimum access imports. Then, in 1998, the government made a second concession to place rice under the same trade rules as other products. This is in surprising contrast with the refusal to make even the smallest concession on forestry and fishery tariffs during the APEC negotiation of 1998.

The Uruguay Round decision to end the rice import ban was only the first change of Japan's rice policies. In 1998 the Japanese government considered whether to continue special treatment with minimum access or change to the general treatment of tariffication. The difference between the two options was that special treatment allowed Japan to main-

---

[118] *Nihon nōgyō shimbun*, 15 November 1998.
[119] Office of the U.S. Trade Representative, *The 1999 National Trade Estimate Report on Foreign Trade Barriers*, 219.

tain its quota for rice imports, which gave greater protection against market fluctuation and maximized government regulatory control. In compensation for this exception to the rule of tariffication, Japan agreed to import a minimum of 4 to 8 percent of domestic consumption. However, continuation of special treatment beyond 1999 was conditional upon Japan's negotiating additional compensation.[120] Switching to tariffication would allow equivalent protection by means of a high tariff, and in exchange for adopting a more market-oriented policy tool, the obligatory amount of minimum imports would be slightly less.[121]

At the same time the government was refusing to consider any tariff cut on forestry and fishery products, it was in the final stages of deciding to accept the tariffication of rice. During the summer and fall of 1998, the government debated the rice issue in trilateral consultation among agriculture cooperatives, MAFF, and the LDP.[122] The government announced in December 1998 that, beginning in April 1999, it would end the rice quota and implement tariff protection.[123]

The decision to accept rice tariffication seems easy — Japan would import less rice, and it would not have to negotiate additional compensation for special treatment in the new trade round. However, the decision was obvious only given the constraints of the Uruguay Round agreement, which bound Japan to minimum access imports and committed it to negotiate more compensation in order to continue special treatment beyond 2000.

The formal nature of the GATT/WTO system with binding commitments facilitates the exchange of concessions. Although GATT treaty obligations certainly do not mandate a specific tariff reduction, the legal framing within the institution endows the entire process with greater authority. When leaders turn to their domestic audience to explain a tariff concession, they can justify that the sacrifice is *necessary* in order

[120] Although the agreement did not specify the nature of such compensation, it would have to satisfy the principal countries, namely, the United States. Mostly likely such compensation would involve tariff cuts on other products or greater rice import obligation.

[121] With the new tariff rate set at about 450 percent, U.S. rice would sell for 429 yen/kg compared with the highest-priced Japanese rice selling at 519 yen/kg and standard Japanese rice selling at 332 yen/kg. As a result, while Japan would continue to import the obligated minimum access rice, foreign rice above that fixed amount is unlikely to be competitive until the tariff is further reduced. USDA, Economic Research Service, "Rice Tariffication in Japan: What Does It Mean for Trade?" *Agricultural Outlook* (April 1999): 14.

[122] According to a senior LDP politician, Nōkyō began discussing the tariffication option as early as December 1997, although the issue only became public in November. *Nikkei shimbun*, 25 November 1998.

[123] *Zenkoku nōgyō shimbun*, 1 January 1999.

to achieve gains on other issues and to support the system of trade rules. This makes it easier for leaders to agree to the concession in the first place. Thus even the most influential lobby group, rice farmers, could not resist liberalization given the constraints of the WTO process.

The problem for liberalization under APEC is that the principle of voluntarism is explicit. Rather than helping leaders persuade constituents that a concession is necessary for the long-term goal of economic cooperation, voluntarism offers a loophole. This makes it more difficult for any leader to make a tariff cut harmful to a powerful domestic constituency. Although fishery and forestry interests do not hold as much political influence as rice farmers, given the weaker constraints of the APEC negotiation structure these interests were sufficient to prevent any concession.

Low Institutionalization and Liberalization in APEC

The refusal by Japan to liberalize forestry and fishery products during the 1998 APEC meeting highlighted the limitations of U.S. pressure and Japanese proliberalization interests to bring about even a small tariff cut. Against a background of high trade dependence and rising friction over Japanese exports, U.S. economic leverage over Japan would presumably have been at its most influential in November 1998. Japan was vulnerable to any U.S. threats of protectionism as declining demand in recession-struck Asia and Japan left the U.S. market as a crucial outlet for Japanese exports. The 1999 *National Trade Estimate Report* prepared by the Office of the USTR comments that "Japan is more dependent on the U.S. market to absorb its exports than it has been for many years. In 1998, the United States bought about 31 percent of Japan's exports, the highest level since 1990, and close to the all-time high of 36 percent in 1986." The report goes on to describe problematic trends in U.S.-Japan trade in 1998, as U.S. exports to Japan decreased by nearly 12 percent from the previous year, the goods trade deficit with Japan rose 14 percent, and import surges from Japan in steel and other sectors damaged U.S. industries. The trade imbalance left Japan more vulnerable and increased the political pressures in the United States to take a tough position against Japan.

How credible was the U.S. threat that Japan would regret its obstinate stance at APEC? Neither the U.S. fish nor timber industries chose to file a petition under section 301 of U.S. Trade Law, and overall industry lobbying remained low profile. The United States was already Japan's top supplier in both markets, and average tariff rates in Japan were low. Furthermore, environmental protection policies had led the

United States to restrict imports of fishery items and exports of forestry products. This made it appear unlikely that the United States would launch sanctions over forestry and fishery trade. Nevertheless, the rising U.S. trade deficit created a tense politicized atmosphere for trade relations. Indeed, the Japanese officials said that they felt political goals rather than industry lobbying drove the U.S. demands.[124] There was potential for friction on issues such as Japan's refusal to reduce forestry and fishery tariffs to fuel anger against Japan's closed market that would build support for U.S. measures in unrelated areas, such as antidumping action against Japanese steel exports. Therefore, while specific retaliation over forestry and fisheries lacked credibility, the general threat of rising protectionism in the United States was very credible.

The broadening of domestic policy participation and presence of domestic groups that stood to gain from the agreement make the negotiation fit a prima facie case for a two-level game explanation of liberalization. The cross-sector package of nine sectors discussed at the Kuala Lumpur meeting established the conditions for internal pressure to complement U.S. pressure as companies that would benefit from the agreement would counter the lobbying against the agreement by forestry and fishery groups. That is, there was the kind of latent support for foreign demands that Schoppa (1997) attributes with better bargaining outcomes. For example, chemical companies, whose exports accounted for 7 percent of total Japanese exports in 1996, stood to gain from priority liberalization.[125] Even in the fisheries sector, processing firms favor liberalization in order to gain cheaper imports for raw materials. More importantly, success on the nine priority areas would also have built momentum for addressing the remaining six EVSL areas in 1999. These sectors included automobiles, which account for 12 percent of all Japanese exports, as a sector in which Japanese exporters could gain from an APEC liberalization agreement. Such divided interests at home should have made Japan more likely to yield under foreign pressure.

Not only were there divided economic interests, but the policy process of APEC included different ministries representing diverse interests. Indeed, MAFF is in a particularly weak position in APEC negotiations because the trade ministerial meetings do not include representation by the Minister of Agriculture.[126] Within the APEC process, MITI has traditionally taken a lead role. This gives it greater authority over the ne-

---

[124] Former MAFF official working for a fisheries association. Interview by author. Tokyo, 17 January 2000.

[125] Export share figures are taken from *Asahi Shimbun, Japan Almanac* 1998, 117.

[126] Indeed, for all other countries only the trade minister attends these meetings, and Japan alone sends both the minister of trade and the minister of foreign affairs.

gotiating position, even with the understanding that MAFF has jurisdiction for agriculture, forestry, and fishery issues.[127] Yet despite the strong position of MITI in the APEC policy process, it could not persuade officials of MAFF, MOFA, or the Cabinet advisor to support its position favoring a small tariff concession.

Given the U.S. pressure, the prospective gains from liberalization, and the MITI role as proponent of APEC, one would expect that Japan would have at least offered a moderate tariff concession on some of the products in forestry and fishery sectors. This could have shown that Japan was contributing to the effort to build a balanced package, while at the same time only imposing a small sacrifice on the vulnerable primary sectors. One must look closer at the negotiation process to understand why the government did not try this approach.

The APEC principle of voluntarism rendered it politically difficult to make concessions harmful to domestic constituencies. How could any Japanese politician justify that they were *forced* to make an *early voluntary* tariff cut? In addition, the Osaka Action Agenda created a weak connection between different issues by pairing the principle of comprehensive liberalization with the principle of flexibility. Voluntarism and flexibility left open the possibility to liberalize only those areas where it was easy to make commitments. This prevented the kind of argument used during the Uruguay Round when politicians justified sacrifices in agriculture as necessary for broader gains and international obligation to support the GATT trade system.

The weakly institutionalized issue linkage also reduced the incentive for lobbying by business to advocate liberalization of sectors outside of their own direct interest. There was not a clear signal from the agenda that the failure to liberalize one sector would prevent agreement on other sectors. Consequently, an industry group expecting that chemicals sectoral liberalization would take place regardless of the outcome on fisheries had little reason to advocate concessions on fisheries. On the other hand, if the same industry group expected that other countries would opportunistically choose to liberalize some sectors and not others, then it had even less reason to lobby during the negotiation given low expectations for much liberalization in any sector. Even if countries did agree to meaningful liberalization commitments, there would be no monitoring or dispute mechanism to hold them to their commitments. In short, while business groups had specific interests in parts of the negotiation, the weakly institutionalized linkage produced uncertainty about the stakes of the negotiation, and lowered incentives for mobilization.

[127] MAFF official. Interview by author. Tokyo, 14 January 2000.

Differences in interpretations over the nature of the APEC forum played a large role in how Japan responded to demands to liberalize sensitive sectors. In the Vancouver meeting, Japan had agreed to the EVSL agenda to negotiate liberalization of fifteen sectors, including forestry and fisheries. From the perspective of Japanese government officials, *voluntary* meant that Japan did not have to reduce tariffs at all if it chose otherwise. This led even the more liberal and internationalist Foreign Ministry to take sides with the Ministry of Agriculture. Officials of the United States and some APEC nations, however, felt that Japan had committed itself in Vancouver to accept comprehensive liberalization. The wide disparity in views about the proper role of APEC meant that Japanese leaders did not feel they had to choose between abandoning APEC or making tariff cuts in fish and forestry sectors. Mexico and Chile had already opted not to participate in the EVSL process in the prior year. The Malaysian trade minister said, "It is wrong to ascribe an APEC meeting as wrecked because one country cannot participate. Here Japan is participating except for two sectors. That's it and we have to accept that."[128]

Japanese decisions on APEC trade liberalization have demonstrated how features of the negotiation structure change the effect of international pressure. Without the leverage of an institutionalized commitment to an all-or-nothing approach, neither U.S. pressure nor potential gains to Japan were sufficient to persuade liberalization of sensitive issues such as forestry and fisheries.

Conclusion

The historical record of the major agricultural negotiations between the United States and Japan over the past three decades shows that, while U.S. pressure has pushed forward liberalization, it has often relied upon the support of international institutions to bring about liberalization of the most sensitive items. In all of the negotiations examined in this chapter and the previous chapter, the United States made demands and Japan resisted liberalization, but the level of liberalization resulting has varied according to the negotiation structure. When the same quota policies were the topic in a series of three negotiations, it was the final negotiation in the GATT dispute settlement process that brought the greatest policy liberalization. In a paired comparison of comprehensive negotiations on different topics, Japan's decision to end the rice ban in

[128] *New Straits Times*, 14 November 1998.

the Uruguay Round in 1993 and accept rice tariffication in 1998 contrasts with its decision during the same period to reject liberalization of fishery and forestry policy in APEC. This chapter has shown how the Uruguay Round generated pressures to counter the domestic opposition to rice liberalization, while U.S. pressure within APEC was unable to credibly broaden the stakes of the negotiation because it was handicapped by the principle of voluntarism in the negotiation structure.

While threats aroused concern among leaders and big business, agricultural negotiations continued to experience deadlock in the face of escalating trade tensions. For example, there were strong threats from the United States against the quota cases during the bilateral negotiations of the early 1980s, but this only produced minor reform, although threats and U.S. pressure biased results to favor U.S. exports. In contrast, more policy liberalization occurred in negotiations like the 1988 GATT 12 settlement, which actually involved a lower level of U.S. threats.

The fact that liberalization outcomes often bring higher budget expenses goes against the hypothesis that budget cutting motivates liberalization. Indeed, liberalization of beef and citrus was contrary to structural reform efforts, which aimed to reduce budget costs by encouraging farmers to shift production from rice to other agricultural commodities. An expensive compensation package accompanied rice liberalization. Moreover, as a consequence of the Uruguay Round, the government fell into a situation where it was spending money to store surplus domestic production of rice and paying Japanese farmers not to produce more rice, while at the same time purchasing imported rice. Budget rationality clearly did not motivate these decisions to accept liberalization.

The decisions that shaped the negotiation structure reflected the strategies of both the United States and Japan, as well as other actors. When Japan had more influence over the agenda, it tried to weaken the issue linkage and legal framing, as it did during the 1995 Osaka meeting of APEC. However, the ability of one nation to shape the negotiation structure depended on the broader consent of other nations and the nature of the existing institution. How did the choices over negotiation forum influence the final outcomes? If the hardest cases were negotiated in bilateral talks, it would not be surprising to find that these negotiations had less liberalization in their policy outcomes. However, in fact, the most difficult negotiation issues were brought up in a trade round or panel negotiation. For example, Japanese politicians wanted to negotiate rice policy in the Uruguay Round rather than in a bilateral negotiation. Leaders clearly hoped to avoid any policy change, and yet in the end, they accepted important changes to the most politically sensitive policy topic in Japan. Some factors favored placing the more controversial cases within a GATT context. For GATT trade rounds, the potential for delays and lower attention on any single issue made it easier for leaders to commit to negotiate about rice trade while hoping to avoid painful reforms. Delegating to a third party in a panel negotiation was another way to reduce the domestic political costs from liberalization. For example, during the height of the beef-citrus negotiation in 1988, some LDP politicians expressed their preference for letting the issue be settled in a GATT panel. Therefore, when political costs from liberalization were the highest, Japan was more likely to encourage a negotiation within a round or panel negotiation. This pattern gives added significance to the finding that the institutional mechanisms of these negotiations promoted more liberalization.

The sequence of events during the negotiations indicates the importance of changes within the negotiation structure. Shifts to increase the level of legal framing or to strengthen the cross-sector linkage were followed by movement toward agreement. The turning point of each phase of the quota negotiations followed closely after changes in negotiation context — the shift to bring beef-citrus talks into the Tokyo Round context in 1978, the move toward seeking GATT panel mediation in 1984, and the establishment of GATT panels during 1987 and 1988. Within the Uruguay Round, the evidence is even stronger. After the Brussels meeting failure and the draft agreement issued by the GATT director-general made the linkage more credible, interest groups responded by increasing their lobbying for agricultural liberalization, and actors within the government also began to change their position.

The level of institutionalization of the negotiation structure feature — issue linkage or legal framing — corresponds with the level of liberalization in the outcome (see table 6.2). For example, the weak issue linkage in the Tokyo Round brought only minor reform of beef and citrus policies, and the weak issue linkage in the APEC negotiations led to a status quo outcome for fish quotas and fish and forestry tariffs. In contrast, the strong issue linkage of the Uruguay Round helped push forward major changes in the basic domestic programs regulating Japanese agriculture, including an end to the ban on rice imports. Establishment of a panel and the subsequent violation ruling led to major policy reform. Across several negotiations, the bilateral agreements involved partial change, and the agreements following the GATT panels and the Uruguay Round involved more comprehensive overhaul of domestic policies. Either a strongly institutionalized linkage or high legal framing is a necessary condition for major liberalization.

Most importantly, in each negotiation, there was evidence that do-

TABLE 6.2
Summary of Japanese Case Outcomes

Negotiation Case	Issue Linkage	Legal Framing	Liberalization
Tokyo Round (beef, citrus, other quotas)	moderate	low	minor
Bilateral (beef, citrus, other quotas)	none	none	minor
GATT DSP (beef, citrus, other quotas)	none	high	major
Uruguay Round (rice)	strong	moderate	major
APEC (fish, forestry)	weak	low	none

Note: The categories measure the institutionalization of the issue linkage and legal framing in the negotiation structure.

mestic actors changed their behavior because of factors related to negotiation structure. Following an increase in the institutionalization of the issue linkage in the Uruguay Round, industry groups intensified their lobbying and made more explicit demands for agricultural concessions. Agricultural interest groups cited more difficulty lobbying for protection in negotiations with a legalistic context. Issue linkage led to a greater role for MITI and the Foreign Ministry as a counterweight to the Agriculture Ministry in government decision-making. At both the interest group and bureaucratic level, the involvement of proliberalization groups varied according to the negotiation structure.

The analysis has shown that legal framing promotes liberalization because it creates a sense of international obligation, which held both economic and political value for politicians. First, there is a tangible economic stake in the broader system of trade rules that maintains open markets for Japanese exports. Hence comments about Japan's international obligation to GATT were often prefaced by statements that "Japan is a trading nation." Second, there is a political interest in whether liberalization represents an international obligation, because both trade interests and normative stakes influence the level of domestic opposition. In societies that respect international law such as Japan, framing a concession in terms of compliance with international law adds legitimacy. Such legitimacy for a liberalization demand increased pressure in favor of a compromise position while isolating opponents. For example, the violation ruling against Japan's quota policies in 1987 increased media and business advocacy for compromise. On the other hand, when U.S. demands in 1984 had lacked such legal force, fierce farm group opposition made it politically too risky for either business groups or

Prime Minister Nakasone to push for compromise. During the 1998 APEC meeting, flexibility of the negotiation made it easier for domestic groups opposing compromise to resist change. Finally, Japanese politicians used the rationale of international obligation to explain decisions, such as when they justified decisions to end quotas and to allow rice imports in terms of duty to support international rules. They also defended their refusal to make trade concessions within APEC in terms of the lack of any obligation to make commitments in a voluntary trade forum. When leaders weigh the economic costs of protection and the political costs of liberalization, international obligation is an important factor in their calculations.

In sum, the U.S.-Japan negotiation cases have shown that changes in the international negotiation structure influenced the mobilization of interest groups and involvement of bureaucratic actors. Issue linkage and legal framing broadened the stakes during the negotiations in ways that made liberalization both necessary for the national interest and possible for political leaders.

Part III

U.S.-EU TRADE NEGOTIATIONS

7

Farm Politics in the European Union

EFFORTS TO OPEN markets encounter stiff resistance when confronting European agricultural trade policies. The nature of policies, the influence of the governments and farm groups backing these policies, and the bias of EU institutions in favor of agricultural interests all contribute to the system supporting the status quo.

Although the EU traces its roots to a customs union for coal and steel, since the formation of the Common Agricultural Policy in 1962, agriculture as much as industry became the central focus. At its founding, the CAP held promise as the model for future integration. Optimists at the time wrote that "the progress made in agriculture will be of definitive importance for the integrative potential for the EEC. It represents the Community's first effort to develop a common policy in a major economic sphere. Such common policies are central to the successful implementation of the broader goal of economic union and the efficient operation of the customs union."[1] For decades CAP was the only working Community policy. CAP subsidies are a central mechanism for redistributive transfers between members and generate political support for integration among influential domestic constituencies in all member states. Even as EU activities have expanded, agriculture has continued to seize a disproportionate share of Community attention and budgets.

At the same time, the budget burden and conflicting interests over reforming CAP have nearly torn asunder the union on many occasions. The Luxembourg compromise of 1966, which allowed members to veto policies they strongly opposed, found its origins in disagreements over CAP financing. Past accession agreements for new members and current plans for enlargement have been delayed and nearly blocked by complications related to agricultural policy questions.

As CAP policies transformed the EU from a net importer into a major exporter of many commodities by the 1980s, they drew the ire of the United States and other agricultural exporters who targeted EU agricultural policies in frequent trade complaints. From 1970 to 1989 under GATT, thirty-one of forty-five complaints against the EC related to agri-

[1] L. N. Lindberg (1963) cited in Wallace and Wallace (1996, 100).

cultural products, while under the WTO from 1995 to 2000, twenty out of thirty-three complaints against the EU related to agricultural products.[2] Clearly, agriculture dominates EU relations within the GATT system. Bilateral disputes and discussions within round negotiations have occurred in addition to these complaints.

This chapter provides the background about the policies and important actors involved in the EU policy process for setting agricultural trade policies. The analysis leads to a base expectation that there would be little liberalization of European agriculture in the absence of pressures arising in international negotiations.

Agricultural Protection

As part of creating a common market for goods, the six original members of the European Economic Community agreed also to unify their agricultural protection policies. CAP originated in the 1957 Treaty of Rome establishing the EEC, which outlines the following objectives of the policy in article 39 to increase productivity through technological progress, provide a fair standard of living for farmers, stabilize markets, guarantee adequate supplies of food for the population, and finally ensure that supplies reach consumers at reasonable prices. The design of the common marketing arrangements for CAP was eventually agreed upon in 1962. Governments in essence relinquished their national agricultural policies when they agreed to implement CAP policies and accept common financial responsibility to pay for them through the EU budget.[3]

The CAP mechanism for protection revolves around a target price for each commodity set by the Council of Ministers at a level expected to give a satisfactory level of return to the farmer.[4] An intervention price provides the floor to the market at which the government guarantees it will purchase goods, and trade barriers ensure that imports cannot un-

[2] All complaints are counted, including when multiple complaints address a single issue. GATT disputes are summarized from Hudec (1993). WTO disputes are summarized from "Overview of the State-of-Play of WTO Disputes" (Geneva: World Trade Organization, 26 February 2001).

[3] The European Court of Justice has ruled that national governments do not have the authority either to enact conflicting national laws in the field or to modify CAP policies when they implement them (Bentil 1985, 353).

[4] However, following the breakdown of fixed exchange rates in 1971, national governments gave extra subsidies to their own farmers by manipulating the complicated "green money" system for adjusting common prices into national exchange rates. The move to monetary union has closed this substantial loophole in the common pricing idea.

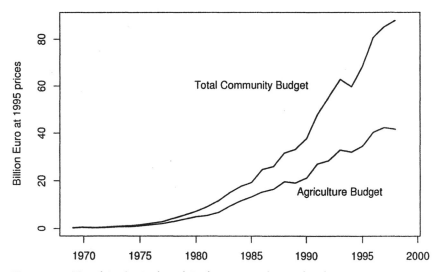

Figure 7.1: Trend in Agricultural Budget Expenditures by the European Union. Community expenditure from 1969 to 1998 (at 1995 prices) showing total budget figures and European Agricultural Guidance and Guarantee Fund section of general budget. *Source*: EC (1999).

dercut internal market prices. These policy tools form a complex network of market arrangements.

Such heavy government intervention creates a burden for the EU budget. Spending for CAP as a share of total Community expenditures ranged from the high of 87 percent in 1970 to 45 percent in 2000 (see figure 7.1). The EU agricultural budget has steadily increased to reach the height of 45 billion Euro (43.7 billion U.S. dollars) in 2001.[5] Its declining share of overall spending reflects the expansion of EU activities into other policy spheres.

Success in achieving objectives to maintain farm incomes and build self-sufficiency also lay the basis for future trade conflicts. EC farm output increased by 30 percent in the first ten years following the establishment of CAP (Larsen 1994, 12). As consumption failed to keep pace with production, surplus stocks accumulated. The solution was to use the CAP budget to finance export subsidies that would enable farmers to sell high-price EU products at internationally competitive prices.[6] Such policies both depressed world prices and took markets from

[5] *International Herald Tribune*, 26 June 2002.
[6] For example, by 1994, the EU held a 47 percent share of the world dairy market with about 2.38 billion U.S. dollars spent on subsidized exports (Grant 1997, 26).

TABLE 7.1
EU: OECD Estimates of Support to Agriculture

Year	86–88	97–99
Producer support estimate (all crops)	44%	44%
PSE (rice)	57	23
PSE (milk)	56	54
PSE (beef)	48	58
Consumer support estimate	40	31
Total support as percent of GDP	2.6	1.5

Source: OECD (2000a, 205–206).
Note: The percent producer support estimate measures the monetary value of transfers to agricultural producers relative to the total value of farm production. The consumer support estimate measures the tax on consumption associated with agricultural policies relative to total consumption of food commodities (negative values are listed in positive terms). The percent total support estimate measures the share of all agricultural support in the GDP.

other exporters. Across all commodities the EU is a net importer of agriculture and food products, while at the same time it is a leading exporter of some commodities.[7] In 1996, agricultural products equaled 11.4 percent of total EU imports and 7.9 percent of total EU exports.[8]

CAP has provided substantial protection for farmers. Support to producers amounts to 44 percent of the total value of all farm receipts, compared with 36 percent for OECD countries in the 1997–1999 period (OECD 2000a, 24). Table 7.1 shows that protection levels in the EU remain high and have experienced only moderate shifts in form and levels.[9] While it appears that there has been no change in the producer protection levels, this masks the shift in policy tools toward less use of market support prices and more direct payments. The OECD publishes a Consumer Support Estimate measuring the consumer burden from high market prices and other policies. According to this measure for the period 1997–99, the implicit consumption tax associated with agricultural support policies formed 31 percent of all consumer expendi-

[7] While the EU imports fruit and vegetables, animal feed, fish, oilseeds and timber, it is a major exporter of cereals, milk products, and alcoholic beverages.

[8] European Commission, The Agricultural Situation in the European Union 1997 Report (Luxembourg: Office for Official Publications of the European Communities, 1998) 174.

[9] The increase in beef support reflects in large part the costs incurred regarding the bovine spongiform encephalopathy (BSE) crisis for European beef farmers and payments made for slaughtered cattle.

tures on domestic agricultural commodities, which was still an improvement from 1986–1988. By another measure, consumers in Europe spent 46 percent more for their food purchases at EU prices in 1997–1999 than they would have spent buying food at world prices, which was also a decline from 66 percent in 1986–1988. Finally, the total support estimate includes both producer and consumer support to measure the share of national wealth used to support agriculture. From this perspective, there has been an overall decline in support for agricultural spending in Europe, although EU members continue to pay above the average 1.4 percent of GDP paid by all OECD member nations (OECD 2000a, 159, 205).

European agricultural policies have important implications for the United States given the impact on U.S. agricultural trade. For many years the EU ranked second behind Japan among top U.S. agricultural export markets with average annual exports by the United States of 7.6 billion U.S. dollars over the years 1990–1996, and in 2000 the EU ranked third behind Japan and Canada with total U.S. exports to the EU worth 6.4 billion U.S. dollars.[10] Oilseeds, grains and feeds, and soybeans are the largest U.S. export items to the EU.

The United States also imported an average of 5.3 billion dollars of agricultural products from the EU over the years 1990–1996, which made the United States the largest market for European agricultural exports.[11] The EU has an interest in continued access to United States markets, and the U.S. can easily target agricultural exports for retaliation in the context of trade negotiations over EU protection barriers. Beverages and spirits compose nearly half of the EU agricultural exports to the United States, and these products have frequently been on target lists in trade disputes. This dynamic distinguishes the EU from Japan's position, since Japan is almost exclusively an importer of agricultural goods.

U.S.-EU relations must also be viewed in the wider context of economic interdependence. The U.S.-EU trade relationship forms 30 percent of world trade and they hold the largest two-way trade and investment relationship. Trade between the United States and the EU is fairly balanced. In 1999 the United States exported 236.5 billion dollars worth of goods and services to the EU and imported 264.4 billion dollars

[10] USDA, "U.S. Agricultural Trade," accessed at www.ers.usda.gov/briefing/AgTrade; USDA, "Outlook for U.S. Agricultural Trade," 22 February 2001.

[11] USDA, "U.S. Agricultural Trade," accessed at www.ers.usda.gov/briefing/AgTrade. In 1998 EU exports to the U.S. equaled 8,034 million ECU and exports to its second largest market, Russia, equaled 4,038 million ECU. Japan was the third largest EU market with exports to Japan worth 3,627 million ECU (European Commission, Eurostat).

worth of goods and services.[12] Investment patterns also reflect large two-way flows. Forty-five percent of U.S. foreign direct investment abroad is in EU members, which also provide 63 percent of all foreign direct investment in the United States.[13] Such high interdependence both gives rise to tension over specific issues and creates incentives to maintain a mutually beneficial economic relationship.

Actors and Interests

The CAP has been referred to as a "self-contained world, following its own logic" (Wallace and Wallace 1996, 100). What are the factors that contribute to this situation, and what forces could bring change?

First, the question arises about whether the EU can be treated as having a foreign economic policy comparable to Japan or other states. Clearly the EU is its own unique form of international organization, with policy processes integrating supranational policies and the national policies of fifteen member countries. Often EU policy-making is characterized as a "three-level game" in which there is the national process of preference determination, then an EU process for aggregating these policies into a single position, and finally an international negotiation (Moyer 1993; Patterson 1997). Consequently, while this study focuses on the EU level and international level, attention must be given as well to the internal politics shaping the EU policy position. Nevertheless, the complexity of EU policy-making does not deny the possibility to study a single foreign economic policy of the EU that represents the collective interests of the members.[14] While the EU falls short of statehood along some policy dimensions, its trade policies affect the international political economy *as if* it were a single nation.

In the WTO, the EU holds the legal status of a contracting party alongside sovereign states, as it did in practice in the 1947 GATT sys-

---

[12] U.S. Department of Commerce, *Survey of Current Business*, July 2000, table 2. Figures are calculated on a balance-of-payments basis. In comparison, U.S. international trade in goods and services with Japan included 56.4 billion dollars of U.S. exports to Japan and 130.9 billion dollars of U.S. imports from Japan.

[13] European-American Business Council, *The United States and Europe: Jobs, Investment and Trade*, seventh edition (Washington, DC, 2001).

[14] Michael Smith (1994, 289) argues the "pulling and hauling" of the EU policy process is similar to the US government or other federal systems. Sophie Meunier (2000, 104) argues that one can consider how distinct EU processes determine its position in a negotiation and analyze the "collective" EU interest in international negotiations.

tem.[15] EU member states also maintain legal status as individual contracting parties, but the European Commission represents the EU at WTO meetings. Since 1970 most trade agreements, with a few exceptions, have been negotiated as "Community agreements" where there was not any need for an additional acceptance by members (Petersmann 1986, 37). Within the international trade system, the EU is a single policy actor comparable to Japan.

Agricultural Politics and National Governments

While the operation of CAP occurs at the EU level, decision making reflects the intergovernmental nature of the EU. National governments determine CAP policies through the price-setting decisions of the Council of Ministers and their approval or veto of reform proposals. Indeed, opposition by governments in the Council diluted major reform proposals from the Commission, such as the Mansholt plan of 1968 to reduce expenditures and encourage structural reforms, and in 1985, the German government vetoed the Commission proposal for price cuts in cereals. The complicated mix of protection policies embodied within the CAP arose as the response to demands of member states.

The agricultural situation across European nations diverges considerably in terms of the structure of the agricultural sector. For the most part, European agriculture faces higher production costs than the United States, Australia, or other major exporters. The average size of European farms is thirteen hectares of land, but this average conceals the presence of many large farms (over fifty hectares) in France and the UK as well as many tiny farms of less than five hectares in southern nations (Larsen 1994, 24). Competitiveness varies considerably — some French grain farmers could be competitive on international markets without government support; Denmark and the Netherlands export value-added agricultural items such as ham and have built a world-leading food-processing industry; on the other hand, some Italian farmers live entirely off EU subsidies by producing for intervention purchases (Grant 1997, 48–57).

This variation in the structure of the agricultural sector across Europe leads to different policy preferences. States with smaller farms favor higher price supports, while those with larger farms would be willing to consider price cuts but resist production controls and want export sub-

[15] The EC never formally acceded to GATT. Nevertheless, the commission participated like a GATT contracting party *sui generis*, and the double membership was never legally questioned (Petersmann 1986, 36–37).

sidies (Moyer and Josling 1990, 57). Exporters insist on continued export subsidies, while importers seek protection from cheap foreign imports that would undermine the system of high prices that support farm incomes. Nevertheless, although states have different preferences over specific policies, there is a broad consensus in favor of using an interventionist farm policy to maintain the family farm as the foundation of European agriculture (Daugbjerg 1999, 417).

There is a strong political marketplace for agricultural protection in nearly all EU members. Although the number of farmers has been more than halved over the past thirty years, farmers remain an important political force, given their strong organization and the identification with farmer interests shared by rural society. On average, farmers hold 5 percent share of civilian employment (see table 7.2). In countries such as Greece, Ireland, and Portugal, farmers are such a large group in absolute numbers that they can shift elections. Yet even in countries where farmers are a smaller share of the population, they often hold political influence as a critical electoral constituency.

In Britain, which has the smallest number of farmers, the outbreak of foot and mouth disease in February 2001 illustrated how an emergency for the farm sector could absorb national energies. Despite the fact that the disease is not a human health concern and is disastrous only due to loss of productivity for the livestock sector, the effort to deal with the problem delayed the calling of a national election. Quarantine policies to halt spread of the disease interfered with the travel plans of British and foreign tourists, at great expense for the tourist industry and the rural economy. The fact that sick pigs, sheep, and cows could bring to a halt British politics and tourism clearly illustrates the high priority given to farmer interests — and this in the European nation that has often been seen as the least captive to its farmers.

A coalition of France and Germany along with other, smaller states have provided the backbone of support for CAP. Ireland is among the most pro-CAP smaller states, with EU aid providing over 41 percent of farm incomes (Grant 1997, 181). Southern states with large but inefficient agricultural sectors are heavily dependent on CAP policies that bring a wealth transfer to them from the EU budget. On the other hand, Britain and the northern European countries (Finland, Sweden, Belgium, and Luxembourg) have had less input on CAP policies given that agriculture is not a central activity in their economies and their farmers are not as politically powerful (ibid., 1997, 42). Occasionally these countries advocate reforms and try to restrain the excesses of CAP costs for taxpayers and consumers. However, the entrenched policies of the CAP and the strong preferences of other states have tended to take

TABLE 7.2
EU Agricultural Statistics (1996)

	Farmer Share in Working Population	Agriculture Share in GDP	Major Product (percent in final ag. production)
EU-15	5.1%	1.7%	milk (17.5%)
Austria	7.4	1.0	milk (21.5)
Belgium	2.7	1.3	pork (26.1)
Denmark	3.9	2.4	pork (35.0)
Finland	7.9	0.8	milk (34.7)
France	4.8	1.9	milk (16.5)
Germany	2.9	0.8	milk (25.4)
Greece	20.3	6.7	vegetables (16.8)
Ireland	11.2	4.1	milk (34.2)
Italy	6.7	2.7	vegetables (13.4)
Luxembourg	2.4	0.7	milk (44.3)
Netherlands	3.8	2.8	milk (20.2)
Portugal	12.2	3.3	pork (23.3)
Spain	8.6	3.5	vegetables (14.1)
Sweden	3.3	0.5	milk (33.3)
United Kingdom	2.0	0.8	milk (23.9)

Source: European Commission, *The Agricultural Situation in the European Union 1997 Report* (Brussels, 1998). Figures are for 1996.

Note: Employment figures are for employment in agriculture, forestry, hunting and fishing sector as a share in total employment. The major product is that with the highest value as a share of the total value of agricultural production in the given country.

priority over their interests. The politics of European agricultural policy can be best understood by taking a closer look at France and Germany, the two countries that most strongly influence developments in European agricultural policy.

FRANCE

The radical protests of French farmers seize international headlines and shape perceptions of the centrality of agriculture in France. *The Economist* described the critical role of farming in French identity as follows: "Farming remains an element not just of the French economy but of the French soul. *La France agricole* is a reality even to millions who form no part of it—while to millions still living in the towns and villages of the countryside, the prosperity of its most visible industry is theirs."[16]

[16] *The Economist*, 19 September 1992, 21, cited in Golino (1995, 3).

Political and economic interests explain the vociferous opposition by France to any limits on production or export subsidies. The leading agricultural union, Federation Nationale des Syndicats d'Exploitants Agricoles (FNSEA), has developed a clientelistic relationship with the French government in which it gains subsidies in exchange for cooperation in the management of policies and restraint of farmer demands and violence (Keeler 1996). The potential outbreak of violent farmer protests and electoral defeat makes it credible when French leaders adopt a tough position against agricultural reform or threaten to exercise a veto.

The failed Socialist effort to change agricultural policy upon their election in 1981 illustrates the obstacles to any French government trying to oppose farmer interests. The new Agriculture Minister Edith Cresson sparked the dispute when she tried to recognize rival agricultural unions and restructure the Agriculture Ministry. During the "hot winter" of 1981–1982, widespread farmer protests were organized across the country, and in what a French magazine described as a "state of siege," farmers dumped manure in city streets and ripped up railroad tracks (Golino 1995, 16). Cresson had to request helicopter evacuation to escape a mob of angry farmers, and soon thereafter she reversed her position to favor government cooperation with FNSEA and was replaced by a new minister who restored close ties with the farm movement (ibid., 17).

Support for farmer interests is an important vote strategy in France. The number of farmers has declined from 2.75 million (13.5 percent of civilian employment) in 1970 to 1.07 million (4.8 percent of civilian employment) in 1996.[17] Nevertheless, farmers are a formidable voting bloc. A French scholar estimated that when considering higher voting participation by farmers and including the broader community of relatives and others with a stake in agriculture, the share of the voting electorate with "strong agricultural attributes" is as large as 17 percent.[18]

French agriculture has a vested interest in the CAP system. Its share of intra-EC trade grew from 40 percent to 74 percent in just the first ten years of CAP (ibid., 11), and it accounted for one-fifth of total EU agricultural production in the 1990s.[19] France is second only to the United States as the largest world food exporter, and exports of agricultural and food products form 13.7 percent of total French exports.[20] While Ger-

[17] *The Agricultural Situation in the European Union 1997 Report*, 113–115.

[18] Bertrand Hervieu of Centre Nationale de Recherce Scientifique, quoted in Golino (1995, 7).

[19] French production accounted for 23 percent of total EU agricultural production in 1994 (Grant 1997, 48).

[20] *The Agricultural Situation in the European Union 1997 Report*, 24–25.

many and the United Kingdom pay more toward financing CAP than they receive, France makes substantial net gains from CAP-related subsidies and trade.[21] Having done so well under CAP support policies, France has vehemently opposed reform proposals. In particular, French farmers resist production restraints and favor continued export subsidies which are necessary to dispose of the excess production that results when French farmers can produce as much as they want for guaranteed prices.

GERMANY

It is often said that the CAP represented a compromise to give France access to the German market for its agricultural exports in exchange for opening its own markets to German manufactured goods. However, in actuality, German leaders were unwilling to sacrifice farmers for the sake of manufactured exports, and they only accepted CAP because the other members agreed to accommodate the German demand that CAP embrace high price supports (Moravcsik 1998, 202). The real compromise embodied in CAP was to support greater production and an open internal market according to French preferences and also to support high prices according to German preferences.

Agriculture plays a much smaller role in the German economy than for France or other member states, and German farmers are not known for their radical activities. However, one should not underestimate the power of German agricultural interests. Indeed, the political and economic characteristics of Germany most closely resemble those of Japan (Sato and Schmitt 1993). In both countries the agricultural sector consists of mostly small and inefficient farms with a high ratio of part-time farmers.[22] A single farmers' organization unites farmer political influence and focuses on high price supports as the preferred policy guarantee. In both countries, their high volume of industrial exports creates a strong interest in free trade for manufactured goods; at the same time their inefficient agricultural sector demands protection.

[21] The net gains arising from the CAP guarantee section for France exceed the gains for all other members except Ireland and the Netherlands. The calculation of a total net transfer to France of 1,241 million ECU is reported in a 1993 study by the Institute of Agricultural Economics. The figure represents the net budget transfer plus the gains from internal trade taking place at EC prices rather than world prices. The United Kingdom and Germany suffer a net transfer *loss* of, respectively, 1,307 million ECU and 2,591 million ECU (Munk and Thomson 1994).

[22] Although the structure of German agriculture is diverse, with some very large farms in northern regions (and in the East after unification), small-scale farming is more common. Thirty percent of farms are under 5 hectares, and 37 percent of farmers work in agriculture part-time and have main employment outside of farming (Grant 1997, 57).

German farmers benefit from the enviable situation of having parties vie for their vote in an electoral system that gives swing vote groups considerable influence. Most farmers vote for the conservative Christliche Demokratische Union (CDU) or its Bavarian ally, the Christliche Soziale Union (CSU), which have jointly served as the ruling party for much of the postwar period. However, the support of smaller parties for farm interests also provides important leverage since the electoral system makes it difficult for any party to attain an overall majority. The smaller Freie Demokratische Partei (Free Democrats Party), which created a base among the small farmers of Bavaria and the larger farmers in the North, has in the past made agricultural support policies a condition for its participation in coalition governments.[23] This fragile political balance gives farmers a decisive role in shaping national politics.

The central farmer union, the Deutscher Bauernverband (DBV), represents 90 percent of all farmers and serves as an umbrella organization for local farmer interest groups. The number of farmers in Germany has halved over the past twenty-five years from 2.26 million (8.6% of civilian employment) in 1970 to 1.05 million (2.9% of civilian employment) in 1996.[24] Nevertheless, the powerful farm union guaranteed the continued attention of politicians to this sector's interests. Gisela Hendriks writes: "There is no doubt that the DBV is one of the most powerful interest groups in West Germany. Demands and objectives articulated by the DBV have effectively determined crucial decisions taken by the Federal Government" (Hendriks 1991, 144).

While Germany suffers a net wealth transfer as it pays more to support CAP than it receives back in subsidies,[25] it has been among the strongest opponents of price-cutting measures that would reduce costs. In 1964 Germany insisted that any change in CAP cereal prices must achieve unanimous support in the Council vote, thereby ensuring that Germany could protect its preference (Moravcsik 1998, 196). On that basis, in June 1985 the German government vetoed a proposal by the Commission to lower cereals prices by 3.6 percent, declaring that the cuts threatened "vital national interests" (Hendriks 1994, 155). Again in 1987, Chancellor Helmut Kohl refused to accept price cuts and weakened a Commission plan for stabilizing the budgetary crisis. Indeed, the government has added on protection for its own farmers above that received from CAP by means of special national subsidies and ma-

[23] Tracy (1997, 90); Field and Fulton (1994, 17).
[24] *The Agricultural Situation in the European Union 1997 Report*, 13–15. Note that figures for 1970 do not include East Germany, and that the percent employment figure for 1996 is from table 2.0.1.2.
[25] See footnote 21, this chapter.

nipulation of the CAP mechanism for compensatory amounts adjusting for currency differences.[26] Since it is the high price-support policies that stimulate excess production and necessitate import restrictions, Germany joins France to oppose liberalization of agriculture.

The Commission as "Single Voice"

The common commercial policy has meant both the uniformity of EU internal trade measures and the need for a "single voice" in international trade negotiations. The EC Treaty designates the Commission to negotiate international trade agreements on behalf of the members.[27] Although member states have challenged the competence of the Commission, the European Court of Justice has confirmed that the EU has exclusive competence for trade negotiations relating to goods.[28] In practice, the Commission negotiates in close cooperation with the Council of Ministers. The Commission submits its negotiating proposal to the Council, which must approve the mandate giving authority to the Commission to start negotiations and approve the final agreement (Elles 2000, 24). Sometimes the Council gives the Commission a relatively free hand to negotiate within a broad scope, while at other times a more narrow mandate requires that the Commission negotiators check back with the Council over every change (Meunier 2000).

For most trade negotiations, the Directorate General for External Relations (DGI)[29] drafts the trade proposal for submission to the Council and conducts the actual negotiations. Given its focus on broad trade relations and attention to implications for foreign affairs, DGI tends to

---

[26] Currency union has ended the use of so-called green money to provide additional protection under the guise of adjusting for different exchange rates while maintaining common prices.

[27] Article 113 of the Treaty of Rome establishing the European Economic Community (now article 133 of the Amsterdam Treaty) states that "Where agreements with one or more states or international organizations need to be negotiated, the Commission shall make recommendations to the Council, which shall authorized the Commission to open the necessary negotiations. The Commission shall conduct these negotiations in consultation with a special committee appointed by the Council to assist the Commission in this task and within the framework of such directives as the Council may issue to it."

[28] The challenge arose at the time of ratification for the Uruguay Round Agreement. In an opinion on 15 November 1994, the court rejected arguments submitted to the Council that the Agreements on Agriculture and Sanitary and Phytosanitary Measures and the Agreement on Technical Barriers to Trade were within the authority of Member States (Elles 2000, 29). For nongoods issues such as services, there is "mixed competence" between the EU-level and member states.

[29] Following revision in 1999, External Relations and Trade became two separate directorates.

put forward more liberalizing trade proposals than sectoral representatives within the Commission, especially in comparison with the agriculture bureaucracy (Moyer 1993, 101).

The Directorate General for Agriculture (DGVI) represents agricultural interests within the Commission and has a reputation for strongly opposing trade liberalization. By tradition, a French national fills the position of director-general and French influence is strong — *The Financial Times* (10 February 1993) referred to DGVI as "an outpost of the Paris farm ministry."[30] Management of CAP policies that form over half of the EU budget automatically places this among the most powerful actors in the Commission (Tracy 1997, 84). Although DGI coordinates trade negotiations for all other issues, DGVI takes the lead role for agricultural trade negotiations. This is an example of the "biased enfranchisement" of agricultural interests within EU institutions (Keeler 1996). DGVI drafts the original policy proposal, which then goes before an interservices committee. During negotiations, DGVI officials and the commissioner for agriculture are the lead negotiators and are accompanied by DGI officials. When agricultural issues arise in discussions of the overall negotiation, the complexity of CAP policies reinforces the dominance of the agriculture commissioner over other Commission actors. In effect, this means that "the organization with the strongest interest in maintaining the CAP is placed in the driver's seat for the actual conduct of negotiations" (ibid., 103).

The Council of Ministers

A similar bias favors agricultural interests within the politics of the Council of Ministers, which is the central EU decision-making body that represents the interests of member states. While there is a single Council of Ministers, it meets in different forms, including a General Affairs Council, a Council of Agriculture Ministers, and an array of technical councils on topics ranging from the budget to tourism. A proposal that requires the approval by the Council of Ministers may appear on the agenda of the Agriculture Council or the General Affairs Council, depending on the nature of the issue and at the discretion of the Council Presidency. Thus within the Council of Ministers, one must consider the range of interests among different national representations as well as policy jurisdictions within each delegation.

Trade policy falls within the jurisdiction of the General Affairs Coun-

---

[30] Cited in Grant (1997, 156).

cil. This is the most powerful council, and it discusses a mix of both internal Community affairs and external economic issues. Membership typically consists of foreign ministers, and trade ministers only attend for discussion of major trade issues. This can lead to the neglect of trade policy, as related in the following comment by an official at the German delegation to the EU:

> There is no trade council. Right now it is foreign ministers in General Affairs, and even when we have trade officials join them, this leads to problems as the foreign affairs minister and trade minister will squabble and the foreign affairs minister will tell him his point is minor and this is foreign affairs business. At the Council meeting yesterday bananas [the WTO trade dispute about the EU banana import regime] was a major issue and I wanted our trade minister there, but he did not go. Our foreign minister was more interested in the talks on [EU] enlargement and the Balkans.[31]

Rather than a formal gathering of trade ministers to address trade policy at the highest levels, there are informal meetings of trade ministers as well as sessions of the General Affairs Council attended by trade ministers. The Council relies on a special committee of trade officials to undertake preliminary discussion and represent the council in consultations with the Commission.[32]

The Agriculture Council brings together national agriculture ministers and assumes a strong profarmer perspective. This council is distinct because a Special Agriculture Committee, which consists of agriculture portfolio officials from the national delegations, conducts the preparatory discussion of proposals prior to their submission to the full Agriculture Council. For all other councils, this preparatory work would be performed by the Committee of Permanent Representatives (Coreper), consisting of the senior official from the national delegation to the EU of member states.[33] Coreper meetings have a broad focus and generally reflect the policy orientation of the foreign ministers (Nugent 1999, 149). Keeping agricultural policy decision-making in the Special Agriculture Committee rather than Coreper reduces the likelihood of cross-

---

[31] Official of Permanent Mission of Germany to the European Union. Interview by author. Brussels, 11 July 2000.

[32] This committee was originally named the 113 Committee, after article 113 of the Treaty of Rome which prescribed the common external trade policy. The committee was subsequently renamed the 133 Committee, after the consolidation of EC treaties in the Treaty of Amsterdam.

[33] Coreper 1 consists of deputy officials and deals with less controversial policy areas, while Coreper 2 consists of the Permanent Representatives, who are the equivalent of ambassadors. See Nugent (1999, 149).

sector tradeoffs. While most CAP policy issues automatically go before the Agriculture Council, agricultural trade issues raise possible overlapping jurisdiction with the General Affairs Council. There is no formal precedence of one council over the other, but for agricultural trade issues, the General Affairs Council tends to wait for the opinion of the Agriculture Council before acting (Moyer 1993, 102).

In theory, it should not matter which Council addresses a policy question because national governments coordinate their position before representation to any of the Council meetings. However, the policy dynamic changes according to which Council address as an issue. An official of the German Federal Ministry of Food, Agriculture, and Fishery commented on the reasons why his ministry gains a stronger hand when agricultural issues are raised in the Agriculture Council:

> In trade negotiations there is the question of where a policy issue is discussed in the EU institutions — the General Council or the Agriculture Council. If it is in the General Council we first discuss the issue in Bonn because it will be handled by the Trade and the Foreign Affairs Ministries and not the Agriculture Ministry. We [the Agriculture Ministry] are then pushing the brake. Their inclination is that tradeoffs must of course come in agriculture and concessions can be made. On the other hand, when an issue is discussed in the Agriculture Council, we [the Agriculture Ministry] make the proposals and if they have complaints they must come to us with objections. There is a big difference.[34]

The voting procedures in the Council of Ministers vary by issue. According to treaty provisions for trade in goods and agricultural policy, a qualified majority vote is sufficient to approve measures.[35] Nevertheless, unanimity voting has been sought in practice for Agriculture Council decisions. The collegial norms and common goals of Agriculture Council members, as well as the threat of a veto, have produced this tendency to vote based on consensus. The three occasions in which states have used the veto in Council decisions were all related to agricultural price decisions.[36] Although it never formally raised the point in Council sessions, in 1993 France said it might invoke its veto right in relation to the Uruguay Round (Sherrington 2000, 65). In trade negotiations, ac-

---

[34] Official of the German Federal Ministry of Food, Agriculture, and Fishery. Interview by author. Bonn, 20 July 1999.

[35] The Treaty of Rome calls for majority voting on agricultural issues, and the 1985 Single European Act explicitly called for majority voting on all economic matters.

[36] As the result of the 1966 agreement referred to as the "Luxembourg Compromise," countries agreed to allow any member to veto a proposal they consider a threat to national interest. A veto was exercised in 1982 (United Kingdom), 1985 (Germany), and 1988 (Greece).

cording to the logic of "tied hands," unanimity voting practices enhance bargaining leverage against liberalization demands because EU negotiators can more credibly insist that they cannot make a certain trade concession in light of the impossibility of gaining approval from all members of the Council (Moyer 1993; Meunier 2000).

One effect of consensus decision making in the Agriculture Council has been to force package deals that satisfy all members. Often this leads to "marathon sessions" and elaborate packages full of special measures as a precondition for agreement (Tracy 1997, 85). For example, in order to reach agreement on the 1988 budget stabilizers plan, the Commission had to continue adding elements to its proposal until they had created a balance of benefits for all — Germany and France were pleased that there would be new CAP funds and little cut in farmer incomes, Mediterranean nations were happy to gain increased structural funds, and the UK and the Netherlands were satisfied by price cuts for overproduction (Moyer and Josling 1990, 97). Without such efforts, one nation is more likely to block the entire proposal. The nature of interlocking policies also makes it useful for the Agriculture Council to bundle together several issues for a single decision, because a change affecting one commodity will have ramifications for other commodities and alter the relative balance of gains among members. "Of all the Councils, the Agriculture Council is perhaps the most reliant on issue linkages and package deals for the conduct of its business" (Nugent 1999, 430).

THE PRESIDENCY OF THE COUNCIL

Each national government takes its turn holding the presidency of the Council, a role which grants influence in the policy process as an agenda-setter. The presidency was intended to enhance coordination without favoring one member state's interests. To achieve this purpose, the short six-month presidency is rotated among members in alphabetical order by country name. The presidency presents a work program at the beginning of its term, calls Council sessions, sets the provisional agenda for each session and chairs the meeting, and summarizes the policy discussion and decisions from sessions (which are conducted behind closed doors). The presidency shapes the day-to-day work of the Council and mediates larger conflicts through its role as broker among member state interests (Sherrington 2000, 43). Timing the call of votes, consulting with smaller groups to find compromise positions, and keeping some issues on the agenda for long discussion and keeping other issues off the agenda are all tactics for a presidency to influence policy making (ibid., 38).

The discretion to determine which Council will address a policy is an important source of influence for the office.[37] For example, a presidency can choose not to raise a foreign trade demand for discussion in a General Affairs Council meeting. Keeping agricultural issues within the Agriculture Council and having the General Affairs Council wait for the opinion of the Agriculture Council reinforces the policy autonomy of the agricultural policy community. While blatant manipulation would bring criticism from other nations and the Council Secretariat, at a smaller level such occurrences may delay settlement or frame issues to avoid an agreement.[38]

Examples of the French presidency actions at the outset of its term as Council president in July 2000 are illustrative of how the presidency can influence policies at the margins. When the Council held a discussion of the WTO dispute regarding the EU banana import regime, France as Council president emphasized its position favoring maintenance of a quota system. It included only this view in the summary report of the meeting and did not include the opposing views expressed by Germany and others who favored a tariff system.[39] In addition, the French presidency increased discussion of sustainable development within the trade committee while reducing the time devoted to trade topics. A different country holding the presidency might actively try to build agreement by packaging different issues with gains for reluctant nations and widening the policy circle.

The EU Farm Lobby

Given that most CAP policies are approved by decisions of the Council of Ministers and managed by the Commission, farmers found it necessary to lobby their home governments and EU-level institutions. Created in 1958 as the first European-level representative organization, the Comité des Organisations Professionnelles Agricoles (COPA) acts as the spokesman for the agricultural sector as a whole. COPA now represents twenty-nine organizations from the fifteen EU members and has a secretariat staffed by forty-five people in Brussels, which makes it among the largest of the EU-level interest groups. It jointly coordinates activities

[37] Official of the European Commission Directorate General for Agriculture. Interview by author. Brussels, 7 July 2000.

[38] Official of the Irish Permanent Mission to the European Union. Interview by author. Brussels, 5 July 2000.

[39] Official of the Permanent Mission of Germany to the European Union. Interview by author. Brussels, 11 July 2000.

with its sister organization, the General Committee for Agricultural Co-operation (COGECA). The lobbying activities of COPA target all of the relevant EU institutions; close cooperation with DGVI officials of the Commission, participation on advisory committees, and presentation of position papers to the Council are some of the many avenues for influence.[40] At the same time, national farm organizations contact their national ministers to request that they speak in favor of COPA positions in the Council. Finally, COPA coordinates demonstrations timed around key decisions.

COPA strives to bridge the diversity of members, which represent both highly productive export-oriented regions and small-scale producers that would not be economically viable without subsidies. The organization argues that agriculture plays a special role in society different from other industries. More specifically, COPA calls for continued price support policies and opposes liberalization. These policies are justified as necessary to achieve a European model of agriculture that promotes both self-sufficiency and the survival of small family farms.

Consumer Groups and Public Opinion

Consumers pay a high cost for agricultural protection policies. *The Economist* (3 March 2001) estimated that the average European family pays 1,200 U.S. dollars a year extra because EU farm policies raise food prices well above world prices. CAP policies make products such as beef and butter cost more than twice as much as they would without the policy. Moreover, this consumption tax is on top of the funds already paid by taxpayers for EU budget expenditures, leading one consumer group leader to complain that "consumers are having to pay twice for the CAP."[41]

The European Consumers' Organization (Bureau Européen des Unions de Consommateurs, BEUC) acts as the "voice of the European consumer." It represents twenty-seven national consumer organizations as a group active lobbying EU institutions since 1962 and has a permanent staff of ten to fifteen in its Brussels office. This makes BEUC smaller than COPA, and it must spread its resources widely to cover the range of issues important to consumers (Nugent 1999, 419). The organization exercises influence by issuing press conference statements and position papers as well as through institutionalized cooperation with EU organi-

[40] COPA secretariat official. Interview by author. Brussels, 7 July 1999.

[41] Jim Murray, director of BEUC, cited in press release titled "Consumers pay too much for an outdated policy! BEUC demands radical reform of the CAP," 28 September 1995.

zations.[42] The Commission sponsors a Consumer Committee, which provides a venue for consultation with consumer groups on Commission proposals. One of the technical councils of the Council of Ministers addresses consumer issues and will request the BEUC opinion on issues before the Council. However, this is a relatively minor Council relative to the Agriculture Council. For example, the Consumer Council met only twice during 1997, whereas the Agriculture Council gathered eleven times in that same year (ibid., 147). In addition, national-level consumer organizations and the sister organization of BEUC, Consumers International, carry out similar efforts. However, while consumer groups have access to European level policy-making, their influence is less than agriculture groups.

The position of European consumer groups toward agricultural issues reflects a mixture of concern for reducing prices and for maintaining high food safety standards, which can often lead to contradictory positions toward trade barriers.[43] In September 1995 BEUC issued a position paper calling for radical reform of the CAP, including an end to export subsidies and cuts in support prices. The report condemned the current agricultural trade policies that "lead to high food prices, the dumping of food exports on world market, overproduction at the expense of environmental protection and prohibitive tariffs on imports."[44] On the other hand, the BEUC strongly supports the EU ban prohibiting hormone-treated beef imports. Moreover, it favors the broader goals of an agricultural policy that supports the environment and rural areas and maintains farm income levels, so long as these policies avoid the inefficiencies and consumer burden of the CAP.

While consumers are not without a voice within EU policy-making, whether comparing the size of their organizations in Brussels, their level of access within the EU institutions, or their influence over national governments, consumer groups are a weak counterweight to the powerful farm lobby. Consumer organizations also have a wide range of policy priorities among which the reform of agricultural policy is only one, whereas these policies represent the livelihood for farmers. Thus one returns to the classic collective action problem of diffuse consumer interests against specific and highly organized farmer interests.

Moreover, the European public is highly sympathetic to the cause of farmers and fails to rally against CAP. A 1988 poll by the European

[42] BEUC official. Interview by author. Brussels, July 2000.
[43] "Consumer Priorities for the Finnish Presidency," submission by BEUC to the Council Presidency (1999).
[44] "CAP," BEUC position paper, 25 September 1995.

Commission showed a majority believe it is better to subsidize European farmers than buy foodstuffs from abroad, and 50 percent favored current or increased spending for agriculture (Moyer and Josling 1990, 50). Most importantly, "seventy-five percent of respondents favoured protection against foreign imports even if the consumer has to pay more for certain products" (ibid., 51). A poll by Gallup Europe conducted for the European Commission in September–October 2000 found that the public in the fifteen EU member states overwhelmingly views agriculture as "important for our future" and supports the goals of EU intervention.[45] For example, 90 percent agreed that the EU should use agricultural policy to support life in the countryside, 86 percent agreed that intervention should provide stable, adequate incomes for farmers, and 85 percent supported the goal to make European agriculture more competitive on the world market. The survey also revealed that respondents had little actual knowledge about specific agricultural protection policies — only half had even heard of CAP. A public that is at the same time sympathetic and uninformed has been willing to leave agricultural policy to the interest groups and government officials who have a more direct stake.

In part these attitudes reflect the perception that farmers uphold a rural culture and environment valued by society. Vacationers visiting the countryside also consider the green fields worth their cost in high food prices. Regardless of its basis in myth or reality, there is a strong appeal in the image of small family farmers of Europe battling against an impending flood of cheap imports from industrial farms of the United States. Farmers have not hesitated to dramatize their own plight and take advantage of this public sympathy.

UNICE and Business Lobbying

The potential for countervailing business group lobbying exists within the EU. Lobbying for business interests at the EU level is led by the Union of Industrial and Employers' Confederations of Europe (UNICE). Created in 1958, the organization currently represents thirty-seven business federations from twenty-nine countries as the "voice of business in Europe." It is one of the largest "Eurogroups" after COPA, with a secretariat staff of forty based in Brussels. UNICE can also draw on the resources of experts from member federations and companies. The or-

---

[45] Gallup Europe, "The General Public's Attitudes Towards the CAP," *Eurobarometer Flash* no. 85 (November 2000). Accessed at europa.eu.int/comm/agriculture/survey/2000/index—en.htm. See questions 1, 2, and 6.

ganization holds a special legal status as one of the social partners, which means that the Commission, Council, and Parliament are obligated to consult with UNICE on issues affecting business.[46] However, consensus decision making norms have made it difficult to put forward strong policy initiatives on controversial issues, especially given the frequent conflict of interests among its broad membership.

The trade interests of UNICE make liberalization one of its top priorities, but agricultural policies are given little attention. For example, in its briefing paper released in September 1999, prior to the WTO Ministerial Conference in Seattle, UNICE lists its own priorities, including the following topics: investment, services, trade facilitation, market access, government procurement, trade and environment, and electronic commerce. The agriculture topic is relegated to the section on "other issues of current WTO concern."[47] Moreover, UNICE does not closely follow or participate in internal debates on CAP reform. Unlike Keidanren in Japan, UNICE does not have a committee specifically focusing on agricultural policy, which means that its positions are largely reactive.

UNICE interest in agriculture arises from the twin concerns that agricultural protection will prevent wider trade agreements for liberalization and lead to trade wars that close off markets. The business community views agriculture as just one among many issues, and certainly not an issue that should be allowed to hijack negotiations.[48] There is also frustration over trade sanctions arising from agricultural trade disputes. A UNICE press release stated that "Companies cannot continuously be held hostage to a situation which has nothing to do with them. This is harmful for employment, EU-U.S. relations, and the world economy."[49] Through contacts with Commission officials and national governments, business leaders urge settlement of the disputes.

Whereas the Japanese business organization Keidanren acted as a voice for food industry interests harmed by agricultural protection, the European food industry has suffered less under agricultural protection policies. This is largely because the CAP system of export refunds compensates for the difference between internal and external market prices of input materials (Harris and Swinbank 1997, 275). This helps companies that export products with a low level of processing, such as pasta or tomato sauce, which have a high share of raw material in the final

---

[46] *Financial Times*, 25 June 1999.

[47] UNICE, "UNICE and the WTO Millenium Round" (Brussels: UNICE, 1999), 11.

[48] UNICE official. Interview by author. Brussels, 6 July 2000.

[49] "UNICE Dismay at Escalation in Hormone Beef Dispute," UNICE press release, 11 May 1999.

product value. CAP compensation payments make it possible to export at world prices even while buying European wheat or tomatoes. Hence high domestic agricultural prices do not handicap the international competitiveness of the agribusiness industry in Europe to the same extent as in Japan. It is notable that even as UNICE calls for convergence in prices, it supports the continuation of the export refund system until European agriculture reaches competitive levels with world market prices.[50] On the other hand, many of the companies engaged in production at a higher level of food processing, especially the competitive multinational firms such as Unilever and Nestle, favor free trade in order to reduce payments for CAP levies and input materials that are not reimbursed (ibid., 280).

There are also mixed interests for agribusiness given that many industries are closely linked to the prosperity of European agriculture. As protection policies have promoted higher productivity, they have also encouraged farmers to use more fertilizer, machinery, veterinary medicines, and seeds and feed. Beneficiaries include the European chemicals industry, pharmaceutical companies, and the manufacturers of agricultural machinery (Grant 1997, 21–22). The organization of the food industry is weak and has been unable or unwilling to present a unified front for its interests regarding agricultural trade (Harris and Swinbank 1997, 280).

Business lobby groups and companies prefer not to take strong positions against agricultural interests. The sympathetic position of farmers in society and their ability to rally protests deters businesses from opposing their interests even without the farm groups having to take action. One business association official stated, "Our members don't want to be seen as advocating the demise of family farms. If the media got hold of something like that there would be protests."[51] However, in contrast with Japanese companies, European business has less reason to fear that statements favoring agricultural reform will lead to farm groups staging boycotts against the products of their companies. A UNICE official said that to his knowledge such boycotts had never taken place.[52] The radical energies of farm groups have been directed toward public demonstrations, or, at their extreme in France, widespread disruption of social order through halting traffic or dumping produce in town squares. While interfering with business, such actions do not target specific companies.

[50] UNICE, "UNICE and the WTO Millenium Round," 56.
[51] Official of Eurocommerce, an association of traders and wholesalers. Interview by author. Brussels, 5 July 2000.
[52] UNICE official. Interview by author. Brussels, 6 July 2000.

In sum, business groups favor liberalization and express concern about agricultural issues harming broader trade prospects. However, industry groups such as UNICE lack any specific interest in agricultural issues. Reluctance to draw the anger of farmers inhibits business associations, related businesses hold a stake in continued protection, and CAP extends protection to help food industry exports. Therefore, for the most part European business has accepted CAP and does not lobby for change. Only in the context of an international negotiation do new incentives lead businesses to advocate agricultural liberalization.

CAP as the Pillar of European Integration

With growing intra-EU trade, the importance of European integration provides a counterweight to the importance of global free trade. For individual EU members, 50–70 percent of their total trade is with their fellow EU members (Hanson 1998, 64). This intra-EU trade provides the equivalent of a large domestic market. Hence exporting firms have substantial interest in European integration even as they also hold an interest in access to world markets.

Contrary to fears that European integration would bring higher trade barriers and create a "fortress Europe," for most sectors in Europe, integration occurred parallel with liberalization (ibid.). However, in the agricultural sector, integration was accompanied with increasing protection. In essence, the protection of agriculture helped to induce European states to accept other aspects of integration, including trade liberalization and infringement on national policy autonomy. For the poor states of southern Europe who are net recipients of CAP funds, subsidies are essential welfare payments for a poor and large sector within their economies. For wealthier states like France and Germany, politics made agricultural protection appealing.

For decades CAP stood out as the only common endeavor, referred to by some as a "proxy for European integration" (Wallace and Wallace 1996, 100). By the early 1970s, the CAP was so securely entrenched within the institutional processes and moral purpose of the European Community that it nearly stopped the UK from joining the Community. British politicians demanded changes in the CAP, which they feared would interfere with their existing bilateral trade relations and raise considerable budgetary costs while providing few benefits to British agriculture. However, CAP proved nonnegotiable, and the UK had to accept existing arrangements in order to gain membership in 1973. Andrew Moravcsik (1991, 32) writes about the internal negotiation that "for those who had worked for decades in the Community and who saw the CAP as part of the initial Franco-German bargain at the heart of the EC, the British demand called into question the very foundation of European cooperation."

The status of CAP as a pillar for integration gives greater legitimacy to its policies. Supporters can "argue from an apparent moral high ground that criticism of the CAP is *non communautaire*,' that is, criticism undermines the symbol of 'unity' and is thus tantamount to an attack on the entire integration venture" (Keeler 1996, 136).[53] An example of such rhetoric can be seen in the statement made by the German Agriculture Minister Josef Ertl when he defended CAP policies: "There are no alternatives. . . . For a number of countries the Community — without the CAP — is of no interest. Shall Europe once again become a region of individual nation states? The Community must be saved."[54] Although sectoral protectionism is a narrow interest harmful to the broader economy and consumer interests, the moral value attached to CAP frames parochial demands as serving a greater cause. In terms of the moral debate, institutional processes, and state preferences, the CAP policies connect agricultural protection with the pursuit of European integration.

Drawing Implications

In light of this analysis of the policy process for agricultural trade decisions in the EU, one would not expect to see any substantial liberalization of European agricultural policies. Nevertheless, there are other sources of pressure for liberalization, including budget costs, U.S. threats, and the leverage exerted by negotiation structure. Each of these factors produces different expectations for the sequence of policy change, the rationalization of the decision, and the form of the policy outcome.

Studies of European agricultural reform frequently emphasize the budget pressures arising from the considerable expense of maintaining the CAP (Moyer and Josling 1990; Paarlberg 1997). From this perspective, liberalization is motivated by the need to reduce costly protection policies. In trade negotiations, the EU may just be trying to get credit on the international stage for liberalization measures that it must pursue for internal budgetary reasons. If true, one would expect the agreements to occur during periods of increasing budget pressure, and one would

---

[53] This point is also made by Nugent (1999, 413)
[54] *Der Spiegel*, 26 May 1980, cited in Hendriks (1991, 76).

expect the EU members that bear the largest budget shares for EU expenditures, such as Germany, to lead the calls for reform from the beginning of the negotiation. Policy justification should refer to the disproportionate share of EU spending on agriculture and the need to reduce costs. Moreover, the final policy outcome should be cost-saving. In particular, one would expect that concerns for reducing the budget burden would emphasize cutting export subsidies, since using EU funds to pay for selling agricultural products more cheaply to foreign countries represents the most wasteful kind of spending.

U.S. threats have also formed a strong pressure for change of EU agricultural trade policies. Whereas the United States has never implemented trade sanctions against Japan with regards to agricultural trade issues, the United States has launched trade sanctions against Europe for its agricultural policies beginning with the chicken war of the 1960s and continuing to the banana and beef wars of the 1990s. One could explain liberalization as a remedy to stop trade sanctions against millions of dollars in targeted export items. Then one would expect liberalization to follow sanctions with evidence of targeted European industries lobbying for a change of the offending policy. Another perspective emphasizes the U.S. alliance with European nations in NATO as a source of additional leverage. In that case, the EU might want to quickly settle a trade war during times when the alliance was of considerable importance, such as during the periods of high tension in Cold War politics, or during the Gulf War. The policy rationalization in either scenario would emphasize the importance of the U.S. market to EU business and the need for supporting a cooperative relationship between the United States and Europe. Reforms favoring those issues of most importance to the United States would provide further evidence supporting this kind of explanation.

Finally, the importance of institutions within the negotiation structure leads one to expect higher liberalization when there is a package negotiation structure. An institutional commitment linking agricultural and industrial liberalization in a negotiation should bring more liberalization of agricultural goods than if there were no such linkage. If true, one would expect to see European business organizations lobbying for agricultural liberalization. Those nations with a larger industrial export sector relative to agriculture, such as Germany, should take the lead in calling for reforms of agriculture. Trade ministers would be expected to become closely involved in agricultural policy and advocate liberalization. Both business and national governments in this case would be expected to appeal to the overall interest in the package as the justification for their decision. A final agreement that the EU could approve would likely take the form of a balanced package with the liberalization in agriculture.

For negotiations in formal adjudication, legal framing will bring pressure for liberalization, with reputation and obligation concerns determining whether liberalization comes earlier or later in the negotiation. If legalism operates through concern for reputation, then one would expect the EU to settle cases early. The calculation of bargaining advantage from early settlement is likely to come from the Commission acting with considerable autonomy over trade policy. On the other hand, if legal framing is effective through concern for international obligation, the EU should comply with rulings by the GATT/WTO against its policies. One would expect that liberalization decisions would occur after rulings and that officials would refer to the duty for compliance with international trade rules.

European agricultural protection and regional integration developed in a process of mutual reinforcement. The privileged position of agricultural interests in EU institutions and the strong support for farmers by key member states long stood as an obstacle to reform. Having the agriculture commissioner and Agriculture Council guide the conduct of negotiations and the approval process gives decision-making power to those actors most opposed to agricultural reform. Meanwhile, the countervailing pressure from consumers and business suffers from divided priorities and less influence in the policy process. As a result, while spiraling costs and trade friction led to many reform proposals, the central protection mechanisms — price supports, a variable levy against imports, and export subsidies — long resisted change.

The EU remains among those spending the most to protect farmers, and its policies are the source of major distortion in world food markets. Nevertheless, some reorientation of CAP occurred in 1992, and other policies have been liberalized at the margins of CAP. Against the backdrop of the political marketplace for protection, this liberalization is surprising. Alongside the many negotiations that end in stalemate, in some negotiations, the EU has responded to trade demands with minor and even major liberalization. The following chapters examine cases of both negotiations that deadlocked and those that produced liberalization.

The analysis will examine how the institutional context of the negotiation influences internal politics in the EU. An external negotiation can counteract the obstacles to agricultural policy reform found at the level of EU institutions by strengthening the role of trade officials over agriculture officials, and by changing negotiation stakes so as to persuade reluctant member states to accept some sacrifices in agricultural policy.

8

Two Rounds of Negotiating CAP

RECIPROCITY UNDERLIES the bargaining dynamic of GATT trade rounds. Countries exchange concessions for greater trade liberalization of their own protected sectors in order to gain access to markets for their export sectors. In this mercantilist approach, each side tries to give as little access to their own markets as possible while gaining the desired access to overseas markets. For Europe, the Tokyo Round (1973–1979) represented its preferred outcome because its protected agricultural sector escaped with nominal changes while its industrial sector gained the benefits of improved access to world markets. The Uruguay Round (1986–1994), on the other hand, represented a more balanced outcome with some agricultural reforms along with the gains in liberalization of industrial goods and service markets. What undermined the demands for reciprocity in the former negotiation but not the latter?

The United States and the European Community dominated the agenda setting and forward progress or lack thereof in agricultural negotiations of the Tokyo Round and Uruguay Round.[1] In both negotiations, the United States demanded liberalization, issued threats, and insisted that a good agricultural agreement was necessary to get congressional approval of the agreements. On the other hand, the European Commission began each negotiation with a mandate from the Council that forbade any change to the principles or mechanisms of the Common Agricultural Policy, and European leaders met U.S. threats with their own threats of counterretaliation. Facing an ongoing budget crisis over the expense of CAP policies, in both periods the EC had incentives to agree to international restraints on subsidy policies. Instead, during the Tokyo Round the EC refused any restriction of subsidies, and during the Uruguay Round it agreed to reduce trade-distorting subsidies and rely more on direct income payments to support its farmers. Consequently, neither the threats of the United States nor the pressures for agricultural policy reform within the EC provide a convincing explanation for the difference in policy outcomes.

---

[1] Since the Tokyo Round and much of the Uruguay Round negotiations took place before the establishment of the European Union, I will refer to the European Community (EC) rather than the EU for this chapter.

Important differences characterized the negotiation structure of the two trade rounds. Whereas the Tokyo Round procedures weakly tied together the disparate negotiating groups during the negotiation and countries adopted separate stand-alone treaties on each issue, the Uruguay Round procedures reinforced the need for parallel progress across negotiating groups and bound the final results into an all-or-nothing decision for members. Descriptions of the two negotiating approaches contrast the Tokyo Round "GATT à la carte" with the Uruguay Round "single package" (Jackson 1997, 47).

These differences in the agenda and procedures influenced the stakes of the negotiation. The EC challenged the linkage between agricultural and industrial liberalization during the Tokyo Round and was able to negotiate an agreement that satisfied both its farmers and businesspeople. However, the linkage during the Uruguay Round withstood EC pressure and forced the EC to consider the tradeoff between agricultural protection and industrial liberalization. In this situation, business lobbying and a broadened policy process led the EC to accept a moderate amount of CAP reform as part of the package for liberalization of agricultural, industrial, and service markets.

The aggregate analysis of chapter 3 showed that linking issues helped to promote liberalization in the EU, leading to a predicted outcome of major liberalization when the linkage was strong. To examine more fully the effect of issue linkage in the policy process, this chapter compares the policy impact of the weakly institutionalized linkage in the Tokyo Round with the highly institutionalized linkage of the Uruguay Round.

The two negotiation cases also offer an opportunity to look more closely at how the agenda and procedures of the negotiation are chosen and how they impact on the domestic process. The case study of the Tokyo Round offers insights into the process of strengthening and weakening negotiation institutions with attention given to the prolonged disagreement between the United States and the EC over the procedural questions related to the linkage. The case then illustrates how the weak linkage increased the difficulty for the United States to get any concessions from Europe. The analysis of the Uruguay Round closely traces the interaction between the negotiation and the EC internal policy process. The shift toward a more institutionalized issue linkage midway through the negotiation led to mobilization by EC export interests and more involvement in the policy process by diplomats and trade officials. These developments, which strengthened the linkage with cross-sector interests, acted as a counterweight to the influence of agricultural interests.

Since the Tokyo Round and Uruguay Round had only relatively low levels of legal framing, this dimension of negotiation structure receives little attention in this chapter. The next case chapter will closely examine why legal framing encounters difficulties within the EU context.

The Tokyo Round

The Tokyo Round took place against the backdrop of rising trade tensions. In 1970 Congress nearly passed a highly protectionist trade bill, and as the United States posted its first trade deficit in the postwar period, in 1971 President Richard Nixon unilaterally implemented a 10 percent surcharge on all imports.[2] The collapse of the Bretton Woods system of fixed exchange rates and efforts to accommodate new monetary policies added urgency behind efforts to restrain protectionist pressures. Increasingly, U.S. officials felt that not only the over-valued dollar, but also the unfair trade policies of its main trade partners were responsible for the U.S. balance of payments crisis (Wolff 1980, 6).

Agricultural liberalization, in particular the reform of European agricultural policies, was a major objective for the United States in the Tokyo Round negotiation. The Kennedy Round GATT negotiation (1963–1967) had brought 50 percent reduction in industrial tariffs but left agricultural policies nearly untouched. The Williams Commission study in the early 1970s pointed to agricultural exports as a major strategy for resolving the balance of payments problem and urged the administration to pursue the issue in trade negotiations (U.S. Senate Committee on Finance 1979b, 5). In the early 1970s the share of exports in total farm cash receipts stood at 25 percent, while the United States held 16 percent of all world agricultural exports (Houck 1980, 268). Hence expansion of export markets would help both farmers and the national trade balance. European agricultural policies stood as the major obstacle because import barriers shut off access to the large European market and subsidized export of European surplus commodities brought Europe into direct competition with U.S. agricultural exports in third markets. Congressional hearings featured complaints about the problems

---

[2] The Mills Bill (H.R. 18970, 91st Congress, 2nd session) called for quotas on billions of dollars of U.S. imports, particularly in the area of textiles but also in other areas, by means of a trigger mechanism. The bill would have been a major reversal in postwar liberal trade policy by the United States. It passed the House and Senate but did not make it out of conference. See Wolff (1980).

generated by EC trade policies.[3] Consequently, U.S. negotiators repeatedly declared that agricultural reform was an essential part of any agreement.

Negotiating the Negotiation Structure

Gathering in Tokyo in September 1973, delegates from one hundred countries formally opened the new round of GATT negotiations with the Tokyo Declaration. The declaration singled out six areas: tariffs, nontariff measures, agriculture, tropical products, multilateral safeguards, and the GATT framework. However, the task remained to determine the more specific procedures for the negotiation.

The place of agriculture within the negotiation agenda led to a standoff that held up the entire negotiation until July 1977. The United States and the EC disagreed on the question of the linkage between agricultural and industrial goods. Anticipation that an institutional linkage in the negotiation structure would influence the outcome led the United States to advocate this arrangement and the EC to oppose it. As Timothy Josling (1977, 11) wrote in an essay reviewing the negotiations in 1977, "The tactical aspects of the question of the 'special' place of agriculture reveal the extent to which form is assumed to influence substance in negotiations."

The Tokyo Declaration settled the issue temporarily by including statements in support of both positions. The U.S. position was reflected in the statement that negotiations "shall cover . . . both industrial and agricultural products," while the EC position found support in the statement that negotiations must "take account of the special characteristics and problems in this [agricultural] sector" (GATT 1979). In the early months of the negotiation in February 1974, it was agreed to create a separate negotiating group for agricultural policy. One year later it was agreed to subdivide the agriculture group into distinct subgroups on beef, dairy, and grains. However, the United States and the EC continued to refuse compromise on procedures for also including agriculture in other groups.

The United States wanted agricultural issues to be considered alongside industrial issues. Indeed, the Trade Act of 1974 explicitly called for this approach: "To the maximum extent feasible, the harmonization, reduction, or elimination of agricultural trade barriers and distortions

---

[3] For example, see 1973 discussions on trade reform in the House of Representatives. House Committee on Ways and Means, *Trade Reform: Hearings on H.R. 6767*, 93rd Congress 1st session, 1973.

shall be undertaken in conjunction with the harmonization, reduction, or elimination of industrial trade barriers and distortions."[4] U.S. negotiators thought that greater agricultural liberalization would be possible only if they could apply leverage from other countries' need for access to U.S. markets. Jointly discussing agricultural and industrial good market access would promote this kind of tradeoff whether through application of a single tariff reduction formula or quid pro quo bargaining offers. Although they accepted formation of the separate agriculture group at the time of the Tokyo Declaration in 1973, U.S. officials continued to insist that the tariff group and subsidy group should address *all* tariffs and subsidies and not just those for industrial goods (Winham 1986, 157).

On the other hand, European negotiators emphasized that agriculture must be treated separately — ostensibly to reflect the distinct nature of agriculture, but in reality to reduce the pressure for reform. The negotiating mandate passed by the Council of Ministers in May 1973 declared that CAP "principles and their mechanisms shall not be called into question and therefore do not constitute a matter for negotiation."[5] Given such a restrictive mandate, Commission negotiators wanted to isolate the area — they assumed that it would be easier for them to control the direction of talks in a single forum, and that they could avoid problems in agriculture delaying other groups (Josling, Tangermann, and Warley 1996, 84). Leaving talks in the hands of agricultural experts would help limit discussion to technical issues and price coordination policies while avoiding questions of greater access. The tariff group and subsidy group were moving forward on the application of a tariff-cutting formula and a broad redefinition of the conditions under which domestic subsidies would be permitted. This was exactly the kind of policy reform that would threaten the mechanisms of the CAP, and therefore EC officials fought against inclusion of agriculture within these groups.

The disagreement over the agriculture group effectively put on hold other negotiations. The tariff group could not go forward to negotiate a tariff formula so long as the United States insisted the formula would cover agricultural products and the EC insisted that agricultural tariffs should only be discussed in the agriculture group (Winham 1986, 158, 163).

Finally, the election of Jimmy Carter in 1976 brought in a U.S. nego-

---

[4] Section 103 of Trade Act of 1974, cited in Cohn (1993, 26).
[5] Directive adopted by the Council of Foreign Ministers, cited in Harris, Swinbank, and Wilkinson (1983, 278).

tiating team determined to push the negotiations forward. Nevertheless, even with a priority to conclude the negotiations, the administration could not set aside U.S. agricultural interests. To do so would have risked the loss of the congressional support necessary to ratify any agreement. The newly appointed USTR, Robert Strauss, emphasized in his early press conferences that "agriculture was going to be put on the front burner and not on the back burner as it had been in previous negotiations."[6]

It appeared that without ending the deadlock over agriculture, the Tokyo Round would end in failure. At a summit meeting of industrialized nations in May 1977, leaders considered whether to continue the negotiations. Japan's Prime Minister Takeo Fukuda reminded leaders of his own memories of the London Economic Conference in the early 1930s when a failed meeting led to adjournment of the conference with promises to reconvene later, but the conferees never held the meeting as nations instead chose greater protectionism and dealt in isolation with the consequences of the Depression (Wolff 1980, 17). Leaders in both the United States and Europe had to consider how much they were willing to risk for the sake of their position on the agricultural negotiation procedures, and they agreed to renew their commitment to continue the trade round.

Two months later, the United States and the EC reached a bilateral accommodation. Meeting in Brussels in what Strauss would later describe as "the most significant day in the history of the Tokyo Round," negotiators agreed to focus talks on agriculture in the separate agriculture group while calling on this group to follow in parallel with the progress of other groups (Winham 1986, 165). As part of this compromise, the tariff reduction formula in the tariff group would only apply to nonagricultural goods. Market access questions for agriculture would go forward in the agriculture group on the basis of request-offer procedures. Under these procedures, countries submit lists of concessions on individual products and then conduct a bilateral exchange of requests and offers on specific items. Concessions between principal suppliers/buyers are then generalized to all countries on the basis of most-favored nation principles. These negotiating procedures allow more flexibility to omit sensitive products than occurs under a formula approach. Refusal to grant a concession on some products will not prevent overall agreement so long as other concessions are produced on different products. This procedural decision therefore represented a major gain for the EC desire to protect CAP mechanisms and restrict liber-

---

[6] Robert Strauss interview in Twiggs (1987, 89).

alization to commodities outside of CAP or of marginal importance. Nevertheless, agricultural issues continued to face some constraints from rules determined in other groups. Notably, discussion of subsidies would apply to issues related to all subsidies, including those GATT articles related to agricultural subsidies.

A key development that allowed this breakthrough was the U.S. agreement not to threaten the fundamental principles of the CAP or its mechanisms, such as the variable levy. Robert Strauss reported that he told EC negotiators: "You have my word there will be no attack on common agricultural policies. Now we could try to open it, to penetrate your markets more. We have got to do that, but we are not going to attack the structure itself; we just want you to open it a bit. We will negotiate hard over it, but we will not destroy it" (Twiggs 1987, 90). This reassurance helped to settle the procedural question, and during the meeting U.S. and EC negotiators drew up a timetable for completing negotiations on all agenda issues by the end of 1978.

The compromise did not represent the U.S. government abandoning its goals for agricultural liberalization. The EC agreed to negotiate agricultural trade issues, including greater access, as long as CAP reform was off of the negotiating table. The report to Congress after the negotiation stated that at this time the United States "agreed to drop the U.S. insistence that agriculture be negotiated along with industry on the condition that there would be a 'substantial result for agriculture' in the MTN" (U.S. Senate Committee on Finance 1979b, 15). This outcome represented a weak institutional linkage between agricultural and industrial sector trade negotiations.

Negotiations about cereal grains were conducted under even weaker constraints from the negotiation structure. At the U.S. initiative, in 1975 the locus for talks on wheat shifted outside of the Tokyo Round framework. The food shortage of 1972–1974 gave momentum to efforts for a new commodity agreement to address developing-nation concern about stable supplies and the U.S. and EC concern about stable world prices. To include the Soviet Union, which was not a GATT member but was becoming a major purchaser on the world wheat market, the United States favored discussing these issues in the sixty-nine-member International Wheat Council in London.[7] The IWC began meetings in 1975 to help bring coordination among exporters and importers on reserve stocks and price bands. The goal was to replace the International Wheat Agreement of 1971, which had established the IWC as a consultative body but had not taken concrete measures to

[7] The talks later moved back to Geneva to continue under the auspices of UNCTAD.

establish market stability. While supportive of this goal, the EC favored keeping the cereals grain talks in the Tokyo Round grains subgroup. The EC had long pursued managed international market arrangements as a way to bring more stability on international markets, and now negotiators hoped to use a commodity agreement as the EC "contribution" to the agriculture negotiations of the Tokyo Round (Josling 1979, 279–280).[8] However, the United States won this procedural point. By 1977 the grains talks of the Tokyo Round were completely subsumed in the IWC (Winham 1986, 252). This reduced the possibility for tradeoffs between issues related to grains and those related to other agricultural products or the broader issues of the trade round.

The separation of the grains discussion from the round was an important development because policy changes in this area were necessary to resolve U.S.-EC trade tensions and the EC budget problem. U.S. trade conflict with the EC over agricultural policy long centered over policies related to the CAP support for cereal grains, which include wheat, rye, oats, barley, maize, and rice. Cereals exports accounted for 30 percent of the total value of U.S. exports to the nine EC member countries in 1974 and 47 percent of the value of all U.S. agricultural exports in that year.[9] As the world's largest wheat exporter, the United States had stated early on the importance of improving market access for American wheat.[10] Moreover, in the 1970s the EC was in transition from being a major importer to becoming a major exporter of wheat as CAP price supports stimulated production and created growing surpluses. In light of the fact that the price level for cereals serves as an indicator for the price levels of other arable crops and livestock, and in the early 1970s production of cereals occupied 60 percent of arable land and 30 to 40 percent of total spending, any serious effort to restrain CAP budget costs would depend on reforming the cereals sector (Harris, Swinbank, and Wilkinson 1983, 61, 64). In short, both U.S. export interests and

----

[8] In May 1977 the European Council called for greater efforts in GATT to stabilize trade in agriculture, and some representatives called for explicit division of global markets among exporting nations (Phillips 1990, 148). International commitments to maintain world commodity prices would reduce the gap between world prices and internal prices, and this would minimize EC budget costs from export subsidies (Harris, Swinbank, and Wilkinson 1983, 278).

[9] Cereals here refers to grains including wheat and feed grains such as barley, corn, and oats. Wheat and wheat flour accounted for 4.4 percent of U.S. export value to the EC-9 in 1974 and 21 percent of U.S. total agricultural exports in that year. USDA, "U.S. Foreign Agricultural Trade Statistical Report, Calendar Year 1974," *Foreign Agricultural Trade of the United States*, tables 1, 2, 12.

[10] *New York Times*, 25 November 1978.

EC budget concerns strongly pushed for more liberalization of cereal grains.

The Second Half

Following the breakthrough in July 1977 on procedures for agriculture, negotiations proceeded rapidly over the next two years. According to the timetable set in July, nations agreed to a tariff-cutting formula in September 1977 that would bring an average tariff reduction of 40 percent for industrial goods.[11]

Subsidy negotiations had been held up until 1977 over the U.S. demand for restraint on the use of subsidies, including those used for agricultural goods. A related issue was the U.S. defense of its right to retaliate against foreign subsidies with countervailing duties.[12] In one 1976 case, the United States initiated countervailing duties on EC beef exports and would have applied them to cheese and ham except that the EC preemptively reduced its export subsidies for products going to U.S. markets (Harris, Swinbank, and Wilkinson 1983, 278). The EC strongly opposed the arbitrary nature of the duties, since the U.S. government did not investigate whether the material injury from subsidized third-country exports was proportional to the countervailing duty. The United States offered to restrain its use of countervailing duties if the EC would accept limits on use of subsidies (Winham 1986, 177). By December 1977 the following compromise on the subsidy negotiations had been reached: first, restraint would be called for in use of subsidies according to their negative impact on third parties; second, countries would agree to condition retaliatory duties upon proof of material damage.

On agricultural export subsidies, the EC agreed to clarification of article 16:3 of the GATT treaty, which prohibited export subsidies on nonprimary goods while allowing their use for primary goods. The clarification stipulated that agricultural export subsidies must not result in "more than an equitable share of world export trade in that product." This fell far short of the original U.S. demand to prohibit or substan-

[11] The so-called Swiss formula was aimed to provide a compromise between the U.S. preference for uniform cuts and the EC desire to reduce tariff peaks. Cuts would be phased in over eight years. Countries later tabled offers for specific products with some offers for over-formula cuts to compensate for other offers of under-formula cuts.

[12] The General Agreement in article 6 defined and restricted the use of countervailing duties, but the U.S. legislation predated GATT and so the United States continued to apply countervailing duties according to its own procedures.

tively reduce levels of export subsidies (Phillips 1990, 147). To gain even this vaguely worded restraint, U.S. negotiators had to promise in a secret letter that they would not use the provision to directly challenge CAP.[13] The compromise promised some control where before there had been none.

In the agriculture group, talks proceeded along the two dimensions of market-access and commodity arrangements. The market access discussions for the most part dealt with exchanging tariff cuts and quota expansion deals through request-offer bargaining conducted on a bilateral basis. In this process negotiators exchanged equivalent concessions so that each bilateral equation would achieve relative balance. For example, the United States granted the EC a concession to allow additional cheese imports valued at 66 million U.S. dollars; the EC granted the United States a concession on beef also valued at 66 million U.S. dollars by creating a new tariff line for "hotel beef" that would not be subject to the variable levy.[14] The flexibility of this kind of bargaining allowed the EC to make some concessions on agricultural trade policies without making any changes to the protection policies of the CAP.

The two commodity subgroups meeting in the Tokyo Round created a plan for an International Dairy Products Council and International Meat Council that would meet to exchange information on production, prices, stocks, and changes in domestic policies likely to affect trade. Minimum prices were agreed upon for dairy products, but no economic provisions were made for beef trade (Houck 1980, 291–292). In general their main achievement was to provide information and try to resolve disputes for better policy coordination, and the agreements did not have direct economic effect.[15]

The IWC negotiation on grains encountered more problems. All shared a mutual interest in cooperation for greater market stability, but each had different preferences about the level of prices and stocks necessary to achieve this goal.[16] By November 1978 the EC and the United States

[13] The letter was never made public but is referred to by Robert Hudec (1988, 56n), who spoke with negotiators about the issue. EC documents refer directly to the existence of such a letter from the United States giving this assurance (EC 1979, 68).

[14] Houck (1980, 284, 286) uses output figures and agreed upon import volumes and estimated per-unit trade value to calculate the value of "new trade" represented by the concessions.

[15] Houck (1980, 290) and Winham (1986, 252).

[16] In a January 1978 meeting of the IWC, the EC and developing nations agreed on a floor price of 115 U.S. dollars per ton for all cereals, and the United States wanted a higher floor price of 145 U.S. dollars per ton for an agreement restricted to wheat and supported by high world stock levels (to reduce EC exports of its surplus production).

were reported to be in agreement on the size of reserve stocks and their use to control price variation.[17] However, when the issue came before the Council of Ministers, France blocked a decision out of fear the measure would restrict its wheat exports (Phillips 1990, 149). By the end of the month, the wheat talks had collapsed with the EC and the United States blaming each other for "intransigence."[18] At the same time, developing countries became more disillusioned and hardened their position against the price range and stock levels the United States and the EC could accept. Thus when negotiators were trying to bring the Tokyo Round to a close, talks in the IWC remained inconclusive and the Tokyo Round subgroup on grains policy adjourned pending results in the IWC. Six months later IWC negotiations concluded with no new agreement.

The United States tried unilaterally to create a linkage between agriculture and the overall trade agreement by insisting that Congress would not ratify the Tokyo Round agreements without substantial agricultural liberalization. In February 1978 the head of the U.S. delegation to the Tokyo Round stated publicly that he thought there was only "about 50-50 chance" of gaining congressional approval.[19] U.S. officials stressed that success in industrial areas of the Tokyo Round depended upon freer trade in agricultural products and regulation of subsidies.[20] Later in October, Strauss said, "Without a good agricultural settlement there is no Tokyo Round" and emphasized the need for concessions on specific agricultural products to help him sell the agreement to Congress (Curran 1982, 124, 206). With such public statements, the United States tried unilaterally to force the linkage but ultimately backed down to accept a weak agricultural settlement.

An informal understanding between the United States and the EC brought the substantive issues together in the final outline of an agreement. All of the issues, ranging from customs valuation to government procurement standards to agricultural policies, were pulled together into a memo of understanding issued in July 1978 by U.S. and EC negotiators. Although vaguely worded, the memo represented the basis for political consensus among the developed nations. Shortly thereafter, at the Bonn G-7 Summit, leaders decided to conclude the Tokyo Round on the basis of this memo (Winham 1986, 210).

Eventually, the United States agreed to include all grains, and the EC became more flexible on reserve stocks after its original reluctance over stock provisions (Phillips 1990, 148).

[17] *New York Times*, 7 November 1978.

[18] *New York Times*, 25 November 1978.

[19] *Wall Street Journal*, 1 February 1978.

[20] *New York Times*, 11 April 1978.

The final hurdle in the Tokyo Round negotiation involved a U.S. threat that backfired. In the Trade Act of 1974, Congress passed an unusual provision calling for countervailing duties against European subsidy policies but waiving the duties pending conclusion of the Tokyo Round by the end of 1978. Crisis loomed in December 1978 when the Tokyo Round agreement was nearly finalized and Congress recessed without changing the provision. In January 1979 the duties would automatically go into effect against 400 million dollars of European exports of ham, biscuits, and other products. The European Commission negotiators reacted angrily to negotiating under the deadline of a threat and refused to conclude the Tokyo Round until Congress restored the waiver, and they threatened to retaliate with duties against U.S. exports.[21] Robert Strauss said that the administration would not enforce the collection of the duties. Nevertheless, EC negotiators refused to conclude the round for fear they would face demands from Congress for additional concessions under threat of the duties after the Tokyo Round. Core issues had been settled in November and an agreement in December was within reach, but instead, three months later the negotiation continued and the EC threatened to withdraw from the talks.[22] Congress ultimately withdrew the duties without having gained anything; the final subsidy agreement closely followed the legal outline reached earlier before the entire episode over retaliatory duties began. The automatic duties built into U.S. legislation created a credible threat but failed to increase bargaining leverage against the EC.

Evaluating the Result of the Tokyo Round

After five and a half years of negotiations, the agreements of the Tokyo Round were signed on 12 April 1979. Nations agreed to an average tariff reduction of 35 to 38 percent for industrial goods.[23] The broad package created new rules and gave further details to back up existing GATT principles. The government procurement code opened new opportunities for foreign competition, the subsidy code clarified restrictions on the use of subsidies and established new dispute settlement procedures, and a standards code addressed health and safety regulations that hinder trade. Other agreements regulated civil aircraft trade and commodity prices for dairy and meat. In all, the Tokyo Round agreements were an assortment of the tariff-reduction protocols, nine special agreements, and four understandings.

[21] *New York Times*, 18 November 1978.
[22] *New York Times*, 4 February 1979.
[23] *New York Times*, 12 April 1979.

In what came to be referred to as "GATT à la carte," individual agreements were optional for contract members to accept or reject (Jackson 1997, 47). Drafters gave each agreement a separate signatory clause and designed the text as a stand-alone treaty. There was some legal uncertainty regarding the relation of these add-on agreements to the original GATT and whether the new agreements would apply to all nations, but the contracting parties acknowledged in a decision in November 1979 that the most-favored-nation clause generalized results such that even the GATT members who had not signed an agreement should be accorded the same treatment (ibid., 77). Although Japan, Europe, and the United States agreed to nearly all of the agreements, a large share of developing nations opted to selectively sign only some agreements or, in some cases, none at all.

The increase in agricultural liberalization was modest. Gilbert Winham (1986, 255) concludes that "the participating nations ended the Tokyo Round about as far apart on agricultural trade policy as they were at the beginning of the negotiation." Analysis of the agreement presented to Congress estimated that agricultural concessions by other countries would produce an annual increase in U.S. agricultural exports worth 407.9 million dollars, which represented less than 2 percent of total U.S. agricultural exports of 23 billion dollars (U.S. Senate Committee on Finance 1979b, 28). These gains were almost entirely from the EC and Japan, which accounted for, respectively, 39.1 percent and 40.8 percent of the increase in expected U.S. agricultural exports (ibid., 19).

The agricultural results vis-à-vis the EC represented liberalization in some areas outside of CAP and exhortatory pressure against the excesses of CAP policies. The tariff and nontariff barrier concessions were estimated to increase U.S. agricultural exports by 168 million dollars (U.S. Senate Committee on Finance 1979c, 48). The impact on trade from the subsidy code was more difficult to evaluate. Deputy USTR Alonzo McDonald declared that gains for agriculture would result from the agreement because "among other things, countries will not be able to use subsidized products to disrupt third country markets."[24] However, key sections of the agreement used vague terminology that did not include the definitions and specific criteria desired by the United States. The request for countries to "seek to avoid" domestic subsidies was not a binding constraint. The warning against using export subsidies to expand market shares did not even call for reduction in their use. The report to Congress predicted that "it may be difficult to prove that the EC is using export subsidies excessively. . . . In the absence of specific

[24] *New York Times*, 15 April 1979.

criteria for judging the appropriateness of export subsidy levels, it may be hard to resolve issues such as this under the new codes" (U.S. Senate Committee on Finance 1979b, 215). Indeed, the EC share of world markets grew rapidly the year after the conclusion of the Tokyo Round Agreement.[25]

The CAP emerged nearly unscathed from the negotiation. EC liberalization occurred through policies such as the new category for beef imports that did not interfere with CAP mechanisms.[26] While the agreement urged restraint in use of export subsidies, at the same time it validated their use as a policy tool.[27] The Commission made the following report to the council on the results of the Tokyo Round: "The Community had stressed that it could not allow the principles and mechanisms of the Common Agricultural Policy to be called into question during the Negotiations. The CAP was not called into question and the basic principle behind, and operation of, its mechanisms, including those most open to attack by our partners, such as levies and refunds, remain intact." (EC 1979, 10).

Although grains are the largest U.S. export sector, the Tokyo Round brought no major changes in this area. The USTR office estimated that duty reduction and subsidy reform by trade partners could produce a 26 million dollar export increase for the U.S. grains exports, but the report to Congress concluded that "the duty concessions offered by U.S. trading partners [on grain and feed products] are generally negligible" (U.S. Senate Committee on Finance 1979a, 25). Figure 8.1 shows the decline of U.S. wheat exports to Europe after the Tokyo Round. Moreover, the weak restraint on export subsidies left U.S. wheat traders to compete with the "predatory export practices" of the EC, which they blamed for displacing U.S. wheat in third markets (U.S. Senate Committee on Finance 1979b, 215).

The commodity agreements for dairy and meat trade held little economic significance. The Arrangement Regarding Bovine Meat had a purely informational role by creating a consultation body. While the International Dairy Agreement had specific measures for minimum prices, it lacked any enforcement mechanism or provision for stock ad-

[25] From 1978 to 1980 the EC share of world markets in beef grew from 6.4 percent to 24.4 percent, and the EC share of world markets in wheat and flour grew from 11 to 14 percent (Harris, Swinbank, and Wilkinson 1983, 281).

[26] Nearly half of the value of EC concessions came from the addition of the new tariff line for high-quality beef, with the important exclusion from the variable levy policies.

[27] Indeed, in the U.S. concession to import more EC cheese, it explicitly permits the use of EC export subsidies on those exports so long as the subsidies do not bring the price below U.S. market price (U.S. Senate Committee on Finance 1979b, 98, 214).

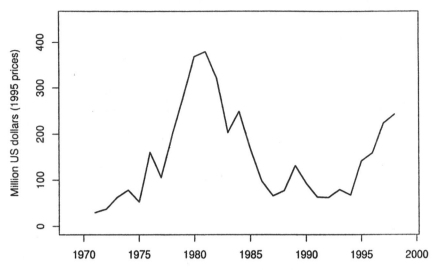

Figure 8.1: U.S. Wheat Exports to the EU, 1971–1998. The figure shows value of U.S. exports of wheat and wheat flour to the EU (member countries differ according to the year). *Source*: USDA, *U.S. Foreign Agricultural Trade Statistical Report*, various calendar years.

justment to maintain the price targets. When prices collapsed a year later, countries reverted to former practice without any joint coordination to maintain price levels (Josling, Tangermann, and Warley 1996). At the end of 1984 the United States withdrew from the Dairy Agreement to protest EC sales of subsidized butter to the Soviet Union (Jackson 1997, 364).

Overall for the United States, the agricultural results offered little gains for key U.S. interests. Disappointed expectations resulted from the failure of the subsidy code to restrain EC subsidies. Also, the EC beef concession that had been among the largest gains of the Tokyo Round was partly nullified by a subsequent health regulation banning most U.S. beef from EC markets (see chapter 9). Twenty years after the negotiation, a U.S. agriculture negotiator expressed the widely held view that "the Tokyo Round was a disaster for U.S. agriculture."[28]

Even as the Community gave up little to the United States in the agricultural negotiations of the Tokyo Round, it achieved large gains on its priorities vis-à-vis the United States in other areas. In the tariff group, EC priorities were for reduction of tariff peaks and greater market access for chemicals, steel, footwear, ceramics, and textiles (EC

[28] Official of USTR office in Geneva. Interview by author. Geneva, 16 July 1999.

1979, 53). In the tariff group the United States and EC agreed to reduce tariffs on industrial trade by about 35 percent on each other's trade (Winham 1986, 267). The United States accommodated EC demands to reduce high tariff peaks by reducing the amount of EC exports subject to high duties in the United States from 16 percent to 6 percent.[29] Regarding those items of specific interest to the EC, both sides reduced their tariffs by 35 percent for chemicals, and the United States made substantial tariff reductions on steel, textiles, and ceramics to the satisfaction of the EC. The EC also gained concessions on several important nontariff issues, such as the end of the American Selling Price, revision of its wine tax, and guarantee that U.S. countervailing duties would be applied less arbitrarily through use of a material injury standard. In summary, the EC achieved many of its objectives in other negotiating groups in spite of not giving up much on U.S. demands for agricultural liberalization.

While there were strong pressures for budget cutting within the EC, they did not bear directly on decisions about trade policy. Facing expanding budget costs of CAP, which then composed over two-thirds of the entire Community budget, the Commission advocated reforms to reduce costs and repeatedly tried to restrain price increases (Neville 1984, 376). Having failed in earlier attempts to get reforms through the Council, the Commission could have seized upon the Tokyo Round for external leverage. Commitments to reduce domestic and export subsidies could have provided an external constraint to hold back CAP expenditures, and strong commodity agreements could have indirectly reduced export subsidy costs. However, Commission proposals did not attempt to combine trade policy proposals with internal reform. Another pressure for budget reform came from the UK entry into the EC in 1973 as a net food importer critical of CAP policies. However, the United Kingdom did not connect its request for a price freeze or its demand for a reduction of its budget contribution with the ongoing trade negotiation.[30] Ultimately, the Tokyo Round Agreement brought little cost restraint — it did not provide any ceiling on subsidies or commodity agreement for grains. Moreover, in the areas where the EC granted concessions for agricultural liberalization, the Commission agreed to compensate those farmers with an increased restitution payment to offset income losses (EC 1979, 70). In sum, there is little evi-

---

[29] A duty over 10 percent was considered high (Winham 1986, 58).

[30] See Neville (1984, 408) on UK pressure against CAP during the five years after it joined the EC.

dence of an effort to combine the international negotiation with internal budget reforms.

Many Issues versus Linked Issues

The difficulties encountered in the Tokyo Round arose directly from the weakening of the linkage between agricultural negotiations and the rest of the negotiation. The EC reduced leverage on agriculture when it won the procedural decision in 1977 to address agricultural market access issues separately in the agriculture group according to bilateral request-offer bargaining rather than in the tariff group according to a multi-lateral-formula approach. The separation of cereal grains, the most important agricultural commodity for U.S.-EC trade relations, to a forum entirely outside of the Tokyo Round represented further weakening of the linkage. In spite of a shared interest in policy coordination to reduce budget costs from export subsidies, agreement proved unreachable. The United States hoped it could gain substantial agricultural reforms without launching a frontal attack on the CAP. Instead, without any leverage over agriculture from other negotiation groups, it could not achieve even moderate liberalization.

The United States tried to increase the stakes in order to make it hard for any country to reject the round. When discussing the fear of collapse of the negotiation and upping the ante, Strauss made the following statement:

> I kept saying, just keep more and more issues on the table and keep putting more things in the pot. The higher the bills, greed will get every participant, and they will all stay in to try to get their share of the pot. I said it's just like drawing to an inside straight in poker, if the pot's big enough you pay whatever it takes to take a shot at it. They are all afraid to walk away. Sure enough, every time they started to walk away and said they were through, they would look back and see all these goodies we put up there.[31]

Adding issues brought the United States, the EC, and Japan to accept the agreement. However, issue *addition* and issue *linkage* are not the same thing. To continue with Strauss's analogy, if the card games were at different tables, negotiators could play conservatively in one game with low stakes while playing hard for the big pot in another game — and folding one hand would not impact the game at the other table. Hence the stakes were only so large as the linkage connecting action at

---

[31] Robert Strauss interview, cited in Twiggs (1987, 92).

both tables. Adding issues could assure reaching an agreement on something, but a stronger linkage was necessary to ensure that this agreement included proportional reductions in sensitive areas.

Some argue that the EC cared more about the CAP than about the
success of the negotiation (Winham 1986, 164). This seems plausible
in view of the early negotiating behavior of the Community. The EC
would have let the round continue in deadlock rather than let the United
States destroy the CAP. One could also say that the United States cared
more about the success of the negotiation than about ending the CAP.
In the face of EC refusal to reform CAP, both the long-term U.S. interest
in the GATT system and its immediate interest in liberalization of other
sectors account for the U.S. compromise to establish a weaker linkage
in the procedures of the round. However, after 1977 the United States
continued to demand substantial progress in agriculture, which was
seen to be important for Congress to ratify the agreement. Furthermore,
while the EC refused to change the principles or mechanisms of CAP, it
did not refuse to negotiate about agricultural trade. The impact of the
U.S. decision to compromise in 1977 was magnified because the procedural arrangements thereafter weakened its leverage on agricultural
issues. As a result, the EC was able to make only nominal agricultural
concessions.

Whether the EC would have accepted *some* reforms of CAP to prevent a failure of the Tokyo Round is the important question. One must
consider a counterfactual scenario in which a credible cross-sector linkage forced the EC to consider tradeoffs between agricultural concessions and the overall agreement. Community exporters stood to gain
considerably from the market-opening agreement, and, conversely, they
had much to lose if the Tokyo Round had failed and the United States
had given in to the protectionist leanings in Congress. Given these
strong EC interests in the overall success of the Tokyo Round, it seems
probable that EC leaders would have accepted more agricultural concessions if they faced such a tradeoff. However, speculation about the
counterfactual is unsatisfying, and in order to provide evidence from
this different kind of scenario, we must turn to the Uruguay Round for
examination of the EC choices in a negotiation when it did face a choice
between CAP reform and successful conclusion of the trade round.

The Uruguay Round

From the beginning, the EC resisted the prospect of an ambitious
agenda for agricultural reform in a new trade round, but it also faced a

tradeoff with other interests. The United States insisted that there could not be any trade agreement without progress in agricultural liberalization, and the newly formed Cairns Group of fourteen agricultural exporting nations threatened to walk out of the negotiations if their goal for agricultural liberalization was not achieved. The desire by European nations to negotiate new rules and liberalization for investment, intellectual property, and service trade built enthusiasm for the new round and led to their reluctant agreement also to negotiate agricultural policies. Then, during the negotiation, the linkage among issues became more credible, and EC business groups and trade officials brought increasing pressure to make concessions in agriculture for the sake of broader gains. The EC moved from a position of steadfast refusal to change CAP policies in 1986 to undertake major reforms of CAP in 1992 that would open the door to accept a Uruguay Round agreement in 1994 that bound agricultural trade within market-oriented GATT rules.

Agreeing to Start the Negotiation

In the early 1980s, while the EC denied the need for a new round, the United States took the lead to push for starting the negotiation. The changes in monetary and trade policies during the 1970s failed to resolve the U.S. balance of payments problem. Although the deficit largely resulted from factors related to macroeconomic policy, the trade policies of other countries received much of the blame. In 1985 nearly three hundred legislative proposals before Congress addressed the need for a more assertive trade policy in pursuit of "fair trade," which led President Reagan to warn against a "mindless stampede toward protectionism" in Congress and USTR William Brock to urge in April 1985 that "we need multilateral negotiations, and we need them now" (Preeg 1995, 51, 53).

At the same time, the GATT faced a crisis as existing rules were widely disregarded and trade barriers in areas not covered by GATT rules were growing. A World Bank report commented that the round was necessary because the GATT system was suffering from "serious and continuing erosions," such that "widely held perceptions in government and business circles are that GATT has become largely irrelevant to today's world" (Finger 1987, 7). In addition to strengthening the system of trade rules, a successful trade round would bring significant economic gains. During the negotiation, U.S. officials stated that a reduction by one-third in tariff levels and removal of many nontariff barriers would be worth five trillion dollars in extra growth for the world economy over ten years.[32] The stakes loomed large because the alternative to a successful trade round was not the status quo, but rather worsening protectionism and disregard of existing GATT rules.

The onset of a subsidy war between the United States and the EC over agricultural trade brought these issues to the forefront. After the Tokyo Round ended without specific restraint on export subsidies, the EC share of world agricultural markets continued to grow as the U.S. share declined, until in 1986 EC agricultural exports exceeded those of the United States (Anania, Carter, and McCalla 1994, 20–21). Although other factors contributed to the reversal of trade fortunes, most in the United States blamed CAP policies.[33] The United States tried to use the GATT panel process to rein in EC export subsidies. In 1981 it filed a complaint that export subsidies made EC wheat exports seize "more than an equitable share of world trade" in violation of the GATT Subsidies Code (Hudec 1993, 491).[34] However, the panel ruled in 1983 that it could not reach a conclusion given the difficulty of defining the *equitable share* concept. The vague outcome of the panel provided no leverage for U.S. demands.

The United States turned to retaliatory actions by applying its own wheat export subsidies, which were justified as a response to EC policies (Yeutter 1998, 64). Export subsidies helped U.S. wheat exporters seize the Egyptian market for a year, displacing about a quarter of EC wheat flour exports. The EC responded with more export subsidies to compete for North African grain markets, and Congress entrenched export subsidies as a new tool in U.S. policy with the Export Enhance-

---

[32] *Financial Times*, 1 November 1991.

[33] Anania, Carter and McCalla (1994) explain that while most blamed CAP, other factors included the slower rate of growth in the developing world and the debt crisis, which reduced import demand; the strong U.S. dollar, which put its exports at competitive disadvantage; and decisions by China and the Soviet Union to buy wheat from other exporters because the United States excluded them from its export subsidy program in the years 1985 to 1987 (these markets returned when the United States included them in the export subsidy program).

[34] The Subsidies Code agreement from the Tokyo Round negotiations had attempted in article 10(1) to clarify the exceptions for agricultural subsidies allowed under article 16 of the GATT by prohibiting subsidies that "displace the exports of another signatory" by "more than an equitable share" (Hudec 1993, 148). EC wheat flour exports had increased from 29 percent of world exports in 1959–1962 to 75 percent in 1978–1981, while the U.S. share fell during that period from 25 percent to 9 percent of world exports. The United States and the EC flooded the panel with data about what should be appropriate shares under free-market conditions, which was difficult to prove due to the unpredictability of markets and the long history of government intervention.

ment Program of the 1985 Food Security Act. Trade retaliation cost the United States 1.6 billion dollars for subsidies given toward wheat sales to North Africa in 1985–1988, and in 1986 both the United States and the EC spent more than 45 billion dollars on export subsidies for a broad range of agricultural commodities (Gardner 1996, 115). Notably, the retaliation measures did not cause the EC to change its policies. However, the futility of the trade war in which the United States and the EC drained their budgets and destabilized markets created pressures for both to talk about changing their agricultural trade policies.

Europe resisted early U.S. efforts to start a new round at the 1982 GATT ministerial meeting largely from concern that any negotiation would bring another attack on the CAP. France in particular remained reluctant to embrace a new round, and the French government indicated it would veto any negotiation proposal that threatened CAP or required restrictions of export subsidies (Vahl 1997, 79, 85). However, in the following years enthusiasm for a new round grew in Europe as it became apparent that a new round would be about more than just agriculture. Europe would be the top beneficiary of liberalization in the new areas being discussed as topics for the round — namely, investments, intellectual property, and services (Paemen and Bensch 1995, 35).[35] Eventually French interest in service sector liberalization as well as increasing consensus within the community and strong support from the United Kingdom and Germany in favor of a multilateral negotiation brought France around to accept reluctantly the start of a new trade round (Meunier 2000, 122). In March 1985 the meeting of European leaders at the Council of European Communities declared itself to favor a new round. This decision received strong backing by European business, which claimed that the improvement of the trade system was necessary to revive economic growth.[36]

Nevertheless, the EC position continued to be defensive on agriculture. The Council Declaration of 1985 stated that the Community was ready to discuss agricultural policies in a new round, but it also warned, "The Council is determined that the fundamental objectives and mechanisms both internal and external of the CAP shall not be placed in question" (Vahl 1997, 81). French opposition continued to closely constrain

[35] This case study of the Uruguay Round draws on the account of the negotiation by Hugo Paemen (1995). Paemen was one of the lead European Commission officials in charge of the negotiation coordination in his role as deputy director-general of the Directorate for External Economic Affairs and head of the Uruguay Round Steering Group.

[36] UNICE, "UNICE Position Paper on a New Round of GATT Multilateral Trade Negotiations," 25 September 1985.

the EC mandate. In a bitter exchange at the Bonn economic summit in May 1985, France tried to delay the setting of a date to begin the new round, and French President François Mitterand accused the United States of trying to destroy the CAP. Secretary of State George Shultz responded, "We intend to move forward in trade, we hope on a multi-lateral basis. But we'll do so on bilateral terms if we have to . . . excluding the French from the resulting benefits of reductions in trade barriers" (Preeg 1995, 54). The appeal of the potential gains from the package deal and possibility of exclusion led France reluctantly to allow the talks to go forward.

Within Europe the budget burden of paying for CAP increasingly made it appear that some kind of policy change was inevitable. The looming budget crisis motivated the Commission to issue a 1981 paper, "Guidelines for European Agriculture," that suggested Community prices should be reduced to levels comparable with U.S. prices (Moyer and Josling 1990, 62). German opposition defeated the idea of reforming prices, and when reforms were eventually passed by the Council in 1984, they introduced quantitative restrictions in the dairy sector, where surplus production was most problematic. Milk production quotas were clearly only a partial solution. The escalating subsidy war with the United States over cereals trade increased budget expenditures. Commission papers continued to urge the need for price discipline. Thus while the EC faced budget pressures to reform, the Council could not agree upon a comprehensive solution. The decision to accept the start of a trade round did not reflect any change in the EC commitment to the fundamental principles of the CAP and use of the variable import levy, export subsidies, and import barriers as a way to uphold high domestic prices in the Community (Ingersent, Rayner, and Hine 1994, 263).

Setting an Ambitious Liberalization Agenda

As in past negotiation rounds, the United States insisted that agriculture was a priority that must be given a central place on the agenda. Producing tangible gains for U.S. agriculture was an essential part of the U.S. strategy to build a free-trade coalition within Congress, and U.S. negotiators repeatedly said that they could not accept any agreement in the Uruguay Round without significant improvement in agricultural trade.

The backdrop to the U.S. negotiating position was a deteriorating situation for U.S. farmers. Low farm prices and depression of rural economies made U.S. farmers eager to increase exports (Hillman 1994,

32). Instead, the high U.S. dollar and competing EC exports contributed to a declining share of world markets for U.S. farmers. Surplus production stimulated by domestic support policies and cheap exports paid for by export subsidies were two factors that put downward pressure on world prices. To counter this distortion of world food markets, the United States and the EC would have to reduce domestic subsidies and export subsidies. U.S. officials estimated that if their proposals for major agricultural liberalization were accepted by their trade partners, world agricultural exports would expand by one-third and U.S. farm incomes would be one to two billion dollars higher in 1996 than the incomes projected under current policies.[37]

Other agricultural export nations provided crucial backing for the need to give high priority to agriculture in the round. In August 1986 Australia, Canada, New Zealand, and eleven developing nations including Brazil and Argentina formed a coalition called the Cairns Group.[38] All were agriculture exporters, and the share of agricultural products within their total exports in 1986 ranged from 18 percent for Canada to 73 percent for Argentina (Higgot and Cooper 1990, 602). The protection policies and subsidy war of the United States and the EC were estimated to depress the export earnings of these countries by as much as 50 percent.[39] The Cairns Group issued a paper calling for agricultural trade liberalization and threatened to walk out of the round negotiations if this goal was not satisfied (Preeg 1995, 58). With a combined GDP of 1.06 trillion dollars, Cairns Group members would be important participants to enable gains in other negotiation groups, such as those on service and industrial goods liberalization (Higgot and Cooper 1990, 604). Hence the United States and the EC could not lightly dismiss their demands or their threat to boycott the entire negotiation if agricultural reforms proved insufficient.

The interests of some developing country members in particular helped to force issue linkage within the negotiation agenda. Brazil and India led developing-country opposition to including on the agenda issues such as services and intellectual property, both of which were new topics for GATT negotiations. Many developing nations feared that service liberalization would only increase the imbalance of world trade in favor of developed countries that dominated key service industries, and

[37] These figures are from a 1991 USDA report and testimony by USTR Carla Hills presented to a congressional hearing in March 1991 (Hillman 1994, 34, 52).

[38] The Cairns Group included: Argentina, Australia, Brazil, Canada, Chile, Colombia, Fiji, Hungary, Indonesia, Malaysia, New Zealand, Philippines, Thailand, and Uruguay.

[39] This figure is from a Tyers-Anderson model for 1990 Cairns Group members' export earnings, cited in Ingersent, Rayner, and Hine (1994, 264).

they believed that patent protection would make access to new technology more difficult (Ricupero 1998, 14). At the same time, many developing countries, such as Brazil, were agricultural exporters who required offsetting gains from agricultural liberalization to make the round beneficial to their interests. From the beginning of the round and through the midterm review in 1988 and the Brussels meeting of 1990, these nations insisted on the cross-sector linkage between parallel progress in agriculture and services (Higgot and Cooper 1990, 619).

Officials who gathered in Punta del Este in Uruguay for the meeting that launched the Uruguay Round in September 1986 faced two major obstacles: European resistance to a strong declaration on agricultural liberalization, and developing country resistance to inclusion of services. The two were not unrelated — the promise of reform in agriculture appealed to developing countries' interests, while the service-sector negotiations appealed to Europe. The final compromise added both agricultural issues and service issues to the agenda while establishing procedures to discuss the former in a separate agriculture negotiation group as part of the negotiations on goods, and to discuss the latter in a separate negotiation track parallel with the negotiations on goods.

The Punta del Este Ministerial Declaration gave an ambitious call for agricultural reform: "Negotiations shall aim to achieve greater liberalization of trade in agriculture and bring all measures affecting import access and export competition under strengthened and more operationally effective GATT rules and disciplines."[40] The declaration went on to call for reduction of import barriers and disciplines on direct and indirect subsidies affecting agricultural trade. This was not the explicit mandate for specific commitments on market access, domestic subsidies, and export subsidies desired by the United States, but it embraced a broader range of policy reform than the EC wanted.

While agricultural issues were placed in a separate negotiating group with primary responsibility for all agricultural topics, progress in this group was linked to the overall package of the Uruguay Round negotiation. The Punta del Este Declaration established the linkage between negotiation groups in the statement that "the launching, the conduct and the implementation of the outcome of the negotiations shall be treated as parts of a single undertaking."[41] Rather than embracing specific cross-sectoral concessions, the declaration appealed for balanced concessions within each negotiation group and recognition that all groups represented an overall balance necessary for the negotiation. In

[40] "Ministerial Declaration on the Uruguay Round," cited in Croome (1995, 387).
[41] Ibid., 383.

practice, during the negotiation this understanding led to the refrain that "nothing is agreed until everything is agreed" (Croome 1995, 34). This kind of package linkage meant that progress toward completing an agreement in one negotiating group would be contingent on equivalent progress toward conclusion in other groups, and at the end of the negotiation there would be joint acceptance of all of the negotiating group proposals.

The decision to accept the Punta del Este Declaration represented a major EC trade policy position, which prevented agricultural interests from dominating the policy process. The Commission Directorate for External Relations produced initial proposals, and all of the important decisions were discussed in the trade committee and Coreper and then forwarded to the General Affairs Council for approval (Vahl 1997, 80). Before participating in these discussions, national governments balanced their own interests between the different issues to produce a common position. These positions were coordinated in discussions by trade officials and ambassadors (i.e., the permanent representatives of each respective EC national delegation) in the trade committee and Coreper and were finally represented in the General Affairs Council by the foreign minister. The Agriculture Council produced an early draft for the negotiation mandate on agricultural issues, and this was cut significantly by the General Affairs Council. Once the international negotiation began, the Commission trade negotiator, Tran Van Thinh, represented the EC. French officials could not even enter the room for the final preparation meetings before the Punta del Este meeting (Vahl 1997, 84). Along each step in this process, agricultural interests were addressed alongside other economic interests at stake in the negotiation as well as the broader concern for the GATT trading system. Those favoring the round, such as the United Kingdom as well as the Commission officials, used the international level to "strengthen their hand" in these discussions of the options (ibid., 78).

The general level of the declaration helped governments accept the ambitious call for liberalization. Clayton Yeutter (1998, 66), who served as U.S. trade representative at the time, later wrote that the discussion of many agenda issues kept the focus off any one issue in a way that made it easier for leaders to handle agriculture. Agricultural concerns could not be ignored, but neither could they exclusively dominate the process. The need for a consensus by all participants to begin GATT trade rounds requires starting out with a general mandate and then working to fill in the details regarding the exact form and level of policy changes (Steinberg 2002). The bland statements of the agenda and inclusion of many issues allow each participant to interpret the agenda as they wish and anticipate gains from some aspect of the negotiation. Hence both the United States and the EC could accept the agenda to start the round even while holding vastly different preferences for the outcome at the end of the negotiation. On 20 September 1986 the General Affairs Council voted to accept the Punta del Este Ministerial Declaration and leave "everything else" — such as defining the Community's objectives in the negotiation — for later decisions (Paemen and Bensch 1995, 56).

Four Years of Resistance: 1986–1990

The record of past failures of GATT negotiations on agriculture undermined the credibility of the linkage in spite of the ambitious goals expressed in the Punta del Este Declaration. In both the Kennedy Round and the Tokyo Round, the United States had insisted that major agricultural liberalization was a prerequisite to agreement and yet, in the end, had accepted marginal reforms. Many in the Commission and national delegations believed that the pattern would repeat itself and the United States would sign a final agreement without any substantial agricultural liberalization (Kay 1998, 59; Josling, Tangermann, and Warley 1996, 172). A Commission negotiator for the agriculture group negotiations of the Uruguay Round said, "We knew agriculture might be a problem, but this was not really clear until the midterm review in 1988. Nobody in Europe thought there could be a negotiation that left out agriculture, but it was hoped that there might not have to be major reforms — like in the Tokyo Round."[42] Even a study by the World Bank at the onset of the Uruguay Round noted that "because of past experience and accumulated cynicism about restoring agricultural trade to the marketplace, failure to make great progress in agriculture probably would not devastate the entire round" (Finger and Olechowski 1987, 11).

The United States and the EC put forward drastically divergent initial negotiating positions. In July 1987 the United States called for a "zero option" to eliminate all import restrictions, domestic subsidies, and export subsidies over ten years. Unveiling the plan at the White House, President Reagan called it "the most ambitious proposal for world agricultural trade ever offered" but warned that the United States would only reform its own agricultural subsidy policies if other nations also

[42] Official of the Commission, Directorate General for Agriculture. Interview by author. Brussels, 4 July 2000.

agreed to do the same.[43] EC Agriculture Commissioner Frans Andriessen dismissed the proposal as unrealistic, and one EC diplomat was
quoted saying, "We've had agricultural subsidies in Europe for more
than a century. We can never accept something that would dismantle
the Common Agricultural Policy in 10 years."[44] Many in the United
States also questioned whether the proposal could be taken seriously.
Representative Dan Glickman, a Democratic congressman from Kansas,
warned that such a policy would cause as much as a 15 percent reduction in the number of American farmers and said, "That just ain't going
to happen. . . . It ain't going to happen in Europe either."[45] By demanding so much, the U.S. proposal lacked credibility. Especially ironic was
the fact that the most protected sectors in U.S. agriculture were the
most adamant that the United States should not retreat from its demand — this unexpected fervor for liberalization by sugar and dairy producers most likely reflected their anticipation that the U.S. "zero option" would stall any possibility for real progress in the negotiations
and thus spare their generous protection programs from any cuts (Paarlberg 1997, 425).

The EC position called for a "global approach" to reduce instability
on world markets by managing markets and lowering subsidies (Coleman and Tangermann 1999, 391). This accepted the need for overall
reductions in support for sectors that received heavy intervention but
resisted binding particular policy instruments. Such a reform program
would leave the CAP intact because reductions in domestic support policies would automatically reduce surpluses and the need for export subsidies without changing the dual pricing and export subsidy mechanisms of CAP. This directly countered the emphasis in the proposals by
the United States and the Cairns Group, which called for specific commitments in the areas of domestic subsidies, export subsidies, and trade
barriers.

The EC proposal prior to the December 1988 midterm review meeting in Montreal endorsed the need for "a significant, balanced reduction
in import barriers" and domestic support measures but added the conditions that each country determine how to reduce domestic support
and that the EC should be allowed to "rebalance" some of its past
GATT concessions on oilseeds (feed substitutes such as soymeal) that
had led to U.S. imports filling major EC feed product markets (Croome
1995, 116). From the beginning of the meeting, the United States in-

---

[43] *Washington Post*, 7 July 1987.
[44] *New York Times*, 7 July 1987; *Washington Post*, 10 July 1987.
[45] *New York Times*, 12 July 1987.

sisted on full liberalization and the EC refused to consider more than gradual reduction.

The Montreal meeting illustrated the potential for disagreements over agriculture to hold up the entire Uruguay Round. Before the meeting, the European government expected that no progress would be made in the agriculture group—EC Agriculture Commissioner Frans Andriessen defended the EC position on agriculture with the statement, "Even if we can't agree in Montreal, that doesn't mean the negotiations would be a failure."[46] Early agreement had been reached in some of the less controversial negotiation groups, such as tropical products and new rules for dispute settlement. In spite of the difficulties, agreement might have been reached on textiles, safeguards, and intellectual property (Croome 1995, 172). The EC tried to "agree to disagree" on agriculture, but the Latin American members of the Cairns Group insisted that negotiations in all groups, even on technical matters, should be put on hold until there was progress on agriculture (Paemen and Bensch 1995, 139). Because GATT norms required consensus to reach agreements, opposition by these countries brought the meeting to an end (Croome 1995, 173). When the agricultural talks stalled, ministers in Montreal temporarily suspended the Uruguay Round as a whole, including both the negotiation tracks for goods and services.

The midterm review meeting reconvened in Geneva in April 1989, and both the EC and the United States relaxed their earlier positions. This produced an agreement that called for creating a fair and market-oriented agricultural trading system by means of "substantial progressive reductions in agricultural support and protection sustained over an agreed period of time, resulting in correcting and preventing restrictions and distortions in world agricultural markets."[47] Both the United States and the EC had compromised, but the declaration still did not involve specific commitments. The midterm review agreement lacked much in the way of substantive significance for agriculture, but it called for members to submit proposals for reduction of support by the end of the year. These proposals issued at the end of 1989 continued to exhibit contrasting philosophies to agricultural reform as the United States and the Cairns Group advocated the opening of agriculture to market forces while the EC favored managing international markets through coordination among nations and continued reliance on import and export mechanisms (Angelidis 1993, 31).

[46] *Financial Times*, 30 November 1988.
[47] Text of April 1989 midterm review agriculture agreement, cited in Croome (1995, 175).

The changes in the U.S. and EC negotiation positions remained marginal. The United States had relaxed the zero option against all government aid to farmers, but the U.S. proposal still represented a strong demand for liberalization; it proposed a ten-year plan for 90 percent reduction of export subsidies and 75 percent reduction of import tariffs and internal support. The final EC proposal in November 1990 recommended reductions of internal support by 30 percent by 1995, while still assuming that this policy reform would automatically obviate the need for export subsidies and render formal restrictions unnecessary. The United States and the Cairns Group still had the stated goal of eliminating export subsidies, while the EC did not plan to make any commitments specifically on export subsidies. From the time of the Punta del Este Declaration in September 1986 until the scheduled "final meeting" of the Uruguay Round in Brussels in December 1990, the divisions between both sides remained intractable.

The hardline position within Europe reflected a strong Franco-German coalition in support of a restrictive negotiation mandate. The large gains for French farmers from privileged access to EC markets and subsidized exports make France's willingness to sabotage the agriculture negotiations less surprising. The position of Germany is more unexpected. The increasing budget costs of CAP and the trade gains from manufactured goods liberalization gave Germany reasons to advocate liberalization, but Germany sided with France to strongly back the CAP status quo policies. The British consistently favored reforming the CAP to be more responsive to world price signals and led the opposition to the Franco-German coalition (Patterson 1997, 149).

German policies toward agriculture have been described as "schizophrenic" in the tendency to support limiting costs while opposing price cuts, and a similar contradiction was apparent in the Uruguay Round as the government favored including agriculture in the agenda but objected to tariffication or subsidy reduction (Hendriks 1991, 80). Although Germany was paying the largest share of the costs of CAP as the largest contributor to the EC budget, during internal discussion of budget reforms in 1988, the German government refused to accept price cuts and quotas on outputs and forced the weakening of the budget stabilizer plans (ibid., 72–73). The consistent element in German policy was support for an incomes-oriented price level and high tariffs, and by the 1980s the government defended the CAP as a valued component of German agricultural policy.

So long as Germany supported France to resist any major reforms, there was little flexibility in the negotiating position of the EC in the Uruguay Round. France refused to consider separate treatment of export subsidies, and Germany supported it on this point; and at the same time, Germany opposed tariffication because it would force price cuts harmful to its farmers, and France supported it on this point (Vahl 1997, 112, 120). Publicly Germany was often outspoken with negative statements about agricultural liberalization even while it strongly supported the Uruguay Round. When the General Affairs Council discussed the midterm review in March 1989 and approved the results in April, France, Germany, Ireland, Italy, and Spain helped push the Council to take a firm stance on agriculture (ibid., 93). The United Kingdom and the Netherlands were the most proreform states, and the Commission also was more flexible in terms of showing willingness to consider parts of the Cairns Group proposal. Yet they were unable to overcome the Franco-German-led coalition in the Council of Ministers, which held the critical decision authority over the negotiation mandate.

In addition to the power struggle among national interests, there was positioning among different jurisdictions of the Council of Ministers. The General Affairs Council formally was the main forum for decisions on the Uruguay Round, but in practice it largely deferred to the Agriculture Council during the first years of the round. In September 1988 the Greek government held the Council presidency and issued a formal decision that the Agriculture Council should discuss the agricultural talks (Vahl 1997, 99).

The lead role taken by the Agriculture Council contributed to the situation from 1988 to 1989 around the midterm review in which the EC and United States talked past each other on agricultural policy. First, the Agriculture Council "recommended" a tough line in the negotiations with a detailed justification of the position written by the French minister of agriculture and supported by his German, Irish, Spanish, and Greek colleagues (Woolcock 1996, 310). Then agriculture ministers attended the Montreal meeting — saying that their trade colleagues would have too many other issues to consider and lacked the knowledge to give proper attention to the agriculture negotiation group (Paemen and Bensch 1995, 126). As it turned out, the added expertise of the agriculture ministers contributed more to an inflexible EC position than to an ability to find places for compromise. In ad hoc meetings of the Agriculture Council during the Montreal meeting, ministers urged the Commission negotiator to persuade the United States to make concessions and said the EC was constitutionally prevented from considering an end to farm subsidies (ibid., 135).[48] Before the meeting in Geneva in April, agriculture ministers issued an "opinion" to Commission negotia-

[48] Their comments alluded to article 39 of the EC treaty, which guarantees farmers a fair standard of living. U.S. demands for the elimination of all support would have challenged the EC ability to meet this goal.

tors again giving their suggestions for the agriculture negotiations (Vahl 1997, 100). While following the strict instructions of the most hardline states in the Agriculture Council, EC negotiators could not make any compromises toward an agreement acceptable to the United States and the Cairns Group.

Some interest groups tried to encourage the EC to take a wider perspective on the negotiations. The food industry was caught in the middle of EC-U.S. trade wars, and prior to the Montreal meeting the Confederation of Food and Drink Industries urged EC negotiators to achieve a mutually acceptable agriculture agreement in the midterm review (ibid., 105). With a more explicit recommendation for major reduction of agricultural support, the consumer group BEUC and the International Organization of Consumers' Unions came out in support of the Cairns Group proposal for the agriculture negotiation group at the Montreal meeting (ibid.). UNICE had also been involved in early industry mobilization urging the EC to consider reform of agriculture.

However, pressure from industry did not emerge as a major factor during the early years of the round. The integration of the food industry into CAP policies and the structure of the market reduced their demand for reforms.[49] Indeed, some of the food-processing companies held vested interests in the export-subsidy programs. This generated cross-cutting pressures within business groups because not all of their members favored agricultural reform. For example, a representative from Eurocommerce, an association of traders and wholesalers, said that his group had been conservative on agriculture because cereals traders are beneficiaries of the export subsidy programs.[50] As long as agriculture did not touch upon other vital interests for industry, such divisions prevented strong lobbying. As one Commission official said, "Business organizations were reluctant to talk about agricultural issues. For the most part, they don't want to get into a fight for something of less importance to their own interests. This changed in the last phase of the Uruguay Round when they began to publicly embrace concessions on agriculture."[51]

The Montreal midterm review meeting began to change how industry saw the role of agriculture in the round. Prior to the Montreal meeting, UNICE statements that touched upon agriculture focused on the need

[49] Official of the European Commission, Directorate General for Agriculture. Interview by author. Brussels, 4 July 2000.

[50] Eurocommerce official. Interview by author. Brussels, 5 July 2000.

[51] Official of the European Commission, Directorate General for Agriculture. Interview by author. Brussels, 4 July 2000.

to address agriculture within the Uruguay Round in order to avoid agricultural trade disputes spilling over to harm industrial trade.[52] Following the breakdown of the Montreal meeting, UNICE emphasized the linkage between agriculture and industry within the negotiation. With the following statement, UNICE called on negotiators to "clear the GATT log jam":

> The agricultural negotiations are not only of direct and significant concern to those industries based on agricultural raw materials — notably the food and beverage manufacturing industries. All enterprises represented by UNICE have an immediate interest in an agreement on agriculture.

> The future of the negotiations on such important issues for industry as TRIPS, services, the reinforcement of GATT rules (for instance access to markets, dispute settlement, safeguards), has been linked to real progress being made on agriculture.

> Industry and services therefore remain by far the major source of wealth creation and employment in the Community. For this reason, UNICE calls for rapid progress in solving the persistent disagreements on agriculture, so that the advantages to be gained by industrial and service enterprises from the Uruguay Round are not jeopardized.[53]

The linkage now had attained sufficient credibility to capture the attention of industry groups. Whereas previous UNICE statements only mentioned agriculture along with all of the other negotiation groups, now it issued statements such as this one, which focused exclusively on the need for compromise in agriculture negotiations.

Despite the fact that the linkage with agriculture repeatedly delayed industrial and service negotiations, business groups did not resist the linkage itself. Not only was it clear that the United States viewed substantial agricultural liberalization as an essential component of the round, but also key developing countries had shown that they would refuse to discuss service liberalization if agricultural talks were abandoned. Moreover, a solution to agricultural disagreements within the Uruguay Round was seen as better than leaving the issues for bilateral disputes outside of the round. UNICE in June 1990 "asked for the opening up of agricultural markets by all GATT partners by establishing multilateral rules for trade" and went on to emphasize that "it seems most important to UNICE that all agricultural products should be included. Thus

---

[52] UNICE, "Ministerial Mid-term Review of the Uruguay Round of Negotiations: The Priorities of European Industry," Brussels, 3 November 1988.

[53] UNICE, " 'Clear the GATT Log Jam,' Says UNICE," Brussels, 17 March 1989.

trade wars that will affect other sectors of the economy can be prevented."[54] In October UNICE officials, along with one hundred business representatives, met European Commission negotiators in a consultation meeting about the Uruguay Round. UNICE President Carlos Ferrer told Frans Andriessen that "Business and industry hope that trade in agricultural products will progressively be governed by stricter rules."[55] As much as business groups lamented the delays resulting from the linkage, they accepted that an agreement on agriculture was a necessary element of the Uruguay Round. Business groups urged the EC to adopt a more flexible agricultural position so that the Uruguay Round could achieve success in other areas.

Toward a Stronger Linkage

The key issue that eventually brought parties toward a compromise was the recognition that major agricultural policy reforms would be necessary for achieving a GATT agreement. Two events caused this strengthening of the linkage. First, the failure of the Brussels meeting revealed that the United States and the Cairns Group were prepared to risk the entire round for the sake of progress in agriculture, and subsequently, the Dunkel Draft brought together a package agreement closing gaps between the United States and the EC and linking all sectors to the single agreement.

The Brussels ministerial meeting of 3–8 December 1990 was scheduled as the final meeting of the Uruguay Round. Over 2,000 delegates, 1,300 journalists, and the top ministers from 100 participating nations gathered at the Heysel conference location outside of Brussels. Yet even before the conference began, problems loomed large. Despite plans to have a "final and complete package" ready by the time of the negotiation, lower-level bureaucratic consultations only produced an outline of points of difference for many negotiation groups (Croome 1995, 275). The main obstacle to progress lay with the EC agriculture proposal.

Political circumstances were extremely unfavorable. French farmers had been protesting since August due to their dire economic situation following a drought and collapse of world prices. The French government of François Mitterand had decided it must take the side of the farmer even if this meant risking the Uruguay Round.[56] Germany took a

[54] UNICE, "*UNICE Comments on 'Agriculture and GATT.'*" Brussels, 8 June 1990.
[55] UNICE, "*Community Businesses Urge Negotiators to Show Realism and Pragmatism*," Brussels, 18 October 1990.
[56] *The Times*, 7 November 1990.

hardline position alongside France. With a regional election in the farming region of Bavaria in mid-October and the first unified election in Germany scheduled for December 2, Chancellor Helmut Kohl took an uncompromising position to support farmers in order to make sure his center-right coalition would not lose any farmer votes.[57]

The interdependence of issues had already begun to emerge in the working-level talks toward a draft final agreement. The situation report sent to Brussels by the EC negotiating team at the July meeting of the Trade Negotiations Committee commented that "our demands for tariff and non-tariff reductions on industrial products vis-à-vis a large number of countries cannot be pressed any harder because of our lack of concrete offers on agriculture" (Paemen and Bensch 1995, 173). EC officials were clearly aware that other countries would delay putting forward serious negotiating proposals in other groups until an agreement in the agriculture group was forthcoming.

In the end, Europe agreed on its negotiating mandate only after seven Council meetings and warnings from the EC representative to GATT that "because of the links established by our partners, the delay in submitting the Community's Agriculture offer is now having negative repercussions on the whole negotiating process" (ibid., 179). Throughout the month of intense discussions on the mandate, the Agriculture Council took the lead with the General Affairs Council "waiting in the wings to give a verdict only after the Agriculture Ministers had taken a position" (Vahl 1997, 133). Germany, France, and Ireland repeatedly blocked approval of the Commission initiative.[58] In an attempt by the Italian presidency to break the Council deadlock, Italian Trade Minister Renato Ruggiero called a joint Council of Trade and Agriculture Ministers for November 5. Ruggiero started off the meeting by warning that the Community would be held responsible for the failure of the Uruguay Round if they did not reach agreement at this meeting.[59] The United Kingdom added a new factor to the balance by threatening to block transition measures to help East German agriculture until the Council agreed on the agriculture offer for the Uruguay Round (Vahl 1997, 137). Finally, the Council approved an agricultural offer for a 30 percent subsidy reduction. The EC proposal did not specify any commitment for reduction of tariffs or export subsidies. Moreover, it included rebalancing demands to reduce previous commitments in a move that

---

[57] *Financial Times*, 24 October 1990.
[58] *Financial Times*, 24 October 1990.
[59] *Journal of Commerce*, 6 November 1990.

would have left oilseeds exporters like the United States, Brazil, and Argentina worse off than before.[60]

The minimalist agreement allowed European states to claim victory back home and also drew immediate criticism from trade partners. The Commission had to enter negotiations with this proposal as the final limit on the reductions that the Council would consider — it had taken nearly two months before the Council would even agree on this proposal. An EC negotiator's report on the final preparations in late November warned that the EC would be blamed for a failure of the round, which seemed imminent given the lack of agreement in several key areas that had been "contaminated by the blockage in agriculture" (Paemen and Bensch 1995, 181). Nevertheless, EC negotiators had no leeway for movement on the proposal.

The Directorate General for Agriculture dominated the Commission decision making. Earlier in 1990 EC Commissioner for External Relations, Frans Andriessen, had suggested the need to accept the U.S. and Cairns Group demands for separate negotiations on internal support and export subsidies. Agriculture Commissioner Ray MacSharry was quick to assert publicly that he, not Andriessen, was "in charge of agricultural negotiations" and that Andriessen's suggestion did not deal with political realities.[61] Now, in the lead-up to the Brussels meeting, Andriessen warned that the EC agriculture proposal did not go far enough to meet the demands of trade partners. However, the influence of Andriessen and the Directorate for External Economic Relations was limited by the explicit division of negotiation portfolios that gave MacSharry jurisdiction over the agriculture negotiation group. Either as a tied-hands negotiation strategy or as a warning of the true situation, MacSharry announced at the beginning of the Brussels meeting, "The only flexibility I have is in explaining in detail the impact which the (30 percent) reductions in internal supports will have on our export restitutions and market access."[62]

Many doubted whether the United States and the Cairns Group would force the linkage rather than accept the modest European reform effort. EC farm officials reportedly regarded it "safe to call the U.S. bluff on farm reform," because they did not think the United States wanted to make severe reforms of its own farm sector either.[63] In particular, the passage of the 1990 U.S. farm legislation, which extended the U.S. export subsidy program and domestic subsidy program without any bud-

---

[60] *Financial Times*, 24 October 1990.
[61] *Financial Times*, 1 June 1990.
[62] *Financial Times*, 4 December 1990.
[63] *Financial Times*, 30 October 1990.

get restrictions, reinforced the image among European policymakers that the United States was bluffing when it called for radical reforms (Kay 1998, 63). Moreover, although Argentina seemed resolved to force the linkage, Cairns Group nations such as Canada said they did not favor such a strategy because "the subject under discussion is too important."[64] As a result, even while making statements that the EC agriculture proposal would not be accepted by its trade partners, in November Andriessen argued against postponement of the Brussels conference and spoke optimistically about the possibility for the meeting to end successfully (Paemen and Bensch 1995, 187–188). At this time, top EC officials still thought the Uruguay Round could be concluded while the EC refused any substantial agricultural policy changes.

The International Chamber of Commerce and UNICE urged the EC to stop delaying serious discussion of agricultural reforms.[65] Industry groups were frustrated to observe that while the EC failed to submit its offer on agriculture, other countries would not take a stance on other parts of the negotiation. Yet at this time, business pressure within France was notably absent. The sympathetic position toward agricultural protection taken by French employer groups prevented the European Roundtable of Industrialists from strongly lobbying for the conclusion of the Uruguay Round (Vahl 1997, 253).[66]

Against the lobbying by industry groups, over thirty thousand European farmers besieged Brussels during the conference meeting as a reminder to negotiators and their governments not to make any last-minute concessions harmful to farmers. Police were driven to use tear gas and water cannons to control protesters who burned tires and tore down traffic signs.[67] Few negotiators wanted to face such angry farm demonstrations back home following any concessions at the international negotiation.

The Brussels ministerial meeting was a negotiation to wrap up *all* negotiation groups, including industrial goods market access, services, and institutional reforms. However, it soon became a negotiation about agriculture. For negotiation groups that required more time working

---

[64] *Financial Times*, 30 October 1990.

[65] *Financial Times*, 30 October 1990; UNICE, "*Uruguay Round Multilateral Negotiations: UNICE Calls on the Twelve to Adopt a Joint Position on Agriculture*," Brussels, 25 October 1990.

[66] Indeed, UNICE noted in its statement in 1986 on the Uruguay Round that the French business organization, Conseil National du Patronat Francais (CNPF), did not agree with its concern about rising trade tensions between the United States and EC over agricultural trade. UNICE, "*UNICE Statement on the New Round of Multilateral Trade Negotiations*," Brussels, 23 May 1986.

[67] *Financial Times*, 4 December 1990.

out details, some substantive discussions took place so the agreement would be ready if a final text reached approval stage. However, governments avoided making important moves until progress was made in the critical sectors to make final agreement possible (Croome 1995, 278). No government wanted to be left having made concessions on politically sensitive questions and later discover that the offsetting gains were inadequate or that no agreement would be reached at all. Consequently, all came to hinge on the agriculture negotiation group.

Swedish Agriculture Minister Mats Hellström chaired the agriculture group and led informal consultations to find a compromise between the large gap in the EC and U.S. proposals. On the opening day of the conference, USTR Carla Hills harshly attacked the EC agriculture proposal, saying it was the source of stalemate in the negotiations, and the Australian delegation declared that they would refuse to negotiate any issues with the EC until it agreed to give precise commitments on export subsidies (Paemen and Bensch 1995, 182). By December 5 lack of progress led the United States to send a message to the EC negotiators informing them that the United States would leave the negotiation unless they made a new proposal on agriculture. Again the Cairns Group nations proved equally determined to call off the negotiation (Paemen and Bensch 1995, 184).

Hopes were raised when, following a Council meeting, Commission negotiators seemed willing to consider specific commitments on export subsidies and to withdraw the demand for rebalancing. Hellström created a draft proposal suggesting 30 percent reduction in support for domestic subsidies and export subsidies and minimum access guarantees to import 5 percent of consumption. This proposal seemed to come quite close to the EC proposal, but it used a 1990 base year for reductions, which would produce greater reductions than the EC proposal for 30 percent reduction of subsidies from a 1986 base year. Also, the Hellström proposal included export subsidies and tariffs as being subject to the 30 percent reduction, while the EC proposal had left out any commitments on these policies. The United States agreed to consider the Hellström proposal as a basis for negotiation—even though it represented far more modest reduction levels than the U.S. original proposal for the Brussels meeting, which called for 75 percent reduction of domestic subsidies and 90 percent reduction of export subsidies. Many thought the breakthrough had arrived, and the *Financial Times* even published an article on December 7 declaring that the "deadlock was broken."[68]

[68] *Financial Times*, 7 December 1990.

However, for the EC, the proposal went too far. Agricultural lobbies fiercely protested against it. France accused the Commission of having exceeded its mandate by even talking about reductions of export subsidies and withdrawal of the rebalancing demand (Vahl 1997, 140). France's Agriculture Minister Louis Mermaz called the Hellström proposal "monstrous."[69] The Agriculture Council and then later a meeting of agriculture and trade ministers unanimously rejected the proposal (ibid.). When the EC along with Japan and South Korea announced that the Hellström proposal was not a basis of discussion, the meeting ended.[70] On signal, the Latin American negotiators withdrew from all negotiating groups. The next day the chairman of the Trade Negotiation Committee and the plenary session in Brussels announced that the ministerial meeting would adjourn without agreement.

The end of the meeting also suspended the agreements in other negotiation groups. Reports indicated that progress had been reached in most other groups to the point where if the blockage in agriculture had been resolved, agreement might have been possible (Preeg 1995, 121). According to a GATT spokesman, agreement had been reached in government procurement, and progress had been made in the controversial negotiations on intellectual property and services so that these areas were on the right track.[71] These potential agreements were set aside as the meeting ended over the agricultural feud.

Headlines clearly placed the blame for the breakdown of the Brussels meeting on the EC. The *Financial Times* declared, "GATT talks break up with row over EC farm reform,"[72] while an editorial in the *New York Times* was titled "The Europeans Sabotage Trade."[73] EC negotiators Hugo Paemen and Alexandra Bensch (1995), in their account of the Uruguay Round, refer to the meeting as a "bloodbath" as the EC was attacked from all sides.

The failure of the Brussels meeting was a tremendous setback for the Uruguay Round and raised the possibility that the round itself would not be concluded. Why did the EC let this happen? Two factors contributed to the outcome. First, some EC actors continued to doubt whether the United States and the Cairns Group would follow through on their threats to hold the round hostage to progress in agriculture. In effect the

---

[69] *Journal of Commerce,* 7 December 1990.

[70] Ray MacSharry said the EC would negotiate only on the basis of its proposal, and that "the text [the Hellström proposal] is not a basis for discussion." *Journal of Commerce,* 7 December 1990.

[71] *Journal of Commerce,* 7 December 1990.

[72] *Financial Times,* 8 December 1990.

[73] *New York Times,* 8 December 1990.

EC tried to call the bluff only to realize too late that the threat was real, at which point the EC could not change course quickly on an issue of such political importance. Second, the resistance of the farm lobby was so great that leaders willingly chose to risk losing the gains of a successful round rather than anger farmers. The interest groups standing to benefit from a successful round had not applied pressure equal to that of the farmers who wanted to see the round fail. Not only were farmers heard protesting outside the conference headquarters, but they also had their own representatives in the EC policy process determining the direction of the EC negotiating position.

EC resistance to compromise was based upon the continued Franco-German coalition. During the discussions on the EC proposal in October, Germany strongly opposed Commission proposals to lower prices. Although German unification raised tremendous costs that increased the fiscal deficit and need for tax hikes, German officials continued to insist that any losses to farmers must be fully compensated.[74] Even when the Commission offered guarantees of compensation payments to address Germany's concerns for farmer incomes, the German agriculture minister said he would not let France become isolated in its opposition.[75] This support for France continued during the course of the Brussels meeting. When the United States issued its ultimatum that it would stop negotiating pending a new EC proposal, Mitterand and Kohl met to discuss further compromises. Kohl had just won a resounding victory in the December 2 election on the eve of the conference. U.S. negotiators expressed their hope that Kohl would intervene to bring some flexibility in the EC position on agriculture, for they feared that the talks would "blow up completely" without leadership from Germany.[76] However, instead of producing compromises, the next day France called for rejection of the Hellström proposal with Germany's support. Despite its economic interest in the successful conclusion of the round and the reduction of spending on CAP, Germany seemed intent on protecting its farmers and standing by France at any cost.

By refusing to reduce export subsidies, the EC rejected the most obvious budget-cutting option. Export subsidies distort trade and also represent the most egregious budget measure. In essence, the policy involves European taxpayers paying to sell food at a lower price to foreign markets while maintaining higher prices for consumers at home. The export subsidy competition between the United States and the EC

---

[74] *Financial Times*, 8 December 1990.
[75] *Financial Times*, 29 October 1990.
[76] *The Independent*, 2 December 1990.

lowered the world price of wheat, which meant more had to be spent on export subsidies as the gap between world and domestic prices grew.[77] However, it was exactly this wasteful policy that proved to be the final sticking point on which the EC refused to compromise at the Brussels meeting.

After the breakdown of negotiations over agricultural issues, GATT Director-General Arthur Dunkel seized the initiative. He declared in January that a framework for proceeding on talks in the agriculture group was necessary before the round could resume. Dunkel put forward a proposal that the agriculture group should seek specific binding commitments in the three areas of internal support, border protection, and export competition. This had been a basic demand of the United States and the Cairns Group and was consistent with the agenda of the Punta del Este Declaration.

However, the EC negotiation mandate was based on the proposal for the Brussels meeting and did not authorize specific commitments, particularly regarding export subsidies. Nevertheless, within Europe, the Brussels ministerial meeting had increased recognition that agricultural liberalization was necessary for a final agreement. Trade officials realized they could not afford to leave agricultural issues to the discretion of agriculture ministers. When considering its response to the Dunkel proposal, the Commission strategically chose to consult with the Trade Committee rather than the Special Agriculture Committee, and it used support in the General Affairs Council to disregard opposition by the Agriculture Council (Vahl 1997, 170). In a diplomatic sleight of hand, the EC changed its negotiation position without explicit acknowledgment of a new negotiation proposal — EC negotiators simply accepted along with thirty other delegations the proposal by Dunkel on February 20 to restart agriculture negotiations on the basis of a framework for binding commitments in the three areas (Croome 1995, 286). With the implicit backing of the General Affairs Council and in the context of a multilateral trade negotiation, this decision escaped veto by the Agriculture Council. This outline opened the door for agricultural negotiations to go forward, thus releasing the other groups to continue negotiations as well.

After a year in which negotiations continued to stall, Dunkel delivered an ultimatum in September 1991. He told a gathering of negotiators that they were about to enter the final stage of negotiations and that he planned to prepare a draft agreement text regardless of whether the chairs of the negotiating groups had submitted their reports (Pae-

---

[77] *Financial Times*, 7 December 1990.

men and Bensch 1995, 199). He said the new package agreement would be put forward "on a take-it-or-leave-it basis. . . . This is it — whether we are going forward or quitting" (Preeg 1995, 135). An EC negotiator reported: "A murmur of panic swept the room. How could delegations defend their interests if they were to be 'bounced' like this? Some questioned whether the Director-General was within his rights to take it upon himself to arbitrate in this way" (Paemen and Bensch 1995, 199). However, he was simply following through on the agreed upon decision by the heads of government that the round should be finalized by the end of the year, and he was building on the agreement after the Brussels failure that he should consolidate positions between countries.

Dunkel further integrated different negotiation groups in December 1991 when he issued the "Draft Final Act Embodying the Results of the Uruguay Round of Multilateral Trade Negotiations," which would become known as the Dunkel Draft. The draft summarized the current state of agreements in all of the negotiating groups, filling in details where no agreements had been reached, as was the case for the agriculture group. The proposal for 36 percent reduction of agricultural export subsidies along with limits on domestic subsidies and elimination of nontariff barriers went further than the EC position while short of the U.S. position, and it ultimately formed the outline of the final agreement (Coleman and Tangermann 1999, 400).[78] It endorsed the formula approach, thus forestalling any shift back to simple request-offer procedures as occurred midway through the Tokyo Round. While eventually the process of filling in the detailed offers of country schedules would involve request-offer style bargaining, the overall formula set the parameters for offers and requests.

In a key development, the draft included all areas of the negotiation to form the charter for a new organization (which later came to be called the World Trade Organization) whose members would accept the Uruguay Round agreements and earlier GATT agreements as a condition for membership. In this step, the "single undertaking" literally became a choice in which nations had to accept both old GATT obligations and all new ones from the Uruguay Round or else "have no trade agreement rights at all" (Hudec 1993, 193).[79] An American negotiator

---

[78] The draft agreement called for a reduction of export subsidies by 36 percent in value, tariffication of all nontariff barriers with minimum access of 3–5 percent, and reduction of tariffs on average by 36 percent, and reduction of domestic subsidies by 20 percent from 1986 levels (Croome 1995, 296).

[79] Legally the "single undertaking" was made effective in article 2:2.3. Article 11:1 limited membership in the WTO to those countries that had submitted schedules of concessions. See Petersmann (1997, 48).

referred to this development as "the ingenious structural incentive of the WTO—by creating the WTO they had to either join or not join."[80] This move was intended to make sure that no nation would try to opt out of tough new commitments by thinking it could continue under the status quo with its existing GATT rights. It was aimed primarily to prevent free riding by developing nations, such as occurred following the Tokyo Round when two-thirds of the participating nations did not sign most of the final agreements. At the same time, the package approach set the tone for all nations to take a more "systemic view" of the negotiation (Petersmann 1997, 52). Previously countries had been reluctant to make concessions in other groups from fear that problems in the agriculture group would prevent an overall agreement. Now, seeing the scope of the full agreement helped negotiators in other groups go forward *as if* an agriculture agreement were possible, while showing negotiators in the agriculture group the cost of failure.

The EC reaction to the Dunkel Draft was cautious overall and critical of the agriculture section. French Prime Minister Edith Cresson rejected it as an American *diktat* on December 18 before the final version had even been released (Paemen 1995, 202). In spite of French efforts urging outright rejection, the Council referred the draft to the Trade Committee for further analysis. In March 1992 the Commission announced over French objections and with the support of Germany and the United Kingdom that the Dunkel Draft provided a basis for agreement (Coleman and Tangermann 1999, 400).

Over the period from December 1990 to early 1992, the cross-sector linkage had grown substantially stronger. At the Brussels ministerial meeting, the United States and developing nations showed that they would let the Uruguay Round collapse rather than accept an agreement with minimal agricultural liberalization. Then Arthur Dunkel brought together a draft agreement that forced governments to consider the potential gains of the Uruguay Round as a package and raised the costs for requesting exceptions. These developments enhanced the credibility of the linkage among the different negotiation groups.

Mobilization to Prevent Failure

The Brussels meeting failure was followed immediately by calls from business groups to restart the negotiation. UNICE issued a sharp call for governments to "face up to their responsibilities and to focus all

---

[80] Official of USTR office in Geneva. Interview by author. Geneva, 16 July 1999.

their efforts on overcoming the current crisis" while reminding them yet again of the small share of agriculture in the European economy.[81] In 1991 business lobbying became more urgent and specific in its focus on agriculture. Meeting in Washington, DC in January, business associations of the United States, Japan, and Europe issued the following statement on the Uruguay Round: "We deplore the fact that the impasse over agriculture has effectively prevented progress in many other areas. At the same time, agricultural trade reform must be a part of the final agreement. We encourage all responsible authorities to reform their agricultural policies, which have led to distortions in international trade."[82]

Even after the dramatic collapse of the Brussels meeting over agricultural issues, business groups did not oppose the linkage itself but continued to urge agricultural reform for the sake of the overall gains. A delegation from European industry met with Commission President Jacques Delors on 5 March 1991. UNICE President Ferrer emphasized that he "particularly hoped that the positions the Community adopts on agriculture will allow progress to be made in this area of the negotiations, without sacrificing the interests of the industry and services sector."[83] In June a group of international business organizations including UNICE endorsed the need for an agriculture agreement addressing the three areas of market access, domestic support, and export subsidies.[84] The next month the European Trade Union Confederation and the European Center for Public Enterprises joined UNICE to lobby for the Uruguay Round and emphasized the employment gains from concluding the round.[85]

The Dunkel Draft also became a focus of industry lobbying. UNICE endorsed the Dunkel Draft as a basis for negotiation and urged negotiators to conclude the Uruguay Round. UNICE sent open letters to the European Council and Commission and also called on its member federations to undertake lobbying at the national level.[86] Appeals continued throughout 1992.

[81] UNICE, "European Business in Favour of Uruguay Round Negotiations Continuing," Brussels, 7 December 1990.

[82] International Private Sector Conference on the Uruguay Round, "Joint Statement of the Conferees," 28 January 1991.

[83] UNICE, "UNICE Delegation Visits President Delors: The Success of GATT Is Crucial and Urgent for European Industry," Brussels, 5 March 1991.

[84] UNICE, "American and European Business Representatives Call for Urgent Efforts to Conclude the Uruguay Round Negotiations," Brussels, 10 June 1991.

[85] UNICE, ETUC, CEEP, "To Create More Jobs, A Successful Outcome to the Uruguay Round Is Essential: Joint Statement by the European Social Partners," Brussels, 25 July 1991.

[86] UNICE, "Uruguay Round: Open Letter to President Delors and the President of the European Council, Mr. A. Cavaco Silva," Brussels, 2 April 1992.

In addition to manufacturing interests, food processing companies, which often bear the brunt of retaliation threats in agricultural issues, urged governments to reach a liberalization agreement and strengthen the GATT system for dispute resolution. Considering that the food industry accounts for about 10 percent of Europe's GDP and is the fifth largest EU exporter, governments cannot lightly dismiss their interests (Harris 1994, 183).

Industry-group lobbying for concessions on agricultural trade was especially pronounced in Germany. Soon after the Brussels meeting, industry groups increased their pressure on the German government to restart the negotiation (Coleman and Tangermann 1999, 395). The Federation of German Industry wrote several times to Chancellor Kohl appealing that he use his influence to persuade other EC states to be more flexible for the sake of the round and warning of the "devastating economic effects" on Germany from a failure of the Uruguay Round (Hendriks 1994, 158).

With the election behind him and increasing industry pressure to show leadership in the Uruguay Round, Kohl was now prepared to help push reforms as he had not done before the Brussels failure. Kohl met with Mitterand in the week following the collapse of the Brussels meeting. The two came away talking about the need for a proposal for the reduction of export subsidies, in what was a remarkable turnaround in just one week (Vahl 1997, 141). In the following year it would be clearly evident that while France remained reluctant on specific commitments to reduce export subsidies, Germany had relaxed its hard-line support for France on export subsidies as well as its own resistance to price cuts. In early 1991 Germany did not side with France to block Dunkel's proposal to negotiate on the basis of specific commitments in three areas, and in October 1991 the German cabinet accepted the Commission proposals to reform CAP with price cuts accompanied by compensation payments. After the decision, German Minister for Economic Affairs Jürgen Möllemann declared that the path to successful conclusion of the Uruguay Round was now clear and that the coalition among Germany, France, and Ireland would no longer block agreement between the United States and the EC in the agricultural negotiations (ibid., 160). When the Agriculture Council addressed the MacSharry reforms in May 1992, German agriculture groups urged the government to veto the price package as it had in 1985 (Hendriks 1994, 160). However, this time Germany sided with Britain to favor reform and France was left isolated. Kohl justified this politically controversial position as advocate of CAP reform, by saying that the reforms "created the conditions for a successful conclusion of the GATT negotiations" (ibid.).

Another critical change in 1991 was the increasing role of trade ministers in key decisions affecting negotiations on agriculture. Following the collapse of the Brussels meeting, trade ministers began to take on an informal role that proved helpful to shift the focus of discussion to the wider community interests (Woolcock and Hodges 1996, 315). The pro-farming states — France, Ireland, and Italy — served as Council presidents in the year and a half leading up to the Brussels meeting. They had been more than happy to leave affairs within the Agriculture Council. On the other hand, more reformist states — Luxembourg, the Netherlands, Britain, and Denmark — served as Council presidents in 1991, 1992, and 1993; they encouraged a larger role by trade ministers. Woolcock and Hodges argue that the Council presidency was an important factor to permit a larger role for trade officials. The Brussels failure and the large stakes of the package agreement created the incentives to bring trade officials into discussions about agriculture, and supportive Council presidencies were able to encourage this development through their control over the agenda for Council decision making. Following the October shift in the German government position, a meeting of EC trade ministers gave indications that the EC would adopt a more flexible negotiating position, although they could not formally revise the negotiation mandate (Vahl 1997, 180).

Immediately following the failure of the Brussels meeting in December 1990, EC Commissioner for Agriculture Ray MacSharry introduced a draft paper suggesting major reforms of the CAP. Although MacSharry and the Commission had begun discussing reform since 1989, plans remained vague, and the Commission had not made public these moves given its anticipation of hostile reaction from member states (Kay 1998, 107). The failure of the Brussels meeting acted as a catalyst prompting quick movement. After only two months, at the end of January the Commission adopted the formal proposal, which called for substantial price reductions and land set-aside commitments by farmers with income compensation payments issued on the basis of historical reference values rather than current production.[87]

The goal of the MacSharry reform plan was to restrain chronic overproduction that was the source of the worst budget and trade problems. Following the release of the Dunkel Draft in December 1991, the Commission made the reform plan more "GATT-able" by adjusting the reforms to better fit the outline by Dunkel (ibid., 71). The new internal policies would make an agreement with the United States in the Uruguay Round easier on several points: reduction of overproduction would reduce the need for export subsidies to dispose of surplus production,

---

[87] The proposal COM (91)100 was passed January 31 by the Commission.

lower prices would make EC cereals competitive with imported cereal substitutes so that there would be less need to demand the rebalancing of the oilseeds tariff, and the shift in orientation toward subsidies decoupled from production would open new options for subsidy reduction (Coleman and Tangermann 1999, 399). Although the EC had declared in 1986 that the principles and mechanisms of the CAP would not be changed, acceptance of the MacSharry reform proposal by the Council in May 1992 represented a major reorientation of CAP. Much of the legislation passed through management committees received little attention given its technical nature, but the sum total represented a "complete overhaul of CAP legislation relating to external trade."[88]

Farm groups vehemently opposed the reforms, and there were multiple bomb attacks against public buildings in France. At the same time, foreign ministers and economic ministers in national governments were increasingly interested in pushing CAP reform. Industry groups urged adoption of the MacSharry reforms, and then, upon passage of the measures, they urged EC leaders to move forward with the negotiation: "Both UNICE and the Round Table of major industrialists issued countless public appeals and bombarded European governments with missives urging them not to allow this 'window of opportunity' to go by" (Paemen 1995, 212).

Even if they were disinterested in the gains for the industrial and service sector from the Uruguay Round, representatives of agricultural interests were concerned that agriculture should not be seen as having caused the sacrifice of those gains. One official of the Directorate General for Agriculture commented that "Agriculture needs the support of society and therefore it could not make the round fail. In the end phase of the negotiation, it was clear that agriculture must move."[89] It was in the agricultural sector's interest to avoid events that could turn public opinion against it or increase critical attitudes among elites and the media.

For political reasons, namely, the agriculture ministers' insistence that CAP was not to be subject to international negotiation, officials stated that CAP reform was entirely independent of GATT negotiations and necessitated by budget constraints. However, in reality this was no more than "window dressing" according to an official who worked for the GATT secretariat. "Of course it [the MacSharry reform plan] was

---

[88] *AgraEurope* (1995), "Agricultural Trading — Post GATT: A Guide to the Implementation of the GATT Uruguay Round Agreement," no. 28: 2.

[89] Official of the European Commission Directorate General for Agriculture. Interview by author. Brussels, 4 July 2000.

driven from the outside, but to admit this would be to declare lack of muscle in negotiations and that they were not masters of their own authority. . . . For big countries it would be a disaster to say that they must do such changes because of the Americans."[90] Most studies conclude that the MacSharry reforms were largely motivated by the need to make changes so that the EC could reach an agreement in the GATT negotiations.[91]

The MacSharry reforms went far toward creating the basis for an agreement in the Uruguay Round while doing little to restrain CAP costs (Grant 1997, 78; Coleman and Tangermann 1999, 398). For example, in the wheat sector, in the first year of the reforms from 1992 to 1993 the expense for export subsidies fell substantially, but the offsetting direct income compensation subsidies meant that the total budget expenditure almost doubled.[92] Most scenarios estimating the medium-term impact of the CAP reform indicated that the EC would produce less, but with higher budget costs and higher farm incomes (Kay 1998, 134).

The United States pushed the agriculture negotiations in the Uruguay Round with pressure on a separate dispute over oilseeds. In an earlier GATT round, the EC had committed to zero-level tariff bindings on oilseeds (soybean, rapeseed, etc.). However, when cheap imported oilseeds came to be used as cereal substitutes providing a protein source in livestock feed, they undermined CAP by reducing demand for EC wheat, barley, and maize (Ames 1996, 100). The EC tried to close this loophole by introducing subsidies to processors for purchasing higher cost EC oilseeds. By 1985 subsidies for oilseeds exceeded 10 percent of total EC expenditure for agriculture and were reducing the U.S. share of the EC market (ibid.). Considering that by the 1980s, half of all U.S. exports to the EC were oilseeds and that Washington said losses imposed on U.S. farmers as a result of the EC oilseeds subsidy program were 1.5–2 billion dollars a year, this was an issue of major concern.[93] In December 1987 the American Soybean Association filed a section 301 petition requesting that the U.S. government negotiate the issue.

The United States tried unsuccessfully to use legal pressure through the GATT dispute settlement proceedings. Following a U.S. complaint, a GATT panel ruled against the EC oilseeds subsidy program in 1990,

[90] WTO official. Interview by author. Geneva, 14 July 1999.

[91] See, for example, Coleman and Tangermann (1999); Patterson (1997); Swinbank and Tanner (1996); Kay (1998). For an opposing view, that the EC CAP reforms were independent of the GATT negotiations, see Paarlberg (1997).

[92] Kay (1998, 134) cites studies showing that for the EU wheat sector comparison of 1992 and 1993, farm prices declined by 25 percent and exports declined by 12.45 percent, while the budget expense rose from 1886.85 million ECU to 2888.63 million ECU.

[93] Journal of Commerce, 20 November 1992; Hudec (1993, 559).

and a subsequent panel ruled in 1992 that the policy adjustments made by the EC after the first panel were inadequate.[94] EC and U.S. negotiators were unable to reach an agreement on the compensation that the EC should provide the United States in order to continue its subsidy program. When the United States requested binding GATT arbitration, the EC refused. Adjudication of the dispute had clearly failed.

The EC wanted to defer the issue to the Uruguay Round in the hope that it could bargain to raise the oilseeds tariff in exchange for agreeing to reduce its subsidies as part of an overall agreement (Ames 1996, 101). This "rebalancing" request had been a consistent element in the various EC proposals, but it met the adamant rejection of the U.S. negotiators. At the opening session of the Brussels meeting in December 1990, USTR Carla Hills said "the notion of rebalancing is *anathema* to reform because it closes markets" (Paemen and Bensch 1995, 182). The Hellström proposal of the Brussels ministerial meeting and the Dunkel Draft both ignored the EC demand for rebalancing.

The EC demands for rebalancing in the Uruguay Round talks and the second panel ruling set the stage for the showdown between the United States and EC. On 5 November 1992, the United States issued a threat that in one month it would impose 200 percent duties on 300 million dollars worth of EC export items, mostly white wine and rapeseed oil from France, Germany, and Italy, unless the EC agreed before then to reform its oilseeds policy. The United States demanded EC production cuts, and it further threatened to escalate its punitive tariffs to include an additional 700 million dollars in products if no resolution was forthcoming. The EC response was to threaten to counter any U.S. sanctions with retaliatory sanctions of its own, and the French began planning a target list (Preeg 1995, 143).

The Final Stage

The U.S. strategy of bilateral retaliation brought the EC to the table for serious talks to make a deal ending U.S.-EC disagreements on all outstanding agricultural issues. Meeting in Blair House in Washington, DC,

---

[94] The panel ruled in favor of the 1988 U.S. complaint that the subsidies violated GATT article 3:4 and impaired U.S. rights under the 1962 tariff concession by the EC in the Dillon Round. The panel issued a violation finding regarding the claim that the subsidy exceeded the difference between internal and external prices. The panel issued a finding of nullification and impairment related to the expectation by the United States when it received the tariff concession in 1960 that it would have open access to the EC oilseeds market and that this expected benefit was not being fulfilled due to the subsidies adopted after the original concession was made by the EC. See Hudec (1993, 247) and Iceland (1994, 220).

TABLE 8.1

Agriculture Commitments in the Uruguay Round

	U.S. vs. EC (Nov. 1990)	Hellström (Dec. 1990)	Dunkel Draft (Dec. 1991)	Final (Dec. 1993)
Internal support reduction	75% vs. 30%	30%	20%	20%*
Border protection reduction	no mention	30%	36%	36%
Export subsidies				
budget reduction	90% vs. none	30%	36%	36%
volume reduction			24%	21%
Oilseeds	cut subsidy vs. raise tariff	no mention	no mention	land set-aside

Sources: Paemen (1995) and Preeg (1995).
*Excludes direct transfer payments.

U.S. and EC negotiators, including the respective trade and agriculture ministers, hammered out the deal they announced on November 20. The agreement ended two years of stalemate after the collapse of the Brussels ministerial meeting and allowed the Uruguay Round to move toward its conclusion. This negotiation represented bilateralism within the multilateral process. The U.S. and EC negotiators produced a mutually acceptable agreement which they then took back to Geneva to *multilateralize* by persuading other countries to accept the terms. Once the other participants gave their consent, the Blair House deal eventually took the form of amendments to the agreement on agriculture in the Dunkel Draft.

Overall, the Blair House agreement represented compromise by both sides. Table 8.1 summarizes the progression of different positions over the course of the Uruguay Round. The agreement made modest adjustments to the Dunkel Draft but confirmed the broader approach and level of commitments.[95] In a face-saving formula, EC agricultural concessions would have to be balanced by "concrete results" in other trade areas such as financial services and market access.[96] For both the United

[95] Direct compensation payments were excluded from subsidy reduction commitments, and the export-subsidy volume reduction was reduced from 24 percent to 21 percent cuts, although the budget reduction requirement remained the same as in the Dunkel Draft. See Paemen and Bensch (1995).

[96] *Financial Times*, 8 December 1992.

States and the EC, the offsetting gains from cross-sector linkages helped them to relax their original positions on agriculture.

Regarding the oilseeds issue, where U.S. interests were very large, the United States dropped its demand for an end to oilseeds subsidies in exchange for EC concessions on other issues. The EC dropped its request for an increase of tariffs on oilseeds and agreed to restrict its production. The American Soybean Association expressed disappointment but also noted that "the agreement has the potential of gradually slowing and possibly reversing the current trade-distorting trends in EC oilseed production," and the American Farm Bureau expressed pleasure with the agreement as a breakthrough for the agricultural talks of the Uruguay Round (Hanrahan 1992, 3). Whereas GATT panel rulings and U.S. trade sanctions had not brought the EC to yield on its oilseeds program, minor liberalization was achieved for the sake of permitting the rest of the negotiation agreement to go forward.

An important change differing from the Dunkel Draft was the decision to exempt compensation payments from subsidy reduction commitments. The rationale was that these represented direct income transfers to farmers that were not trade distorting.[97] This left open the option for unrestricted amounts of income transfers to the farm sector and reduced the effectiveness of the Uruguay Round agreement as a spending cap. However, by restricting the form of transfers, the concession remained consistent with the goal of making market-oriented reforms.

French politicians eager to earn votes seemed unanimous in their intent to reject the deal. On November 21, French Prime Minister Pierre Beregovoy said the Blair House agreement was "unacceptable" and that "France [would] continue to refuse, whatever the consequences" (Paemen and Bensch 1995, 236). Angry French farmers invaded the Paris stock exchange to halt trading, burned the American flag, vandalized a Paris MacDonald's restaurant, and held mass demonstrations in front of the National Assembly.[98] However, France stood alone in its opposition. Despite the hostility toward the Blair House accords expressed by German farmers, Chancellor Kohl's government endorsed the deal as a good basis for completing the Uruguay Round. This increased the pressure on France; prior to the Blair House agreement, President Mitterand

[97] The agreement specifically referred to the U.S. deficiency payments and the new EC compensation payments that were part of the MacSharry CAP reform. The agreement permits such payments that are decoupled from production insofar as the payment amounts are linked to past production and do not give incentives for greater current production (Ingersent, Rayner, and Hine 1994, 288).

[98] *Journal of Commerce*, 1 December 1992.

said on French television that "it would be very dangerous for France to become isolated" (Preeg 1995, 144).

The EC followed the package approach in its own decision making by not voting on the agricultural component separate from the Uruguay Round. At the time of the Blair House agreement, the Commission consulted with the Council but did not put the agreement to a vote. "In the name of globality, the Uruguay Round was to be seen as a whole, of which agriculture formed only a part. The Council would not take any decisions until the Round was concluded" (Paemen and Bensch 1995, 237). This procedural decision avoided an immediate French veto of the Blair House agreement, as France was unable to vote on the agricultural package alone. France would not invoke a veto in the Council of Ministers without German support, which at the time was not forthcoming.[99] Moreover, French interests in the industrial and service sector agreements also favored a successful conclusion of the Uruguay Round. French employer groups, which had long backed the French government's position, began to pressure the government to be flexible and accept the agreement (Vahl 1997, 253). UNICE and others strongly warned against interference in an agreement that was seen as finally clearing the way for resumption of negotiations.[100] The package approach helped the Blair House agreement on agriculture gain EC acceptance in spite of public rejection by France.

Although the Blair House agreement was voted on later as part of the entire Uruguay Round package, it was necessary to make an earlier decision on the oilseeds section of the agreement. Both the panel rulings and the possibility that the United States would try to renegotiate the understanding motivated the Commission to try quickly to finalize this part of the agreement. However, the Agriculture Council sat on the issue for "procedural reasons" as it tried to delay approval, and it was only when the Danish presidency used its agenda authority to move the oilseeds issue into the General Affairs Council that the Council approved the agreement (ibid., 242, 246). Although the oilseeds subsidy regime itself was an integral CAP commodity regime that normally would have fallen under the jurisdiction of the Agriculture Council, the U.S. sanctions and implications for the Uruguay Round permitted a shift in policy forum to the General Affairs Council.

In the last months of the negotiation in the fall of 1993, France was unable to separate the agriculture section from the overall package, and

---

[99] *Financial Times*, 21 November 1992.

[100] UNICE, "Industry and Services Are Poor Relations in the Negotiations," 3 December 1992.

the pressure against vetoing the entire Uruguay Round was too great. At a September joint Council meeting of agriculture and foreign ministers, France tried to demand renegotiation of the agriculture section of the Uruguay Round but received only limited support from other states. French Prime Minister Edouard Balladur threatened to veto the entire Uruguay Round agreement unless his concerns over the agriculture agreement were allayed, and the United Kingdom in turn threatened to paralyze EC decision making if France blocked the Uruguay Round (Hanrahan 1994, 2; Bossche 1997, 64). German farmers protested against the agreement, but German industrial groups also exerted pressure at the national level, and the German government was not willing to have agriculture block the GATT agreement in this final stage. The government withheld its customary support for France and argued that seven million German jobs depended on the successful conclusion of the Uruguay Round (Vahl 1997, 240, 248). After thirteen hours of continuous discussion, the Council rejected French demands for renegotiation of agriculture. Rather than reopen the agriculture negotiations, Commission negotiators were told to try to "clarify" the Blair House agreement with the United States (Bossche 1997, 65). These follow-up talks led to minor adjustments that were also desired by U.S. agricultural groups.[101] In the context of the large package, the EC traded off concessions in other areas for this adjustment of the agricultural agreement (Paemen and Bensch 1995, 245).

Industry pressure strengthened government resolve at this final juncture. At the EC level, UNICE urged an early agreement of all final issues to conclude the Uruguay Round. UNICE Secretary General Zygmunt Tyszkiewicz said in advance of a meeting of the Council,

> Becoming bogged down in bilateral and sectoral disagreements is not the way forward for the Uruguay Round. . . . It is quite unacceptable for individual dossiers, however sensitive they might be, to compromise the chances of developing together, the rules, which will provide the framework for future international trade. . . . [A Uruguay Round agreement] is an essential component of any Community strategy for a recovery in competitiveness, growth and employment in Europe.[102]

---

[101] The compromise, which satisfied both governments and responded to concerns of American and French grain producers, allowed the use of a later reference period (1992 instead of 1986–1990) as the basis for making reductions. The change opened the way for the EC and the United States to export an additional seven to eight million tons of grain over what would have been allowed by the original Blair House agreement. Extension of the "peace clause" also met a European demand (Hanrahan 1994, 2, 5).

[102] UNICE, "All Sides Must Intensify Efforts in GATT Talks," Brussels, 22 October 1993.

Perhaps more importantly, German industrial groups exerted particular pressure at the national level (Vahl 1997, 252). Even French employer groups, which had long backed the French government's position, began to pressure the French government to be flexible and accept the agreement (ibid., 253).

Final decisions to conclude the round were made by the foreign ministers in the General Affairs Council as a single vote in December on the entire Uruguay Round Agreement. The Agriculture Council could neither veto the agriculture section of the agreement nor persuade other ministers to reject the entire package with such high stakes (Patterson 1997, 162). France tried to push for a Jumbo Council with a joint meeting of agriculture ministers together with foreign ministers, but the Belgian Council presidency, with the backing of other countries, refused (Vahl 1997, 242). The agreement retained its character as a "single undertaking" throughout the approval process. On 15 April 1994, at the time of the formal signing of the Agreement in Marrakesh, Morocco, in a meeting of the Council, member states insisted that the implementing legislation also follow the form of a single legislative package — it would help to sell the agreement back home to emphasize the package nature of the deal in which there were offsetting gains and losses (Bossche 1997, 87). Therefore, the Commission submitted implementing acts jointly for a single Council decision to adopt the Uruguay Round Agreement and approve the simultaneous entry of all implementation measures. In December 1994 the European Parliament gave its assent and the Council of Ministers unanimously approved the agreements and adopted the implementing legislation. Each member nation undertook the national procedure for approving the agreement, and at the end of the month the EC and member states' instruments of ratification were deposited in Geneva, taking effect by the 1 January 1995 deadline.

The successful conclusion of the Uruguay Round brought large overall gains. In the traditional area of industrial tariffs, a 40 percent average tariff cut continued the postwar liberalization trend. Rules comparable to those for industrial goods were established to regulate the world service trade that amounts to almost $1 trillion (Schott 1994, 13). Institutional improvements included greater legalization of the dispute settlement procedures and establishment of the World Trade Organization. When considering all aspects of the agreement, studies forecast a net contribution to economic growth that will increase world income over a ten-year period by over 200 billion dollars.[103]

---

[103] A GATT study estimates an increase of world GDP $230 billion (in 1992 dollars) by 2005 when looking at the actual concessions of the Final Act. Other studies by the OECD

The final package of agricultural reform addressed subsidy policies, market access, and export competition. The most important result of the agreement for U.S.-EC agricultural trade was the establishment of a ceiling on export subsidies with an obligation for 36 percent reduction in expenditure (ibid., 47). In addition, the mean tariff on EC agricultural products was scheduled to decline from 11.5 in the base period of 1986–1988 to 7.6 in the final year of implementation in 2000 (Wainio, Gibson, and Whitley 1999, 29). The agreement called for reduction of total domestic support by 20 percent over six years from the base period of 1986 to 1988.[104] This imposed discipline on internal farm subsidy programs that had never before fallen within the scope of GATT rules.

In a comparison of the period 1986–1988 with 1997–1999, the total support estimate of the share of national wealth Community members used to support agriculture shows a decline from 2.6 percent of GDP to 1.5 percent (OECD 2000a, 159). From this perspective, there has been a significant decline in protection for farmers in Europe. Looking more closely at specific commodities also shows evidence of policy changes. For wheat, the ratio between the average price received by producers and the world price nearly halved from 2.1 in 1986 when the Uruguay Round began to 1.1 in the year 2000.[105] Relative to the Tokyo Round agreement that failed to rein back EC intervention for wheat production, the Uruguay Round results were a remarkable success. While dairy products continue to be among the most highly protected commodities, the gap between internal and world prices for milk declined from 3.3 in 1986 to 1.7 in the year 2000.

The agreement was a disappointment for any who had hoped the negotiation would fix the EC budget problems. Other countries accepted the U.S.-EC compromise from the Blair House meetings, which accommodated their programs to provide income support to farmers by not counting these measures in their spending reduction commitments.[106] The Uruguay Round Agriculture Agreement would help to restrain fur-

---

and scholars are reported in Schott (1994, 17). These studies all rely on aggregate estimates of the reduction of protection and compute a general equilibrium model estimating the impact on global income.

[104] The fact that the figures are not inflation adjusted will bring further real reductions.

[105] These figures are the producer nominal protection coefficients reported by the OECD as an indicator of the nominal rate of protection (OECD 2000b).

[106] As long as direct payments are made in conjunction with production-limiting programs and are based on a fixed yield, they fall within annex 2, paragraph 1, of the agreement, which exempts from reduction those subsidies that "have no, or at most minimal, trade distorting effects or effects on production." Other subsidies include research support, food aid, environmental programs, and other such programs (Schott 1994, 49).

ther growth of market support spending, but the exemption for income payments meant that there would be no ceiling on total spending.

An American official at the USTR office in Geneva who was closely involved in the negotiation evaluated the outcome for U.S. agricultural trade with the EC as a modest success: "Our objective in the Uruguay Round was to limit export subsidies and we did get this done. There was not a major increase in access overall. However, binding tariffs was an achievement and there were real tariff cuts on the less sensitive items."[107] Reviewing the first three years following the agreement, a USDA study concluded that the EC along with other countries had fulfilled their commitments to reduce domestic subsidies and export subsidies.[108] Good market conditions and the modest levels of cuts meant that countries easily met their export subsidy reduction commitments during the first years of implementation, while domestic subsidy reduction largely consisted of changing the policy orientation away from price supports and toward direct payments. Tariffication rules allowed sufficient latitude for the EC to comply even while providing high protection for some products.[109] The agriculture agreement was important because it showed the willingness of governments to subject even the most sensitive sector to more market-oriented policies. The built-in agenda of the agreement mandated that new negotiations on both agriculture and services would begin in 2000 and thus guaranteed that the liberalization process would continue.

Conclusion

The Tokyo Round and the Uruguay Round represented large multilateral negotiations on a broad range of issues at times when the trade system was viewed to be under threat from rising protectionist pressures. Despite their significance for the world economy, the two negotiations moved forward—and backward—according to the status of talks about agriculture. The Tokyo Round and the Uruguay Round both began with the EC insisting that it would not change the principles or mechanisms of the CAP and with the United States insisting that it

---

[107] Official of USTR office in Geneva. Interview by author. Geneva, 16 July 1999.

[108] Indeed, of the twenty-four countries submitting reports, nearly all were shown to be in compliance. See Normile (1998).

[109] The agreement mandated the conversion of existing nontariff measures into tariffs. Such tariffication in some cases simply meant translating a quota into a high tariff with little real market access achieved, although minimum access commitments ensured that at least 3–5 percent of consumption would be imported.

would not accept an agreement without major agricultural reform. From similar beginnings, the end results differed. The Tokyo Round brought only marginal changes in the level of protection for a few agricultural policies of Europe and was followed by the EC increasing its production levels and the volume of subsidized exports. In contrast, during the Uruguay Round the EC conducted the largest overhaul of CAP policies since its establishment in 1962. Both EC production and export subsidies were reduced in line with the agreement.

Variation in the strength of the linkage between agriculture and the overall agreement for the two negotiations helps to explain the different outcomes. In the Tokyo Round, the negotiation structure was characterized by a weak linkage between agriculture and the rest of the negotiation. Not only were agriculture negotiations isolated for special treatment in the agriculture group, but the wider package of agreements in the Tokyo Round were loosely connected with each other, and informal agreements between the United States and EC provided the direction for how to conclude the round. The weakly institutionalized linkage facilitated EC intransigence on agriculture. Those products such as wheat where the linkage was weakest were also where policies did not change. In contrast, the cross-sector linkage established in the Uruguay Round was institutionalized and forced the EC to choose between accepting major agricultural reform or losing the gains from conclusion of the Uruguay Round.

Only after being brought to the brink of negotiation failure over agriculture disagreements did the Uruguay Round linkage attain sufficient credibility to shape decision making within the EC. The collapse of the Brussels meeting in 1990 showed that the United States as well as key developing nations would not conclude the negotiation without agricultural reform. The follow-up by Arthur Dunkel to create a draft agreement formalized the single undertaking approach. In contrast to the Tokyo Round, the Dunkel Draft, rather than a U.S.-EC memo of understanding, formed the political consensus upon which the final agreement would build. Changes in the behavior of domestic actors closely followed the timing of these developments that shaped the nature of the linkage. In the end, the EC agreed to liberalization measures that far exceeded the results for agriculture in the Tokyo Round.

Linking agricultural liberalization within a multisector package exerted pressure through two mechanisms: increasing the incentives for liberalization and shifting the policy process to include wider interests. Europe had much to gain from service sector liberalization, industrial sector liberalization, and strengthening of trade rules. The failure of the Uruguay Round would have denied European economies these gains while raising the specter of more bilateral disputes over agriculture and rising protectionism under a weakened trade system. These high stakes persuaded many within the EC that agricultural concessions were necessary for broader gains; business groups, the external economic relations section of the Commission led by Andriessen, and even the German government began to advocate compromise in the agriculture negotiations. However, neither farm groups nor agriculture ministers changed their opposition to reform.

Therefore the second aspect — changes in the policy process — played a crucial role. The politics of the Agriculture Council allow those most reluctant to reform agriculture to veto reform. To the extent that the negotiation shifted decision making outside of the Agriculture Council, liberalization became more likely. The Agriculture Council dominated decisions for the agriculture group negotiations throughout the Tokyo Round and in the early years of the Uruguay Round. However, in the concluding half of the Uruguay Round, the Commission and proreform presidencies of the Council restricted the influence of the Agriculture Council. Two conditions arising from the negotiation context made this possible. First, the large negotiation stakes provided the motivation for such leadership efforts. Second, the cross-sector range of issues provided the opening — it was possible to justify that a comprehensive negotiation should fall in the jurisdiction of foreign ministers and trade ministers rather than agriculture ministers, and it was possible to have a vote on the entire package at the end of the negotiation when even France could not afford to veto the package deal. In this way, the negotiation structure determined the stakes of the negotiation and shaped the internal political process.

The Tokyo Round negotiation highlighted the importance of the choice of procedures. The fact that negotiators spent two years trying to agree on the procedures for how to talk about agricultural trade policy indicates that they believe negotiation structure will have an impact on outcomes. The choice of procedures can become a negotiation over preferred outcomes where the preference intensity and bargaining leverage of the United States and the EC determine the outcome. This makes it difficult to separate the influence of the institutional feature from the configuration of interests that led to its establishment. However, the comparison of the Tokyo Round and Uruguay Round has shown how, once established, the negotiation structure amplified the effect of the initial choice. Even when the United States agreed to weaken the procedures for agricultural negotiations midway through the Tokyo Round, the United States continued to pressure for liberalization, but with little success. Similarly, during the Uruguay Round, when the EC accepted the Dunkel Draft as the basis for negotiation toward a package agreement with a strong linkage, it still resisted CAP reforms, although it thereafter undertook those reforms.

The strength of the linkage reflected in part the preferences of the actors but was also determined by other factors. In both rounds, the EC negotiators tried to avoid the linkage for agriculture while American negotiators tried to insist that equivalent gains for agricultural and industrial liberalization were a necessary condition for agreement. However, the role of other countries and the GATT director-general influenced the balance between these two conflicting positions. For example, the negotiation on wheat and grains moved outside of the Tokyo Round to the IWC in order to include the Soviet Union. The effect was to weaken the linkage, and the negotiation ended in stalemate. During the Uruguay Round, an organized group of developing nations refused to negotiate other sectors in the round without agricultural reform, which added credibility to the linkage. Such pressure was absent in the Tokyo Round when developing nations were more disengaged. In the Uruguay Round, GATT Director-General Arthur Dunkel also intervened as an active mediator creating a draft agreement that forced countries to consider a single package agreement. The choices that determine the linkage can arise from multiple sources, and those decisions will influence outcomes.

The importance of the single undertaking approach was emphasized by both EC and U.S. negotiating officials. A senior official at the U.S. delegation to the EC said that "if the Uruguay Round had not been an 'all or nothing' approach, then we could not have achieved so much."[110] EC negotiators Hugo Paemen and Alexandra Bensch allude to both the power and the risk entailed by this approach, referred to as "globality" in the EC discussions of the round:

> When the European Community talked of globality, it was not referring to the structural dimension typical of all multi-subject negotiations, but to a negotiating principle having the force of a legal obligation. In other words, in the Uruguay Round, it was a question of all or nothing. Right up to the very last minute, one comma, a single footnote could have caused the whole edifice to collapse. The raising of globality to the level of a legal principle was what caused the crises in the Uruguay Round to be so numerous and acute. Matters came to a head whenever there was the prospect of all being lost. (Paemen and Bensch 1995, 98)

[110] Official of U.S. delegation to the EU. Interview by author. Brussels, 7 July 1999.

The issue linkage had become so highly institutionalized that it supported such analogies with a legal style of negotiation. Although the
bargaining of the Uruguay Round never approached the legal framing
seen in GATT/WTO dispute-settlement proceedings, moderate legal
framing augmented the leverage of the cross-sector linkage by making it
more than just a unilateral negotiating tactic by the United States.

Neither threats nor budget constraints explain the policy outcomes.
Contrary to the hypothesis that the United States used its influence and
threats to coerce agricultural liberalization in favor of U.S. interests, the
Tokyo Round demonstrated the inability of the United States to achieve
gains in agricultural negotiations without the support of institutional
arrangements. Efforts by the United States to insist that a good agricultural settlement was necessary to gain ratification in Congress failed
to add enough bargaining leverage for additional concessions from the
EC. It was difficult for the United States credibly to threaten to throw
away the substantial gains from the round for the sake of agriculture.
Where U.S. interests were the greatest — wheat — the Tokyo Round ended with no agreement. Moreover, European leaders were unwilling to
make concessions under threats. In the closing months of the Tokyo
Round, when Congress threatened punitive duties to retaliate against
EC agricultural subsidies, this move delayed the negotiations and
brought no additional concessions. Then during the Uruguay Round,
the United States engaged in trade sanctions over the oilseeds subsidy
issue, but even then it achieved less liberalization on the oilseeds policy
relative to other areas of the agriculture agreement. Repeatedly the EC
called the U.S. bluff by refusing the major changes in agricultural policy
demanded by the United States. U.S. threats and attempts to use its own
domestic political constraints as a commitment failed to convince EC
leaders that agricultural reform was necessary for their broader economic interests.

There is little indication that budget constraints influenced decisions
on trade policy. During the Tokyo Round, while in the midst of a budget crisis over CAP spending and facing UK demands for change, the
EC fought against any international agreement to reduce subsidies. The
outcome was an expensive subsidy war between the United States and
the EC during the 1980s. The form of policy changes reveals that cost
cutting was also not the primary force for change in the Uruguay
Round — the EC and the United States chose to exempt direct payments
to farmers rather than jointly agree upon a ceiling for these costs. Even
after the Uruguay Round, agriculture remains heavily subsidized. Rather
than U.S. interests or budget constraints dictating the terms of the
agreement, the context of the GATT negotiation led EC officials to

make compromises because they believed that agricultural liberalization was necessary to conclude the trade round.

The achievement of the Uruguay Round was the integration of agriculture within GATT rules. Agricultural protection remains a priority for governments, but it is now subject to free trade principles, as evidenced by the shift away from protecting farmers with price supports and production subsidies and toward supporting farmers with tariffs and direct payments. This is a step toward the goal of protecting farmers as much as possible while distorting markets as little as possible.

In the complicated balance of interests within Europe, package deals are a common occurrence. Linking issues helps promote an agreement acceptable to all members. Similarly, a package negotiation structure facilitates liberalizing trade agreements.

9

Battles over Beef

BEGINNING IN 1989, the EC banned hormone-treated beef, in effect excluding U.S. beef from the European market. EC officials declared that consumer health concerns motivated the ban, while U.S. officials insisted that there was no scientific evidence of a health risk and the ban represented a trade barrier motivated by the desire to reduce beef imports. In the first negotiation from 1989 until 1996, the dispute remained a bilateral affair without mediation from GATT. In what was soon labeled the beef war, the United States launched unilateral sanctions against the EC. In the second negotiation from 1996 until 1999, the United States took the case before a WTO dispute panel, which ruled against the policy and authorized U.S. sanctions. The EU continues to ban hormone-treated meat in spite of annual sanctions of over $100 million dollars against EU exports to the United States and in spite of a clear legal ruling against the policy according to the new rules created by the Uruguay Round and accepted by the EU. Although scientific evidence has not substantiated a clear risk to human health from hormone-treated meat, the EU has taken a precautionary approach and refused to adjust its regulation.

Whereas the previous chapter focused on the role of institutions to promote package deals in trade rounds, this chapter will focus on the role of institutions to use legal framing in the adjudication of trade disputes. The GATT/WTO dispute proceedings apply legal framing in the negotiation structure as negotiations that evaluate the legal status of policies and publicize rule violations. In a negotiation structure very different from the trade rounds, this process begins with a country filing a formal legal complaint, then enters a consultation phase, and in some cases continues to the establishment of a panel of judges who rule on the policy.

The statistical analysis of chapter 3 showed that lower levels of legalism predicted EU liberalization in agricultural trade negotiations. As shown in model 1 in table 3.6, negotiations that involved a complaint and consultations in the early stage of the GATT dispute settlement process were significantly more likely to bring liberalization. This corresponds with the expectation that concern for reputation motivates liberalization. By compromising during the early stages of the dispute settlement process, the EU avoids a formal panel ruling against its policy and thereby reduces the potential harm to its reputation. Indeed, it is generally true for all nations that concessions are more likely during the consultation phase (Busch 2000). However, at the higher level of legal framing after a violation ruling, the EU resisted liberalization. Model 2 in table 3.6 showed that a violation ruling had no significant relationship with the negotiation outcome. Further analysis is necessary since there were only five cases with a violation ruling against an EU agricultural policy during the sample period of the analysis from 1970 to 1999.

Why does the higher level of legal framing encounter such problems in the EU policy process? Trade interests to support the credibility of the system of trade rules call for compliance with panel rulings, and normative pressure from international obligation would be at its greatest following a legal ruling against a policy. Both factors should make liberalization more likely after a GATT/WTO panel releases a ruling that recommends changing the policy. The evidence contrary to this expectation raises the question of whether there are any systematic factors that interfere with the influence of trade rules in the EU political context.

This chapter examines why the highest level of legal framing following a violation ruling sometimes fails to bring liberalization by the EU. In the case study, the failure of legal framing to bring liberalization of the EU ban against hormone-treated beef points to two general findings about the potential conflict between legal framing and EU institutions. First, the narrow focus of legal framing is not conducive to forming the kind of package deal that is often necessary for a policy to gain approval in the Council of Ministers, and particularly in the Agriculture Council. This sharply contrasts with the negotiation structure of a trade round that has a broad focus and facilitates linking different issues. Second, when policies supportive of EU integration conflict with those supportive of GATT rules, EU officials are likely to favor the former. While none in the EU openly challenge GATT legitimacy, they support GATT-illegal policies such as the beef hormone ban in the name of European unanimity. Whether judged on its political, normative, or economic importance, the project of European integration takes precedence over any individual GATT case. Tensions between CAP and GATT as well as the nature of consensus decision making prevent Europe from being more responsive to a ruling by a GATT panel against a single policy.

Integration versus Free Trade

Is the pursuit of European integration complementary with the pursuit of free trade? This section discusses sources of tension between EU policies and GATT rules that may contribute to the difficulty of negotiations characterized by legal framing in dispute settlement proceedings.

Although formation of the EU does not itself conflict with GATT rules, subsidiary policies central to European integration are often problematic. In particular, the CAP and preferential trade agreements repeatedly give rise to legal challenges by trade partners (Farrell 1999, 22). Created to protect the internal market, the CAP is supported by policy measures such as import quotas, import licensing schemes, and export subsidies that have rendered CAP "contentious from an international trade law perspective" according to one European legal scholar (Scott 2000, 170). In addition, preferential trade arrangements involve deviations from the principle of nondiscrimination in market access. Although the EU has used article 24 to justify its many preferential trade agreements, their conformity with GATT is debatable, and the management of these agreements has been a frequent source of criticism in WTO trade policy reviews (Hine 1985, 45; Farrell 1999, 21). In one controversial trade dispute, a GATT panel ruled against the EU banana import policies on the grounds that the preferential trade association, the Lome Convention, did not justify the discrimination between imports of a product from some developing countries in Africa over imports of the same product from developing countries in Latin America.[1] Given the structure of trade between these developing countries and Europe, many of the cases regarding preferential trade arrangements

---

[1] The Lomé Convention established a preferential trade agreement with former colonies among African, Caribbean, and Pacific (ACP) states. It forms the basis for the EU import regime that favors imports of bananas from these states over lower-cost imports from Latin America. Until creation of the Single European Market in 1992, there had been separate national tariff regimes to allow France and Britain to favor imports of bananas from the ACP states while Germany imported bananas from Latin America. The different prices in national markets would have been a problem for the Common Market, and so a new Banana Protocol was created by a February 1993 decision that extended the preference for the entire Common Market to allow ACP bananas duty-free status while other bananas faced a tariff quota to limit them from expanding market share. See Stevens (1996). The banana regime became the center of trade disputes initiated by complaints to GATT from Latin American banana exporters and the United States. U.S. multinational firms involved in the banana trade held interests in selling Latin American bananas to Europe that were impaired by the EU system for allocation of licenses to distributors.

that have been addressed in dispute settlement proceedings involve agricultural products.

These two areas of EU policy play important roles in the integration process. Preferential trade agreements act as a "quasi-foreign policy" serving development and political goals between EU members and those countries with special historical ties, often former colonies (Stevens 1996, 340). The CAP policies were central to European integration as the only working common policy during the first decades of Community development, and CAP continues to hold importance today as "an integral part of the West European welfare state" (Rieger 1996, 100). Consequently, policies related to preferential trade agreements with developing states and the CAP have their own moral legitimacy and institutional stakes within the EU that lend further support when they are challenged as contradictory to EU commitments to the GATT.

The CAP long held an uneasy legal status within international trade law. In the first frontal attack against a central CAP policy, in 1961, Uruguay filed a complaint to GATT, claiming that the variable levy along with a wide range of other CAP policies violated the GATT rules. The panel concluded that the contracting parties had not sufficiently settled the legality of CAP policies in the terms of the GATT and refused to give a ruling on the legality of the variable levies (Hudec 1993, 445–447). The outcome neither exonerated the CAP policies as compatible with GATT nor found them to be in violation. Thereafter, EC negotiators had to wage a defensive battle to uphold CAP policies against ongoing legal challenges.

Since then, the EU has established a poor record within the dispute settlement process when it comes to agricultural topics. It has frequently used delaying tactics, and twice it blocked the formation of a panel (when this was possible under the more lenient rules of the 1947 GATT system).[2] The EC also blocked the adoption of three panel reports in the early 1980s.[3] In some cases the EC made only minor adjustments to the

---

[2] The EC blocked the formation of a panel on the 1972 complaint by the United States against EC compensatory taxes paid for imports of processed agricultural products that were not within the CAP, but it then eliminated the tax system unilaterally. The 1976 case, *United States v. European Community: Programme of Minimum Import Prices, Licenses, etc. for Certain Processed Fruits and Vegetables*, offered a "textbook lesson in the many ways a GATT lawsuit could be obstructed" (Hudec 1993, 48). After the 1987 U.S. complaint against the EC Animal Hormones directive, the EC blocked a technical panel (ibid. 48, 453, 462, 545).

[3] The three cases, all initiated in 1982, were *United States v. European Community: Production Aids on Canned Peaches, Canned Pears, Canned Fruit Cocktail and Dried*

policy after a violation ruling, and then, after further negotiations with additional panel rulings, it finally agreed to more concessions to conclude the dispute.[4] Under the new WTO rules, the EU no longer can block panels or reports. However, in two notable cases, the EU refused to comply with violation rulings.[5] A frustrated USTR official said, "The Europeans still don't pay attention to the rules."[6]

The interlocking nature of the CAP policies means that a negative panel ruling holds wider implications beyond any single issue. A ruling on a mechanism such as the levy or subsidy policies would unravel the core operation of the CAP. For example, the legal issue in the case against export subsidies for the raw material component of pasta products threatened to destroy the export markets of EC food processors, which depended on export restitution payments to compensate for the high prices they paid to buy European agricultural products (Hudec 1988, 33). Even marginal adjustments threatened to upset the precarious balance of common prices and exacerbate the problem of surplus production. For example, when the EC agreed to a zero tariff binding for oilseeds in an early GATT round (the Dillon Round, 1960–1961), there was no expectation that imported oilseeds would displace EC grains in the internal market (Iceland 1994, 211). However, the high price support for EC grains, dairy, and meat led to development of an internal demand for oilseeds as a feed substitute, and soon EC livestock farmers were using U.S. soymeal cake while EC grains piled up in surplus paid for by EC budgets. This became a major point of contention in later negotiations as the EC tried to renegotiate its earlier tariff concession. The CAP stood at risk of unraveling from the development of such holes within the complex network of protection. Any single case had to be viewed in terms of its wider effect on the entire agricultural sector.

Grapes, United States v. European Community: Tariff Treatment of Citrus Products from Certain Mediterranean Countries, and *United States v. European Community: Subsidies on Exports of Pasta Products* (ibid. 496–498, 502, 493).

[4] In *United States v. European Community: Payments and Subsidies on Oilseeds and Animal-Feed Proteins*, the panel ruling against the EC oilseeds subsidy program was adopted January 1990. A second panel was convened to evaluate implementation and ruled that the new EC oilseeds regime was also in violation. In the end, two GATT rulings, U.S. threat of sanctions, and the wider context of the Uruguay Round were all part of the final solution (ibid., 560).

[5] The WTO violation rulings against both the banana import regime in 1997 and the beef hormone directive in 1998 did not bring a change in EU policy by the end of the implementation period, although the United States and the EU reached agreement on the banana dispute in April 2001.

[6] Interview by author. Washington, DC, 4 April 2000.

This often magnified the threat of accepting the precedent set by a ruling. In one case against EC subsidies to growers and processors of canned fruit, the EC blocked the panel report but settled the dispute with concessions to the United States on condition that the United States agree to withdraw the panel report (Hudec 1993, 498). Sometimes, even when the EC accepted a ruling, it registered a reservation noting legal objections to the content of the ruling.[7]

The narrow focus necessary for the legal evaluation of a dispute may work against its eventual success in the EU policy process. Cases for dispute settlement necessarily address an isolated policy in order to present legal arguments on the status of a particular policy within trade law. Linking together multiple policy areas would be inconsistent with the standard of legal evaluation and render the case unmanageable. However, this also means that on the domestic agenda the issue is more likely to be addressed as a single policy. Even linkages within the agricultural sector are constrained. Typically a dispute settlement recommendation will call for a policy change, such as ending an import ban or eliminating a subsidy for a given commodity. Such discrete decisions contrast with the tendency within the Agriculture Council to bundle issues together, such as when passing a price package or broad reform measure. Given the EU context where a broad policy package has become the way to get any policy change through the Agriculture Council, the narrow focus of the legalistic approach becomes a liability.

European integration complicates the question of legitimacy and international obligation. Preferential trade arrangements and the CAP are central pillars of European integration. Yet these same policies create tension with the world trade rules. On trade issues related to these topics, European member nations must choose whether to favor European rules over international rules. While EU treaty law recognizes the primacy of international law and the fact that GATT law is binding on EU institutions, there has still been uncertainty on this point.[8] Some EU legal scholars argue that GATT law should automatically take direct effect in EU law — which would represent a higher degree of compliance than most states — but early decisions by the European Court of Justice indicate that GATT rules do not have the legal status to become binding

---

[7] See, for example, *United States v. European Community: Restrictions on Imports of Apples*, in Hudec (1993, 564). The EC ended the import quota, which was found to be in violation of GATT article 11:2(c), and did not block the report when it was adopted by the GATT Council in June 1989. However, the EC reserved the right to challenge the panel's interpretation.

[8] EC treaty provisions in articles 228 and 234 state the primacy of international law over secondary EC law (Petersmann 2000, 277).

obligations within internal law (Hudec 1988, 43). In a prominent decision on 5 October 1994, the European Court of Justice stated that the Community did not have to take into consideration GATT rules when evaluating the legality of a regulation.[9] According to Robert Hudec (1988, 43), the vulnerability of important EU policies to criticism on the basis of international law and the uncertainty regarding the status of GATT law within the EU account for its resistance to legal settlement of trade disputes.

EU officials commonly profess to oppose the legalistic approach of the United States in favor of a diplomatic settlement of disputes, even blaming the U.S. "lawyer-ridden society" for its abnormal pursuit of lawsuits as a means to settle trade problems (ibid., 42). In 1986 EC Commissioner DeClerq declared that "GATT is a consensus body, one cannot transform it into a Court of Justice" (Peters 2000, 267). However, one must question whether the reluctance to embrace a legalistic approach lies in the problematic implications held for important policies like CAP. Over time, the EU has accepted legalized settlement of trade disputes due to continued U.S. pressure. Often European officials initiated disputes against the United States in retaliation for the disputes filed against Europe (Hudec 1988, 44). The EU also consented to increased legalization within the WTO because "there was resignation that without strengthening the dispute settlement proceedings, the United States would not get rid of the section 301 law."[10] Although the acceptance in practice of legal settlement of trade disputes represented an important shift in EU foreign policy, it has not ended the resistance against specific rulings. EU officials still voice complaints about the litigative approach of the United States and the need for political decisions on some issues for which they consider it inappropriate for a legal judgment to determine the outcome.[11]

Fundamentally, the competing obligations within the EU represent different priorities over the goals for further integration and the goals for freer trade. The tradeoff is associated with large economic and normative stakes. With growing intra-EU trade, the importance of European integration provides a counterweight to the importance of global

[9] In this case, the German government, supported by Belgium and the Netherlands, argued that the banana import regulation of the Community infringed GATT provisions and was contrary to the intent to uphold international obligations. Case C-280/93, Germany v Council [1994] ECR I-4973. See Petermann (2000, 272–277).

[10] Official of the Directorate General for Agriculture. Interview by author. Brussels, 4 July 2000.

[11] Officials of the Directorate General for Agriculture. Interviews by author. Brussels, 5 July 1999; 4 July 2000.

free trade. Intra-EU trade represents two-thirds of individual members' total trade.[12] This intra-EU trade provides the equivalent of a large domestic market. At the same time, the EU represents the largest trade entity in the world market. When excluding the intra-EU trade, in 1999 the EU had an 18.8 percent share of world merchandise exports, greater than the 16.4 percent share of the United States and 9.9 percent share of Japan.[13] Clearly the EU has strong economic interests in both the internal and external markets.

The EU policy process and interests both account for its difficulty to liberalize agricultural policies within dispute settlement proceedings. Legal framing applies normative pressure and uses the trade interests in international trade rules for leverage. However, for the EU there is a conflict between the importance of CAP, a pillar of integration, and the trade rules. Since the EU policy process for agricultural decision making is biased to favor CAP, liberalization is only possible if the negotiation lifts the issue outside of the normal policy trajectory. Package negotiations in trade rounds create such an opportunity because issue linkages force a broader policy agenda and increase the influence of trade officials. However, the narrow focus of the legalistic approach fails to broaden the EU policy process. The next section will examine these problems as they arose in the context of one of the most controversial trade disputes between the United States and the EU.

The Beef Hormone Dispute

Mad cow disease captured headlines in 1996 when the British government announced there was a link between a cow ailment and a rare but fatal human brain disease.[14] Stories of people dying from eating beef struck fear in the hearts of consumers and caused devastation for beef producers in Britain. A British psychologist said the crisis crystallized "all our fears about what goes into food, about hormones and chemicals and genetically engineered tomatoes and all the other things in the

[12] In 1999 the share of intraregion exports for the EU–15 was 63.4 percent of total exports, and the share of intraregion imports for the EU–15 was 62.6 percent of total imports. World Trade Organization Secretariat, "International Trade Statistics, 2000" (Geneva: WTO, 2000), table II.4; online database at www.wto.org.

[13] Ibid., table I.6.

[14] After years of suspicion that there was a link between bovine spongiform encephalopathy (BSE) and a rare but fatal human brain disease, Creutzfeldt-Jakob, in March 1996 the British government admitted that scientists had demonstrated the link did exist. *Financial Times*, 30 March 1996.

environment that we can't control."[15] This was but the most recent example of a food safety issue transforming debates over agricultural policy. Indeed, food safety issues in Europe about beef go back two decades to when European governments first began to discuss restrictions on the use of growth-promoting hormones in beef production. Facing consumer fears about the health effects on humans from eating hormone-treated meat, and at a time when the Community also had to deal with mountains of excess beef within European markets, it seemed an easy decision to ban the use of growth-promoting hormones in beef production in order to have a common regulatory standard across the Community. However, while mad cow disease remained strictly a food safety issue, the question of hormones raised trade problems because of the ban against the import of beef treated with hormones. This soon developed into one of the most serious trade disputes between the United States and the EC.

Financial incentives motivate farmers to use growth hormones in their livestock production.[16] A cow treated with hormones will reach market weight faster and consume less feed. Up until the 1980s growth hormones were frequently used within Europe, particularly in the United Kingdom and Ireland, and they continue to be used by farmers in the United States, Canada, Australia, New Zealand, and other live-stock-producing nations. As much as 50 percent of British cattle were being given growth hormones, and it was estimated that farmers would lose forty million pounds a year by stopping the use of hormones.[17]

The concern of Europeans about hormone-treated meat began in 1980 with horror stories about the irresponsible use of hormones. In Italy babies exhibited early sexual development after being fed baby food containing veal that had received large doses of the hormone stil-benes. Soon European consumer groups seized upon hormone-treated meat as a public health threat and urged the ban of all hormones. West Germany led the opposition to hormone use, and its government along with the Belgian and Italian governments banned hormone use with national legislation while the EC discussed whether to implement a Community-wide ban.[18] In 1981 the Commission proposed a directive to ban hormones. After much debate in the Council of Ministers, it was

[15] *New York Times*, 31 March 1996.
[16] The trade dispute dealt with six hormones. Three of the hormones are naturally occurring (oestradiol-17, progesterone, and testosterone), and three are synthetic hormones that mimic the function of natural hormones (trenbolone, zeranol, and melengestrol acetate).
[17] *The Guardian*, 15 November 1985.
[18] *Financial Times*, 31 October 1985.

decided to ban the hormone stilbenes that had been the source of problems, but to postpone action on a prohibition of all hormones pending results from a scientific study appointed by the Commission.[19]

Then, in October 1985, the European Parliament took the initiative when it passed a resolution for a ban on all hormones. While the European Parliament has no authority over trade policy, the hormone policy related to consumer health and regulation of the Common Market where the Parliament has a larger voice in the institutional process.[20] The strong endorsement of a complete ban by the Parliament led the Commission to withdraw a proposal to allow use of natural hormones and instead put before the Council a proposal to ban all hormones.[21] In December 1985 the Agriculture Council adopted the directive to ban the use of hormones within EC livestock farming and the import of meat produced with such hormones. The UK agriculture minister voted against the proposal, and the representatives of Ireland and Denmark voiced their objections.[22]

Agriculture Commissioner Frans Andriessen said the major factor in support of the ban was the democratic verdict reflected by the European Parliament vote, and he stated publicly that it would not matter whether scientific studies found evidence of harm from the hormones.[23] He also advocated the ban as a way to help curb the growing beef surplus problem. In view of the 800,000 ton "beef mountain" filling EC intervention stocks in 1985, it was easy to advocate a regulation that would in effect limit domestic production and imports. CAP price supports guaranteed that the European Community would buy at intervention prices all meat that could not be sold for a better price in the depressed market. This left the EC budget to pay cold storage costs and export subsidies — the beef sector in 1986 received 16 percent of all EC expenditure for agriculture and over half of expenditure for intervention purchasing.[24]

[19] *Financial Times*, 9 June 1984.

[20] The Council directive subsequently passed by the Council (no. 85/649, 31 December 1985, OJ L 382/228, 31 December 1985) was based on article 43, which gave the Parliament a formal consultative role. In 1985 this remained a nominal policy role since the Council could ignore the input from the Parliament, but later, as EU institutions developed, the ban was based on article 95 regarding approximation of laws, and the Parliament gained a veto role over the policy under co-decision procedures (Baroncini 1998, 219).

[21] *Financial Times*, 18 October 1985; 26 November 1985.

[22] *The Times*, 21 December 1985.

[23] *Financial Times*, 26 November 1985.

[24] European Commission Directorate General for Agriculture, "Situation and Outlook: Beef," CAP 2000 Working Document, Brussels, April 1997.

TABLE 9.1
World Beef Market, 1995

	Production (million tons)	Consumption (million tons)	Exports (million tons)	Imports (million tons)	Prices (ecu/ton)
EU	8.0	7.5	1.2	0.4	2,944
United States	11.6	11.7	0.9	1.6	1,775
Argentina	2.5	1.9	0.6	—	1,100
Australia	1.7	0.6	1.1	—	1,145

Source: European Commission (1997), "Situation and Outlook: Beef," pp. 9, 28.
Note: Figures for 1995 quantity of beef production, consumption, exports, and imports for the major traders of beef.

Farmers supported the ban as long as it would level the playing field so that neither farmers within Europe nor those overseas could gain a competitive advantage by means of growth-promoting hormones. The Commission assured them that imports would also be banned. Prohibiting European farmers from using the cost-saving hormones only further reduced the competitiveness of this sector, which became one more factor contributing to the international price differential shown in table 9.1. Nevertheless, surplus production continued, and with the generous use of export subsidies, Europe became the largest beef exporter despite prices well above its competitors.[25] With such policies protecting both domestic and foreign market shares, farmers had little need to worry about a loss in competitiveness. Even British farmers, who were the most reliant on use of hormones in their livestock production, did not oppose the ban. Britain's National Farmers' Union said it could not take a position because many members believed the ban would help improve farmers' image with the public.[26]

While consumer concerns were cited as the motive for national regulations, the justification in the directive emphasized the need to harmonize policies in order to uphold equal trade conditions within the Common Market.[27] Although different national regulations to protect public health are allowed within the Common Market, differential regulation of hormones would distort trade because some countries could use hormones to produce more beef at less cost while other countries could use

[25] In 1995 beef received 12 percent of all agriculture expenditures, and 43 percent of expenditures for export subsidies were allocated to beef (ibid.)

[26] *Financial Times*, 26 November 1985.

[27] Council directive (EEC) no. 85/649, on prohibiting the use in livestock farming of certain substances having a hormonal action, OJ L 382/228, 31 December 1985.

the health standard as a trade barrier to isolate their national market. Creating a single hormone policy for the Common Market was indirectly part of the Single European Act plan to integrate the product standards of member states, including harmonization of sanitary and phytosanitary standards (Vogt 1989, 5). Five years after the directive was first issued in 1985, the European Court of Justice upheld the hormone ban against a legal challenge and stated that the policy was necessary to prevent different rules in member states from forming barriers that distort trade.[28]

European officials have known they lacked the scientific evidence to support the policy and have emphasized the democratic pressure for it. The Commission-appointed scientific study finally completed its research after the ban had already been approved. Its conclusion that hormone implants did not pose a health danger was dismissed, and Andriessen said, "Scientific advice is important, but it is not decisive. In public opinion, this is a very delicate issue that has to be dealt with in political terms."[29] The Danish agriculture minister, who had reluctantly voted for the ban in 1985, later came out to criticize it, saying that "There are no scientific arguments against hormones. It is difficult to argue in favour of a ban."[30] However, consumer groups have strongly upheld the necessity of the ban on the grounds that science cannot provide complete certainty that the substances are safe.

A Failed Attempt to Seek GATT Mediation

The United States issued early warnings that any restriction in the absence of scientific evidence would violate GATT rules. It was widely viewed that the United States would retaliate against the ban if it were implemented.[31] U.S. officials viewed the policy as a test case for new EC product standards under the plan for creation of the European Union in 1992 (Hudec 1993, 545). Moreover, it was essential for the United States to defend the safety of American meat. A spokesman for the Farm Bureau Federation warned that the hormone issue "could become a snowball in other markets," both abroad and at home.[32] Eliminating the use of hormones in the U.S. livestock industry would cost the beef and sheep retail industry two to four billion dollars according to a

[28] *Financial Times*, 14 November 1990.
[29] *New York Times*, 1 January 1989.
[30] *The Times*, 30 December 1988.
[31] *Financial Times*, 31 October 1985; 1 November 1985.
[32] *New York Times*, 1 January 1989.

USDA study (Vogt 1989, 3). The United States contended that the meat was safe and therefore the ban an unnecessary trade barrier illegal under GATT.[33] The EC officials defended the ban as a nondiscriminatory policy that applied equally to EC and foreign producers. They rejected the U.S. position that the scientific standard should apply and that the measure fell under GATT regulations (Roberts 1998, 6).

Where a dispute panel could have resolved these questions, in a bizarre legal battle that made a farce of GATT dispute settlement, the two sides blocked establishment of a panel and the legal interpretation remained uncertain. In 1987 the United States called for establishment of a technical experts group (under article 14.9 of the Standards Code of the GATT Tokyo Round Agreements) to evaluate whether there was any scientific justification for the hormone ban. However, the EC objected to establishment of the technical panel on the grounds that accepting the applicability of the Standards Code and experts panel would prejudge the relevance of scientific evidence (Hudec 1993, 545). The EC reluctance to consider scientific evidence reflected the fact that in 1987 evidence from studies supported by international organizations favored the U.S. position.[34] The United States in turn refused to accept the EC suggestion for a legal panel and broke off the dispute settlement procedures. Both sides were locked into positions on the desired composition and evaluation standard of the panel. The GATT 1947 rules gave both sides the right to block dispute proceedings, and consequently no panel was established.

Faced with deadlock of the dispute proceedings in GATT, the United States moved forward on unilateral sanctions. In November 1987 the United States proposed imposition of 100 percent duties on a list of mostly agricultural items that amounted to a value of approximately $100 million dollars, which the USTR estimated as the comparable value of exports that the United States would lose as a consequence of

[33] The GATT 1947 agreement in article 20 states that a policy may be given a general exception from GATT rules if the measure is "necessary to protect human, animal or plant life or health" and subject to the requirement that "such measures are not applied in a manner which would constitute a means of arbitrary or unjustifiable discrimination between countries where the same conditions prevail, or a disguised restriction on international trade." The United States argued that lack of scientific evidence meant this was not a *necessary* ban, but the EC officials disputed this.

[34] In June 1987 the Joint Expert Committee on Food Additives of the World Health Organization and the Food and Agriculture Organization had established standards for acceptable levels for synthetic hormones and declared natural hormones not to need any regulation as they posed no hazard. In December 1987 the Committee on Veterinary Drugs of the Codex Alimentarius Commission confirmed this decision.

the EC hormone directive.[35] The U.S. secretary of agriculture hinted that the United States could block the import of all EC meat in the amount of $450 million.[36] However, in spite of the rising threats, the hormone directive went into effect on 1 January 1989. U.S. retaliatory tariffs against European exports immediately followed.

Escalation continued as the Commission drew up its own list of counterretaliatory measures. A USTR spokesman warned that "if the European Community goes forward with counterretaliation, the United States will have to consider a further response."[37] At this point media headlines frequently referred to the dispute as a trade war. In the end, European foreign ministers stepped back from an all-out trade war. In the General Affairs Council meeting in January 1989, they rejected the Commission proposal for immediate counterretaliation. The Council agreed to postpone sanctions subject to progress in negotiations with the United States.

Although it was the EC that stood accused of having an unfair trade barrier, the weight of normative pressure from GATT condemned the United States rather than the EC. At a February 1989 GATT Council meeting, the EC was joined by most other member nations to condemn the U.S. unilateral sanctions.[38] In the view of most GATT members, use of section 301 provisions of U.S. trade law as the basis for sanctions threatened the principles of the multilateral trade system. At the meeting, GATT Director-General Arthur Dunkel said that discriminatory tariffs went against the General Agreement.[39] Because the United States had resorted to unilateral sanctions without the basis of a panel ruling, this opened the door for EC claims that the United States, rather than the EC, was acting to undermine the GATT system with illegal sanctions.

At this point, leaders on both sides were trying to defuse tensions. European Commission President Jacques Delors urged negotiators to find a solution, and President Bush in an address to Congress said industrial countries must "rise above fighting about beef hormones to

[35] Office of the United States Trade Representative, "Unfair Trade Practices; European Community Hormones Directive," The Federal Register 52 [FR 45304], 25 November 1987.

[36] This threat involved use of a "reciprocal mean inspection." The 1988 U.S. trade law allowed for a ban from countries that forbid the import of U.S. meat without scientific support of a health concern. Recent news of illegal hormones used in European meat production could be used to justify the reciprocal ban accusing European meat of not being safe (Financial Times, 3 November 1988).

[37] New York Times, 6 January 1989.

[38] Financial Times, 9 February 1989.

[39] Ibid.

build a better future, to move from protectionism to progress."[40] Eventually, an accommodation was reached when both sides agreed upon measures that would allow U.S. producers to ship hormone-treated beef as pet food and to certify certain shipments of meat as hormone-free for use in human consumption. The United States said that while it would continue its sanctions on $100 million value of trade, it would not escalate with its own ban against all EC meat imports into the United States.[41] The EC laid to rest discussion of any EC sanctions. The trade conflict had reached a cease-fire that would persist for the next six years while ongoing talks in the Uruguay Round became the focus of concerns regarding agriculture. The Uruguay Round results would set new institutional parameters to shape the next phase of the dispute.

Creating New Rules: The Sanitary and Phytosanitary Agreement

The Uruguay Round agreement included ambitious new regulations for policies motivated to protect human, plant, or animal health. The Agreement on the Application of Sanitary and Phytosanitary (SPS) Measures encourages harmonization of SPS policies on the basis of international standards. However, the SPS agreement recognizes the right of nations to set a higher standard for protection of health and environment than would be achieved by the international standard as long as they follow three criteria: the measures should be based on scientific assessment of risks, their application should be nondiscriminatory between domestic and foreign producers, and interference with trade should be kept to the minimum level necessary to maintain the given health and environmental standard.

Negotiations for the SPS agreement proceeded smoothly without any of the deadlock seen in the other parts of the agriculture negotiation group of the Uruguay Round. This was the "one aspect of agricultural liberalization on which most countries saw eye to eye: the need to keep to a minimum the effects on trade of government actions taken to ensure the safety of food and the protection of animal and plant health" (Croome 1995, 117). Even though the new rules would influence highly politicized cases, the SPS negotiation remained low-profile — it was seen as a "sleeper issue," where "only the pros understood its importance and closely followed the negotiation."[42] Whereas EC negotiators had blocked application of the Standards code and a technical panel in the

---

[40] *New York Times*, 19 February 1989.

[41] *Los Angeles Times*, 19 February 1989.

[42] Former Senate Agriculture Committee staff member. Interview by author. Washington, DC, 3 April 2000.

U.S. complaint to GATT in 1987, they did not interfere with the effort to set new SPS standards that would clearly establish scientific criteria as a condition for health and environmental regulations. The EC proposal to the SPS negotiation group insisted upon the right of countries to have standards higher than international standards, but the EC accepted the requirement that scientific evidence must support such standards (Croome 1995, 237). According to a U.S. negotiator of the SPS agreement, the EC was not a major player in these negotiations: "The Europeans were never able to articulate a coherent position."[43]

The European Parliament did not exhibit strong interest in the negotiation. When it passed a resolution on the progress in the Uruguay Round in September 1990, of the ninety-six items providing detailed commentary on the agriculture negotiations, only one touched upon an SPS related topic — a statement urging that biotechnology rules should be determined by the FAO rather than the GATT.[44] Similarly, the Parliament's resolution in March 1994 on the outcome of the Uruguay Round made no specific mention of the SPS agreement even while it devoted six paragraphs of commentary to the Agriculture Agreement.[45] The lack of intervention by the Parliament into the SPS negotiations reflected the relatively small role of the Parliament in the entire Uruguay Round negotiation. The negotiations on agriculture, including the SPS negotiation, were considered to fall within the scope of article 113 of the EC treaty, which provides for decision making without parliamentary involvement.[46] Parliamentarians did not have the authority to influence the negotiation mandate or the conduct of negotiations, and they could not veto any individual part of the Uruguay Round agreement.

Whereas the hormone directive had occupied the full attention of the Council and Parliament as a single issue, the negotiations for the SPS agreement had little political intervention. Framed as a trade issue within the Uruguay Round, the SPS agreement fell outside of the jurisdiction of the European Parliament and was overshadowed by the Agriculture Agreement. Despite the relative ease with which the EU agreed

---

[43] Former USDA official. Interview by author. Washington, DC, 5 April 2000.

[44] Extracts from the European Parliament Resolution of September 1990 (session document A3-215/90, OJ C284, 11 November 1990), cited in Angelidis (1993, 88).

[45] Text of European Parliament Resolution of 17 March 1994 on the outcome of the Uruguay Round of GATT multilateral trade negotiations (Resolution on GATT multilateral trade negotiations, A3-0149/94), in Angelidis (1994, 64–70).

[46] Shortly before the signing of the Uruguay Round agreements, on 15 November 1994 the Court issued an opinion (Op. 1/94) that all of the multilateral agreement on trade in goods, including the Agreement on Agriculture and the SPS agreement, were to be concluded on the basis of article 113 (Bossche 1997, 37).

to the new SPS rules, it was later unwilling to accept the implications of this agreement for the beef hormone dispute.

Refusal to Follow a WTO Ruling

In light of the new international rules as well as internal implementation problems, the EU undertook a review of its hormone regulation in 1995. According to the SPS agreement, scientific evidence of risk should form the criteria for evaluating the hormone ban and international standards could provide one benchmark for the current scientific consensus. In 1995, the Codex Alimentarius Commission, the body that sets international food standards, established minimum residue levels for the safe use of synthetic hormones and declared no regulation necessary for the natural hormones because they did not pose any health risk (Roberts 1998, 14). The SPS agreement did not mandate that the EU follow the existing international standards. Nevertheless, these standards raised questions regarding whether the EU policy to ban all six hormones was based on scientific evidence and whether the ban represented the minimal amount of trade distortion necessary to protect human health.

In spite of the new SPS rules, the European Parliament and Agriculture Commissioner again rejected scientific evidence as the criterion for a policy reevaluation in 1995. The European Parliament had raised concerns about poor implementation of the ban and adopted a resolution calling on the Commission and Council to make it clear that the hormone ban would be maintained under the current WTO rules.[47] In November, the EU sponsored a Scientific Conference on Growth Promotion in Meat Production that was intended to guide the upcoming decisions. However, even before the meeting, Agriculture Commissioner Franz Fischler declared that the ban should continue, citing consumer resistance to hormone-treated beef and the beef surplus within Europe.[48] Although the scientists at the conference confirmed that when properly used hormones did not pose a human health threat, the Commission reaffirmed the hormone ban and said it would defend the policy against any U.S. challenges within the WTO.[49] On 18 January 1996 the European Parliament voted unanimously in favor of a resolution that the EU should work "steadfastly to oppose the import of hormone-treated meat in the EU."[50] Four days later the Agriculture Council discussed the

[47] European Commission, Memo/95/153, Brussels, 21 November 1995.
[48] *The Guardian*, 22 November 1995.
[49] *Financial Times*, 13 January 1996.
[50] *Journal of Commerce*, 19 January 1996.

studies from the conference and restated its commitment to uphold the ban.

Fear that consumers would not want to eat hormone-treated beef as well as the desire to avoid competition from cheaper imported beef made farmers continue to support the ban.[51] A spokesperson for the British National Farmers Union said, "We are against additives and want the ban to stay. The consumer's wishes must be respected."[52] The mad cow disease outbreak in 1996 further unified EU resistance to lifting the hormone ban — the United Kingdom no longer had any authority to speak on food safety issues, consumer fears were skyrocketing, and declining consumption produced greater beef surplus stocks.[53]

After the SPS agreement went into effect 1 January 1995, U.S. livestock and meat producers lobbied the U.S. government to challenge the ban, and trade analysts argued it was a clear violation of the SPS agreement (Hanrahan 1999). In January 1996 the United States filed a complaint to initiate dispute settlement proceedings on the beef hormone dispute with the European Union. The United States was not alone in its objections to the EU policy — Australia, New Zealand, Chile, and Argentina asked to join the United States, while Canada filed its own complaint on the same policy. Under the new WTO dispute settlement procedures, each step in the process went forward according to a series of deadlines, and the EU could not block the panel or ruling.[54] The WTO panel was established 20 May 1996. After hearing legal arguments from both sides and evidence from five scientists, the three panelists issued their report on 18 August 1997.[55] The ruling, which was upheld by an Appellate Body report, found that the ban was inconsistent with the SPS agreement because the EU had not performed any kind of risk assessment showing scientific justification for the ban.[56] The Appellate Body

---

[51] *The Independent*, 19 March 1996; Hanrahan (1999, 2).

[52] *The Guardian*, 22 November 1995.

[53] Within a week of the March 1996 announcement by the British government concerning mad cow disease, consumption of beef across Europe dropped by 30 percent, and the EU voted a ban on British beef to halt the panic (*Financial Times*, 30 March 1996). As demand fell, intervention purchasing increased and the EU stock of beef rose from 6,000 metric tons in 1995 to 230,000 metric tons in just the first six months of 1996 (Klein and Tai 1996, 5).

[54] For a comparison of the GATT and WTO dispute settlement procedures, see Jackson (1998).

[55] WTO, Report of the Panel on "EC Measures Concerning Meat and Meat Products (Hormones)," WT/DS26/R/USA, 18 August 1997.

[56] Ibid.; "EC Measures Concerning Meat and Meat Products (Hormones) Report of the Appellate Body," WT/DS26/AB/R), 16 January 1998. The Appellate Body report cited articles 5.1 and 2.2 of the SPS agreement in its finding that the EU measures were at

ruling recognized the EU right to have a higher standard than existing international standards, but only if that decision was based on risk assessment. Since there had not been such an evaluation, the panel recommended that the EU change its ban to bring it into conformity with its obligations under the SPS agreement. This ruling was adopted by the Dispute Settlement Body of the WTO on 13 February 1998, and the EU announced that it "intended to fulfill its obligations under the WTO."[57]

Having accepted the ruling, the EU faced the question of how it would comply. The Commission used the WTO decision to frame an option paper to the Council and Parliament, which it premised on the assumption that any policy must ensure consumer health and respect obligations under the WTO.[58] The Commission paper presented the following three options: enter negotiations for compensation through increased access to EU agricultural markets for the United States while continuing to ban hormone-treated beef; change the ban to a provisional measure pending further risk analysis and accept that the United States would impose sanctions while the EU remained in noncompliance, or end the ban and use a labeling scheme to allow consumers to choose whether to buy hormone-treated meat. On the question of whether to end the ban, the Commission gave the following discussion of the pros and cons:

> Option (3) [ending the ban] has the advantage that it would bring the Community as quickly as possible into a position where, in the eyes of all relevant parties, it was in conformity with its obligations. This would avoid the need to provide compensation or suffer loss of concessions and it would enhance the Community's own ability to insist on the strict application of WTO agreements by other countries. But this option has the disadvantage (depending on the preliminary results of the scientific studies which are now in progress) that it might involve allowing on to the market a product which, hitherto we have considered to pose a potential risk.[59]

The violation ruling raised concerns about the ramifications for future trade policy negotiations from refusal to cooperate in the beef hormone case. A Commission official commented on the utility of the ruling to clarify the potential consequences of policy choices: "When we

---

present inconsistent with the SPS agreement, but it allowed that future scientific evidence could justify regulating hormone-treated imports. See Stewart (1998).

[57] Commission of the European Communities, "Communication from the Commission to the Council and the European Parliament: WTO Decisions Regarding the EC Hormones Ban," COM (1999) 81 final, 10 February 1999.

[58] Ibid.

[59] Ibid.

go to the Council or Parliament, the ruling shows them more clearly what are the options and helps them to decide. We can present it as a choice to implement or not, with knowledge that if not [implementing], we then risk retaliation, lose the credibility of the organization, and run the risk that next time Japan stops pork imports, it will use similar arguments."[60] Although reputation and obligation to the rules appear as factors in the internal decision process, they did not persuade the EU to change the policy. Refusing to end the ban, EU negotiators tried to negotiate compensation on other issues. They were unable, however, to persuade either the United States or Canada to accept a compensation package with the indefinite continuation of the ban.[61] When the May 13 deadline expired, WTO arbitrators authorized the United States to implement sanctions against goods up to the value of $116.8 million.[62]

U.S. officials were quick to emphasize the dual economic and normative stakes. USTR Charlene Barshefsky commented after the final WTO ruling and authorization of sanctions that "the EU must pay a price for failing to comply with its WTO obligations. . . . I would urge the EU to reconsider its damaging actions and to demonstrate a real commitment to the rules-based multilateral system."[63] An official of the USTR delegation to the WTO in Geneva said "Our best argument is to tell the EU they weaken the organization when they don't follow the rulings. . . . The [WTO] membership more broadly will pressure — we raise the issue in every [WTO] meeting."[64] Considering that countries are eager to avoid being "branded as a rule breaker" (Jackson 1998, 175), these tactics by the United States raised the costs to the EU for its hormone ban.

None of the major EU policy actors rejected the principle that the EU should comply with WTO rules. Even when informing the WTO that the EU could not lift the ban by the deadline, the Commission spokesperson said, "We want to comply with our WTO obligations. We believe the best way forward on this is a dialogue with the Americans about compensation."[65] The European Parliament passed a resolution

[60] Official of Directorate General for External Economic Relations. Interview by author. Brussels, 26 July 1999.

[61] *Financial Times*, 27 May 1999.

[62] In their submissions to the WTO arbitration panel, the EU estimated that the ban only cost U.S. beef exporters $53 million, while the United States estimated its producers lost $202 million a year (WTO, "Recourse to Arbitration by the European Communities under Article 22.6 of the DSU: Decision by the Arbitrators," WT/DS26/ARB, 12 July 1999.)

[63] USTR Press release no. 99–58, 12 July 1999.

[64] Interview by author. Geneva, 16 July 1999.

[65] *Journal of Commerce*, 14 May 1999.

on 4 May 1999 that called for the Commission to maintain the ban on
hormone-treated meat but also said that any acceptable solution must
both provide the "highest possible level of food security for European
consumers" and represent "fulfillment by the EU of its international
obligations under the WTO."[66] An EU official commented that not even
the most radical minister would say in Council discussions that the EU
should not follow WTO rules.[67] Yet while officials expressed a general
belief that the EU policies should conform with WTO rules, in this case
even a violation ruling did not persuade them to change the policy
measure.

Consumer groups were the most hostile to the WTO and continued
to lobby for keeping the ban. Although consumers favor liberalization
in general, food safety has been given higher priority in the beef hormone case. The WTO ruling had little impact on consumer groups' position toward the issue. Following the panel ruling, the consumer organization BEUC issued a press release on the outcome that challenged
both the narrow interpretation of the SPS obligations and the evaluation of scientific evidence.[68] In a 1999 policy memo to the incoming
president of the Council of Ministers, "Consumer Priorities for the
Finnish Presidency," BEUC appealed, "We hope that the Finnish Presidency will apply all its political weight to the maintenance of the EU
ban on hormones, and to resist WTO pressures."

U.S. officials drew up the sanctions list in order to mobilize lobbying
against the WTO-illegal policy. The target list imposed 24 percent of the
sanction value on the industries of Germany and France, such as French
Roquefort cheese and German fruit juices, and exempted the UK from
any sanctions because its government already opposed the ban.[69] In an
effort to increase the leverage of sanctions for both the beef hormones
and banana disputes, Congress authorized "carousel retaliation"
whereby the target list would rotate to spread the pain of sanctions
across more industries while not exceeding the fixed amount of trade
value.[70] Although it was not utilized at first, this new measure threatened the prospect of more damaging sanctions in the future.

[66] European Parliament, "Resolution on the Transatlantic Economic Partnership and
EU/United States — Trade Disputes, Especially Hormones, Bananas, and Hushkits," Brussels, 4 May 1999; www.europa.eu.int/comm/trade/miti/dispute/hormones/0605hormb.htm.

[67] Official of Secretariat to the Council of Ministers. Interview by author. Brussels, 7
July 2000.

[68] BEUC, "BEUC Comments on the Report of the (WTO) Panel on EC Measures Concerning Meat and Meat Products (Hormones)," number 320/97, 24 September 1997.

[69] Former USTR official. Interview by author. Washington, DC, 3 April 2000; Agra-
Europe, no. 1859, 23 July 1999.

[70] The measure calls for modification of the product lists and is mandated by section

Contrary to U.S. expectations, neither big business nor the victims of trade sanctions lobbied against the ban. For the business association UNICE, there was not enough at stake to mobilize for a change in the ban. The total value of the sanctions authorized by the WTO was a small package of $116.8 million worth of EU exports to the United States. In the original list of potential target items submitted by the United States as part of the WTO arbitration process, only 13 percent of the trade value came from nonagricultural products such as yarn and motorcycles.[71] The rest of the potential targets were agricultural products ranging from beef and pork to chocolates and juices. UNICE expressed dismay at the increased tension in trade relations, and in private officials said they generally felt that unless scientific evidence showed a clear risk, labeling should be preferred over a ban.[72] However, UNICE did not publicly advocate any position on the issue of the ban. This pattern contrasts with industry behavior during the Uruguay Round, when UNICE and other business groups explicitly advocated agricultural liberalization for the sake of the comprehensive agreement.

The targeted industries lobbied the commission and national governments, but they fought against the linkage of their interest with the hormone ban rather than oppose the policy itself. An EU official at the delegation to the WTO in Geneva said that groups did not pressure for a change in the policy because "none question that the EU is entitled to have the ban on hormone beef."[73] An official of the Directorate General for External Economic Relations in Brussels said that victims of retaliation came to his office and sent letters expressing anger that they had to suffer losses, but "so far there has not been any requests to liberalize agriculture as such. Mostly they resist the connection between their product and agriculture."[74] In this case, the issue linkage became so narrow that it tied Austrian auto-bikes with beef hormone policy. Therefore it was easier for industry groups to protest that there should be no relationship between the issues than to lobby against a policy backed by the consensus of European institutions. Consequently, there

---

407 of the Trade and Development Act of 2000, which went into effect 18 May 2000 (USTR, "USTR Announces Procedures for Modifying Measures in EC Beef and Bananas Cases," Press release 00-41, 26 May 2000).

[71] Author's calculation. WTO, "Recourse to Arbitration by the European Communities," WT/DS26/ARB, 12 July 1999.

[72] UNICE official. Interview by author. Brussels, 6 July 2000; "UNICE Dismay at Escalation in Hormone Beef Dispute." UNICE press release, 11 May 1999.

[73] Official of EU delegation to Geneva. Interview by author. Geneva, 15 July 1999.

[74] Interview by author. Brussels, 6 July 1999.

was a notable absence of strong cross-sectoral pressures within the EU pushing for a change in the beef hormone ban.

The case is currently listed in "implementation stage," but each side views this status differently.[75] For the United States, the EU is in violation, and ongoing U.S. sanctions provide temporary compensation until the EU ends the ban. On the other hand, the EU continues to examine scientific evidence in the hope that results will show a health risk that would justify the ban according to the requirements of the SPS agreement.

The European Parliament as an Obstacle to Reform

Shifting policy jurisdiction beyond the control of agriculture ministers can promote liberalization if it leads to including trade and foreign ministers in decision making and the mobilization of export industries. However, the new actors in this case — the Parliament, the Directorate-General for Health and Consumer Protection, and consumer groups — had no direct stake in trade rules. None was routinely involved in other trade negotiations, which meant they had less experience and concern about the effect of this case on future trade negotiations. Indeed, for these actors, their own involvement in the policy process was only justified insofar as the issue was defined in terms of health rather than agricultural or trade interests.

Involvement by the European Parliament constrained EU decision making and made this negotiation especially difficult. An official of the Directorate for External Relations of the Commission commented: "This is the first time when the European Parliament flexed its muscles and opposed the Commission saying that this was a consumer concern and making the Commission toe the line they wanted. It is a warhorse for them."[76]

This was a new role for the European Parliament. In the first two decades of European integration, the Parliament was generally "regarded as a somewhat ineffective institution" with a policy role limited to informal influence and consultation (Nugent 1999, 205). Beginning with the Single European Act of 1986, the Parliament gained "conditional agenda setting power" by means of a new cooperation procedure that allowed it to amend and reject Council proposals (Garrett and Tsebelis 1996, 285). However, decision authority remained the exclu-

[75] See the Directorate General for Trade website at http://europa.eu.int.

[76] Official of Directorate General for External Economic Relations. Interview by author. Brussels, 26 July 1999.

sive domain of the Council, which could override a parliamentary decision. Beginning in November 1993 under the Treaty of European Union, co-decision rules empowered Parliament with shared legislative authority to amend and block proposals in certain policy areas: public health, educational and cultural measures, environmental programs, consumer protection, and some internal market legislation (Earnshaw and Judge 1996, 109).

The Parliament remains largely a passive observer of most agricultural trade negotiations, since both agricultural policy and trade policy are outside of the domain for co-decision. Indeed, for agricultural policy the Parliament only offers an opinion in a consultation procedure and lacks the authority derived from the stronger cooperation procedure (Nugent 1999, 209). The Parliament's position is weakest for trade policy given that the Council is not even obligated to consult with Parliament in this area. For negotiations on trade in goods, treaty provisions do not give the Parliament any role in authorization of the mandate or monitoring of progress in negotiations, although informal consultation arrangements include the Parliament (Bossche 1997, 70).

The Parliament could assert itself on the hormones case because this was a public health issue. Even before the strengthening of European Parliament's institutional role in 1993, member states had been more favorable to consider input from the European Parliament on social policy issues (Sherrington 2000, 22). Under the Treaty of European Union, so long as the policy was defined as a health issue, any change in the policy would be subject to co-decision. During the WTO proceedings this became a central point in the determination of the "reasonable period" for implementation. The United States and Canada argued that the policy was an agricultural measure where only consultation was necessary, and the EU argued that as a health measure it related to approximation of laws and any change would require more time for the lengthy co-decision procedure (Baroncini 1998, 219). The WTO accepted the EU argument that implementation of its ruling could require the co-decision procedure and granted a longer time period to reflect this.[77] Parliament must explicitly emphasize framing the case outside of the trade context in order to justify its own involvement — if the ban is treated as a trade or agriculture issue, then the Parliament does not have co-decision rights.

Strong advocacy by the Parliament endowed the ban with democratic legitimacy. Even before Parliament had gained the formal institutional

[77] Commission of the European Communities, "Communication from the Commission to the Council and the European Parliament," COM(1999) 81 final, 10 February 1999.

powers of co-decision in 1985, Frans Andriessen, the commissioner for agriculture, advocated adopting the ban because of Parliament's vote in favor of the comprehensive ban.[78] When questioned about why the EU did not change the ban following the WTO ruling, an official from the Agriculture Directorate said, "The Commission cannot put forward a proposal to end the ban because we know we could not get support of either Council or Parliament. How to persuade an entire people?"[79] This unanimity was also emphasized by a staff member of a senior European Parliament member, who said the ban would continue because "there is no conflict between the Council and Parliament on this—we all agree we don't want the meat."[80]

The case is a precedent for other regulatory battles to come. The definition of the issue in terms of food safety opened the door for the European Parliament to influence this negotiation. Future trade negotiations are likely to address other issues within the jurisdiction of parliamentary oversight, such as health, labor, and environmental standards. In particular, the difficulties encountered on the beef hormone dispute foreshadow the upcoming negotiations about biotechnology that will have even larger economic stakes. In a broad trade round, the parliamentary oversight will be limited, whereas in a legalized dispute on the single issue, the Parliament may have a veto role. The evidence from this case provides a warning that WTO adjudication is likely to be ineffective against EU trade barriers, especially for nontrade topics with greater politicization.

Conclusion

Achieving agricultural liberalization of any kind in Europe is challenging. Doing so without an understanding of the internal processes is impossible. Agricultural protection in Europe has reached high levels for economic and political reasons, and EU institutions and norms have helped to maintain those policies. Once established, the CAP became one of the most entrenched policies within EU institutions. The autonomy of agricultural representatives to make key decisions about agricultural policy even during trade negotiations often prevents reform. The interlocking policies of CAP make it difficult for other actors to

[78] *Financial Times*, 26 November 1985.

[79] Official of the European Commission Directorate General for Agriculture. Interview by author. Brussels, 4 July 2000.

[80] Staff member of European Parliament Representative. Interview by author. Brussels, 10 July 2000.

interfere and increase the ramifications of even small changes. More-over, the role of CAP as a central pillar of European integration out-weighs other appeals to trade interests and international obligation.

The analysis of the agriculture negotiations of the Uruguay Round in chapter 8 demonstrated that while difficult, agricultural liberalization in Europe is not impossible. Liberalization occurred when the interna-tional institution helped to broaden the policy agenda within the EU. Issue linkage countered the autonomy of agricultural interests that in so many other cases prevented CAP reform. By giving something to every-one, it made it easier to find an agreement that all would accept and to avoid the problem of multiple veto players in the fragmented internal EU institutions.

In this chapter, the case analysis of the beef hormone dispute corrobo-rated the statistical finding from chapter 3 that while the EU does not entirely disregard the trade rules, they are not a decisive factor deter-mining trade policy. The first beef hormone negotiation highlighted the weakness of the old GATT legal system. With the legality of the policy undetermined, the Community did not face normative criticism for un-dermining the trade rules. Policy discussion within the EC remained focused on the tradeoff between keeping the ban and increasing trade tensions with the United States. The Commission rejected the scientific standard and called off further studies. However, the second negotiation in the WTO dispute settlement proceedings brought the highest level of legal framing with a violation ruling against the ban. As expected, legal framing shaped which options were considered by European policy-makers. Reputation and the interest to support the rules system emerged as a factor in policy discussion. This time, the Commission accepted the scientific standard and funded additional scientific studies while saying it would comply with the rules after the full risk assessment had been completed. The negotiation context shaped incentives, but nevertheless, it failed to bring liberalization of the ban.

The legalistic approach to negotiations relies on narrowing the focus to apply pressure on one policy, but this is ineffective against EU institu-tions. When possible, the EU settles cases early. However, when political opposition is strong, this is not an option. Since the legal ruling fails to change the domestic political process, these cases are unlikely to end with any substantial liberalization. The hormone case represents an issue where political consensus against lifting the ban prevented any early settlement. The legal adjudication of the dispute did not offer any specific gains that would convince the Agriculture Council, the Euro-pean Parliament, or consumer groups to change the ban. Indeed, the narrow focus of legal framing made it less likely that policymakers would find a compromise through combining issues. Nor did the ruling shift the policy discussion to increase the authority and involvement of trade ministers. A key obstacle to reform lay in the involvement of the European Parliament and dominance of the Agriculture Council for most decisions. In this case, the actors with the least involvement in trade policy played the lead role in the negotiation.

In both phases of the negotiation, sanctions were ineffective. The narrow focus also reduced the economic pressure — the potential economic loss was not as large and far-reaching as when a broad economic package in a round was at stake. Meanwhile, the targeted industries lacked both the influence and motivation to directly oppose the agricultural policy.

In this case, budget concerns did not clearly favor liberalization and were not a decisive factor in policy decisions. On the one hand, there were financial incentives behind the beef hormone ban given the oversupply problem draining CAP revenues. To the extent that banning hormones for domestic farmers and keeping out cheaper imports reduced the surplus problem, it helped reduce those expenditures. On the other hand, denying European farmers the use of growth-promoting hormones also increased the price differential with world markets, and this increased expenditures for export subsidies. The comments of officials when the ban was established indicated that officials considered the surplus and budget constraints as an additional reason to support the ban, but that this was secondary to the consumer health and democratic pressures.

Changing the ban would have had serious implications for the European integration project. To defy the Parliament by weakening the ban would have provoked an institutional crisis. Without the Community-wide ban, different national regulations would have remained in place, which could impede the free movement of goods in the Common Market. This gave rise to a conflict between the interests of European integration and the interests of upholding the WTO.

The comparison of the SPS negotiations in the Uruguay Round and the beef hormone dispute illustrates that accepting general rules within a broad framework can be easier than accepting the overturn of a specific policy. When faced with the decision on beef hormone imports in 1985, the EC dismissed the scientific standard. However, in the broader context of the Uruguay Round, it negotiated a new agreement to strengthen the rules mandating that sanitary and phytosanitary regulations must be based on risk assessment. The EC did not attempt to block these negotiations even though the scientific standard that emerged would place it on the defensive later in the hormone beef dispute. Having the SPS negotiation subsumed in the package of the Uruguay Round promoted consideration of policy gains from the broader agreement and reduced political intervention.

This chapter has shown that not only the interests at stake but also the process and norms of the negotiation account for why Europe has been so uncooperative in legal adjudication of agricultural trade disputes. A general conclusion is that the EU policy-making process is more conducive to liberalizing a wide range of issues than a narrow and politically sensitive policy. An insight derived from the specific case leads one to anticipate difficulties for negotiations that provide increased influence to the Parliament and societal groups which are less responsive to pressure from trade rules.

International institutions should not be seen as one size fits all — the complementarity between the international and EU-level institutions influences policy outcomes. Herein lies the answer to the puzzle of EU willingness to conduct major overhaul of CAP policies in the Uruguay Round while resisting cooperation in case after case of dispute settlement. The high complementarity between Council decision making for CAP and the package approach of a comprehensive trade round with a strong issue linkage makes liberalization more likely. The conflict between these same decision processes and the legalistic approach of GATT/WTO dispute settlement prevents liberalization.

Part IV

CONCLUSION

10

Comparative Perspectives

THE GENEROUS support for the agricultural sector in Japan and Europe represents the classic story of how protection policies develop. Because that most Japanese and European farmers could not compete on international markets without government support, they sought government protection and organized an effective lobby. Wealthy industrial societies like Japan and Europe have been willing and able to pay the cost of supporting a group that holds a valued societal role and electoral power. The interest groups, bureaucrats, and politicians who represent farmers closely cooperate in the policy process and enjoy considerable autonomy. This domestic political dynamic allowed agricultural protection to reach high levels in Japan and Europe.

Consequently, persuading Japan and the EU to lower their agricultural trade barriers has produced some of the most contentious trade negotiations. Yet even while several negotiations ended in failure and farmers continue to be the beneficiaries of government subsidies, the reduction of some of the most trade-distorting protection measures has brought substantial liberalization. The central puzzle is why similar U.S. demands for agricultural liberalization produced different policy responses across negotiations, despite the strong political preference in Japan and Europe to protect farmers.

Traditional explanations that retaliatory threats and budget constraints forced governments to open agricultural markets insufficiently account for the variation in negotiation outcomes. Some liberalization resulted from negotiations that did not involve specific threats and when the compensation to farmers would raise budget costs. For example, Japan's decision to allow rice imports came after the U.S. government decided against taking any unilateral measures and was accompanied by a fifty billion dollar rural aid package. In other cases, repeated threats yielded no change in policy, such as in the beef hormone trade dispute with the EU. In fact, the EU has been the most resistant to changing export subsidy policies that are an expensive budget cost and the focus of the greatest U.S. pressure. Both Japan and the EU have demonstrated their willingness to risk both heightened trade tension with the United States and rising budget costs in order to defend their agricultural sectors.

The conclusion of this book is that rules persuade more than power. Liberalization took place when the agenda, rules, and procedures of international negotiations changed the aggregation of domestic interests to favor agricultural liberalization. Features of the negotiation structure added more leverage to U.S. demands for liberalization than did threats of retaliation. Even in the sensitive area of agricultural trade, international institutions can influence state decisions about domestic policies.

Negotiation structures matter because they determine who participates in the decision process and what they consider when calculating the best policy choice. Two different kinds of institutional arrangements in the negotiation structure promote liberalization by increasing negotiation stakes and empowering proliberalization interests in the domestic policy process. The first, cross-sector issue linkage, unites a broad range of issues in a package deal. This both increases the potential economic gains and expands the policy jurisdiction by creating a tradeoff between exporting more industrial or service goods and importing more agricultural goods. As a result, trade ministers and big business join discussions of agricultural policy, and governments are more likely to offer concessions for agricultural liberalization. Institutionalizing the linkage by means of the agenda, rules, and procedures of the negotiation adds credibility and signals that the refusal to liberalize agricultural policies will threaten the prospects for liberalization of other issues. This provides incentives for business groups and trade officials to apply pressure for compromise on agricultural issues for the sake of the greater gains from the overall negotiation. The need for a final decision on the package as a whole encourages a broader decision-making process that is more likely to favor liberalization.

The second negotiation structure, legal framing, relies on the narrow focus on one issue in order to apply established legal principles to judge whether a country has an obligation to reduce a given trade barrier. This formal process raises both reputation costs and the value of the rules system as additional negotiation stakes and thus gives export industries and trade officials motivation to encourage agricultural liberalization. To the extent that a state benefits from the system of trade rules, leaders will not want to damage the credibility of these rules through open defiance. Finally, a legal ruling legitimizes liberalization as the necessary policy choice in the eyes of both leaders and the public.

Not all countries will respond identically to similar negotiation strategies. Trade interests and perceptions of international obligation lead some countries to value the trade rules more than others. This book provides evidence that Japan is more responsive to international legal pressure than the EU. In addition, some negotiation strategies will be more effective given a particular domestic political context. For example, in the EU, segmentation of the policy process can block liberalization of single issues in adjudication. Yet at the same time, this kind of policy process is very responsive to advancing liberalization via an issue linkage. The interaction between international institutions and domestic structures and the variation across countries is too often neglected by studies that either focus exclusively on one country or pool all countries for aggregate analysis. As a step to fill this gap, this book has engaged in two levels of comparison, first asking how different negotiation structures influence liberalization in Japan and the EU, and second asking how the political context in Japan and the EU influences their responsiveness to a given negotiation structure. This chapter summarizes the findings of the book and extends the comparative analysis.

Findings

Five explanations for the variation in policy liberalization were evaluated comparing U.S. agricultural trade negotiations with Japan and the EU over the period 1970 to 1999. Table 10.1 provides an overview of the key findings. The two central hypotheses about negotiation structure examined issue linkage and legal framing. The other three hypotheses addressed whether liberalization could be explained by U.S. threats of retaliation, domestic political constraints or financial constraints related to budget conditions.

The combination of quantitative and qualitative methodologies draws upon the advantage of each. The statistical findings confirm that the hypotheses about linkage and legalism are generally true across agricultural negotiations, and the case studies verify that actors involved in the negotiation process behaved as expected.

Statistical analysis demonstrated the importance of negotiation structures. Controlling for several variables, negotiations with high institutionalization of the issue linkage were the most likely to bring liberalization in both Japan and the EU. Negotiations with high legal framing in the form of a legal ruling against the policy by a GATT/WTO dispute panel provided substantial leverage for opening agricultural markets of Japan. However, this same negotiation structure was not a significant explanation of EU policy. Only during the early consultation phase with low levels of legal framing did legalistic dispute procedures promote EU

TABLE 10.1
Empirical Results

Hypothesis	Japan
Issue linkage	Strong linkage increases probability of major liberalization by 0.82.
	• In Uruguay Round, *Keidanren* calls for rice liberalization.
	• MITI and MOFA advocate agricultural liberalization.
	• Diet votes on Uruguay Round as a single package.
	• Liberalization justified for larger gains and international obligation.
Legal framing	GATT ruling increases probability of major liberalization by 0.67.
	• 1987 ruling brings intervention by senior politicians.
	• Media increases criticism after ruling.
	• Liberalization justified as international obligation.
Threats	Strong threat increases probability of major liberalization by 0.46.
	• Business groups call for concessions.
	• Backlash as farmer opposition remains strong; risk of boycotts
Domestic politics	10% increase in LDP seats increases probability of major liberalization by 0.39.
	• LDP resists more when politically weak during 1984 quota negotiation.
Budget	Budget growth has no significant effect.
	• Large compensation packages follow liberalization.

	European Union
Issue linkage	Strong linkage increases probability of major liberalization by 0.39.
	• In Uruguay Round, UNICE calls for CAP reform.
	• Trade officials and General Affairs Council take larger role.
	• Germany shifts to favor CAP reform in Uruguay Round.
	• Council and Parliament vote on single package.
Legal framing	GATT ruling has no effect. Consultations increase liberalization by 0.31.
	• Agriculture Council and Parliament uphold beef ban despite ruling.
Threats	Strong threat increases probability of major liberalization by 0.29.
	• Threats bring EU to the table on oilseeds dispute in 1992.
	• But no industries call for lifting hormone ban in 1996.

TABLE 10.1
(*continued*)

Hypothesis	European Union
Domestic politics	French Council Presidency reduces probability of major liberalization by 0.31.
	• France threatens to veto negotiation directives on agriculture.
	• As Council President, France shapes agenda against CAP reform.
Budget	20% growth of EU expenditures decreases probability of major liberalization by 0.19.
	• Budget constraints used to justify need for reform.
	• Reduce market support but increase direct compensation.

Note: See chapter 3 for full statistical results. The figures reported are the average predicted probabilities of major liberalization from tables 3.5 and 3.7.

liberalization. Such differences between the Japanese and European responses suggest that the domestic context influences the impact of any given negotiation structure.

The negotiation case studies examined the causal mechanism in the negotiation process. Changes in the scope of issues and international context influenced the nature of the domestic bargaining process in comparison both during the course of an individual negotiation and across different negotiations. An institutionalized issue linkage increased the mobilization by export industries for agricultural liberalization and expanded the jurisdiction of the decision-making process. In Japan the legalized context of the GATT dispute process added legitimacy to demands for liberalization, which placed agricultural groups on the defensive in the domestic debate and brought intervention by senior political leaders to accept liberalization for the sake of Japan's trade interests and international obligation. Interviews with politicians and officials, government documents, and newspaper accounts at the time of the negotiations provide a close-up view of how the negotiation structure influenced the options that were considered.

Cross-Sector Issue Linkage in Japan and the European Union

A highly institutionalized, cross-sector linkage provides the most leverage for opening sensitive agricultural markets in both Japan and the EU. In aggregate analysis a highly institutionalized issue linkage predicted major liberalization. When controlling for other characteristics of the negotiation and product, a change in the kind of issue linkage led to a change in the predicted outcome of the negotiation.

The Uruguay Round illustrated the process by which an institutionalized cross-sector linkage influences policy decisions. This multisector negotiation promised large gains to Japanese and European export sectors with its agenda for liberalization of goods, services, and investment. Both the European and Japanese governments committed to an agenda for comprehensive liberalization across sectors despite preferences against agricultural liberalization because other countries made inclusion of agriculture a prerequisite for their participation. In addition, faced with the choice of whether to discuss rice policy in a bilateral forum or in the Uruguay Round, both the United States and Japan favored the latter option in order to defuse political tension on this controversial issue.

The single undertaking embraced in the Uruguay Round agenda created a package approach, which gained credibility after important meetings on the overall negotiation in 1988 and 1990 failed because of deadlock in the agriculture group. The issue linkage became further institutionalized in 1991, when the GATT director-general produced a draft text binding together all parts of the negotiation into one agreement. The main business associations in Japan and the EU, Keidanren and UNICE, increased their lobbying for agricultural liberalization as the cross-sector linkage became stronger in 1990 and 1991. Their policy statements endorsed the linkage itself and specifically recommended agricultural liberalization for the sake of the gains from the overall negotiation package. In this period EU trade ministers began to play a larger role in the decision making, and Germany switched sides to favor agricultural concessions. Both the change in the Council presidency and the pressures arising from the linkage helped to push the balance against antireform agriculture ministers and France. Similar forces were at work in Japan, where trade officials and senior politicians intervened to urge a more flexible position in the agriculture negotiation group for the sake of a successful conclusion of the round. In 1991 several prominent LDP politicians began to make statements about a possible concession to allow partial opening of Japan's rice market.

Many of the changes made by the Uruguay Round Agriculture Agreement reduced trade-distorting policies in favor of more market-oriented policies. Given the entrenched nature of agricultural policies, such a major reorientation represented a politically risky decision that was strongly opposed by farmers. At the same time, the generous compensation to farmers through direct payments or other measures demonstrated that farmers continued to exercise considerable influence to resist financial pressures for budget cuts. The final form of liberalization reduced the negative external costs from the distortion of international markets by agricultural protection even as it only made a marginal contribution to reduce budget costs.

The Tokyo Round and APEC negotiations provided counterexamples. Both negotiations were comprehensive in the scope of the agenda and included a large number of countries like the Uruguay Round, but there was also less institutionalization of the cross-sector issue linkage. As expected, problems arose because interest groups and leaders thought they could achieve gains from the agreement on industrial goods while refusing liberalization of agriculture. In the end, this is exactly what happened in the Tokyo Round, when an agreement was concluded for substantial industrial liberalization and very modest agricultural reforms. On the other hand, the effort by Japan to pursue industrial liberalization while refusing to lower tariffs on fish and forestry imports caused the 1998 APEC meeting to collapse in failure. MITI ministers found themselves unable to overcome the opposition of primary sectors to any liberalization, and neither senior politicians nor the business community pushed for the concessions that were a condition for concluding the comprehensive agreement across nine sectors. In both of these negotiations, the weak connection among the different parts of the negotiation in the agenda was used to resist any kind of parallel liberalization across negotiation groups.

The number of countries involved in the negotiation was less important than the nature of the institutions that generally accompany multilateral negotiations (e.g., broad agendas and common rules). The statistical evidence showed that when controlling for other features of the negotiation context, multiple countries making a demand for liberalization did not increase the likelihood of liberalization. Indeed, for Japan liberalization was less likely when multiple countries participated in the negotiation. Certainly the number of countries and the nature of institutions of the negotiation are interrelated since the larger number of countries gives rise to the demand for multilateral institutions. However, peer pressure alone is not enough. This was witnessed at the 1998 APEC meeting when strong pressure from the United States, Australia, and ASEAN countries failed to persuade Japan to accept any liberalization of its fishery and forestry markets.

Threats also changed the negotiation stakes and brought in a wider set of policy actors, but the effect was smaller than an institutionalized issue linkage. Strong threats increased the probability that Japan would accept major liberalization by about half the increase from a strong issue linkage. Moreover, threats had relatively less effect on Europe.

Both politics and trade interests account for the lower effectiveness of threats relative to linkage. First, the trade value of sanctions rarely approached the trade value of a comprehensive liberalization agreement. Especially when sanctions targeted agricultural goods rather than industrial goods, there was insufficient cross-sectoral pressure to counter the strong agricultural interests. Second, it was politically difficult to make a unilateral concession under threat from the United States. Japanese and European business associations and trade officials strongly opposed U.S. unilateralism as represented by section 301, and they were reluctant to urge concessions in response to such threats.

The greater imbalance in trade flows between Japan and the United States may explain why a coercive strategy by the United States wielded more influence over Japan than the EU. Hostile statements from members of Congress about the trade deficit with Japan and protectionist legislative proposals gave credibility to U.S. threats. Statistical analysis showed that a larger trade deficit predicted greater liberalization by Japan, and business groups favored agricultural liberalization as one way to reduce trade tensions with the United States. Dependence on U.S. markets made it more difficult for Japan to risk ongoing trade tensions let alone propose counter-retaliation against U.S. sanctions. With a more balanced two-way trade relationship, the EU was able to resist threats where Japan could not. In the 1980s Europe risked a trade war with the United States by escalating export subsidies on wheat and issuing threats of counterretaliation against the United States at the height of the beef hormone dispute in 1988. Even when the United States implemented sanctions with WTO authorization in 1998, neither the targeted groups nor UNICE lobbied for a change in the ban against hormone-treated beef. The trade balance with the United States made Japan vulnerable to U.S. threats and allowed the EU to selectively ignore them.

EU resistance to agricultural liberalization is also strengthened by the political constraints arising from EU institutions. The burden from retaliatory trade sanctions as well as the financial cost of agricultural protection are shared among all members, but consensus decision-making often allows one member to dictate terms. France lives up to its reputation as an obstinate opponent of agricultural liberalization. Its capacity to interfere with negotiations is greater when it has a position of authority in the EU institutional context; France holding the presidency of the Council of Ministers reduced the likelihood of major liberalization. The

Uruguay Round illustrated the ability for France to use the agenda-setting role of the presidency to let agriculture ministers dominate the policy process. Only when the Dutch and British Council presidencies promoted a larger role for trade officials in the final years of the negotiation did a more conciliatory EU position in the agriculture negotiation group allow the Uruguay Round to move forward.

In further evidence that domestic political constraints provide bargaining leverage, the results showed a significant decrease in the probability of liberalization when the LDP had a narrow majority. Political weakness allowed LDP leaders to credibly argue that they must appeal to the party's farmer base. For example, during the second beef–citrus negotiation in 1983 and 1984, the LDP only narrowly held onto its majority in the Lower House. Japanese officials appealed to the United States with the argument that they could not liberalize because it would harm their electoral prospects. In spite of hinted threats about protectionist legislation in Congress during a period of heightened tension over the rising trade deficit, this negotiation only brought minor liberalization. LDP electoral gains in 1986 prevented a repetition of this argument during the third negotiation on beef and citrus from 1986 to 1988, and pressure from a GATT panel persuaded Japan to accept major liberalization.

The considerable financial cost of agricultural protection has provided internal pressure for policy changes. In the statistical analysis, budget conditions had different effects on Japan and the EU; the EU was more likely to liberalize during years with reduced spending levels, but changes in budget growth had little impact on Japanese policies. Yet even while the high cost of CAP made the EU cost-conscious, it nevertheless accepted less liberalization for expensive export subsidy policies than for other measures. In the Uruguay Round, governments did not choose the most budget-saving option available, and they offered compensation to relieve most of the downward pressure on farmer incomes that could result from liberalization. This mix of evidence makes it difficult to draw conclusions about the relationship between budgets and trade negotiations. Nevertheless, it is noteworthy that even while controlling for budget spending in statistical analysis, the negotiation structure exerts independent influence over outcomes.

The strength of the support for the issue linkage hypothesis gives insight into the nature of politics in Japan and the EU. The policy process in Japan, and even more so in the EU, grants considerable autonomy to agricultural interests. When the actors least willing to reform have the authority to block reforms, it is not surprising that little change happens. Issue linkage is important for overcoming the obstacles of segmented policy-making because it promotes greater policy integration. The international negotiation structure confronts decision-makers with the tradeoffs that too often are ignored in the domestic policy process. In this way, the international institution compensates for a weakness in the domestic institutions.

Legal Framing in Japan and the European Union

Japan and Europe reacted very differently to negotiations characterized by legal framing of the trade dispute. The strong legal tradition in European society relative to Japan might lead one to expect the EU would be more responsive to adjudication than the latter. In contrast, the evidence from agricultural trade negotiations reveals Japan as far more responsive to legal pressure than the EU. The statistical analysis of chapter 3 showed that high legal framing, represented by a violation ruling in a GATT/WTO dispute settlement proceeding, caused substantial increase in the likelihood of liberalization by Japan. The effect of a ruling was greater than either threats or strengthening of the LDP majority, and only an institutionalized issue linkage had a slightly larger effect. In contrast, a violation ruling had no significant effect on Europe. Typically the EU either made an early concession during the consultation phase of the dispute settlement process in order to avoid a ruling, or it engaged in legal obstructionism; and in some cases, it refused to change a policy even after a panel ruled that the policy violated GATT.

Table 10.2 shows the difference between the Japanese and EU rate of liberalization in agricultural trade negotiations where the United States issued a formal complaint under the dispute settlement proceedings. For the EU there is little difference between the frequency of liberalization for disputes with such a complaint and those without one. In contrast, there is a significant difference for Japan, which has a higher frequency of liberalization for those cases where a legal complaint is filed.[1] This presents a clear pattern that Japan is responsive to legal framing, while Europe is resistant.

How do Japan and the EU compare with other countries in their

[1] The tabular analysis of the two columns of EU data shows there is no statistically significant difference between the DSP versus non-DSP cases (Pearson $\chi^2 = 0.2165$, p-value = 0.64). The analysis of the two columns of Japan data shows the difference between DSP and non-DSP cases is statistically significant to the 1 percent confidence level (Pearson $\chi^2 = 6.72$, p-value = 0.01).

TABLE 10.2

Outcomes for Dispute Settlement Proceedings, U.S. Agricultural Negotiations with Japan and EU, 1970–1999

	EU		Japan	
	DSP	*Not DSP*	*DSP*	*Not DSP*
No change	14	21	7	39
	(33%)	(29%)	(15%)	(36%)
Liberalization	28	51	39	69
	(67%)	(71%)	(85%)	(64%)
Total cases	42	72	46	108

Note: The table shows the frequency that Japan and the EU offered a concession in a negotiation where the United States filed a complaint in GATT Dispute Settlement Proceedings (DSP) compared with all other non-DSP negotiations. Liberalization includes either minor or major liberalization. The table includes all DSP cases where a complaint was filed, whether the negotiation ends in consultations or following a panel ruling.

overall record in GATT disputes? Examination of Japan and the EU as defendants across the full record of GATT disputes through 1994 (not just limited to agricultural issues or limited to complaints initiated by the United States) reveals a similar pattern; in comparison with all GATT members, Japan is more cooperative on average and the EU is less cooperative.[2] GATT members made concessions to remedy partially or fully the alleged violation of GATT rules in two-thirds of all complaints and refused to make a concession in only one-third of the cases. The U.S. response to complaints was close to this average ratio. In comparison, Japan refused to make a liberalization concession for only 12.5 percent of the cases when it was a defendant. Although Japan has often been portrayed as a country that does not play by the rules (e.g., Lincoln 1999), this provides additional support to those who have disputed that claim (e.g., Schoppa 1999).[3] Japan's record is better than most

[2] I thank Marc Busch for sharing his dataset of GATT disputes. See Busch (2000) for the full description of the data. Cases include all complaints filed under GATT 1947 dispute procedures from 1948 to 1994, whether the negotiation ended in consultations or following a panel ruling. There are 252 cases in total, and 64 with the United States as defendant. There are 24 cases of Japan as defendant over the period from its membership in 1956 until 1994. The EU was a defendant for 57 cases, beginning in 1960 when the European Community became fully active as a GATT member.

[3] Leonard Schoppa (1999) uses the Bayard and Elliott (1994) data on U.S. section 301 negotiations and finds that Japan was one of the countries most responsive to U.S. demands through the end of the 1980s.

countries when it comes to playing by GATT rules in dispute settlement proceedings.

On the other hand, the EU refused to offer any concession in 56 percent of the GATT dispute cases when it was a defendant. The uncooperative position of the EU is also highlighted in the study by Bayard and Elliott (1994). They conclude from analysis of negotiations initiated under U.S. section 301 trade law that GATT procedures do not significantly improve outcomes for the United States. However, they note that this is largely due to including the EU, which lowers GATT success from an average of 71 percent of cases to 54 percent of cases (Bayard and Elliott 1994, 90). This places Japan and the EU at the two extremes in their response to legal framing when compared with all GATT members. Rather than try to evaluate whether the GATT rules are effective in general, it is necessary to consider how the rules work more or less effectively in different political settings.

One possibility is that differences at the domestic level account for variation in response to similar negotiation structures. Does state behavior toward international institutions mimic their domestic institutions? If countries externalize norms developed within their own political context, then more legalized societies may also be more responsive to resolving international disputes through legal processes.

The above conjecture finds little support in Japan. Although Japan is responsive to international legal pressure, this is not based on high use of legalistic policy-making at the domestic level. Japan (and Asia more generally) has often been characterized as having less developed social norms for legalism and judicial dispute resolution than other societies (e.g., Green 1995). In Japan, governance by administrative guidance and informal consensus has been common. Gerald Curtis (1999, 119) says the policy-making process in Japan revolves around informal party committees that "emphasize informality, privacy, implicit understandings" and operate outside of the public committee process. Some argue that legislation is left vague to discourage litigation against the government, and much legislative activity occurs through regulations rather than laws, or even more informally through a "system of understandings" called administrative guidance (Richard 1997, 112–113). Judicial oversight of government policies is strictly constrained by a system of incentives that punish judges who rule against the preferences of the ruling party (Ramseyer and Rosenbluth 1993). At the societal level, some have remarked that Japanese people have a lower "law-consciousness" as reflected in the low number of civil suits and lawyers (Tanaka 1988). Many of these characterizations are no longer appropriate as trends toward more legalization emerge in Japan. Nevertheless, in a comparative perspective, Japan has a weaker legal tradition than most European nations or the United States for using legalistic procedures in its domestic policy process.

Strong legal traditions in domestic society would lead one to expect the EU to be more, not less, responsive to pressure from legal rulings than other governments. Moreover, the process of integration has given European states unique opportunities to develop a habit of compliance with supranational law. EU institutions delegate considerable authority to the judiciary, as seen by the large role of the European Court of Justice and national courts to review decisions and shape the day-to-day operation of the internal market (Garrett and Weingast 1993). Some argue that legal oversight by the judiciary has fundamentally shaped the direction of EU policies and even the nature of the European polity (Alter 1998, Weiler 1999). While debates continue over the degree to which such judicial decisions have reflected state interests or represent independent judicial influence, few challenge the notion that the power of law has been central to the integration process or that the EU represents high levels of legalization.[4]

Thus the examination of legal framing at the societal level leads one to expect that if state behavior toward international institutions mimics the behavior they have toward their domestic institutions, then the EU should be more cooperative with legal framing than Japan. Indeed, the EU is an active user of the trade rules as a complainant (second only to the United States), while Japan was long one of the least active in terms of filing disputes and only in the 1990s began to use the rules as a complainant (Pekkanen 2001). This makes it all the more surprising to observe the uncooperative record of the EU in GATT disputes and its refusal to accept the WTO ruling against the beef hormone policy.

The value of CAP for EU integration and the privileged position of agriculture in EU policy-making account for the poor performance of the EU in adjudication of trade disputes. The large majority of all complaints filed against the EU in GATT disputes relate to agricultural issues. These cases arise because the CAP relies on many policies that have had questionable legal status within the GATT. Yet, at the same time, it has been difficult for the EU to change these policies. The interconnected policies of CAP's protective wall around European agriculture magnify the potential impact from even small liberalization measures. Given the central role in European integration played by the CAP, its maintenance serves both economic interests and normative goals for European states. This weighs against the trade interests at stake in a

---

[4] See, for example, Mattli and Slaughter (1998) and Abbott et al. (2000).

single GATT dispute and even the long-term importance of the system of trade rules.

Moreover, the segmented nature of EU policy-making allows the Agriculture Council and Directorate General for Agriculture to dominate decision making on agricultural policies. In legal cases, the narrow focus on a single agricultural policy fails to reduce the autonomy of these representatives of agricultural interests. Since they prioritize CAP over trade rules, their influence reduces the likelihood of agricultural liberalization. In the beef hormone case, the European Parliament and the Agriculture Council jointly blocked any policy reform, and not even the WTO violation ruling persuaded them to modify the policy. In contrast, in the Uruguay Round, the EU undertook CAP reform and accepted the SPS agreement mandating that science must guide standards for health regulations. Not only did the negotiation promise large gains, but the linkage in the negotiation structure forced the European Parliament and Council of Ministers to evaluate the final agreement as a whole package rather than vote on each isolated policy measure. Foreign ministers and trade officials advising the General Affairs Council made the final decisions. Whereas the issue linkage in the Uruguay Round brought agricultural issues into a wider context in EU policy-making, legal framing left the Agriculture Council in control with a veto over the single issue.

On the other hand, the interests and domestic institutions of Japan make it particularly responsive to pressure from GATT rules. First, there is a strong economic interest in maintaining free-trade rules. Not only is Japan trade dependent, but the structure of its trade—the large trade surplus with industrial economies and dependence on imports for essential raw materials—makes Japan more vulnerable to protectionism. The unequal market dependency prevents Japan from combating discrimination against its goods with threats of counterretaliation. This leaves the trade rules to play a vital role to maintain open markets for Japanese goods. Appreciation for its vulnerable position without GATT is greater because of the fact that Japan experienced widespread trade discrimination against its exports when it was denied GATT relations by many countries through the 1970s, and it had to negotiate to gain full acceptance in GATT.[5] Unlike the EU and the United States, Japan

---

[5] When Japan was admitted as a contracting party to GATT in 1955, fourteen countries, including the United Kingdom and France, refused to have GATT relations with Japan. Article 35 of the GATT allowed the option not to apply GATT rules to a state. Many of these states accepted Japan for full GATT relations as a result of bilateral negotiations during the 1960s, but as late as 1972 Austria, Ireland, and Portugal still refused to accord GATT relations to Japan (Komiya and Itoh 1988, 178).

has not pursued other free trade agreements until recently, and it has instead relied entirely on GATT to uphold its trading rights.

Second, in the Japanese political context, international legal pressure is treated with special importance. Legal framing of the demand for liberalization raises the issue to a higher level in the policy process. In Japan, senior politicians and the prime minister are more likely to intervene in favor of liberalization than lower-rank politicians or officials. Such intervention occurred during the negotiations on agricultural quotas in 1988, when a complaint to GATT by the United States led Prime Minister Takeshita to order reluctant agriculture ministry officials and rank-and-file rural district politicians to accept elimination of beef and citrus import quotas. Senior politicians favor trade interests and diplomacy because they must represent broad national interests in order to earn the support of business and party elites. The legitimacy accorded to international law in Japan can increase support for what would otherwise be an unpopular decision. The Japanese Constitution privileges international law over domestic law, most politicians support the need to follow international rules, and opinion polls show that a majority of the public favors following international law to settle trade disputes. Thus both trade interests and political context make Japan responsive to GATT law, even when it mandates liberalization of agricultural markets.

The pattern of liberalization reflects the degree of complementarity between the causal mechanism of the international institution and domestic institutions. Issue linkage promotes liberalization in the EU because it transforms segmented EU policy-making into a more integrated process and presents larger interests so that every member gains some benefit. Legal framing often fails because it relies on a narrow focus that is susceptible to becoming blocked in the process of EU agricultural decision making. In Japan, issue linkage promotes liberalization through increasing the proliberalization lobby as trade officials and business groups advocate liberalization and more senior levels of politicians become involved. Legal framing is more effective to promote liberalization in Japan than Europe because of the large interest Japan holds in the system of trade rules, and because domestic politics privileges international law. Whereas agricultural representatives retained a veto role over disputes about agricultural policy and trade law in the EU, in Japan legalizing the process led trade officials and senior politicians to force representatives of agricultural interests to accept concessions.

Specific domestic institutions and interests are more important than the social tradition for legalism, and this explains why Japan is more cooperative than the EU within GATT dispute settlement proceedings.

More generally, this suggests that, rather than countries having a consistent policy type, their behavior toward international cooperation will vary according to the fit between international and domestic interests and institutions for a given issue. Future research should consider which governments are more likely to cooperate in an institutional setting. For example, are presidential or parliamentary governments more willing to delegate to an international adjudication process? Are centralized governments with the capacity to make the calculation of tradeoffs among national interests more willing to make cross-sector linkage agreements than federal governments? Do governments with frequent coalition governments or high party turnover cooperate more within institutions that provide formal binding commitments to lock in policy choices? This kind of research agenda will reveal how a particular international institution can compensate for specific features of a domestic policy setting to change outcomes.

Multistage Negotiation Analysis

Having compared how different types of negotiation structures and domestic contexts can influence liberalization outcomes, this section steps back to view the wider context of the negotiation. Each trade negotiation occurs within a series of negotiations, the results of which constrain participants in later negotiations. First, bargaining established the GATT rules in 1947, and subsequent negotiations have revised the content of the rules as the trade system has developed to its current form as the WTO. Second, when a given trade topic arises on the international agenda, there is the choice of negotiation forum. Following selection of the negotiation forum, there may be need for a negotiation over the procedures. Third, there is the negotiation about specific trade issues that occurs in the institutional context established by these earlier stages in the negotiation process. The third stage has been the primary focus of this book. To examine how the institutional context of a negotiation influenced liberalization outcomes, the general system of trade rules and the specific choice of negotiation structure were taken as given.

However, questions remain concerning what determines the negotiation structure. It is conceptually and methodologically difficult to separate the independent effects of one negotiation in this process of sequential bargaining. Factors important for one decision indirectly influence later decisions. Some of the case studies revealed this dynamic of an endogenous process in which the choice of the negotiation structure anticipates the effect it will have on outcomes. In the Tokyo Round negotiation, the United States and the EC disagreed over the procedures for negotiating agricultural issues alongside industrial issues, in essence engaging in a negotiation over the negotiation structure. The EC was able to weaken the institutionalization of the issue linkage, and this in turn reduced the ability of the United States to force more liberalization in the agriculture group of the negotiation. The EC was also able to refuse the legal framing of the beef hormone dispute during the first phase of the negotiation under GATT rules at the time. Japan helped to reduce the institutionalization of APEC, and the principle of voluntarism later made it easier for Japan to resist liberalization. These examples point to the importance of viewing the relationship between the choice of negotiation structure and the impact of any given structure on liberalization outcomes.

One concern is whether states choose to raise only easy issues in GATT disputes or trade rounds. The research design of this book attempted to minimize this risk by showing the effects of institutional constraints on negotiations in the agricultural sector, which has long been one of the hardest areas to achieve trade liberalization. Closely examining one sector allowed comparison of negotiations where the constellation of interest groups remained relatively similar. Looking only at cases initiated by U.S. demands for liberalization further narrowed cases to share a common element of international pressure. Hence the research design partly controlled for some of the variation that complicates efforts to isolate the causal mechanism. Furthermore, the statistical models included variables specific to the negotiation and product in order to account for remaining differences in the pressure from the United States and resistance by Japan and the EU. Finally, the cases showed little evidence of a systematic selection effect. Indeed, the rice case with Japan and beef hormone dispute with the EU both indicate that some of the most difficult issues have been addressed in trade rounds or dispute settlement proceedings in the GATT context. This strengthens the confidence in the conclusions about issue linkage and legal framing.

The choice of negotiation structure is bounded by the existing institutional procedures and the demands of other countries, so that the negotiation structure does not simply reflect the preferences and bargaining power of the United States, the EU, or Japan. For example, in the Uruguay Round the demands of agricultural exporters of the Cairns Group and the actions of the GATT director-general were key factors strengthening the issue linkage. Second, even where the choice of negotiation structure is largely determined by bargaining among the principal countries, once it has been established, the negotiation structure subsequently exerts its own leverage that influences the amount of liberalization. Indeed, it is because actors anticipate that the negotiation structure will increase or decrease the pressure for agricultural liberalization that they care about the choice of the negotiation structure. Studying the effect of the negotiation structure will help to better inform our understanding of why governments make the choices they do. The evidence presented here — that the institutional design of a negotiation influences the policy outcome — calls for further study into the decisions that shape the form of institutions.

Future research toward a theory of negotiation should take into account the record of past negotiations and the cumulative process whereby interests and power become reflected in each step of institutional evolution. It would be useful to specify the constraints that leaders face when choosing a given institutional arrangement and the information that determines how they anticipate the effects of different institutional arrangements. The findings here contribute to this effort by increasing our understanding of how the choices over institutional rules can impact policy outcomes.

Another direction of future inquiry would be to examine the influence of negotiation structure on implementation. After the negotiation produces the agreement on policy changes, the next stage in the policy process is the actual implementation by governments. In some cases, problems at this stage provoke yet another international negotiation. On the one hand, James Fearon (1998) argues that countries anticipate whether others will implement the policy change, and that the difficulties over enforcement are brought into the negotiation over the policy agreement. However, this bargaining is influenced by the institutional context, and features of the negotiation structure may facilitate making enforceable agreements. For example, agreements reached in a GATT trade round are public agreements with specific schedules covering the agreed-upon liberalization measures. Greater formality in the agreement could reduce uncertainty later about exactly what each side has agreed it will do. The less institutionalized form of a bilateral agreement, which may consist of an exchange of letters, could contribute to conflicts over implementation after the negotiation settlement.[6] Although greater pressure for implementation of the binding agreement could reduce the amount of liberalization in the agreement, the conclusions of this book help to dismiss this concern by showing that more

---

[6] Negotiators on both sides of U.S.-Japan trade negotiations have made this observation. See Arai (1998). A senior USTR negotiator stated about Japan's record implementing agreements: "Japan honors its commitments to the letter. Sometimes I think the problem is whether the bilateral agreements are specific enough. There are ambiguities and both are walking away declaring victory. They may both have different interpretations. One can fault the agreement." Interview by author. Washington, DC, 6 April 2000.

institutionalized negotiations brought more liberalization. Future research should analyze the form of the agreement and long-term implementation success in order to evaluate this conjecture that institutionalized negotiations produce agreements with better implementation.

Implications

The rise and fall of protection in the agricultural sector defies explanation by arguments that focus exclusively on either U.S. power or farmer power. If the United States can dictate outcomes, why have America's closest allies and trade partners risked trade wars to maintain high agricultural trade barriers? On the other hand, in view of the formidable domestic lobbying power of farmers, why do we observe any liberalization? Comparative politics theories about interest groups explain high protection for agriculture while international relations theories about international bargaining power help to explain liberalization. However, to understand the variation observed in negotiations, it was necessary to examine the institutional context of the decisions between conflicting international and domestic demands.

This book has demonstrated how the variation of the institutional context at the international level shapes the aggregation of interest and actors at the domestic level. Doing so required relaxing the common assumption in international relations that the state is a unitary actor. At the same time, the emphasis on the structure of international negotiations departs from other studies of political economy that disregard the variety of international institutions that shape the options for state strategies. New insights will be possible from examination of the nexus between international relations and comparative politics. Institutions are equally important in the domestic and international political arenas.

Many studies have supported theories that international institutions promote cooperation, but less is understood about the way norms, principles, and procedures of the institution change state behavior. Disaggregating features of institutions to examine their role in trade negotiations revealed that issue linkage and legal framing represent two distinct means to promote liberalization. These features are not exclusive to GATT negotiations, but rather are dimensions that vary in degree across different GATT negotiations and those outside of the GATT context.

Issue linkage and international law are fundamental diplomatic tools that have long held an important place in theory and practice. Looking at their application in agricultural negotiations has highlighted that sometimes the constraints from the institutional context of the negotiation can overcome the most entrenched domestic interests. Agriculture was a good starting point given the strength of domestic opposition to liberalization in Japan and Europe. However, the framework for negotiation analysis is not limited to agriculture. Further research could extend the analysis to other sectors in order to generalize the findings more broadly. All trade negotiations should exhibit a similar process in which liberalization depends upon whether the negotiation structure broadens the stakes and shifts the domestic process to consider wider interests.

What are the limits of using cross-sector linkage to continue promoting trade liberalization? One is saturation. If industries that have a stake in expanding trade achieve full liberalization in their sector, they are likely to withdraw from future trade negotiations. Over time, liberalization will reach a plateau that freezes the gap between the level of openness of different sectors. Optimistically, one could foresee continued use of cross-sector linkage strategies bringing industrial tariffs down to zero and halving current levels of agricultural protection. Yet thereafter, cross-sector linkage would be ineffective. Since substantial agricultural protection remains in Japan and the EU, this is a worrisome possibility.

This points to the danger of single-sector trade liberalization. Pursuit of single-sector liberalization agreements where liberalization may be easier to achieve will bring closer the time when cross-sector linkages are no longer available. The economic gains from rapid liberalization of select sectors may outweigh the need for liberalization of highly protected sectors in the short term. However, over time greater losses may accumulate if persistent pockets of protection remain as sources of trade distortion and diplomatic tensions. This scenario would be the most harmful to developing countries that must rely on agricultural exports as a foundation for a broader development strategy. To avoid getting left without any source of leverage, developing nations may need to demand a greater proportion of liberalization of agricultural and textile markets by developed nations relative to measures they agree to undertake for service sector or investment liberalization. When developing nations cooperate as a coalition, they may be able to utilize cross-sector issue linkage and consensus norms of the WTO to their advantage. The role of the Cairns Group to reinforce the linkage in the Uruguay Round illustrates the potential for such a strategy.

Another limit on the future use of cross-sector linkages is strategic anticipation. Each time a linkage brings liberalization, groups opposed to liberalization may become more hostile to the establishment of a linkage. The negotiators of the Uruguay Round themselves anticipated this likelihood when they created the "built-in agenda" that mandated that the next trade round would automatically include negotiations on agriculture and services. Consequently, during the period leading up to the start of the Doha Round in 2001, agricultural interest groups in Japan and the EU, as well as officials promoting U.S. agricultural exports, all favored a comprehensive agenda that would add more issues to the table along with agriculture — each hoping to get more leverage from the addition of other sectors.

What about the potential for different kinds of linkages? The focus on cross-sectoral linkages has given less attention to intrasectoral divisions of interest that could be exploited through a linkage strategy. Whether high-skill and low-skill labor in manufacturing or feedgrain and livestock producers in agriculture, liberalization will have differential impacts on producers within sectors. Just as cross-sector linkage mobilizes one sector for the liberalization of another, it may be possible to use focused design of an agreement to create tradeoffs within a sector. The difficulty with intrasectoral linkage, however, is that decision making remains narrow in scope. As a result, regulatory capture of a ministry by one set of interests is unlikely to be overturned by an intrasectoral linkage.

Introducing linkages with nontrade issues to trade negotiations is less likely to succeed. For many issues related to security or environmental policies, the central mechanisms for issue linkage and legal framing — mobilization of export interests and inclusion of trade officials — will no longer apply. As seen in the beef hormone case, which raised both health and trade issues, the introduction of new policy actors can reduce prospects for liberalization if they do not share an interest in the trade system. Therefore analysis of issue linkage and legalization in nontrade policy spheres requires reexamination of the effects of negotiation structure. This is increasingly important as pressure grows to use the WTO dispute-settlement procedures and trade rounds as a forum to jointly address environmental and labor concerns as they relate to trade.

The evidence that legal framing helps to promote liberalization provides optimism for the future settlement of trade disputes. Increasingly countries are settling their trade disputes by means of adjudication. However, if expectations rise too high it may undermine the system. WTO adjudication cannot resolve all trade disputes. Cases such as the EU refusal to change its beef hormone ban make it easier for other countries also to disregard rulings — both the reputation effect and normative effect of rules depend upon others following them. If major countries ignore rules too often, the only leverage left for the WTO dispute settlement proceedings is the authorization of sanctions. This would make trade liberalization more difficult to achieve, for the evidence indicates that the legal procedures of the dispute process have greater impact than threats of retaliation. Yet at the same time, strategic rulings by judges to avoid ruling against the sensitive policies of powerful countries would undermine the legitimacy of the rules and thereby erode their effectiveness. It is up to the United States and other governments to consider the consequences of initiating a case that may be too difficult for the other country to liberalize in a legal setting. Against some controversial policies, winning the ruling may mean losing the rules system. Attention to how different governments respond to particular negotiation structures will promote better negotiation outcomes for all concerned.

This book has explained negotiation strategies to promote liberalization, but it is beyond its scope to evaluate the consequences of liberalization. Trade protection is deplored by many as a source of economic inefficiencies, financial burdens, and trade conflicts. When it comes to agricultural protection, the distortion of world market prices and the loss of economic opportunities have particularly severe consequences for many developing nations. It represents the worst double standard to demand that poor countries open their markets to services and manufactured goods while rich nations protect their well-to-do farmers. However, the goal to support a vulnerable sector that represents a valued way of life cannot be lightly dismissed. Does a fallow rice field represent a greater loss to society than an empty factory? Is it unreasonable for a government to worry about importing more than half of its food? These are the important questions that scholars and policymakers must grapple with.

A dairy farmer in Tochigi prefecture of Japan said liberalization of dairy and beef products had made it difficult for him to make enough income to continue farming. But with a look of resignation, he added that since his son worked for a local factory exporting cars to the United States, he could not oppose free trade. Even the families whose livelihoods are at stake have divided interests, and the dilemma is harder at the national level. As leaders weigh these questions during future trade negotiations, one hopes they will make a balanced decision between the economic interests of many groups and the value of both the farming tradition and international trade law. The structure of the international negotiation will play a critical role to determine which tradeoffs they consider.

Appendix

DESCRIPTIVE STATISTICS

TABLE A.1
Negotiation Outcomes, Japan

Liberalization	*Frequency*	*Percent*
None	46	29.87
Minor	46	29.87
Major	62	40.26

Note: Summary of dependent variable used for statistical analysis in chapter 3, table 3.4.

TABLE A.2
Negotiation Outcomes, EU

Liberalization	*Frequency*	*Percent*
None	35	30.70
Minor	39	34.21
Major	40	35.09

Note: Summary of dependent variable used for statistical analysis in chapter 3, table 3.6.

TABLE A.3
Descriptive Statistics, Japan (154 cases)

Variable	Mean	Standard Deviation
Liberalization	2.10	0.83
Cross-sector linkage	1.94	1.09
GATT dispute consultation	0.12	0.32
GATT dispute violation ruling	0.13	0.34
Threat	1.70	1.02
Trade balance	− 31.89	26.57
U.S. export priority	1.99	3.99
LDP strength	51.81	5.79
Budget growth	6.84	7.48
Economic growth	2.81	2.19
Multicountry demand	0.53	0.50

Note: Summary of variables used for statistical analysis in chapter 3, table 3.4.

TABLE A.4
Descriptive Statistics, EU (114 cases)

Variable	Mean	Standard Deviation
Liberalization	2.04	0.81
Cross-sector linkage	2.13	1.33
GATT dispute consultation	0.20	0.40
GATT dispute violation ruling	0.04	0.21
Threat	1.93	1.15
Trade balance	− 9.03	13.46
U.S. export priority	0.04	0.07
French Council presidency	1.28	0.52
Export subsidy case	0.36	0.48
Budget growth	4.53	17.23
Economic growth	2.49	0.99
Multicountry demand	0.46	0.50

Note: Summary of variables used for statistical analysis in chapter 3, table 3.6.

Bibliography

Abbott, Kenneth W., Robert Keohane, Andrew Moravcsik, Anne-Marie Slaughter, and Duncan Snidal. 2000. "The Concept of Legalization." *International Organization* 54 (3): 401–419.

Abbott, Kenneth W., and Duncan Snidal. 2000. "Hard and Soft Law in International Governance." *International Organization* 54 (3): 421–456.

Abbott, Philip. 1998. "Tariff Rate Quotas: Structural and Stability Impacts in Growing Markets." *Agricultural Economics* 19:257–267.

ACCJ (American Chamber of Commerce in Japan). 1997. *Making Trade Talks Work: Lessons from Recent History*. Tokyo: ACCJ.

Aggarwal, Vinod K., and Charles E. Morrison, eds. 1998. *Asia-Pacific Crossroads: Regime Creation and the Future of APEC*. New York: St. Martin's.

Aghion, Philippe, and Jean Tirole. 1997. "Formal and Real Authority in Organizations." *Journal of Political Economy* 105:1–29.

Akao, Nobutoshi. 1994. "Kōshō tantōsha ga kataru Uruguai Raundo seiritsu no butai ura" (The backstage of completing the Uruguay Round as told by a negotiator). *Gaikō Forum* 67.

Aldrich, John H. 1993. "Rational Choice and Turnout." *American Journal of Political Science* 37 (1): 246–278.

Allison, Graham. 1971. *Essence of Decision: Explaining the Cuban Missile Crisis*. Boston: Little, Brown.

Alt, James, and Michael Gilligan. 1994. "The Political Economy of Trading States: Factor Specificity, Collective Action Problems, and Domestic Political Institutions." *Journal of Political Philosophy*, 2:165–192.

Alter, Karen. 1998. "Who Are the 'Masters of the Treaty'?: European Governments and the European Court of Justice." *International Organization* 52 (1): 121–147.

Ames, Glenn, Lewell Gunter, and Claudia Davis. 1996. "Analysis of USA-European Community Oilseeds Agreements." *Agricultural Economics* 15:97–112.

Anania, Giovanni, Colin Carter, and Alex McCalla, eds. 1994. *Agricultural Trade Conflicts and GATT: New Dimensions in U.S.-European Agricultural Trade Relations*. Boulder: Westview Press.

Angelidis, Angel. 1993. "The Agricultural Negotiations within the Uruguay Round of GATT." Working document W-6/Part I, European Parliament Directorate General for Research.

———. 1994, July. "The Agricultural Negotiations within the Uruguay Round of GATT." Working document W-6/Part II, European Parliament Directorate General for Research.

Arai, Yutaka. 1998. "A Path to Freer Trade in Agricultural Products." Working paper 98-05, Harvard University Program on U.S.-Japan Relations.

Asano, Naonobu. 1988. "Kankitsu jiyūka to kokunai taisaku" (Citrus liberalization and domestic policy). *Nōrin tōkei chōsa* (Agriculture and forestries statistics survey) 11:10–13.

Bagwell, Kyle, and Robert Staiger. 1999. "An Economic Theory of GATT." *American Economic Review* 89 (1): 215–248.

Bailey, Michael, Judith Goldstein, and Barry Weingast. 1997. "The Institutional Roots of American Trade Policy: Politics, Coalitions, and International Trade." *World Politics* 49:309–338.

Baroncini, Elisa. 1998. "The European Community and the Diplomatic Phase of the WTO Dispute Settlement Understanding." *Yearbook of European Law* 18:157–220.

Baumgartner, Frank, and Bryan Jones. 1993. *Agendas and Instability in American Politics*. Chicago: University of Chicago Press.

Bawn, Kathleen. 1995. "Political Control Versus Expertise: Congressional Choices about Administrative Procedures." *American Political Science Review* 89:62–73.

Bayard, Thomas, and Kimberly Ann Elliott. 1994. *Reciprocity and Retaliation in U.S. Trade Policy*. Washington, DC: Institute for International Economics.

Becker, Gary. 1983. "A Theory of Competition among Pressure Groups for Political Influence." *Quarterly Journal of Economics* 98 (3): 317–400.

Bendor, Jonathan, Serge Taylor, and Roland Van Gaalen. 1987. "Stacking the Deck: Bureaucratic Missions and Policy Design." *American Political Science Review* 81 (3): 873–896.

Bentil, J. Kodwo. 1985. "Attempts to Liberalize International Trade in Agriculture and the Problem of the External Aspects of the Common Agricultural Policy of the European Economic Community." *Case Western Reserve Journal of International Law* 17 (3): 335–387.

Bergin, Anthony, and Marcus Haward. 1996. *Japan's Tuna Fishing Industry: A Setting Sun or New Dawn?* Commack, NY: Nova Science Publishers.

Bergsten, Fred, and Marcus Noland. 1993. *Reconcilable Differences? United States-Japan Economic Conflict*. Washington, DC: Institute for International Economics.

Bhagwati, Jagdish, and Hugh T. Patrick, eds. 1990. *Aggressive Unilateralism: America's 301 Trade Policy and the World Trading System*. Ann Arbor: University of Michigan Press.

Bossche, Peter Van den. 1997. "The European Community and the Uruguay Round Agreements." In *Implementing the Uruguay Round*, edited by John H. Jackson and Alan O. Sykes, 23–102. Oxford: Clarendon Press.

Brownlie, Ian. 1990. *Principles of Public International Law*. Fourth edition. Oxford: Oxford University Press.

Burley, Anne-Marie, and Walter Mattli. 1993. "Europe before the Court: A Political Theory of Legal Integration." *International Organization* 47 (1): 41–76.

Busch, Marc. 2000. "Democracy, Consultation, and the Paneling of Disputes under GATT." *Journal of Conflict Resolution* 44 (4): 425–446.

Busch, Marc, and Eric Reinhardt. 2002. "Testing International Trade Law: Empirical Studies of GATT/WTO Dispute Settlement." In *The Political Economy* of *International Trade Law: Essays in Honor of Robert E. Hudec*, edited by Daniel Kennedy and James Southwick, 457–481. Cambridge: Cambridge University Press.

Butler, Monika, and Heinz Hauser. 2000. "The WTO Dispute Settlement System: A First Assessment from an Economic Perspective." *The Journal of Law, Economics, & Organization* 16 (2): 503–533.

Calder, Kent. 1988. *Crisis and Compensation*. Princeton: Princeton University Press.

———. 1997. "The Institutions of Japanese Foreign Policy." In *The Process of Japanese Foreign Policy*, edited by Richard Grant, 1–24. London: The Royal Institute of International Affairs.

Chayes, Abram, and Antonia Handler Chayes. 1995. *The New Sovereignty: Compliance with International Regulatory Agreements*. Cambridge: Harvard University Press.

Coase, Ronald. 1960. "The Problem of Social Cost." *Journal of Law and Economics* 3:1–44.

Cohn, Theodore. 1993. "The Changing Role of the United States in the Global Agricultural Trade Regime." In *World Agriculture and the GATT*, edited by William P. Avery, 17–38. Boulder: Lynne Rienner Publishers.

Coleman, William D., and Stefan Tangermann. 1999. "The 1992 CAP Reform, the Uruguay Round and the Commission: Conceptualizing Linked Policy Games." *Journal of Common Market Studies* 37 (3): 385–405.

Conybeare, John A. C. 1987. *Trade Wars: The Theory and Practice of International Commercial Rivalry*. New York: Columbia University Press.

Cowhey, Peter, and Mathew McCubbins, eds. 1995. *Structure and Policy in Japan and the United States*. Cambridge: Cambridge University Press.

Croome, John. 1995. *Reshaping the World Trading System: A History of the Uruguay Round*. Boston: Kluwer Law International.

Curran, Timothy J. 1982. "The Politics of Trade Liberalization in Contemporary. Japan: The Case of the Tokyo Round of Multilateral Trade Negotiations, 1973–79." Ph.D. dissertation, Columbia University.

Curtis, Gerald. 1988. *The Japanese Way of Politics*. New York: Columbia University Press.

———. 1999. *The Logic of Japanese Politics: Leaders, Institutions, and the Limits of Change*. New York: Columbia University Press.

Daugbjerg, Carsten. 1999. "Reforming the CAP." *Journal of Common Market Studies* 37 (3): 407–428.

Davis, Christina. 2001. "Beyond Food Fights: How International Institutions Promote Agricultural Trade Liberalization." Ph.D. dissertation, Harvard University.

DeSombre, Elizabeth. 2000. *Domestic Sources of International Environmental Policy: Industry, Environmentalists, and U.S. Power*. Cambridge: MIT Press.

Domon, Takeshi. 1993. "Kome 'bubunkaihō' de toku suru no ha dare ka (Who gains from the 'partial liberalization' of rice?). *Shūkan Tōyō Keizai*, December 18:40–43.

———. 1994. "Shōeki ni hashitta nōrinshō no hyaku nichi (In pursuit of interest: The one hundred days of the Ministry of Agriculture). *Chūō Kōron* 6: 128–135.

Downs, Anthony. 1957. *An Economic Theory of Democracy*. New York: Harper and Row.

Downs, George, and David M. Rocke. 1995. *Optimal Imperfection? Domestic Uncertainty and Institutions in International Relations*. Princeton: Princeton University Press.

Drezner, Daniel. 2001. September. "State Power and the Structure of Global Regulation." Paper presented at the annual meeting of the American Political Science Association, San Francisco.

Earnshaw, David, and David Judge. 1996. "From Co-operation to Co-decision." In *European Union: Power and Policy-making*, edited by Jeremy Richardson, 96–126. London: Routledge.

EC (Commission of the European Community). 1979. "Final Report on the GATT Multilateral Trade Negotiations in Geneva (Tokyo Round) and Proposal for Council Decision." COM(79) 514 final, Commission of the European Communities, October 8.

———. 1999. *The Community Budget: The Facts in Figures*. Luxembourg: Office for Official Publications of the European Communities.

Eckstein, Harry. 1975. "Case Study and Theory in Political Science." In *Strategy of Inquiry*, edited by N. W. Polsby. Volume 7 of *Handbook of Political Science*, 79–137. Reading, MA: Addison–Wesley Publishing.

Eichengreen, Barry, and Jeffry Frieden. 1993. "The Political Economy of European Monetary Unification: An Analytical Introduction." *Politics and Economics* 5:85–104.

Eichmann, Erwin. 1990. "Procedural Aspects of GATT Dispute Settlement: Moving Toward Legalism." Technical Report 14. Palo Alto: Stanford Center on Conflict and Negotiation.

Elles, Diana. 2000. "The Role of EU Institutions in External Trade Policy." In *The European Union and World Trade Law*, edited by Nicholas Emiliou and David O'Keeffe, 19–30. Oxford: Oxford University Press.

Epstein, David, and Sharyn O'Halloran. 1999. *Delegating Powers: A Transaction Cost Politics Approach to Policy Making under Separate Powers*. Cambridge: Cambridge University Press.

Evans, Peter, Harold Jacobson, and Robert Putnam, eds. 1993. *Double-Edged Diplomacy: International Bargaining and Domestic Politics*. Berkeley: University of California Press.

FAO (Food and Agricultural Organization). 2001. *FAOSTAT* [database online]. Rome: FAO (apps.fao.org).

Farrell, Mary. 1999. *EU and WTO Regulatory Frameworks: Complementarity or Competition?* London: Kogan Page.

Fearon, James D. 1994. "Domestic Political Audiences and the Escalation of International Disputes." *American Political Science Review* 88:577–592.

———. 1998. "Bargaining, Enforcement, and International Cooperation." *International Organization* 52 (2): 269–306.

Field, Heather, and Murray Fulton. 1994. "Germany and the CAP: A Bargaining Model of EC Agricultural Policy Formation." *American Journal of Agricultural Economics* 76:15–25.

Finger, J. Michael, and Andrzej Olechowski, eds. 1987. *The Uruguay Round: A Handbook on the Multilateral Trade Negotiations*. Washington, DC: World Bank.

Finnemore, Martha, and Stephen Toope. 2001. "Alternatives to 'Legalization': Richer Views of Law and Politics." *International Organization* 55 (3): 743–758.

Fitchett, Delbert. 1987. "Agriculture." In *The Uruguay Round: A Handbook on the Multilateral Trade Negotiations*, edited by J. Michael Finger and Andrzej Olechowski, 162–170. Washington, DC: World Bank.

FPRC (Food Policy Research Center). 1999. *Shokuryō hakusho (heisei jyūichi nenban): aratana gyogyō chitsujo e no taido* (Food White Paper 1999: Movement toward a New Fisheries Order). Tokyo: Nōsan Gyoson Bunka Kyōkai.

Franck, Thomas. 1990. *The Power of Legitimacy among Nations*. Oxford: Oxford University Press.

Frieden, Jeffry. 1994. "International Investment and Colonial Control: A New Interpretation." *International Organization* 48:559–593.

Fukui, Haruhiro. 1978. "The GATT Tokyo Round: The Bureaucratic Politics of Multilateral Diplomacy." In *The Politics of Trade: US and Japanese Policymaking for the GATT Negotiations*, edited by Michael Blaker, 75–169. New York: Columbia University East Asian Institute.

Fukushima, Glen. 1992. *Nichibei keizai massatsu no seijigaku* (The politics of U.S.-Japan economic friction). Tokyo: Asahi Shimbun.

Funabashi, Yoichi. 1995. *Asia Pacific Fusion: Japan's Role in APEC*. Washington, DC: Institute for International Economics.

Gardner, Brian. 1996. *European Agriculture: Policies, Production and Trade*. London: Routledge.

Garrett, Geoffrey, and George Tsebelis. 1996. "An Institutional Critique of Intergovernmentalism." *International Organization* 50 (2): 269–299.

Garrett, Geoffrey, and Barry Weingast. 1993. "Ideas, Interests, and Institutions: Constructing the EC's Internal Market." In *Ideas and Foreign Policy*, edited by Judith Goldstein and Robert Keohane, 269–300. Ithaca: Cornell University Press.

GATT (General Agreement on Tariffs and Trade). 1979. *The Tokyo Round of Multilateral Trade Negotiations*. Geneva: GATT.

Gawande, Kishore, and Wendy Hansen. 1999. "Retaliation, Bargaining, and the Pursuit of "Free and Fair" Trade." *International Organization* 53 (1): 117–159.

George, Aurelia. 1988. "Rice Politics in Japan." Pacific Economic Paper 159, Australia-Japan Research Centre.

———. 1990. *The Last Bastion: Prospects for Liberalizing Japan's Rice Market*. Tokyo: Food and Agriculture Policy Research Center.

Gerschenkron, Alexander. 1943/1989. *Bread and Democracy in Germany*. Ithaca: Cornell University Press.

Gilligan, Michael. 1997. *Empowering Exporters: Reciprocity, Delegation, and Collective Action in American Trade Policy*. Ann Arbor: University of Michigan Press.

Gilpin, Robert. 1981. *War and Change in World Politics*. Cambridge: Cambridge University Press.

Goldberg, Pinelopi, and Giovanni Maggi. 1999. "Protection for Sale: An Empirical Investigation." *The American Economic Review* 89 (5): 1135–1155.

Goldstein, Judith. 1993. "Creating the GATT Rules: Politics, Institutions, and American Policy." In *Multilateralism Matters: The Theory and Praxis of an Institutional Form*, edited by John G. Ruggie, 201–32. New York: Columbia University Press.

Goldstein, Judith, and Robert Keohane, eds. 1993. *Ideas and Foreign Policy: Beliefs, Institutions, and Political Change*. Ithaca: Cornell University Press.

Goldstein, Judith, and Lisa L. Martin. 2000. "Legalization, Trade Liberalization, and Domestic Politics: A Cautionary Note." *International Organization* 54 (3): 603–632.

Golino, Louis R. 1995. "French Farmers and French Agricultural Policies: An Overview." Report for Congress. 96-8. Washington, DC: Congressional Research Service, December 20.

Goto, Junko, and Naraomi Imamura. 1993. "Japanese Agriculture: Characteristics, Institutions, and Policies." In *Japanese and American Agriculture: Tradition and Progress in Conflict*, edited by Luther Tweeten et al., 11–29. Boulder: Westview Press.

Gourevitch, Peter. 1996. "Squaring the Circle: the Domestic Sources of International Cooperation." *International Organization* 50 (2): 349–373.

Gowa, Joanne. 1994. *Allies, Adversaries, and International Trade*. Princeton: Princeton University Press.

Grant, Richard. 1993. "Against the Grain: Agricultural Trade Policies of the U.S., the European Community and Japan at the GATT." *Political Geography* 12 (3): 247–262.

Grant, Wyn. 1997. *The Common Agricultural Policy*. London: Macmillan.

Green, Carl. 1995. "APEC and Trans-Pacific Dispute Management." *Law and Policy in International Business* 26 (3): 719–734.

Grossman, Gene M., and Elhanan Helpman. 1994. "Protection for Sale." *The American Economic Review* 84 (4): 833–850.

Haas, Ernst B. 1958. *The Uniting of Europe: Political, Economic and Social Forces, 1950–57*. Stanford: Stanford University Press.

———. 1980. "Why Collaborate? Issue-Linkage and International Regimes." *World Politics* 32 (3): 357–405.

Hanrahan, Charles E. 1992. "Oilseeds, Agriculture, and the Uruguay Round." Report for Congress 92-904S. Congressional Research Service, 4 December.

———. 1994. "Agriculture in the GATT." Report for Congress IB89027. Congressional Research Service, 28 February.

———. 1999. "The European Union's Ban on Hormone-Treated Meat." Report for Congress RS20142. Congressional Research Service, 9 December.

Hanson, Brian T. 1998. "What Happened to Fortress Europe? External Trade Policy Liberalization in the European Union." *International Organization* 52 (1): 55–85.

Harris, Simon. 1994. "The Food Industry Perspective." In *Agriculture in the*

Uruguay Round, edited by K. A. Ingersent, A. J. Rayner, and R. C. Hine, 182–202. New York: St. Martin's Press.

Harris, Simon, and Alan Swinbank. 1997. "The CAP and the Food Industry." In *The Common Agricultural Policy*, edited by Christopher Ritson and David Harvey, 265–283. Wallingford, UK: CAB International.

Harris, Simon, Alan Swinbank, and Guy Wilkinson. 1983. *The Food and Farm Policies of the European Community*. Chichester: John Wiley and Sons.

Hayami, Yujiro. 1988. *Japanese Agriculture under Siege: The Political Economy of Agricultural Policies*. London: Macmillan.

Hayami, Yujiro, and Kym Anderson. 1986. *The Political Economy of Agricultural Protection: East Asia in International Perspective*. London: Allen and Unwin.

Hayami, Yujiro, and Yoshihisa Godo. 1995. "Economics and Politics of Rice Policy in Japan: A Perspective on the Uruguay Round." *NBER Working Paper Series*, 5341.

Hemmi, Kenzo. 1982. "Agriculture and Politics in Japan." In *U.S.-Japanese Agricultural Trade Relations*, edited by Emery Castle and Kenzo Hemmi, 219–274. Washington, DC: Resources for the Future.

Hendriks, Gizelle. 1991. *Germany and European Integration — The Common Agricultural Policy: An Area of Conflict*. Oxford: Berg.

———. 1994. "The National Politics of International Trade Reform: The Case of Germany." In *Regulating Agriculture*, edited by Philip Lowe, Terry Marsden, and Sarah Whatmore, 149–162. London: David Fulton Publishers.

Higgott, Richard A., and Andrew Fenton Cooper. 1990. "Middle Power Leadership and Coalition Building: Australia, the Cairns Group, and the Uruguay Round of Trade Negotiations." *International Organization* 44 (4): 589–632.

Hillman, Jimmye S. 1994. "The US Perspective." In *Agriculture in the Uruguay Round*, edited by K. A. Ingersent, A. J. Rayner, and R. C. Hine, 26–54. New York: St. Martin's Press.

Hine, R. C. 1985. *The Political Economy of European Trade*. New York: St. Martin's Press.

Hiscox, Michael J. 2002. *International Trade and Political Conflict: Commerce, Coalitions, and Mobility*. Princeton: Princeton University Press.

Hoekman, Bernard M. 1989. "Determining the Need for Issue Linkages in Multilateral Trade Negotiations." *International Organization* 43 (4): 693–714.

Honma, Masayoshi. 1994. *Nōgyō mondai no seijikeizai gaku* (The political economy of agriculture). Tokyo: Nihon Keizai Shimbunsha.

Houck, James. 1980. "U.S. Agricultural Trade and the Tokyo Round." *Law and Policy in International Business* 12:265–295.

Hudec, Robert. 1988. "Legal Issues in US-EC Trade Policy: GATT Litigation 1960–1985." In *Issues in U.S.-EC Trade Relations*, edited by Robert Baldwin, Carl Hamilton, and Andre Sapir, 17–58. Chicago: University of Chicago Press.

———. 1993. *Enforcing International Trade Law: The Evolution of the Modern GATT Legal System*. Salem, NH: Butterworth.

Hungerford, T. L. 1991. "GATT: A Cooperative Equilibrium in a Noncooperative Trading Regime?" *Journal of International Economics* 31:357–369.

Hurd, Ian. 1999. "Legitimacy and Authority in International Politics." *International Organization* 53 (2): 379–408.

Iceland, Charles. 1994. "European Union: Oilseeds." In *Reciprocity and Retaliation in U.S. Trade Policy*, edited by Thomas Bayard and Kimberly Ann Elliott, 209–232. Washington, DC: Institute for International Economics.

Iida, Keisuke. 1993. "When and How Do Domestic Constraints Matter? Two-Level Games with Uncertainty." *Journal of Conflict Resolution* 37:403–426.

Imamura, Naraomi, ed. 1995. *Ajia gyogyō no hatten to Nihon* (Asian fisheries development and Japan). Tokyo: Nōsangyōson Bunka Kyōkai.

Ingersent, Ken, A. J. Rayner, and R. C. Hine, eds. 1994. *Agriculture in the Uruguay Round*. New York: St. Martin's Press.

Ingersent, K. A., and A. J. Rayner. 1999. *Agricultural Policy in Western Europe and the United States*. Northampton, MA: Edward Elgar.

Ishikura, Teruka. 1988. *Nōsanbutsu jiyūka no sōtenken* (An examination of agricultural liberalization). Tokyo: Fumin Kyōkai.

Jackson, John H. 1997. *The World Trading System: Law and Policy of International Economic Relations*. 2d edition. Cambridge: MIT Press.

———. 1998. "Designing and Implementing Effective Dispute Settlement Procedures: WTO Dispute Settlement, Appraisal and Prospects." In *The WTO as an International Organization*, edited by Anne O. Krueger, 161–180. Chicago: University of Chicago Press.

Jackson, John, Jean-Victor Louis, and Mitsuo Matsushita. 1984. *Implementing the Tokyo Round*. Ann Arbor: University of Michigan Press.

Janow, Merit. 1996/97. "Assessing APEC's Role in Economic Integration in the Asia-Pacific Region." *Northwestern Journal of International Law and Business* 17 (2–3): 947–1013.

Johnson, Chalmers. 1982. *MITI and the Japanese Miracle*. Stanford: Stanford University Press.

Johnson, D. Gale. 1991. *World Agriculture in Disarray*. 2nd edition. London: Macmillan.

Johnston, Alastair Iain. 2001. "Treating International Institutions as Social Environments." *International Studies Quarterly* 45 (4): 487–515.

Josling, Timothy. 1977. September. "Agriculture in the Tokyo Round Negotiations." Thames essay 10, Trade Policy Research Centre.

———. 1979. "The CAP and International Commodity Agreements." In *Prospects for Agriculture in the European Economic Community*, edited by M. Tracy and I. Hodac, 275–292. Bruges, Belgium: College of Europe.

Josling, Timothy, Stefan Tangermann, and T. K. Warley, eds. 1996. *Agriculture in the GATT*. New York: St. Martin's Press.

Jussaume, Raymond. 1994. "An Introduction to the Japanese Juice Industry: Trading Firms, the State, and New Liberalization Policies." In *From Columbus to ConAgra*, edited by Alessandro Bonanno, 160–183. Lawrence: University Press of Kansas.

Kahler, Miles. 1992. "Multilateralism with Small and Large Numbers." *International Organization* 46 (3): 681–708.

———. 2000. "Legalization as Strategy: The Asia-Pacific Case." *International Organization* 54 (3): 549–571.

Kajikawa, Chikako. 1999. *Ringo keizai no tōkei bunseki* (Statistical analysis of the apple economy). Tokyo: Norin Tōkei Kyōkai.

Karube, Kensuke. 1997. *Nichibei kome kōshō* (U.S.-Japan rice negotiations). Tokyo: Chukō Shinshō.

Kay, Adrian. 1998. *The Reform of the Common Agricultural Policy: The Case of the MacSharry Reforms*. Wallingford, UK: CAB International.

Keeler, John. 1996. "Agricultural Power in the European Community." *Comparative Politics* 28 (2): 127–149.

Keidanren. 1991. "Nihon nōgyō, uchinaru kaikaku, sotonaru kaizen" (Japanese agriculture, reform from within and improvement from without). *Keidanren geppō* 6:10–27.

———. 1999. *Keizai dantai rengōkai gojūnenshi* (Fifty-year history of the Japan Federation of Economic Organizations). Tokyo: Keidanren.

Keohane, Robert. 1984. *After Hegemony: Cooperation and Discord in the World Political Economy*. Princeton: Princeton University Press.

Keohane, Robert, and Lisa Martin. 1999. "Institutional Theory, Endogeneity and Delegation." Working paper 99-07, Weatherhead Center for International Affairs, Harvard University.

Keohane, Robert, and Joseph Nye. 1977. *Power and Interdependence*. Boston: Little, Brown.

Kherallah, Mylene, and John Beghin. 1998. "U.S. Trade Threats: Rhetoric or War?" *American Journal of Agricultural Economics* 80:15–29.

Kindleberger, Charles P. 1986. *The World in Depression*. Berkeley: University of California Press.

King, Gary, Michael Tomz, and Jason Wittenberg. 2000. "Making the Most of Statistical Analyses: Improving Interpretation and Presentation." *American Journal of Political Science* 44 (2): 341–355.

Kirshner, Jonathan. 1995. *Currency and Coercion: The Political Economy of International Monetary Power*. Princeton: Princeton University Press.

Klein, Mark, and Wendy Tai. 1996. "The World Trade Organization Cuts Its Teeth on a Beefy Trade Dispute." *The Cargill Bulletin*, 1–8.

Kobayashi, Yoshiaki. 1991. *Gendai nihon no senkyo* (Contemporary Japanese elections). Tokyo: Tokyo University Press.

Koizumi, Sadahiko. 1994. "Raundo gōi e itaru haikei to naigai no jitsujō" (Background to the round agreement and the domestic and foreign circumstances). *Nōgyō to Keizai* 4:21–27.

Komiya, Ryutaro, and Motoshige Itoh. 1988. "Japan's International Trade and Trade Policy, 1955–1984." In *The Political Economy of Japan*, edited by Takashi Inoguchi and Daniel Okimoto. Volume 2, 173–224. Palo Alto: Stanford University Press.

Koremenos, Barbara, Charles Lipson, and Duncan Snidal. 2001. "The Rational

Design of International Institutions." *International Organization* 55 (4): 761–799.

Kovenock, Dan, and Marie Thursby. 1992. "GATT, Dispute Settlement and Co-operation." *Economics and Politics* 4 (2): 151–170.

Krasner, Stephen, ed. 1983a. *International Regimes.* Ithaca: Cornell University Press.

———. 1983b. "Regimes and the Limits of Realism: Regimes as Autonomous Variables." In *International Regimes,* edited by Stephen Krasner, 355–368. Ithaca: Cornell University Press.

———. 1991. "Global Communications and National Power: Life on the Pareto Frontier." *World Politics* 43 (3): 336–356.

———, ed. 1999. *Sovereignty: Organized Hypocrisy.* Princeton: Princeton University Press.

Krauss, Ellis. forthcoming. "The U.S. and Japan in APEC's EVSL Negotiations: Regional Multilateralism and Trade." In *Beyond Bilateralism: The U.S.-Japan Relationship in the New Asia Pacific,* edited by Ellis Krauss and T. J. Pempel.

Krueger, Anne O. 1996. "The Political Economy of Controls: American Sugar." In *Empirical Studies in Institutional Change,* edited by Lee Alston, Thrainn Eggertsson, and Douglass North. Cambridge: Cambridge University Press.

———, ed. 1998. *The WTO as an International Organization.* Chicago: University of Chicago Press.

Kuo, Cheng-Tian, and Takuya Yanagisawa. 1992. "The Politics of Japan's Rice Trade." *The Journal of Northeast Asian Studies* 12:19–39.

Kusano, Atsushi. 1983. *Nichibei orenji kōshō* (Japan.-U.S. orange negotiations). Tokyo: Nihon Keizai Shimbunsha.

Lake, David, and Robert Powell, eds. 1999. *Strategic Choice and International Relations.* Princeton: Princeton University Press.

Larsen, Arne, ed. 1994. *The Economics of the Common Agricultural Policy (CAP).* Volume 5. Brussels: European Commission Directorate General for Economic and Financial Affairs.

Lee, Jong-Wha, and Phillip Swagel. 1997. "Trade Barriers and Trade Flows across Countries and Industries." *Review of Economics and Statistics* 79:372–382.

Lieber, Robert. 1970. *British Politics and European Unity: Parties, Elites, and Pressure Groups.* Berkeley: University of California Press.

Lincoln, Edward. 1999. *Troubled Times: U.S.-Japan Trade Relations in the 1990s.* Washington, DC: Brookings Institution.

Lindberg, L. N. 1963. *The Political Dynamics of European Economic Integration.* Palo Alto: Stanford University Press.

Lindert, Peter. 1991. "Historical Patterns of Agricultural Policy." In *Agriculture and the State,* edited by Peter Timmer, 29–83. Ithaca: Cornell University Press.

Lohmann, Susanne. 1997. "Linkage Politics." *Journal of Conflict Resolution* 41 (1): 38–67.

Lohmann, Susanne, and Sharyn O'Halloran. 1994. "Divided Government and U.S. Trade Policy: Theory and Evidence." *International Organization* 48 (4): 596–632.

MAFF (Ministry of Agriculture, Forestry, and Fisheries). 1997. *The Statistical Yearbook of the Ministry of Agriculture, Forestry, and Fisheries.* Volume 73. Tokyo: MAFF.

———. 1999. *Nōgyō hakusho, heisei 10 nen* (Agriculture white paper 1998). Tokyo: Norin Tōkei Kyōkai.

Maggi, Giovanni. 1999. "The Role of Multilateral Institutions in International Trade Cooperation." *The American Economic Review* 89 (1): 190–214.

Martin, Lisa. 1992a. *Coercive Cooperation: Explaining Multilateral Economic Sanctions.* Princeton: Princeton University Press.

———. 1992b. "Interests, Power, Multilateralism." *International Organization* 46 (3): 765–792.

———. 2000. *Democratic Commitments: Legislatures and International Cooperation.* Princeton: Princeton University Press.

Masuda, Yoshitaka. 1998. *Gendai nōgyō seisakuron* (Contemporary agriculture policy). Tokyo: Nōrin Tōkei Kyōkai.

Mattli, Walter, and Anne-Marie Slaughter. 1998. "Revisiting the European Court of Justice." *International Organization* 52 (1): 177–209.

Mayer, Frederick. 1992. "Managing Domestic Differences in International Negotiations: The Strategic Use of Internal Side-payments." *International Organization* 46 (4): 793–818.

McMillan, John. 1990. "Strategic Bargaining and Section 301." In *Aggressive Unilateralism: America's 301 Trade Policy and the World Trading System*, edited by Jagdish Bhagwati and Hugh Patrick. Ann Arbor: University of Michigan Press.

Mearsheimer, John. 1994–95. "The False Promise of International Institutions." *International Security* 19:5–49.

Meunier, Sophie. 2000. "European Institutions and EU-U.S. Trade Negotiations." *International Organization* 54 (1): 103–135.

Mikanagi, Yumiko. 1996. *Japan's Trade Policy: Action or Reaction?* London: Routledge.

Milgrom, Paul R., Douglass C. North, and Barry R. Weingast. 1990. "The Role of Institutions in the Revival of Trade: The Law Merchant, Private Judges, and the Champagne, Fairs." *Economics and Politics* 2 (1): 1–23.

Milner, Helen. 1988. *Resisting Protectionism: Global Industries and the Politics of International Trade.* Princeton: Princeton University Press.

———. 1997. *Interests, Institutions, and Information: Domestic Politics and International Relations.* Princeton: Princeton University Press.

Mizoguchi, Michio, and Masahiro Matsuō. 1994. *Uruguai Raundo* (Uruguay Round). Tokyo: NHK.

MOF (Ministry of Finance). 1999. "Financial Statistics of Japan 1999." Technical Report, Ministry of Finance.

Moore, Richard H. 1990. *Japanese Agriculture: Patterns of Rural Development.* Boulder: Westview Press.

Moravcsik, Andrew. 1991. "Negotiating the Single European Act: National Interests and Conventional Statecraft in the European Community." *International Organization* 45 (1): 19–56.

———. 1997. "Taking Preferences Seriously: A Liberal Theory of International Politics." *International Organization* 51 (4): 513–553.

———. 1998. *The Choice for Europe: Social Purpose and State Power from Messina to Maastricht*. Ithaca: Cornell University Press.

———. 1999. "A New Statecraft? Supranational Entrepreneurs and International Cooperation." *International Organization* 53 (2): 267–306.

Morrison, Charles. 1998. "APEC: The Evolution of an Institution." In *Asia-Pacific Crossroads: Regime Creation and the Future of APEC*, edited by Vinod K. Aggarwal and Charles Morrison, 1–22. New York: St. Martin's Press.

Morrow, James. 1992. "Signaling Difficulties with Linkage in Crisis Bargaining." *International Studies Quarterly* 36 (2): 153–172.

———. 1994. "The Forms of International Cooperation." *International Organization* 48 (3): 387–423.

Moyer, H. Wayne. 1993. "The European Community and the GATT Uruguay Round: Preserving the Common Agriculture Policy at All Costs." In *World Agriculture and the GATT*, edited by William P. Avery, 95–119. Boulder: Lynne Rienner Publishers.

Moyer, H. Wayne, and Timothy Josling. 1990. *Agricultural Policy Reform: Politics and Process in the EC and the USA*. New York: Harvester Wheatsheaf.

Mulgan, Aurelia George. 1997a. "Electoral Determinants of Agrarian Power: Measuring Rural Decline in Japan." *Political Studies* 45:875–899.

———. 1997b. "The Role of Foreign Pressure (*Gaiatsu*) in Japan's Agricultural Trade Liberalization." *The Pacific Review* 10 (2): 165–209.

———. 2000. *The Politics of Agriculture in Japan*. London: Routledge.

———. 2001. "'Japan Inc.' in the Agricultural Sector: Reform or Regression." Pacific Economic Papers 314, Australia-Japan Research Centre.

———. Forthcoming. *The Challenge to Vested Interests: Contesting Agricultural Policies and Policymaking in Japan*. London: Routledge.

Munk, Knud, and Ken Thomson. 1994. "The Economic Costs of Agricultural Policy." In *The Economics of the Common Agricultural Policy (CAP)*, edited by Arne Larsen. Volume 5. Brussels: European Commission Directorate General for Economic and Financial Affairs.

Murata, Takeshi, ed. 1995. *Towareru gatto nōsanbutsu jiyū bōeki* (Considering GATT agriculture commodities free trade). Tokyo: Tsukuba Shobō.

Nagao, Satoru. 1990. "Nihon keizai gaikō no henyō: kokusai seisaku katei to nichibei gyūniku/orenji kōshō" (Japanese foreign policy change: The international process and U.S.-Japan beef/orange negotiations). *Kokusai Mondai* 93: 82–97.

Neville-Rolfe, Edmund. 1984. *The Politics of Agriculture in the European Community*. London: Policy Studies Institute.

Normile, Mary Anne. 1998. "Uruguay Round Agreement on Agriculture: The Record to Date." *Agricultural Outlook* (December): 29–33.

North, Douglass C. 1990. *Institutions, Institutional Change and Economic Performance*. Cambridge: Cambridge University Press.

———. 1994. "Economic Performance through Time." *American Economic Review* 84:359–398.

Nugent, Neill. 1999. *The Government and Politics of the European Union*. 4th edition. Durham: Duke University Press.

Odell, John. 1993. "International Threats and Internal Politics: Brazil, the European Community, and the United States, 1985–1987." In *Double-Edged Diplomacy: International Bargaining and Domestic Politics*, edited by Peter Evans, Harold Jacobson, and Robert Putnam, 233–264. Berkeley: University of California Press.

———. 2000. *Negotiating the World Economy*. Ithaca: Cornell University Press.

OECD (Organization for Economic Co-operation and Development). 1999. *Agricultural Policies in OECD Countries: Monitoring and Evaluation*. Paris: OECD.

———. 2000a. *Agricultural Policies in OECD Countries: Monitoring and Evaluation 2000*. Paris: OECD.

———. 2000b. Producer and Consumer Support Estimates Database on CD-ROM. Paris: OECD.

Olson, Mancur. 1965. *The Logic of Collective Action*. Cambridge: Harvard University Press.

Orden, David, Robert Paarlberg, and Terry Roe. 1999. *Policy Reform in American Agriculture: Analysis and Prognosis*. Chicago: University of Chicago Press.

Oxfam. 2002. *Rigged Rules and Double Standards: Trade, Globalisation, and the Fight against Poverty*. Oxford: Oxfam.

Paarlberg, Robert. 1985. *Food Trade and Foreign Policy: India, the Soviet Union, and the United States*. Ithaca: Cornell University Press.

———. 1997. "Agricultural Policy Reform and the Uruguay Round: Synergistic Linkage in a Two-Level Game?" *International Organization* 51 (3): 413–444.

Paemen, Hugo, and Alexandra Bensch. 1995. *From the GATT to the WTO: The European Community in the Uruguay Round*. Leuven, Belgium: Leuven University Press.

Patterson, Lee Ann. 1997. "Agricultural Policy Reform in the European Community: A Three-level Game Analysis." *International Organization* 51 (1): 135–165.

Pekkanen, Saadia. 2001. "International Law, the WTO, and the Japanese State: Assessment and Implications of the New Legalized Trade Politics." *The Journal of Japanese Studies* 27 (1): 41–79.

Petersmann, Ernst-Ulrich. 1986. "The EEC as a GATT Member—Legal Conflicts between GATT Law and European Community Law." In *The European Community and GATT*, edited by Meinhard Hilf, Francis Jacobs, and Ernst-Ulrich Petersmann. Volume 4, 23–71. Deventer, The Netherlands: Kluwer.

———. 1997. *The GATT/WTO Dispute Settlement System*. London: Kluwer Law.

———. 2000. "The GATT Dispute Settlement System." In *The European Union and World Trade Law*, edited by Nicholas Emiliou and David O'Keeffe, 253–277. Oxford: Oxford University Press.

Phillips, Peter. 1990. *Wheat, Europe and the GATT*. London: Pinter Publishers.

Pollack, Mark. 1997. "Delegation, Agency, and Agenda Setting in the European Community." *International Organization* 51 (1): 99–134.

Porges, Amelia. 1994. "Japan: Beef and Citrus." In *Reciprocity and Retaliation in U.S. Trade Policy*, edited by Thomas Bayard and Kimberly Ann Elliott, 233–266. Washington, DC: Institute for International Economics.

Preeg, Ernest H. 1995. *Traders in a Brave New World*. Chicago: University of Chicago Press.

Putnam, Robert. 1988. "Diplomacy and Domestic Politics: the Logic of Two-level Games." *International Organization* 42 (3): 427–460.

Raiffa, Howard. 1982. *The Art and Science of Negotiation*. Cambridge: Harvard University Press.

Ramseyer, Mark, and Frances Rosenbluth. 1993. *Japan's Political Marketplace*. Cambridge: Harvard University Press.

Ray, Edward. 1981. "Tariff and Nontariff Barriers to Trade in the United States and Abroad." *The Review of Economics and Statistics* 63 (2): 161–168.

Ray, Edward J., and Howard P. Marvel. 1984. "The Pattern of Protection in the Industrialized World." *The Review of Economics and Statistics* 66 (3): 452–458.

Reich, Michael, and Yasuo Endo. 1983. "Conflicting Demands in U.S.-Japan Agricultural Negotiations." Working paper 83-01, Harvard University Program on U.S.-Japan Relations.

Reich, Michael, Yasuo Endo, and Peter Timmer. 1986. "Agriculture: The Political Economy of Structural Change." In *America Versus Japan*, edited by Thomas K. McCraw, 151–192. Boston: Harvard Business School Press.

Reinhardt, Eric. 2001. "Adjudication without Enforcement in GATT Disputes." *Journal of Conflict Resolution* 45 (2): 174–195.

Richardson, Bradley M. 1997. *Japanese Democracy: Power, Coordination, and Performance*. New Haven: Yale University Press.

Ricupero, Rubens. 1998. "Integration of Developing Countries into the Multilateral Trading System." In *The Uruguay Round and Beyond*, edited by Jagdish Bhagwati and Mathias Hirsch, 9–36. Ann Arbor: University of Michigan Press.

Rieger, Elmar. 1996. "The Common Agricultural Policy: External and Internal Dimensions." In *Policy-making in the European Union*, edited by Helen Wallace and William Wallace, 97–123. Oxford: Oxford University Press.

Riker, William H. 1986. *The Art of Political Manipulation*. New Haven: Yale University Press.

Roberts, Donna. 1998. "Implementation of the WTO Agreement on the Application of Sanitary and Phytosanitary Measures: The First Two Years." Working paper 98-4, International Agricultural Trade Research Consortium.

Rodrik, Dani. 1995. "Political Economy of Trade Policy." In *Handbook of International Economics*, edited by Gene Grossman and Kenneth Rogoff. Volume 3. Amsterdam: North-Holland.

Rogowski, Ronald. 1989. *Commerce and Coalitions: How Trade Affects Domestic Political Alignments*. Princeton: Princeton University Press.

Romana, Elpidio R. Sta. 1991. "The Politics of Liberalization of the Japanese Agricultural Market." Report 12, Department of Japanese Studies, National University of Singapore.

Rosendorff, Peter, and Helen Milner. 2001. "The Optimal Design of International Trade Institutions: Uncertainty and Escape." *International Organization* 55 (4): 829–857.

Rothacher, Albrecht. 1989. *Japan's Agro-Food Sector*. London: Macmillan.

Ruggie, John Gerard. 1982. "International Regimes, Transactions, and Change: Embedded Liberalism in the Postwar Economic Order." *International Organization* 36 (2): 379–415.

Saito, Takahiro, 1997. *Kaihatsu yunyū to fūdo bijinesu* (Development imports and the food business). Tokyo: Nōrin Tōkei Kyōkai.

Sakuma, Naoki. 1988. "Gatto tainichi jiyūka kankoku no sujikaki" (The plan of the GATT liberalization recommendation to Japan). *Nōrin Tōkei Chōsa* 2:2–8.

Sano, Hiroya. 1987. "Nichibei nōsanbutsu kōsō no seiji keizaigaku" (The political economy of U.S.-Japan agriculture negotiations). *Economia 95*, Yokohama University Economics Department.

———. 1988. "Waga kuni nōsei shijyō no kakki to shite no 1988nen" (1988 as an epoch-making year in the history of our country's agriculture politics). *Nōgyō to Keizai* 54:6–13.

Sato, Hideo, and Timothy Curran. 1982. "Agricultural Trade: The Case of Beef and Citrus." In *Coping with U.S.-Japan Economic Conflicts*, edited by I. M. Destler and Hideo Sato, 121–183. Lexington, MA: Heath.

Sato, Hideo, and Gunther Schmitt. 1993. "The Political Management of Agriculture in Japan and West Germany." In *The Politics of Economic Change in Postwar Japan and West Germany*, edited by Haruhiro Fukui and Peter H. Merkl, 233–280. New York: St. Martin's Press.

Sato, Yoichiro. 1996. "Sticky Efforts: Japan's Rice Market Opening and U.S.-Japan Transnational Lobbying." In *Japan Engaging the World: A Century of International Encounter*, edited by Harumi Befu. Denver: Center for Japan Studies, Teikyo Loretto Heights University.

Schattschneider, E. E. 1935. *Politics, Pressures, and the Tariff*. New York: Prentice-Hall.

Schelling, Thomas. 1960. *The Strategy of Conflict*. Cambridge: Harvard University Press.

Schoppa, Leonard. 1993. "Two-Level Gaines and Bargaining Outcomes: Why Gaiatsu Succeeds in Japan in Some Cases but Not Others." *International Organization* 47 (3): 353–386.

———. 1997. *Bargaining With Japan: What American Pressure Can and Cannot Do*. New York: Columbia University Press.

———. 1999. "The Social Context in Coercive International Bargaining." *International Organization* 53 (2): 307–342.

Schott, Jeffrey. 1994. *The Uruguay Round: An Assessment*. Washington, DC: Institute for International Economics.

Schultz, Kenneth. 1998. "Domestic Opposition and Signaling in International Crises." *American Political Science Review* 92 (4): 829–844.

Scott, Joanne. 2000. "Tragic Triumph: Agricultural Trade, the Common Agricultural Policy and the Uruguay Round." In *The European Union and World*

Trade Law, edited by Nicholas Emiliou and David O'Keeffe, 165–180. Oxford: Oxford University Press.

Sebenius, James. 1983. "Negotiation Arithmetic: Adding and Subtracting Issues and Parties." *International Organization* 37 (2): 281–316.

Sek, Lenore. 2002. "Trade Retaliation: The 'Carousel' Approach." Report for Congress RS20715. Congressional Research Service, 5 March.

Sheingate, Adam. 2001. *The Rise of the Agricultural Welfare State*. Princeton: Princeton University Press.

Shepsle, Kenneth, and Barry Weingast, eds. 1995. *Positive Theories of Congressional Institutions*. Ann Arbor: University of Michigan Press.

Sherrington, Philippa. 2000. *The Council of Ministers*. London: Pinter.

Shiwaku, Jirō. 1994. "Gatto uruguai raundo nōgyō kōshō no keika to ketsumatsu" (The progress and conclusion of the GATT Uruguay Round agriculture negotiation). *Nōson to Toshi o Musubu* 6 (515): 4–31.

Simmons, Beth. 1994. *Who Adjusts? Domestic Sources of Foreign Economic Policy During the Interwar Years*. Princeton: Princeton University Press.

———. 2000. "International Law and State Behavior: Commitment and Compliance in International Monetary Affairs." *American Political Science Review* 94 (4): 819–835.

Sloof, Randolph. 2000. "Interest Group Lobbying and the Delegation of Policy Authority." *Economics and Politics* 12 (3): 247–274.

Smith, Brendan. 2001. Constitution Building in the European Union: *The Process of Treaty Reforms*. The Hague: Kluwer Law International.

Smith, Michael. 1994. "The European Union, Foreign Economic Policy and the Changing World Arena." *Journal of European Public Policy* 1 (2): 283–302.

———. 1996. "The EU as an International Actor." In *European Union: Power and Policy-making*, edited by Jeremy Richardson, 247–262. London: Routledge.

Sorifu (Office of the Prime Minister), ed. 1999. *Gaikō ni kan suru yoron chōsa* (Opinion polls on foreign policy). Yoron Chōsa Nenkan (Annual of public opinion surveys). Tokyo: Office of the Prime Minister.

Staiger, Robert W. 1995. "International Rules and Institutions for Trade Policy." In *Handbook of International Economics*, edited by Gene Grossman and Kenneth Rogoff. Volume 3, 1497–1551. Amsterdam: North-Holland.

Stein, Arthur. 1980. "The Politics of Linkage." *World Politics* 33:62–81.

Steinberg, Richard. 2002. "In the Shadow of Law or Power? Consensus-Based Bargaining and Outcomes in the GATT/WTO." *International Organization* 56 (2): 339–374.

Stevens, Christopher. 1996. "EU Policy for the Banana Market: The External Impact of Internal Policies." In *Policy-making in the European Union*, edited by Helen Wallace and William Wallace, 325–351. Oxford: Oxford University Press.

Stewart, Terence, ed. 1993. *The GATT Uruguay Round: A Negotiating History (1986–1992)*. Volume 1. Cambridge, MA: Kluwer Law and Taxation Publishers.

———. 1998. *Agricultural Sanitary and Phytosanitary and Standards Reports: The WTO Beef Hormone Dispute*. Geneva: World Trade Organization.

Stigler, George. 1971. "The Theory of Economic Regulation." *The Bell Journal of Economics and Management Science* 2 (1): 3–21.

Strange, Susan. 1982. "*Cave! hic dragones*: A Critique of Regime Analysis." *International Organization* 36 (2): 479–518.

Sweet, Alec Stone, and Thomas Brunell. 1998. "Constructing a Supranational Constitution: Dispute Resolution and Governance in the European Community." *American Political Science Review* 92 (1): 63–81.

Swinbank, Alan, and Carolyn Tanner, eds. 1996. *Farm Policy and Trade Conflict*. Ann Arbor: University of Michigan Press.

Takase, Tamotsu. 1997. *Gatto nijūnen no genba kara* (Twenty-nine years on site at the GATT). Tokyo: Chūō Kōron.

Tanaka, Hideo. 1988. "The Role of Law and Lawyers in Japanese Society." In *Inside the Japanese System: Readings on Contemporary Society and Political Economy*, edited by Daniel Okimoto and Thomas Rohlen, 194–196. Palo Alto: Stanford University Press.

Tarar, Ahmer. 2001. "International Bargaining with Two-Sided Domestic Constraints." *Journal of Conflict Resolution* 45:320–340.

Taussig, Frank. 1964. *The Tariff History of the United States*. 8th edition. New York: Capricorn Books.

Terasawa, Tatsuma. 1984. "Tenkanki no seisansha beika no kettei" (A turning point in the process of setting the rice producer price). Technical Report, Ministry of Finance, Tokyo.

Tollison, Robert D., and Thomas D. Willett. 1979. "An Economic Theory of Mutually Advantageous Issue Linkages in International Negotiations." *International Organization* 33 (4): 425–449.

Tracy, Michael. 1997. *Agricultural Policy in the European Union*. Brussels: Agricultural Policy Studies.

Trefler, Daniel. 1993. "Trade Liberalization and the Theory of Endogenous Protection: An Econometric Study of U.S. Import Policy." *The Journal of Political Economy* 101 (1): 138–160.

Twiggs, Joan E. 1987. *The Tokyo Round of Multilateral Trade Negotiations*. Lanham, MD: University Press of America.

U.S. Senate Committee on Finance. 1979a, August. *Agreements Being Negotiated at the Multilateral Trade Negotiations in Geneva — U.S. International Trade Commission Investigation No. 332-101 (Industry/Agriculture Sector Analysis)*. Volume 6, part 5, of *MTN Studies*. 96th Congress, 1st sess. Committee Print 27.

———. 1979b. *Results for U.S. Agriculture*. Volume 1 of *MTN Studies*. 96th Congress, 1st sess. Committee Print 11.

———. 1979c, June. *Tokyo-Geneva Round: Its Relation to U.S. Agriculture*. Volume 2 of *MTN Studies*. 96th Congress, 1st sess. Committee Print 12.

USDA (U.S. Department of Agriculture). 1999. *Foreign Agricultural Trade of the United States*. Washington, DC: USDA.

Vahl, Remco. 1997. *Leadership in Disguise: The Role of the European Commission in EC Decision-Making on Agriculture in the Uruguay Round*. Aldershot, England: Ashgate.

Vogel, Steven. 1999. "When Interests Are Not Preferences: The Cautionary Tale of Japanese Consumers." *Journal of Comparative Politics* 31:2 187–207.

Vogt, Donna. 1989, January 3. "U.S.-European Community Trade Dispute Over Meat Containing Growth Hormones." Report to Congress 89-6, Congressional Research Service.

Wainio, John, Paul Gibson, and Daniel Whitley. 1999. "Implementation of Uruguay Round Tariff Reductions." *Agricultural Outlook* 267 (November): 26–30.

Wallace, Helen, and William Wallace. 1996. *Policy-making in the European Union.* Oxford: Oxford University Press.

Weber, Katja. 2000. *Hierarchy amidst Anarchy.* Albany: State University of New York Press.

Weiler, Joseph H. H. 1999. *The Constitution of Europe: Do the New Clothes Have an Emperor? And Other Essays on European Integration.* Cambridge: Cambridge University Press.

Williamson, Oliver. 1985. *The Economic Institutions of Capitalism: Firms, Markets, Relational Contracting.* New York: Free Press.

Winham, Gilbert. 1986. *International Trade and the Tokyo Round Negotiation.* Princeton: Princeton University Press.

Wolff, Alan. 1980. "The Larger Political and Economic Role of the Tokyo Round." *Law and Policy in International Business* 12:1–19.

Woolcock, Stephen, and Michael Hodges. 1996. "EU Policy in the Uruguay Round." In *Policy-making in the European Union,* edited by Helen Wallace and William Wallace, 301–351. Oxford: Oxford University Press.

Yaguchi, Yoshio. 1988. "12 hinmoku ni yuderu painappuru sangyō" (Pineapple industry is shaken by 12 commodities case). *Nōrin Tōkei Chōsa* (Agriculture and Forestries statistics survey), no. 1:2–8.

Yamaji, Susumu, and Shoichi Ito. 1993. "The Political Economy of Rice in Japan." In *Japanese and American Agriculture: Tradition and Progress in Conflict,* edited by Luther et al. 349–365. Boulder: Westview Press.

Yarbrough, Beth, and Robert Yarbrough. 1992. *Cooperation and Governance in International Trade: The Strategic Organizational Approach.* Princeton: Princeton University Press.

Yasuhara, Kazuo. 1985. *Keidanren kaichō no sengoshi* (Postwar history of the Keidanren chairmen). Tokyo: Bijinesusha.

Yeutter, Clayton. 1998. "Bringing Agriculture into the Multilateral Trading System." In *The Uruguay Round and Beyond,* edited by Jagdish Bhagwati and Mathias Hirsch, 61–77. Ann Arbor: University of Michigan Press.

Yoshimatsu, Hidetaka. 1998. "Japan's *Keidanren* and Political Influence on Market Liberalization." *Asian Survey* 38 (3): 328–345.

Zeng, Ka. 2002. "Trade Structure and the Effectiveness of America's 'Aggressively Unilateral' Trade Policy." *International Studies Quarterly* 46:93–115.

Index

Abe Shintarō, 166

Agricultural Basic Law of 1961 (Japan), 8–9, 117–18

agricultural commodity definition, 29n.45

agricultural liberalization: expectations according to negotiation structure, 58fig-64; global economic benefits of, 6; insufficiency of traditional explanation of, 345–46; international institutions and facilitation of, 26–28, 216–19; legal framing as facilitating, 27–28, 74–77, 222–23, 346–47; opposition in Japan and Europe to, 11–13; patterns of, 70–85, 134, 353–54; recent progress made in, 1–2; role of reputation in, 51–53, 74–77; statistical analysis of, 93–110; trade policy preferences and, 15–18; two types of negotiation structure likely to lead to, 3, 26–27, 346–47. See also negotiated policy liberalization

agricultural liberalization findings: on cross-sector issue linkage in Japan and EU, 349–54; empirical results, 348t-49t; implications of, 363–66; legal framing in Japan and EU, 354–60; methodologies/statistical analysis used in, 28–30, 93–110, 347, 349

agricultural liberalization hypotheses: 1: cross-sector linkages and package negotiations, 71–74; 2a: positive impact on liberalization by GATT settlement prior to ruling, 75–76; 2b: GATT violation ruling and positive effect on liberalization, 76–77, 133; 3: U.S. influence through threats and appeals, 79, 133–34; 4a: Japanese domestic politics and liberalization patterns, 82–83, 134; 4b: EU internal politics and liberalization patterns, 83; 5: budget constraints and liberalization patterns, 85, 134

agricultural liberalization patterns: influence of budget on, 83–85; influence of Japan/EU domestic politics on, 80–83,

134, 353–54; impact of negotiation structure on, 70–77; influence of U.S. threats and appeals on, 77–80. See also agricultural liberalization

agricultural negotiation data: base model for estimating liberalization, 89t; data collection on, 85–93; description of, 85–88; negotiation context, 88t; operationalization of hypotheses, 88–93; ten cases of beef negotiations, 87t

agricultural negotiations: analysis of multistage, 360–63; areas of future research on, 362–63; choosing structure for, 64–68; domestic politics and international, 20–22; expectations for liberalization and structure of, 58fig-64; GATT DSP framework for, 3–4, 37; institutional context of, 22–26; outcomes of Tokyo Round/Uruguay Round, 1–2, 13–14, 146–47, 151–54, 222t; strategic dependence/relationships and, 18–20; two structures likely to liberalize agricultural policies, 3, 26–27. See also negotiated policy liberalization; negotiations

agricultural negotiation structure: actor strategies and decisions shaping, 220–21; of APEC, 206–10; choice bounded by existing institutional procedures/actor demands, 361–62; considerations in selecting, 64–68; decision to include rice negotiation in Uruguay Round, 179–89; effects on predicted liberalization (U.S.-EU), 105fig; hypotheses on liberalization patterns and, 70–77; negotiating Tokyo Round, 154, 257–62, 361; two types likely to lead to liberalization, 3, 26–27, 346–47; U.S.-EU negotiations on Tokyo Round, 254, 257–62, 264–65, 271. See also issue linkage negotiation structure; legal framing negotiation structure

agricultural protection: by CAP (Common Agricultural Policy) [EU], 228–32; de-